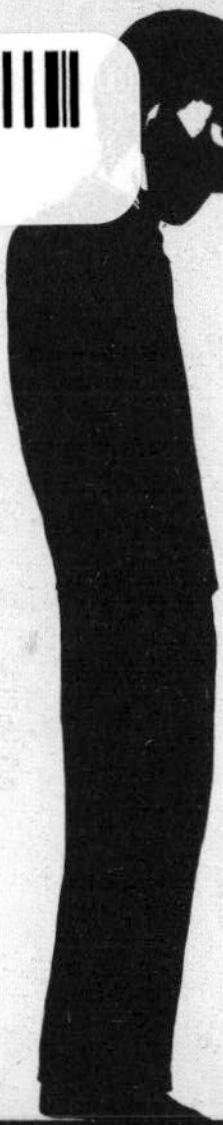

ONE
PRESENTS

モブサイコ100

MOB PSYCHO 100

VOLUME 6

DARK HORSE MANGA

MOB PSYCHO 100
VOLUME 6

Translated by
KUMAR SIVASUBRAMANIAN

Lettering and Retouch by
JOHN CLARK

Edited by
CARL GUSTAV HORN

CHAPTER 44: RESPECT

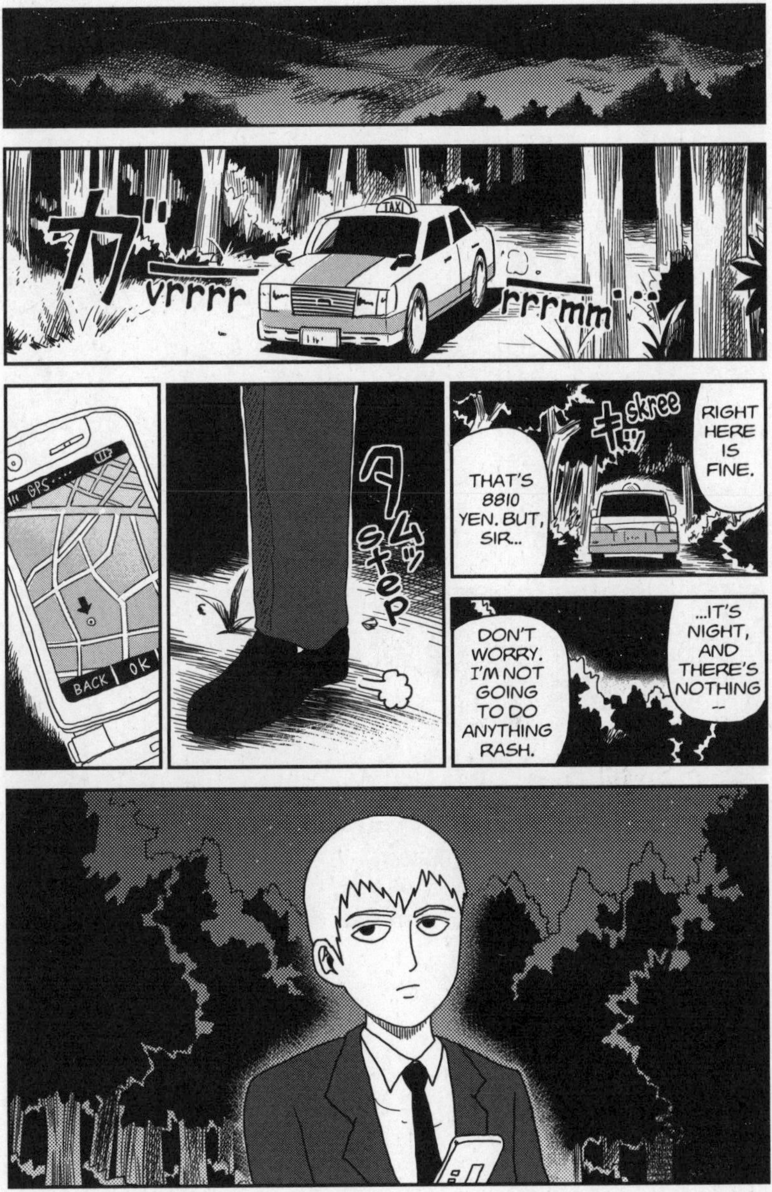

vrrrr
rrrmm
RIGHT HERE IS FINE.
skree
THAT'S 8810 YEN. BUT, SIR...
...IT'S NIGHT, AND THERE'S NOTHING --
DON'T WORRY. I'M NOT GOING TO DO ANYTHING RASH.
step
GPS
BACK
OK

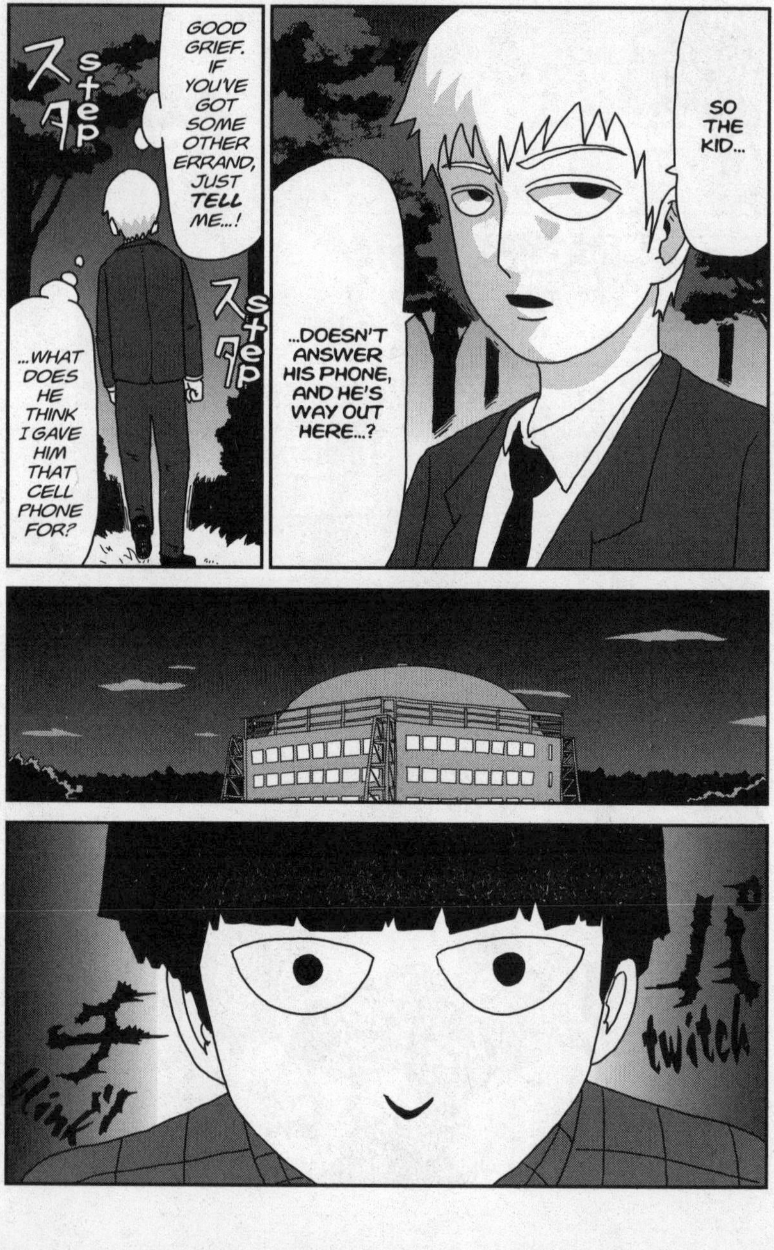
SO THE KID...
...DOESN'T ANSWER HIS PHONE, AND HE'S WAY OUT HERE...?
スタ step
GOOD GRIEF. IF YOU'VE GOT SOME OTHER ERRAND, JUST TELL ME...!
スタ step
...WHAT DOES HE THINK I GAVE HIM THAT CELL PHONE FOR?
twitch

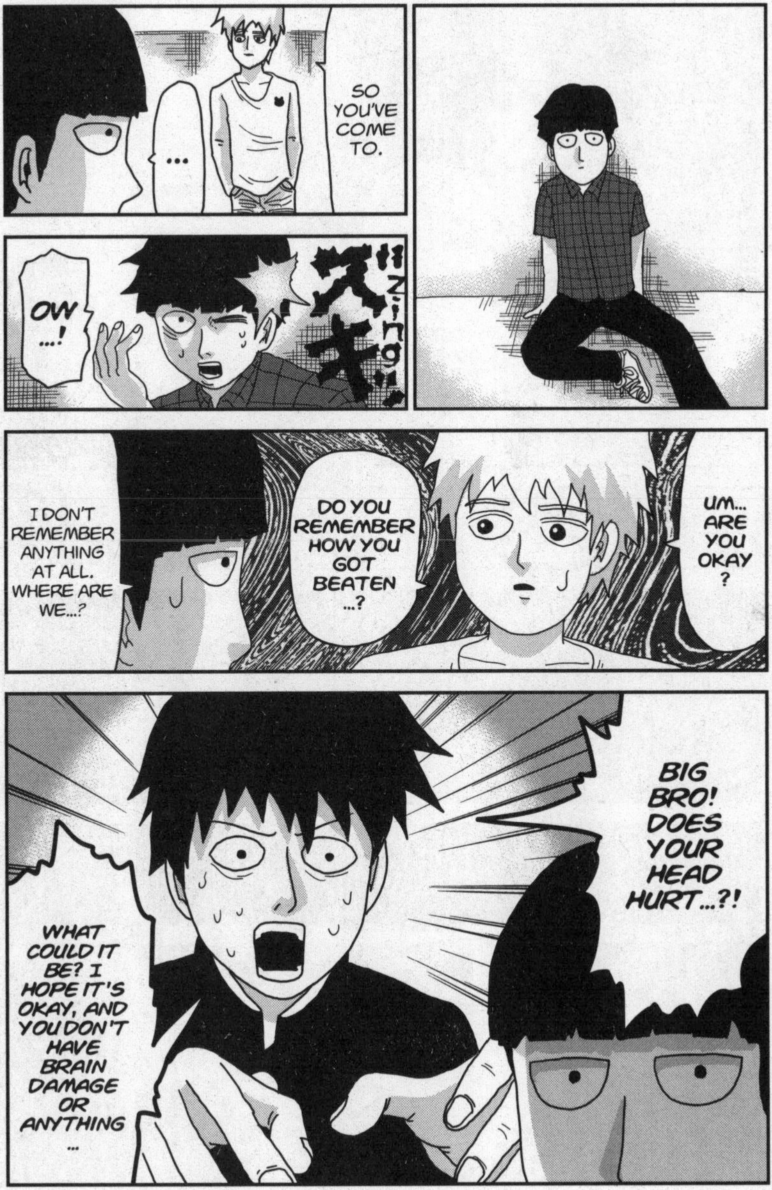
SO YOU'VE COME TO.
...
zing!!
OW ...!
UM... ARE YOU OKAY ?
DO YOU REMEMBER HOW YOU GOT BEATEN ...?
I DON'T REMEMBER ANYTHING AT ALL. WHERE ARE WE...?
BIG BRO! DOES YOUR HEAD HURT...?!
WHAT COULD IT BE? I HOPE IT'S OKAY, AND YOU DON'T HAVE BRAIN DAMAGE OR ANYTHING ...

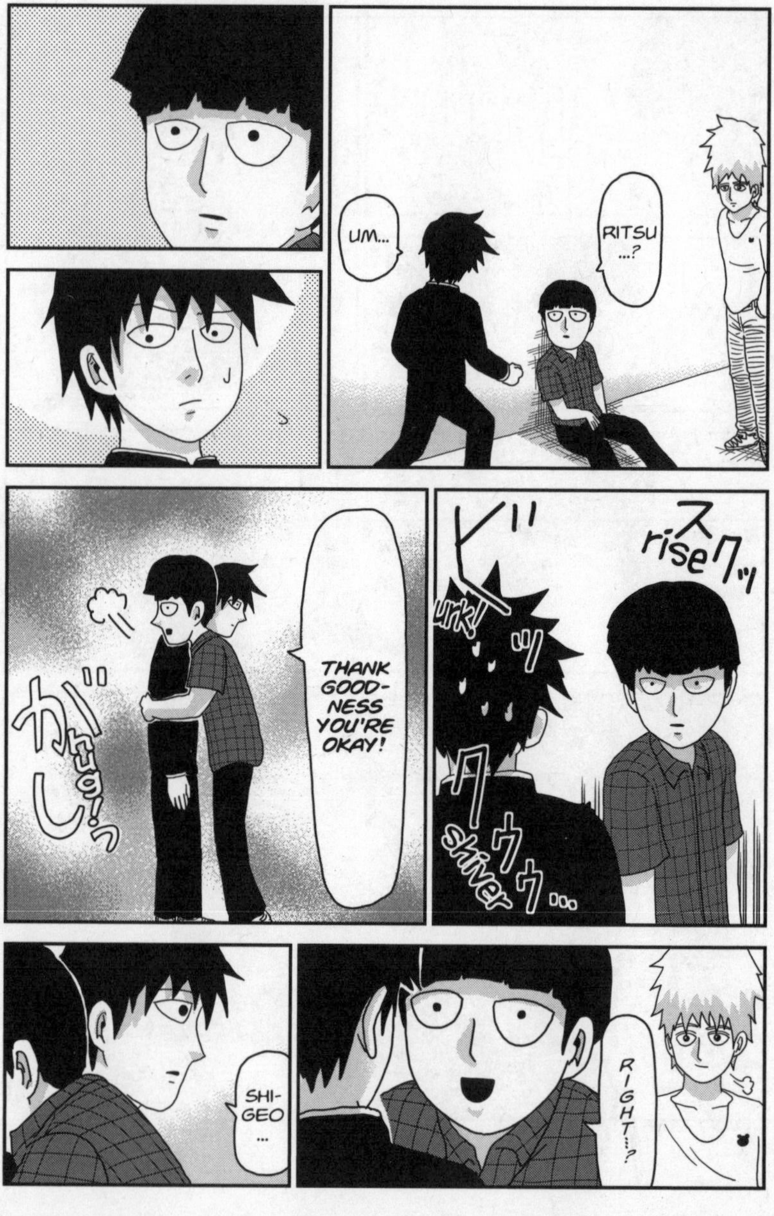
RITSU ...?
UM...
スクッ
rise
ビクッ
urk!
クゥゥ...
shiver
THANK GOODNESS YOU'RE OKAY!
がしっ!
RIGHT...?
SHI-GEO ...

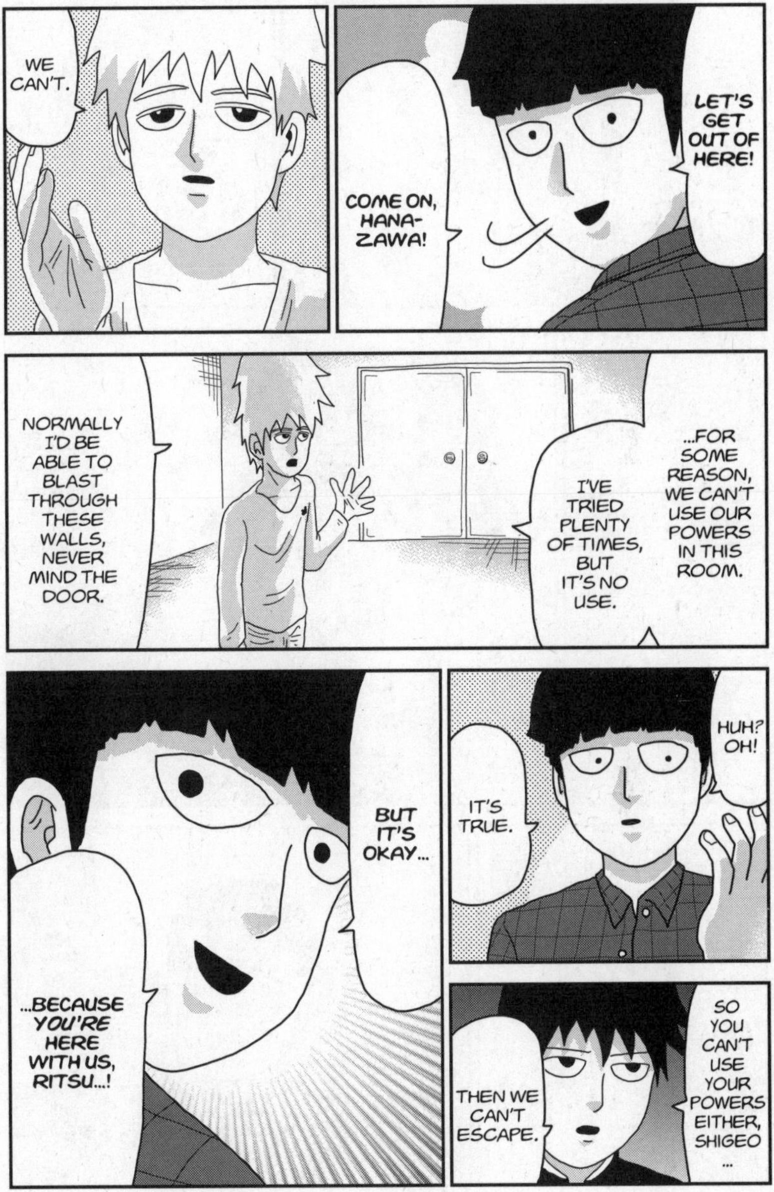
LET'S GET OUT OF HERE!
COME ON, HANAZAWA!
WE CAN'T.
...FOR SOME REASON, WE CAN'T USE OUR POWERS IN THIS ROOM.
I'VE TRIED PLENTY OF TIMES, BUT IT'S NO USE.
NORMALLY I'D BE ABLE TO BLAST THROUGH THESE WALLS, NEVER MIND THE DOOR.
HUH? OH!
IT'S TRUE.
SO YOU CAN'T USE YOUR POWERS EITHER, SHIGEO...
THEN WE CAN'T ESCAPE.
BUT IT'S OKAY...
...BECAUSE *YOU'RE* HERE WITH US, RITSU...!

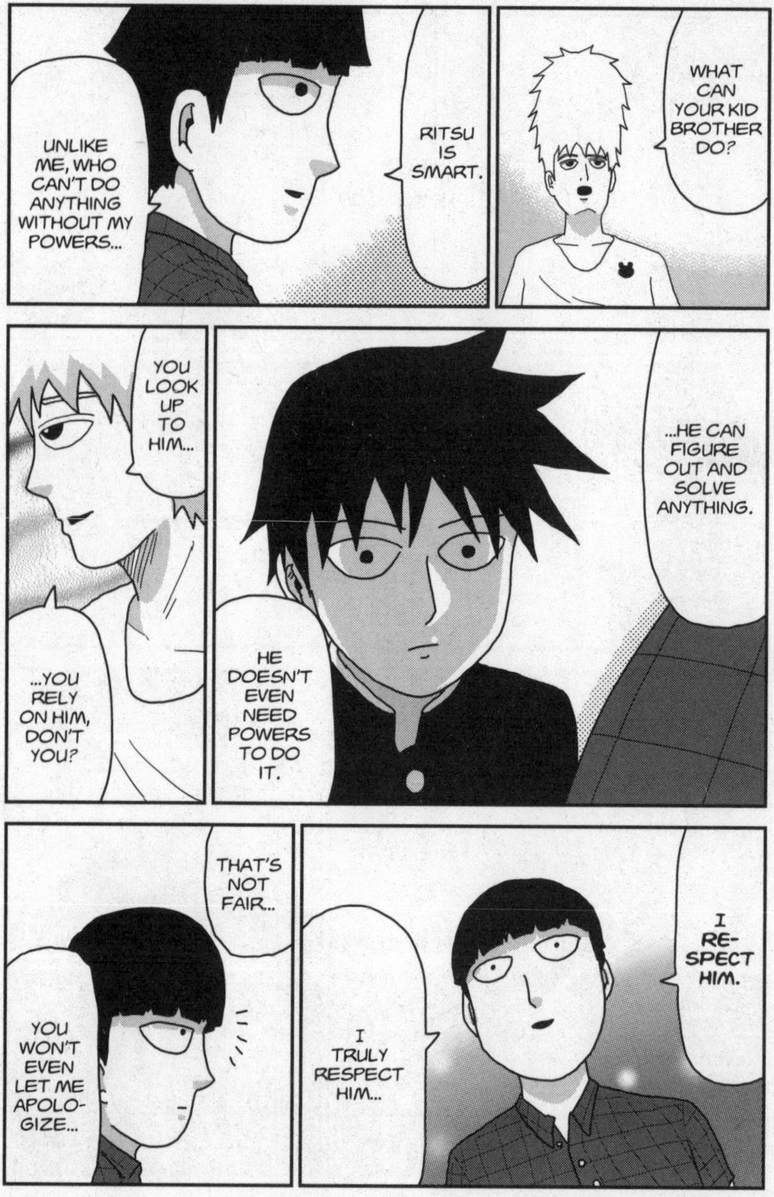
WHAT CAN YOUR KID BROTHER DO?
RITSU IS SMART.
UNLIKE ME, WHO CAN'T DO ANYTHING WITHOUT MY POWERS...
...HE CAN FIGURE OUT AND SOLVE ANYTHING.
HE DOESN'T EVEN NEED POWERS TO DO IT.
YOU LOOK UP TO HIM...
...YOU RELY ON HIM, DON'T YOU?
I RE-SPECT HIM.
I TRULY RESPECT HIM...
THAT'S NOT FAIR...
YOU WON'T EVEN LET ME APOLO-GIZE...

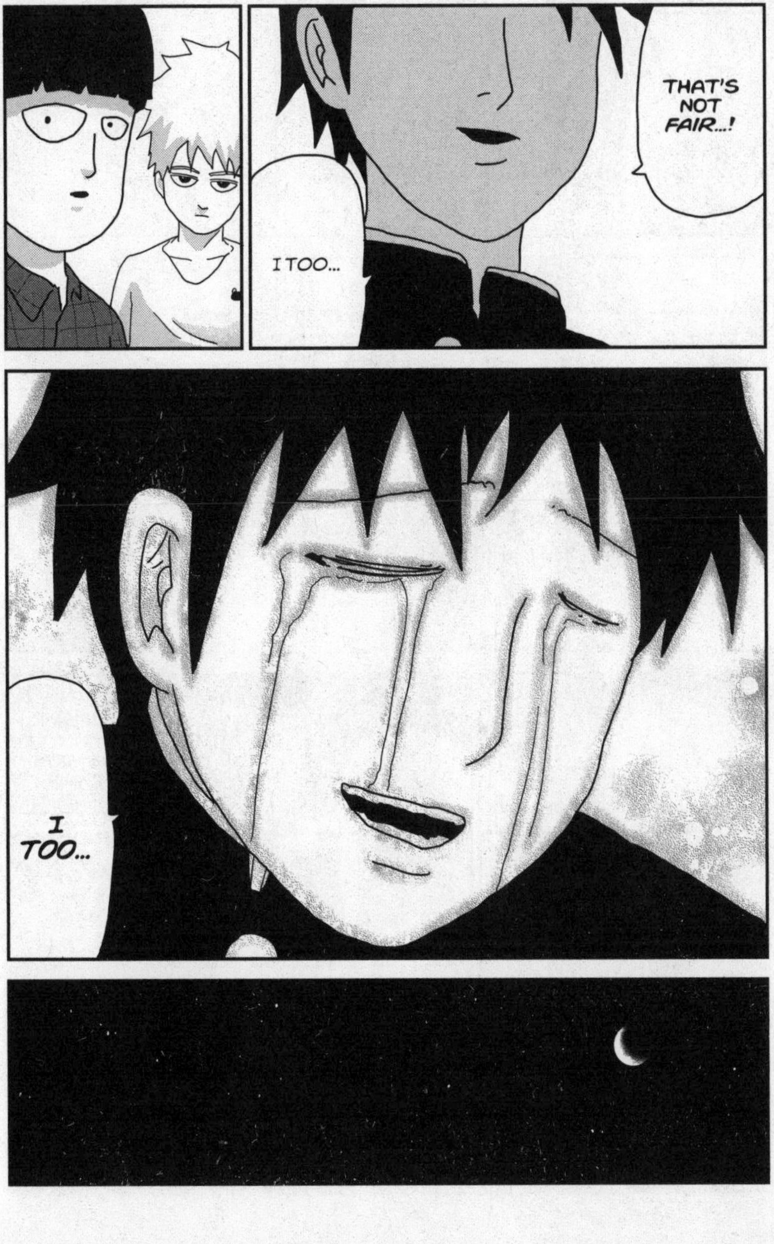
THAT'S NOT FAIR...!
I TOO...
I TOO...

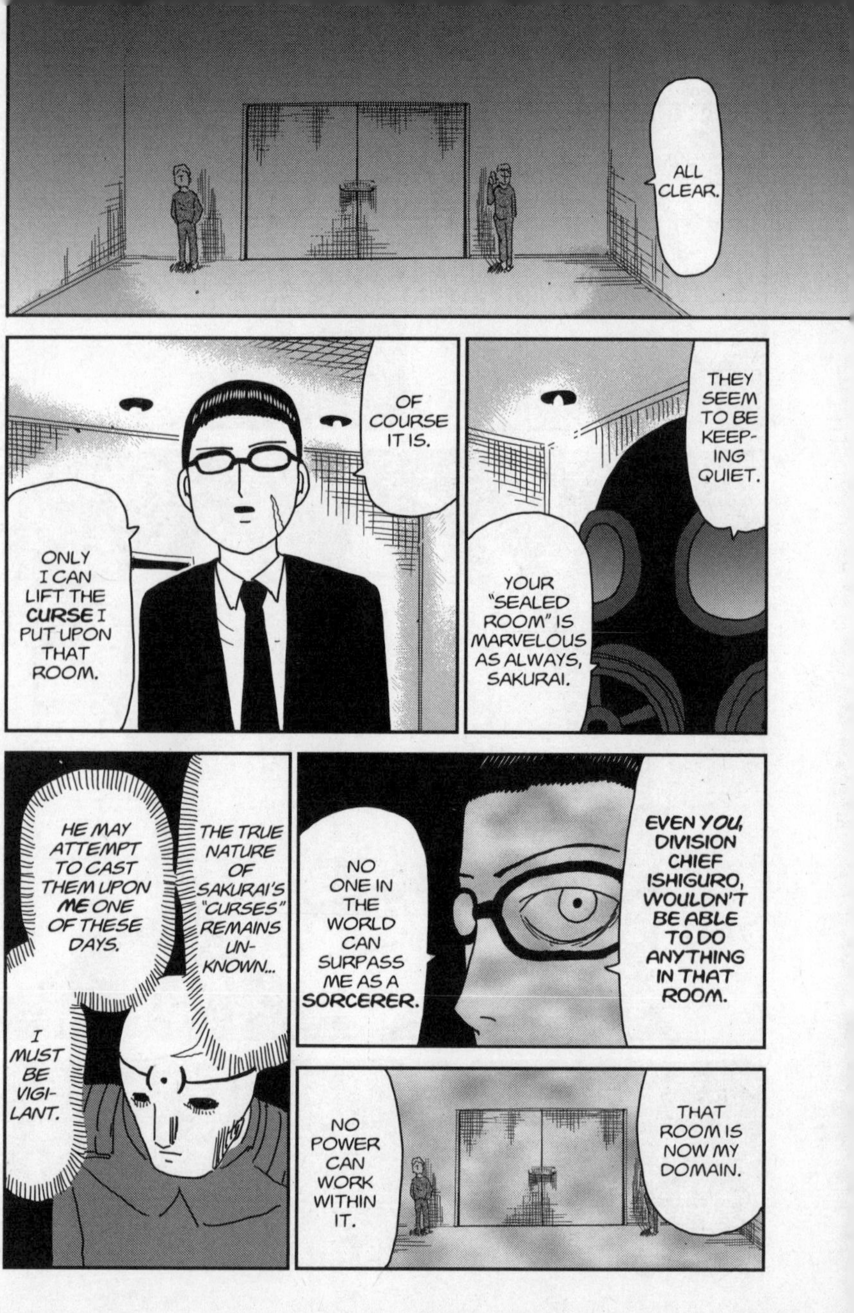
ALL CLEAR.
THEY SEEM TO BE KEEPING QUIET.
YOUR "SEALED ROOM" IS MARVELOUS AS ALWAYS, SAKURAI.
OF COURSE IT IS.
ONLY I CAN LIFT THE CURSE I PUT UPON THAT ROOM.
EVEN YOU, DIVISION CHIEF ISHIGURO, WOULDN'T BE ABLE TO DO ANYTHING IN THAT ROOM.
NO ONE IN THE WORLD CAN SURPASS ME AS A SORCERER.
THAT ROOM IS NOW MY DOMAIN.
NO POWER CAN WORK WITHIN IT.
THE TRUE NATURE OF SAKURAI'S "CURSES" REMAINS UNKNOWN...
HE MAY ATTEMPT TO CAST THEM UPON ME ONE OF THESE DAYS.
I MUST BE VIGILANT.

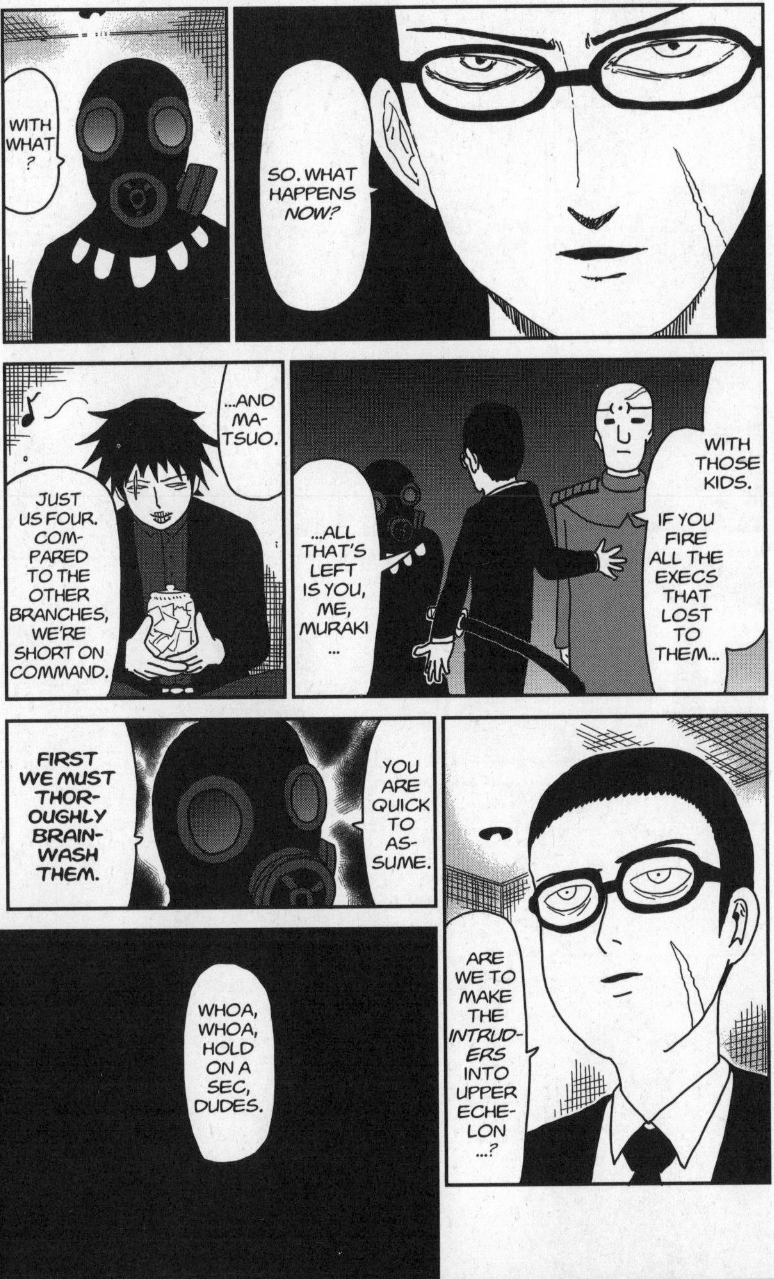
SO. WHAT HAPPENS NOW?
WITH WHAT?
WITH THOSE KIDS.
IF YOU FIRE ALL THE EXECS THAT LOST TO THEM...
...ALL THAT'S LEFT IS YOU, ME, MURAKI...
...AND MATSUO.
JUST US FOUR. COMPARED TO THE OTHER BRANCHES, WE'RE SHORT ON COMMAND.
ARE WE TO MAKE THE INTRUDERS INTO UPPER ECHELON...?
YOU ARE QUICK TO ASSUME.
FIRST WE MUST THOROUGHLY BRAINWASH THEM.
WHOA, WHOA, HOLD ON A SEC, DUDES.

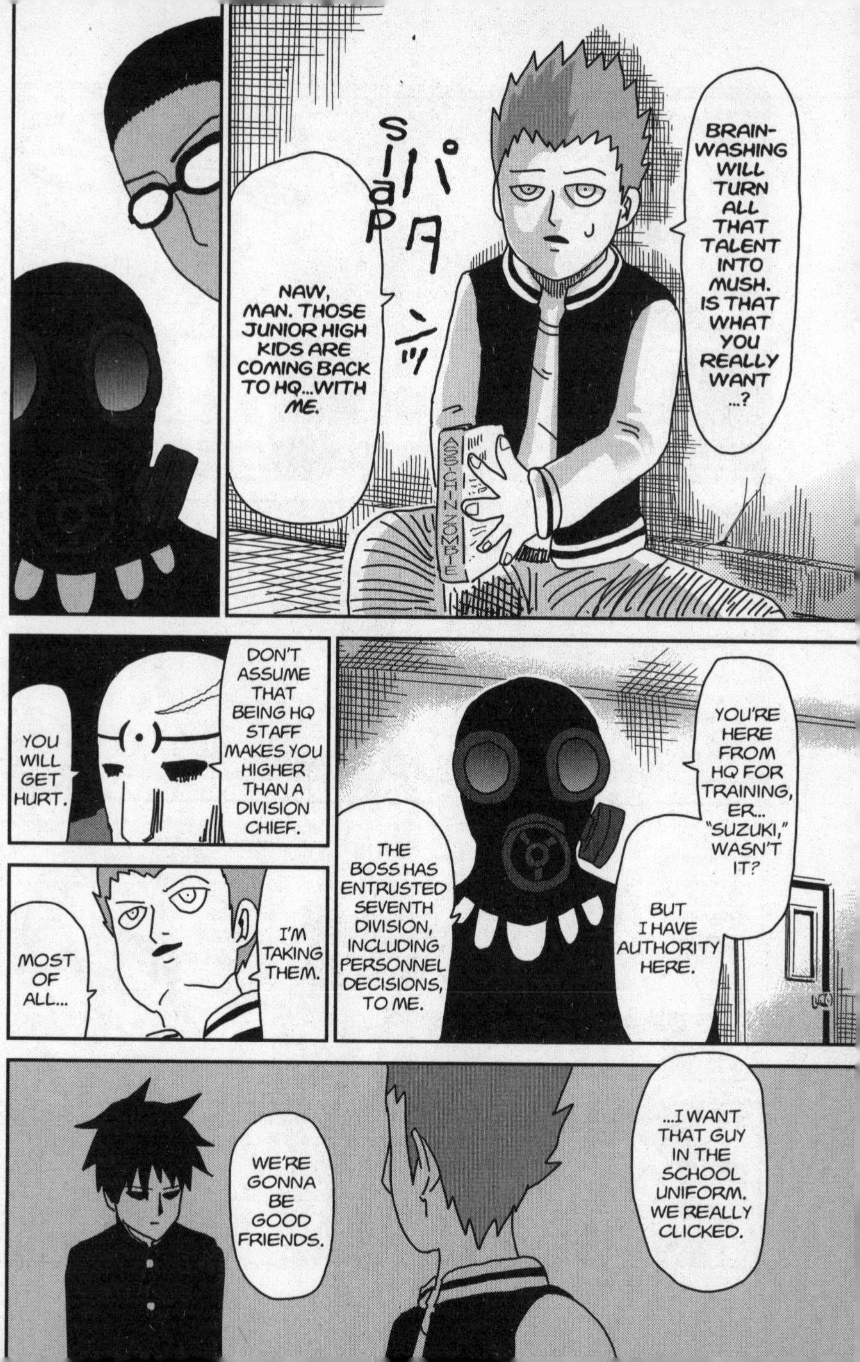
BRAIN-WASHING WILL TURN ALL THAT TALENT INTO MUSH. IS THAT WHAT YOU REALLY WANT ...?
パタンッ
slap
ASS-CHIN ZOMBIE
NAW, MAN. THOSE JUNIOR HIGH KIDS ARE COMING BACK TO HQ...WITH ME.
YOU'RE HERE FROM HQ FOR TRAINING, ER... "SUZUKI," WASN'T IT?
BUT I HAVE AUTHORITY HERE.
THE BOSS HAS ENTRUSTED SEVENTH DIVISION, INCLUDING PERSONNEL DECISIONS, TO ME.
DON'T ASSUME THAT BEING HQ STAFF MAKES YOU HIGHER THAN A DIVISION CHIEF.
YOU WILL GET HURT.
I'M TAKING THEM.
MOST OF ALL...
...I WANT THAT GUY IN THE SCHOOL UNIFORM. WE REALLY CLICKED.
WE'RE GONNA BE GOOD FRIENDS.

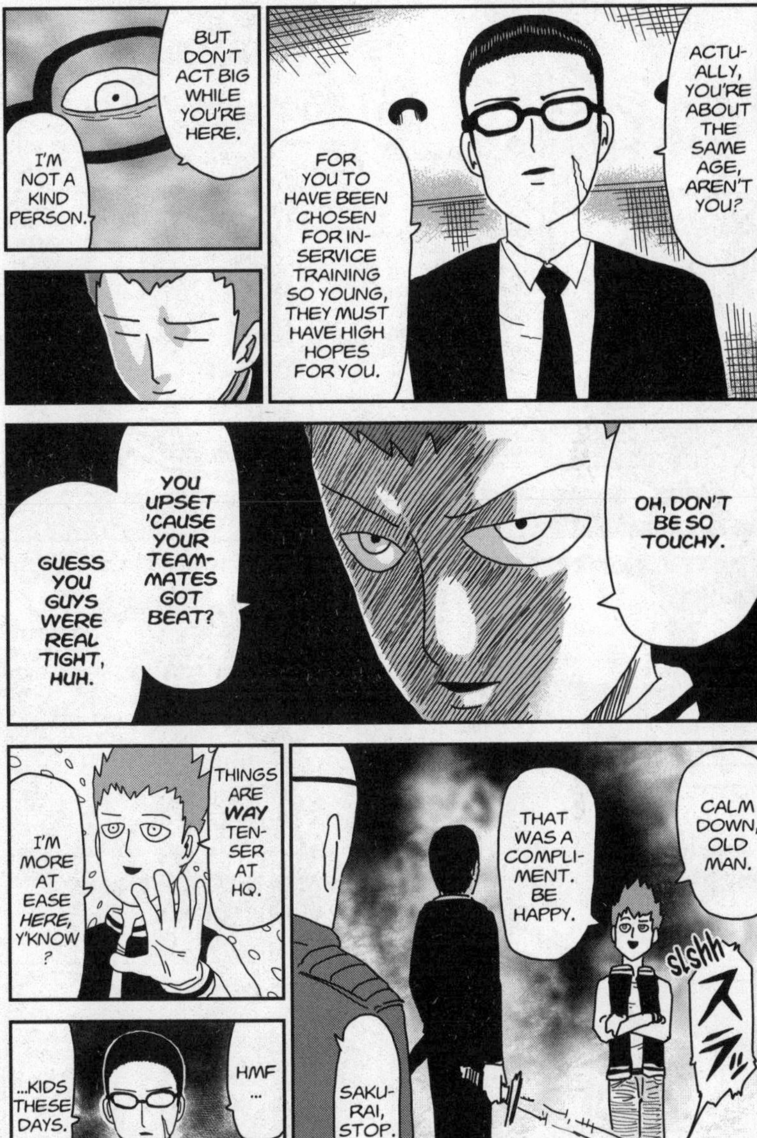

ACTUALLY, YOU'RE ABOUT THE SAME AGE, AREN'T YOU?
FOR YOU TO HAVE BEEN CHOSEN FOR IN-SERVICE TRAINING SO YOUNG, THEY MUST HAVE HIGH HOPES FOR YOU.
BUT DON'T ACT BIG WHILE YOU'RE HERE.
I'M NOT A KIND PERSON.
OH, DON'T BE SO TOUCHY.
YOU UPSET 'CAUSE YOUR TEAMMATES GOT BEAT?
GUESS YOU GUYS WERE REAL TIGHT, HUH.
CALM DOWN, OLD MAN.
THAT WAS A COMPLIMENT. BE HAPPY.
slshh
スラッ
SAKURAI, STOP.
THINGS ARE *WAY* TENSER AT HQ.
I'M MORE AT EASE *HERE*, Y'KNOW?
HMF...
...KIDS THESE DAYS.

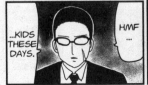

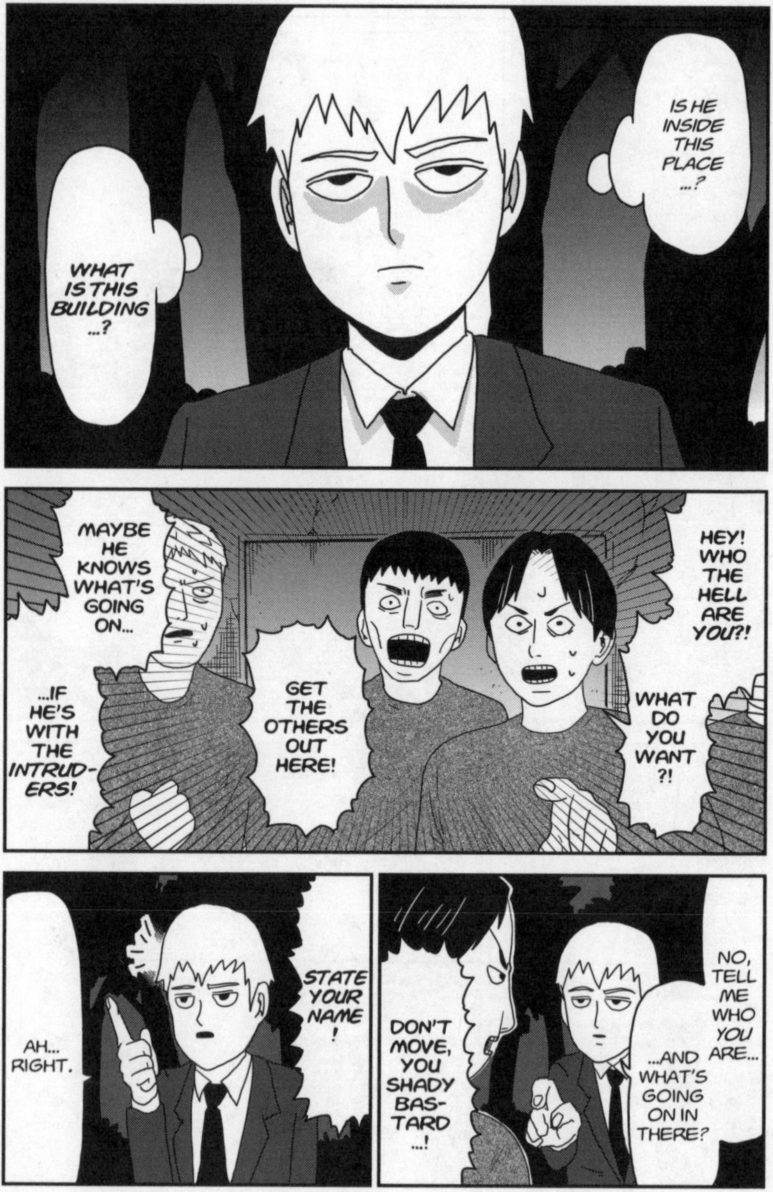
IS HE INSIDE THIS PLACE ...?
WHAT IS THIS BUILDING ...?
HEY! WHO THE HELL ARE YOU?!
WHAT DO YOU WANT ?!
GET THE OTHERS OUT HERE!
MAYBE HE KNOWS WHAT'S GOING ON...
...IF HE'S WITH THE INTRUD-ERS!
NO, TELL ME WHO YOU ARE...
...AND WHAT'S GOING ON IN THERE?
DON'T MOVE, YOU SHADY BAS-TARD ...!
STATE YOUR NAME !
AH... RIGHT.

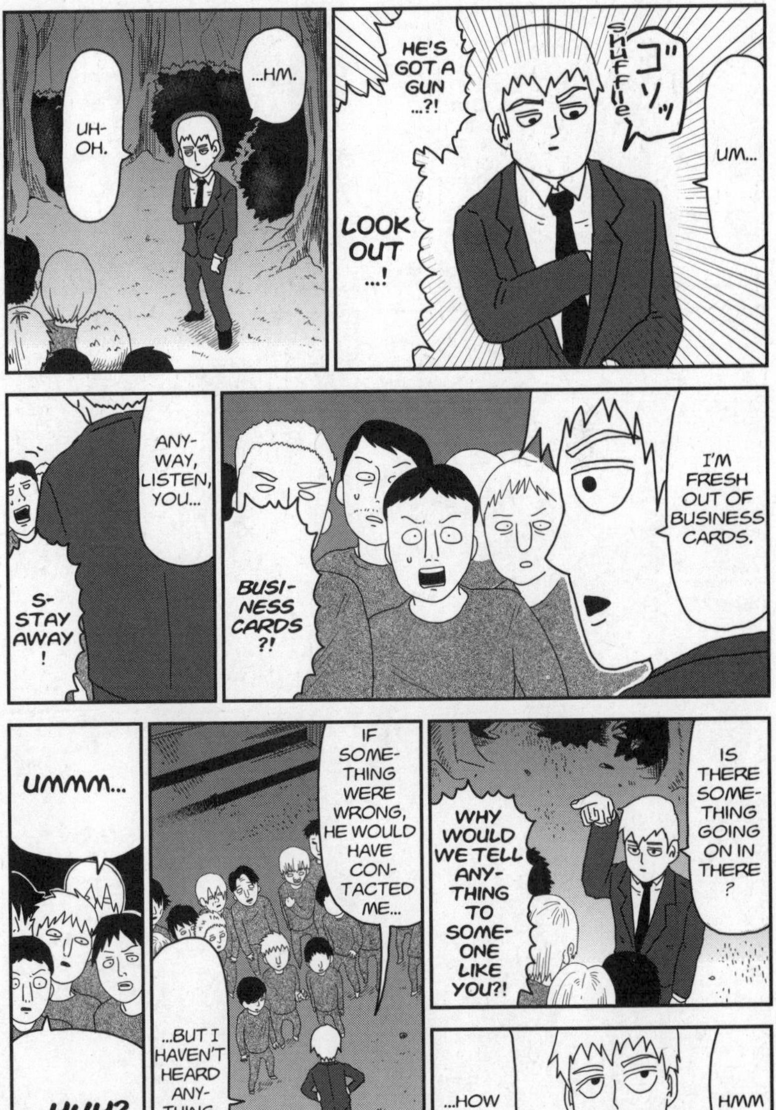
ゴソッ
shuffle
UM...
HE'S GOT A GUN ...?!
LOOK OUT ...!
...HM.
UH-OH.
I'M FRESH OUT OF BUSINESS CARDS.
BUSINESS CARDS?!
ANYWAY, LISTEN, YOU...
S-STAY AWAY!
IS THERE SOMETHING GOING ON IN THERE?
WHY WOULD WE TELL ANYTHING TO SOMEONE LIKE YOU?!
HMM...
...HOW ODD.
IF SOMETHING WERE WRONG, HE WOULD HAVE CONTACTED ME...
...BUT I HAVEN'T HEARD ANYTHING.
UMMM...
...HUH?

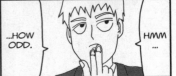

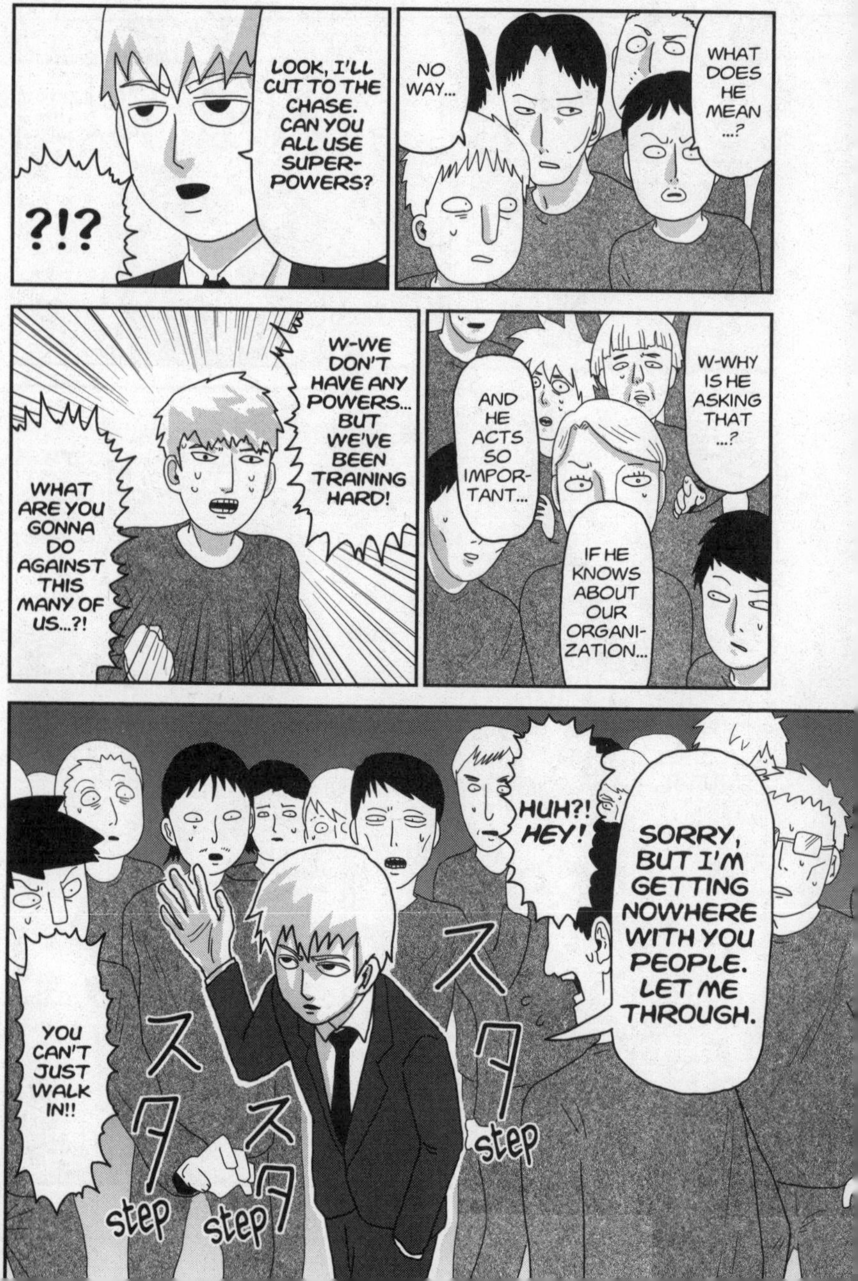
WHAT DOES HE MEAN ...?
NO WAY...
LOOK, I'LL CUT TO THE CHASE. CAN YOU ALL USE SUPER-POWERS?
?!?
W-WHY IS HE ASKING THAT ...?
AND HE ACTS SO IMPOR-TANT...
IF HE KNOWS ABOUT OUR ORGANI-ZATION...
W-WE DON'T HAVE ANY POWERS... BUT WE'VE BEEN TRAINING HARD!
WHAT ARE YOU GONNA DO AGAINST THIS MANY OF US...?!
SORRY, BUT I'M GETTING NOWHERE WITH YOU PEOPLE. LET ME THROUGH.
HUH?! HEY!
スタ
step
YOU CAN'T JUST WALK IN!!
スタ
step
スタ
step

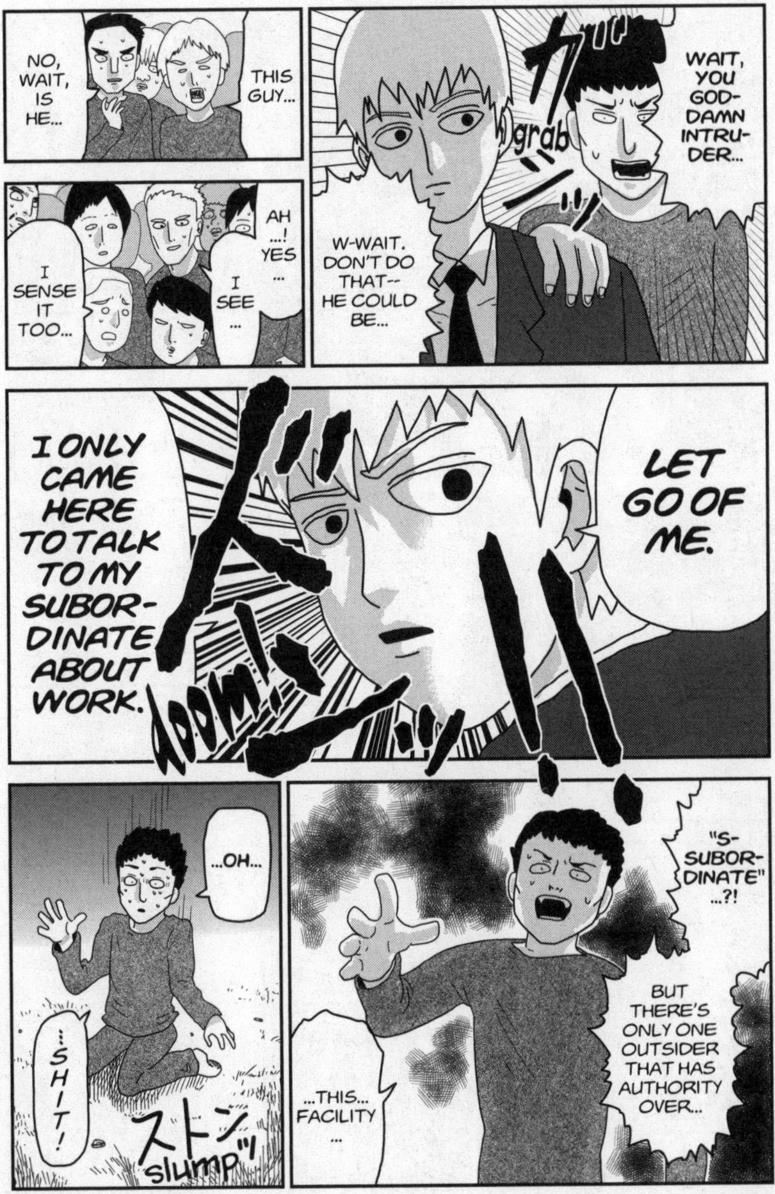
WAIT, YOU GOD-DAMN INTRU-DER...
grab
W-WAIT. DON'T DO THAT-- HE COULD BE...
THIS GUY...
NO, WAIT, IS HE...
AH ...! YES ...
I SEE ...
I SENSE IT TOO...
LET GO OF ME.
I ONLY CAME HERE TO TALK TO MY SUBOR-DINATE ABOUT WORK.
doom!!
"S-SUBOR-DINATE" ...?!
BUT THERE'S ONLY ONE OUTSIDER THAT HAS AUTHORITY OVER...
...THIS... FACILITY ...
...OH...
...SHIT!
ストンッ
slump

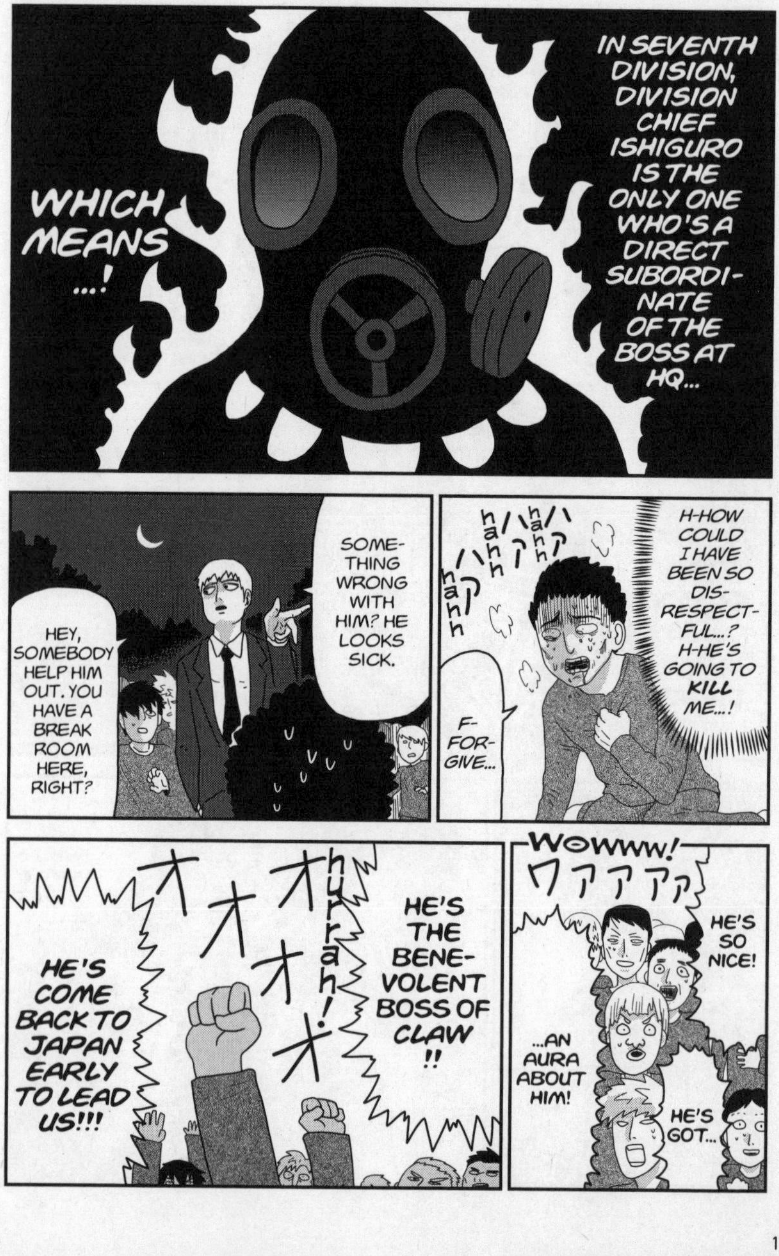
IN SEVENTH DIVISION, DIVISION CHIEF ISHIGURO IS THE ONLY ONE WHO'S A DIRECT SUBORDINATE OF THE BOSS AT HQ...
WHICH MEANS ...!
H-HOW COULD I HAVE BEEN SO DISRESPECTFUL...? H-HE'S GOING TO KILL ME...!
hahh hahh hahh hahh
F-FORGIVE...
SOMETHING WRONG WITH HIM? HE LOOKS SICK.
HEY, SOMEBODY HELP HIM OUT. YOU HAVE A BREAK ROOM HERE, RIGHT?
WOWWW!
ワアアアア
HE'S SO NICE!
HE'S GOT...
...AN AURA ABOUT HIM!
HE'S THE BENEVOLENT BOSS OF CLAW!!
hurrah!
オオオオ
HE'S COME BACK TO JAPAN EARLY TO LEAD US!!!

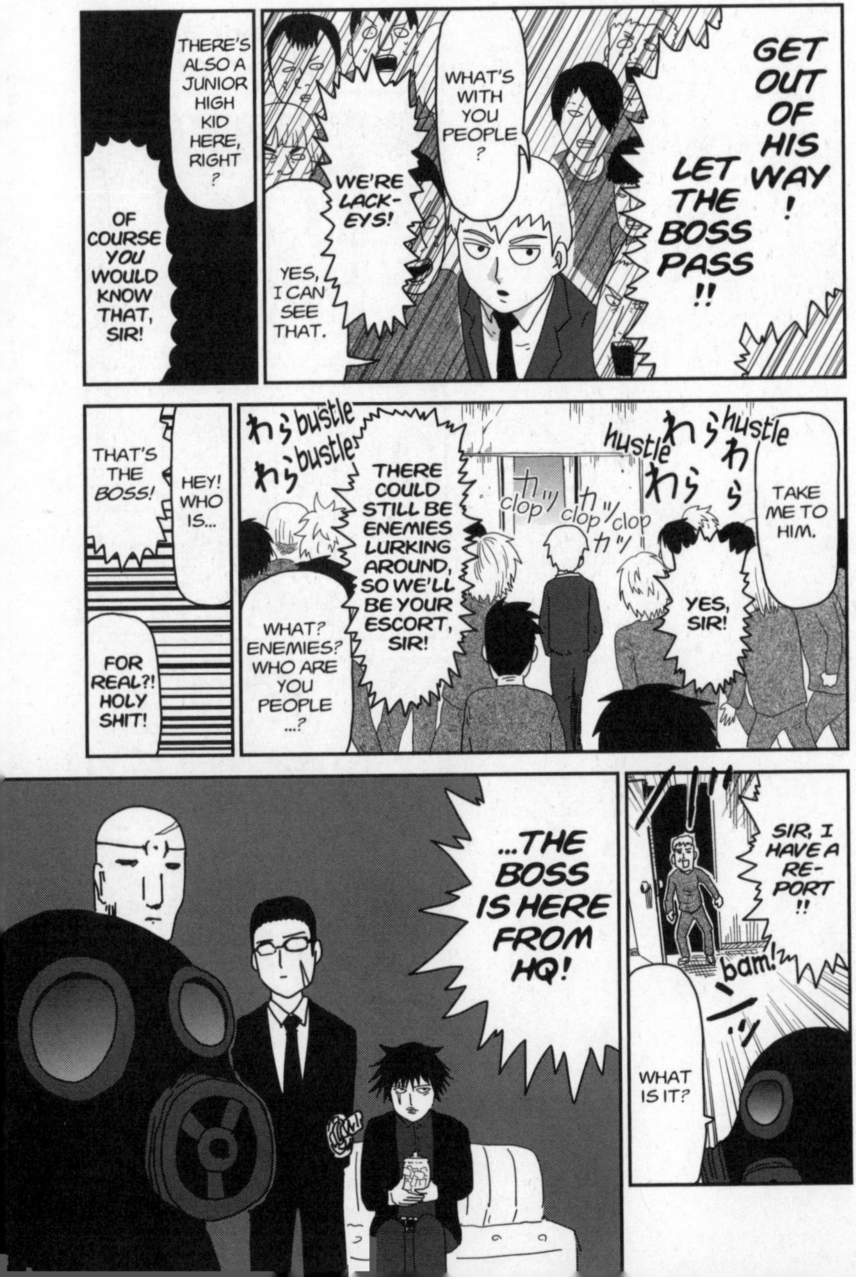
GET OUT OF HIS WAY!
LET THE BOSS PASS!!
WHAT'S WITH YOU PEOPLE?
WE'RE LACKEYS!
YES, I CAN SEE THAT.
THERE'S ALSO A JUNIOR HIGH KID HERE, RIGHT?
OF COURSE YOU WOULD KNOW THAT, SIR!
TAKE ME TO HIM.
わら hustle わら
わら hustle わら
わら bustle
わら bustle
カッ clop カッ clop カッ clop
YES, SIR!
THERE COULD STILL BE ENEMIES LURKING AROUND, SO WE'LL BE YOUR ESCORT, SIR!
WHAT? ENEMIES? WHO ARE YOU PEOPLE...?
HEY! WHO IS...
THAT'S THE BOSS!
FOR REAL?! HOLY SHIT!
SIR, I HAVE A REPORT!!
bam!
WHAT IS IT?
...THE BOSS IS HERE FROM HQ!

Matsuo's Evil Spirit Observation Log (#1)

Each night ...
...we go for a walk.
Cookie is excited when we find a spirit.
STAY!
NO! BAD COOKIE! YOU DON'T KNOW WHERE IT'S BEEN!
munch
munch
chomp
Cookie then eats the spirit.
glorrk
Cookie grows more eyes.

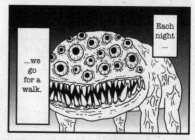

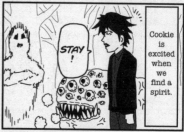

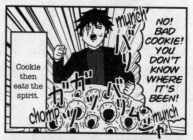

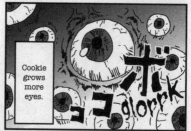

CHAPTER 45: LEADER

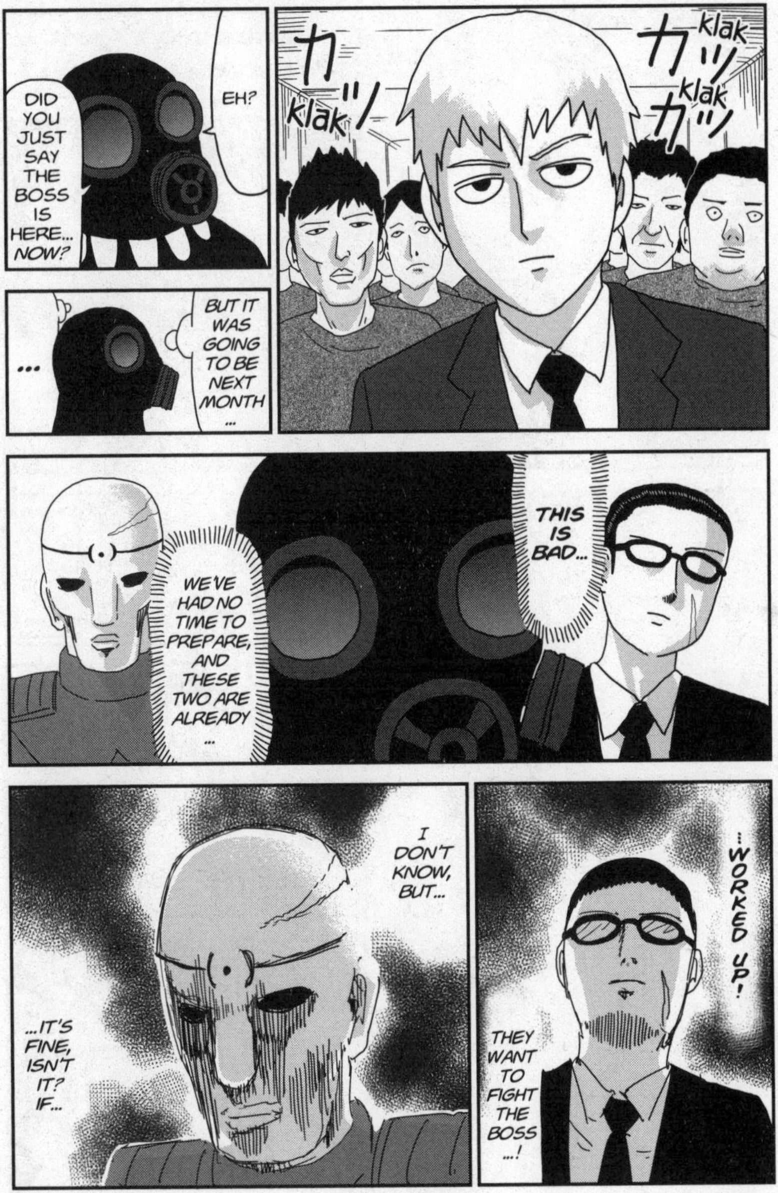
klak
klak
klak
EH?
DID YOU JUST SAY THE BOSS IS HERE... NOW?
BUT IT WAS GOING TO BE NEXT MONTH...
...
THIS IS BAD...
WE'VE HAD NO TIME TO PREPARE, AND THESE TWO ARE ALREADY...
...WORKED UP!
THEY WANT TO FIGHT THE BOSS...!
I DON'T KNOW, BUT...
...IT'S FINE, ISN'T IT? IF...

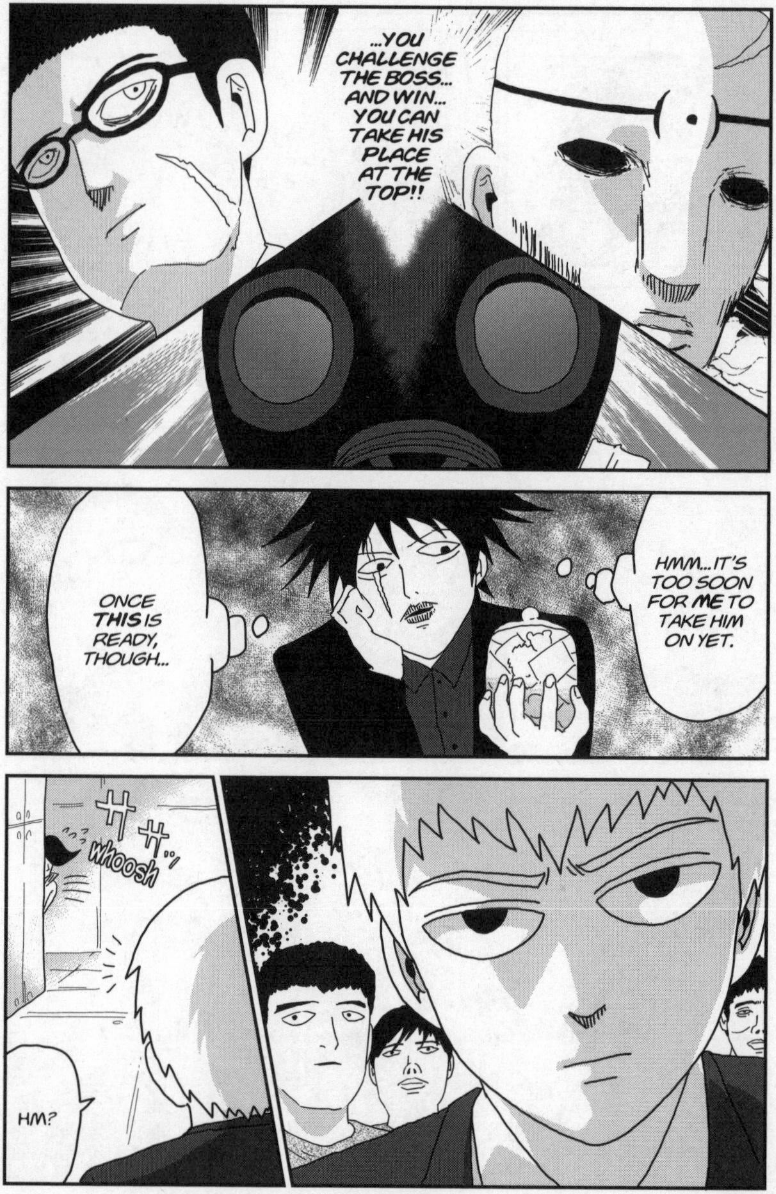
...YOU CHALLENGE THE BOSS... AND WIN... YOU CAN TAKE HIS PLACE AT THE TOP!!
HMM...IT'S TOO SOON FOR ME TO TAKE HIM ON YET.
ONCE THIS IS READY, THOUGH...
whoosh
HM?

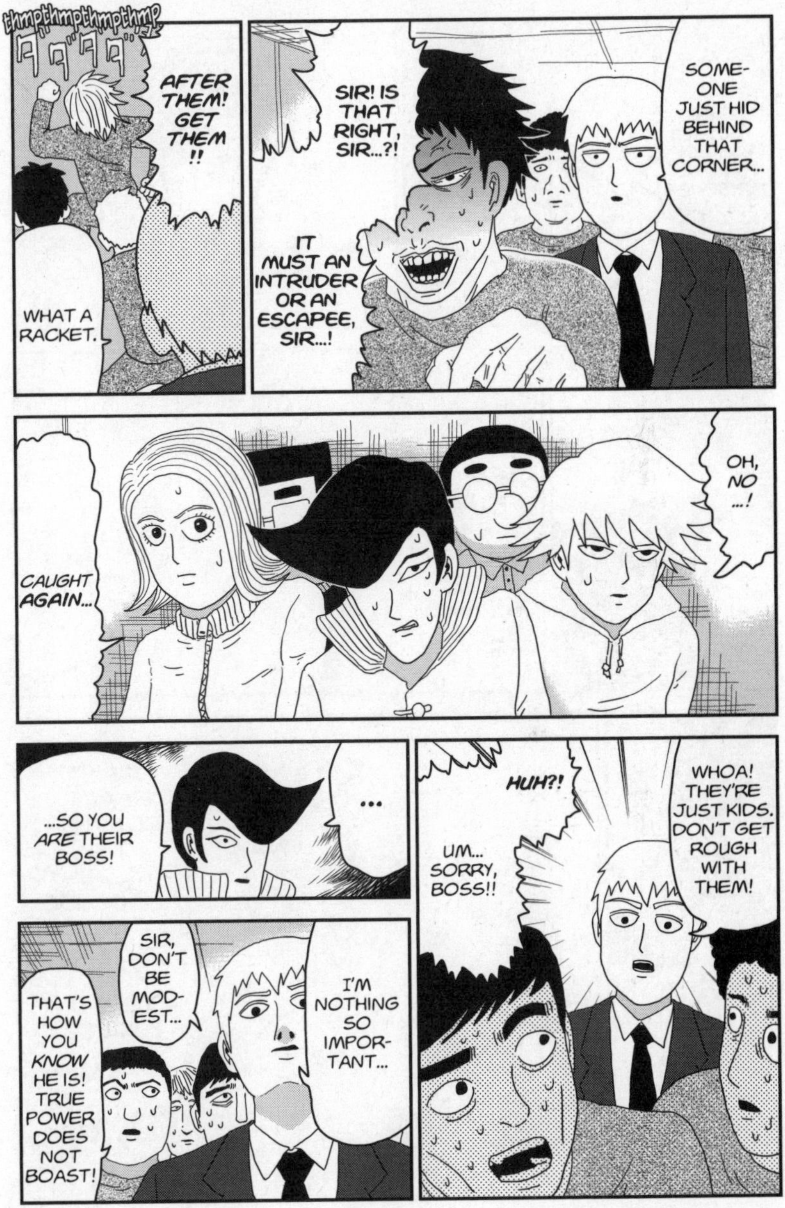
SOME-ONE JUST HID BEHIND THAT CORNER...
SIR! IS THAT RIGHT, SIR...?!
IT MUST AN INTRUDER OR AN ESCAPEE, SIR...!
thmpthmpthmpthmp
タダタダ
AFTER THEM! GET THEM!!
WHAT A RACKET.
OH, NO...!
CAUGHT AGAIN...
WHOA! THEY'RE JUST KIDS. DON'T GET ROUGH WITH THEM!
HUH?!
UM... SORRY, BOSS!!
...
...SO YOU ARE THEIR BOSS!
I'M NOTHING SO IMPORTANT...
SIR, DON'T BE MOD-EST...
THAT'S HOW YOU KNOW HE IS! TRUE POWER DOES NOT BOAST!

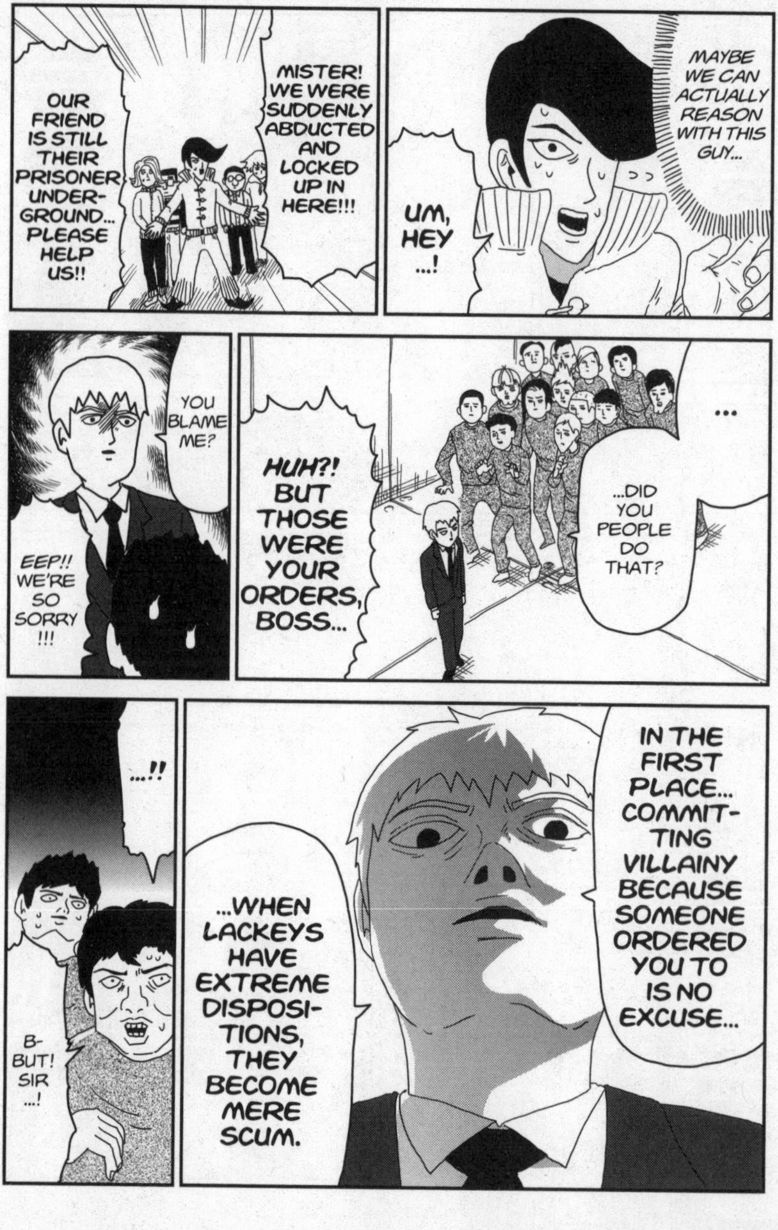
MAYBE WE CAN ACTUALLY REASON WITH THIS GUY...
UM, HEY ...!
MISTER! WE WERE SUDDENLY ABDUCTED AND LOCKED UP IN HERE!!!
OUR FRIEND IS STILL THEIR PRISONER UNDER-GROUND... PLEASE HELP US!!
...
...DID YOU PEOPLE DO THAT?
HUH?! BUT THOSE WERE YOUR ORDERS, BOSS...
YOU BLAME ME?
EEP!! WE'RE SO SORRY !!!
IN THE FIRST PLACE... COMMIT-TING VILLAINY BECAUSE SOMEONE ORDERED YOU TO IS NO EXCUSE...
...WHEN LACKEYS HAVE EXTREME DISPOSI-TIONS, THEY BECOME MERE SCUM.
...!!
B-BUT! SIR ...!

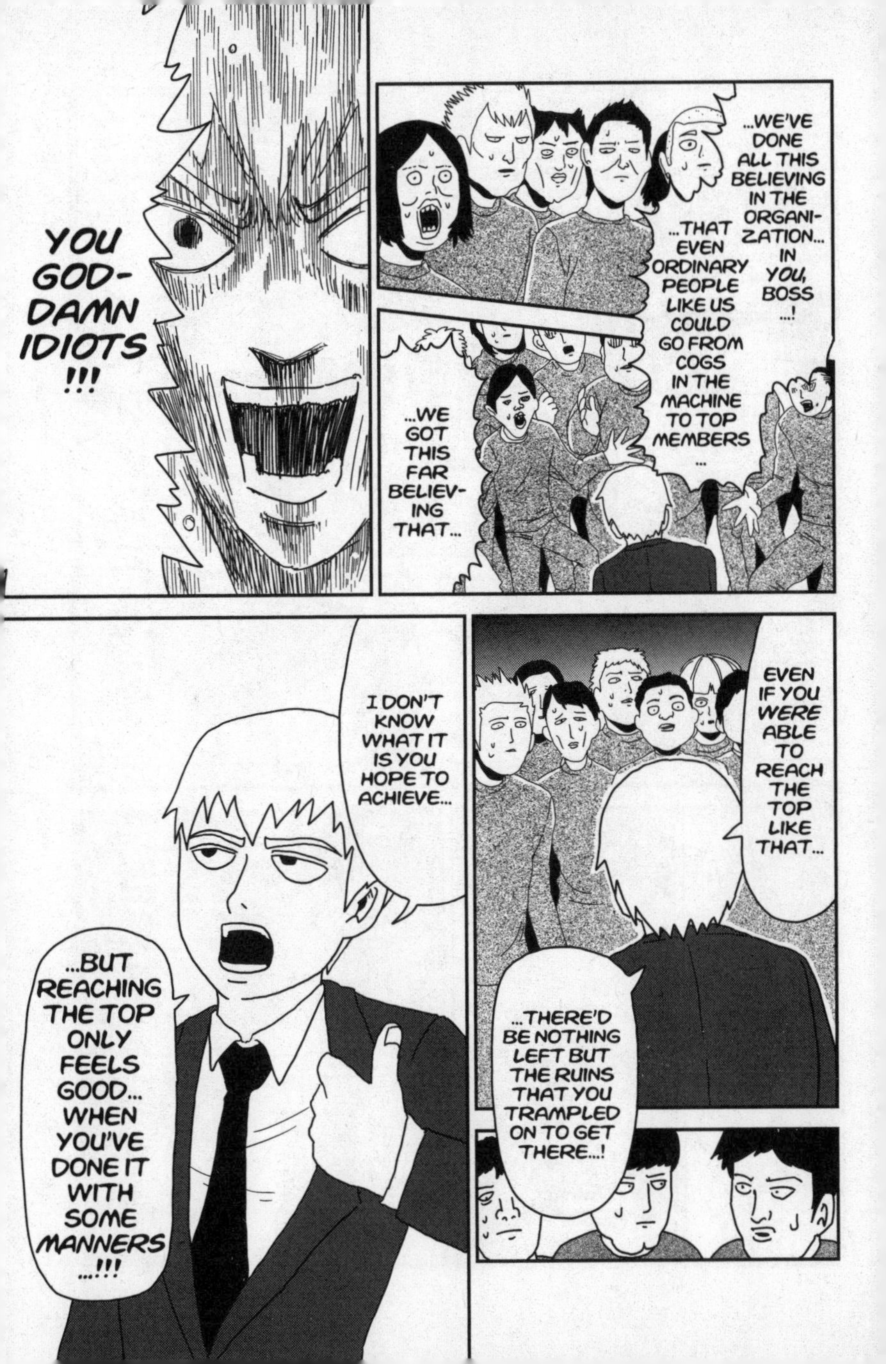
...WE'VE DONE ALL THIS BELIEVING IN THE ORGANIZATION... IN YOU, BOSS...!
...THAT EVEN ORDINARY PEOPLE LIKE US COULD GO FROM COGS IN THE MACHINE TO TOP MEMBERS...
...WE GOT THIS FAR BELIEVING THAT...
YOU GODDAMN IDIOTS!!!
EVEN IF YOU WERE ABLE TO REACH THE TOP LIKE THAT...
...THERE'D BE NOTHING LEFT BUT THE RUINS THAT YOU TRAMPLED ON TO GET THERE...!
I DON'T KNOW WHAT IT IS YOU HOPE TO ACHIEVE...
...BUT REACHING THE TOP ONLY FEELS GOOD... WHEN YOU'VE DONE IT WITH SOME MANNERS...!!!

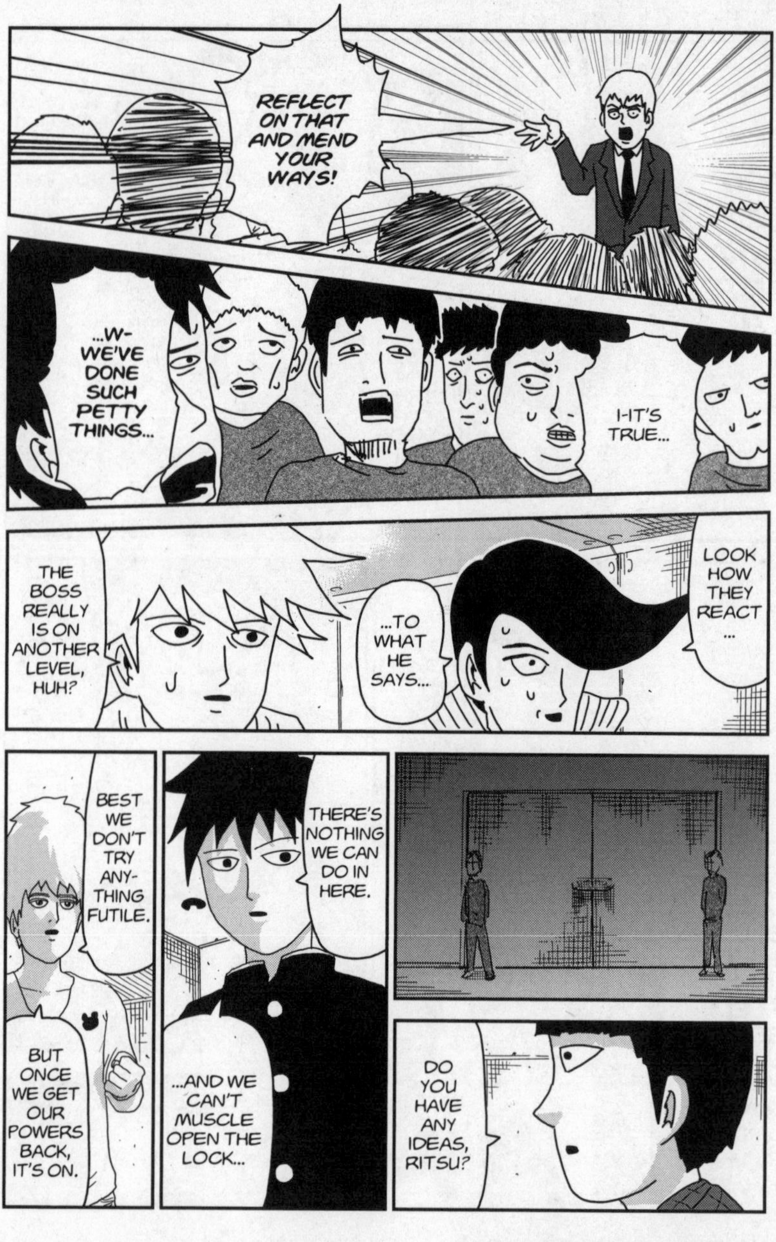

REFLECT ON THAT AND MEND YOUR WAYS!
I-IT'S TRUE...
...W-WE'VE DONE SUCH PETTY THINGS...
LOOK HOW THEY REACT ...
...TO WHAT HE SAYS...
THE BOSS REALLY IS ON ANOTHER LEVEL, HUH?
DO YOU HAVE ANY IDEAS, RITSU?
THERE'S NOTHING WE CAN DO IN HERE.
...AND WE CAN'T MUSCLE OPEN THE LOCK...
BEST WE DON'T TRY ANY-THING FUTILE.
BUT ONCE WE GET OUR POWERS BACK, IT'S ON.

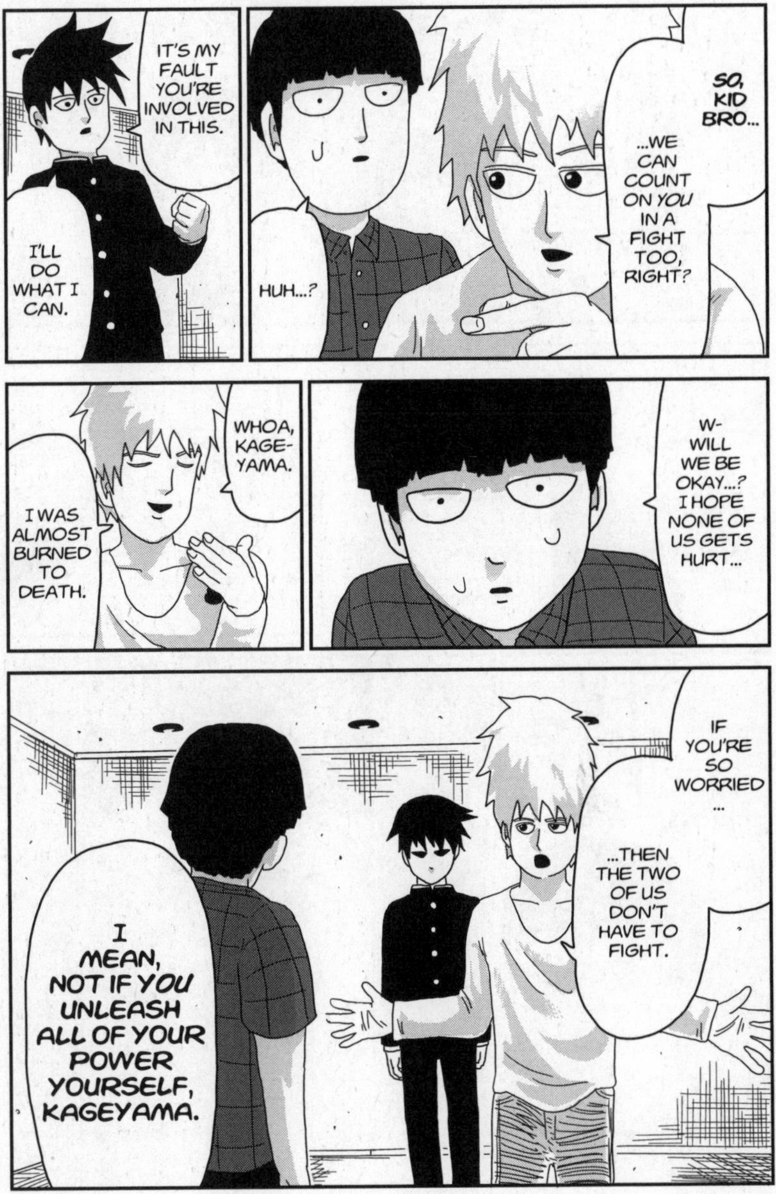
SO, KID BRO...
...WE CAN COUNT ON YOU IN A FIGHT TOO, RIGHT?
HUH...?
IT'S MY FAULT YOU'RE INVOLVED IN THIS.
I'LL DO WHAT I CAN.
W-WILL WE BE OKAY...? I HOPE NONE OF US GETS HURT...
WHOA, KAGE-YAMA.
I WAS ALMOST BURNED TO DEATH.
IF YOU'RE SO WORRIED...
...THEN THE TWO OF US DON'T HAVE TO FIGHT.
I MEAN, NOT IF YOU UNLEASH ALL OF YOUR POWER YOURSELF, KAGEYAMA.

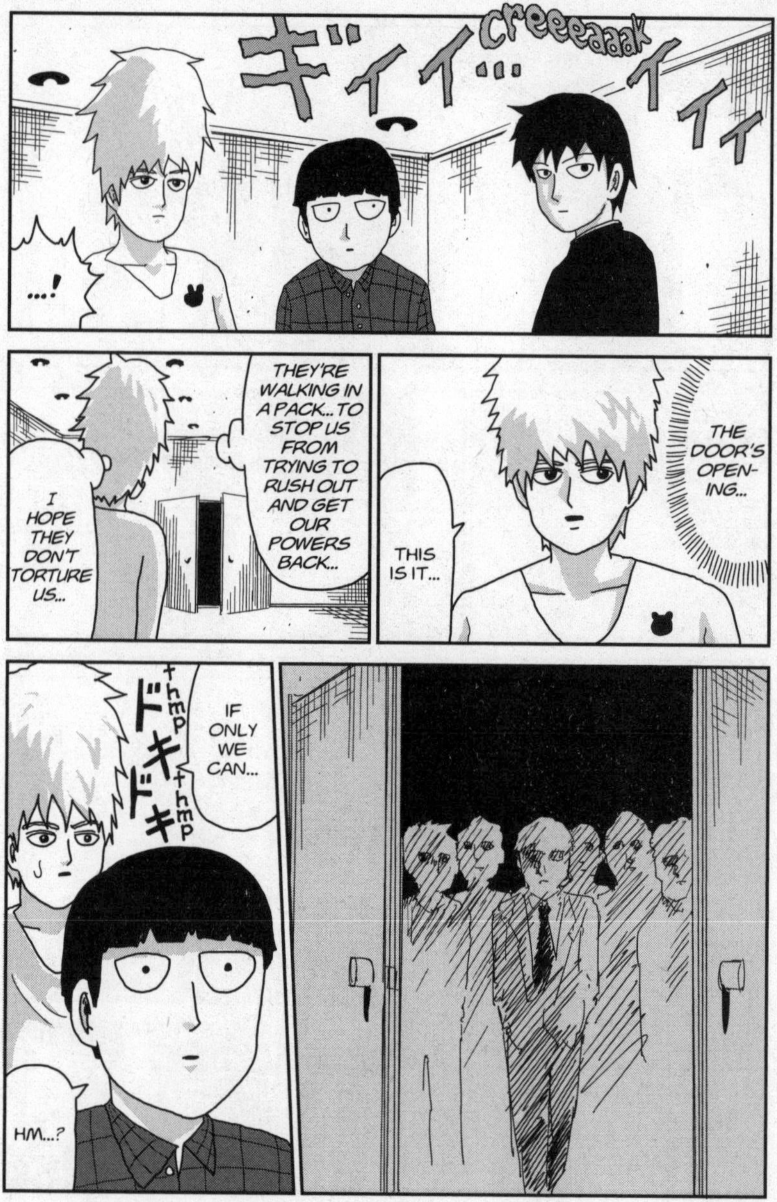
ギイイ…イイイ
creeeaaak
...!
THE DOOR'S OPENING...
THIS IS IT...
THEY'RE WALKING IN A PACK...TO STOP US FROM TRYING TO RUSH OUT AND GET OUR POWERS BACK...
I HOPE THEY DON'T TORTURE US...
IF ONLY WE CAN...
ドキドキ
thmp thmp
HM...?

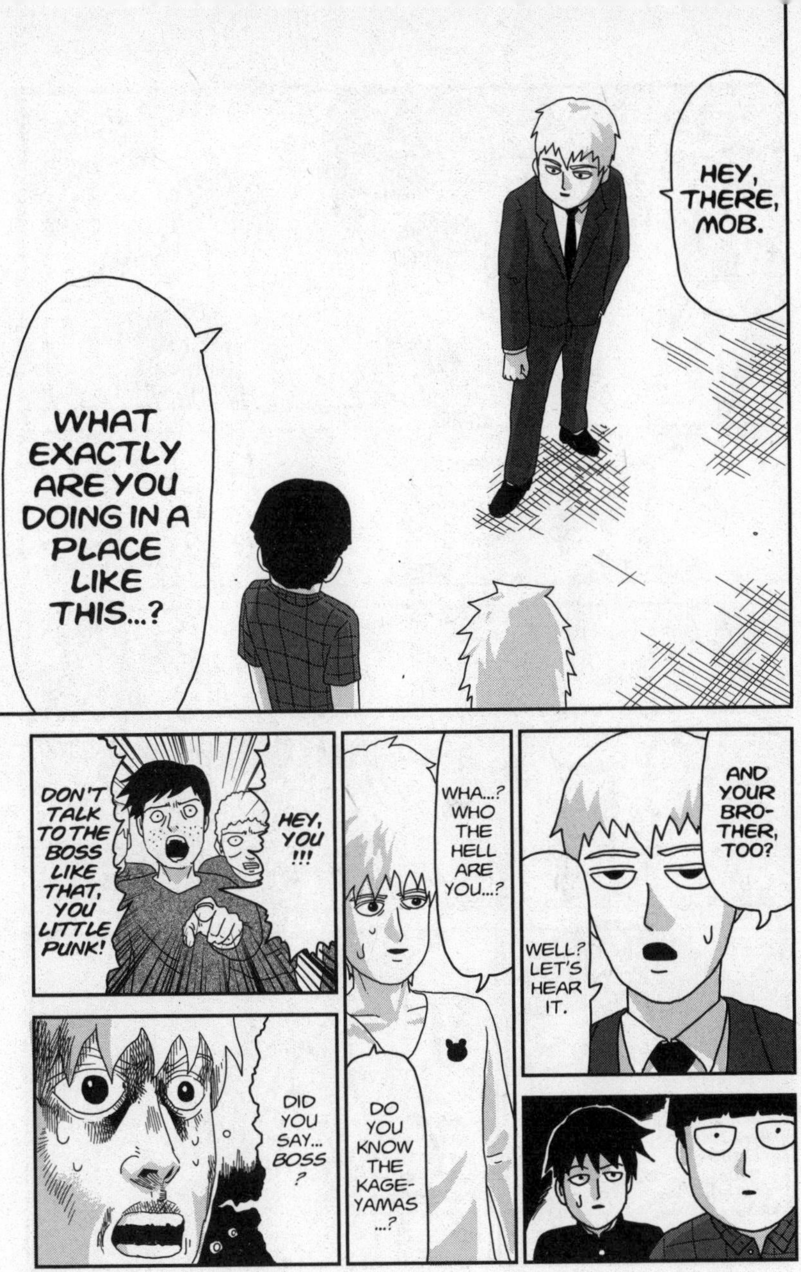
HEY, THERE, MOB.
WHAT EXACTLY ARE YOU DOING IN A PLACE LIKE THIS...?
AND YOUR BRO-THER, TOO?
WELL? LET'S HEAR IT.
WHA...? WHO THE HELL ARE YOU...?
DO YOU KNOW THE KAGE-YAMAS...?
HEY, YOU!!!
DON'T TALK TO THE BOSS LIKE THAT, YOU LITTLE PUNK!
DID YOU SAY... BOSS?

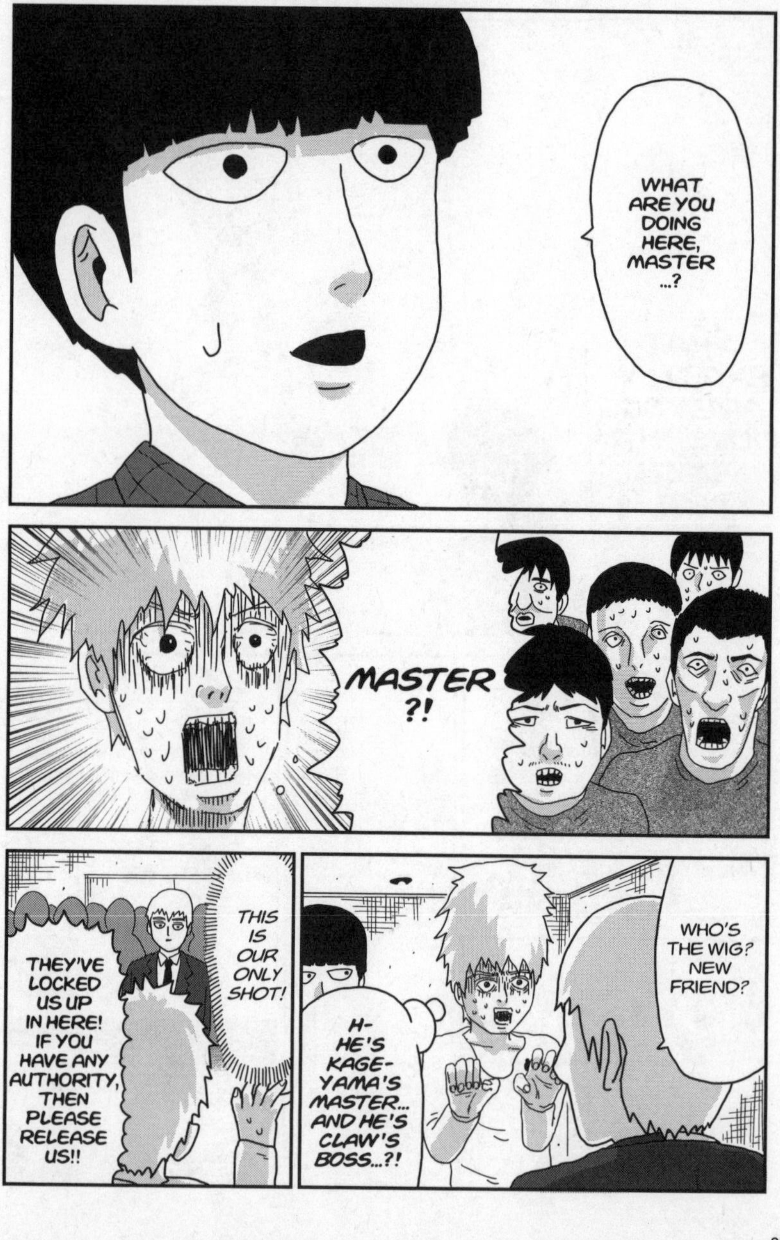
WHAT ARE YOU DOING HERE, MASTER ...?
MASTER ?!
WHO'S THE WIG? NEW FRIEND?
H- HE'S KAGE-YAMA'S MASTER... AND HE'S CLAW'S BOSS...?!
THIS IS OUR ONLY SHOT!
THEY'VE LOCKED US UP IN HERE! IF YOU HAVE ANY AUTHORITY, THEN PLEASE RELEASE US!!

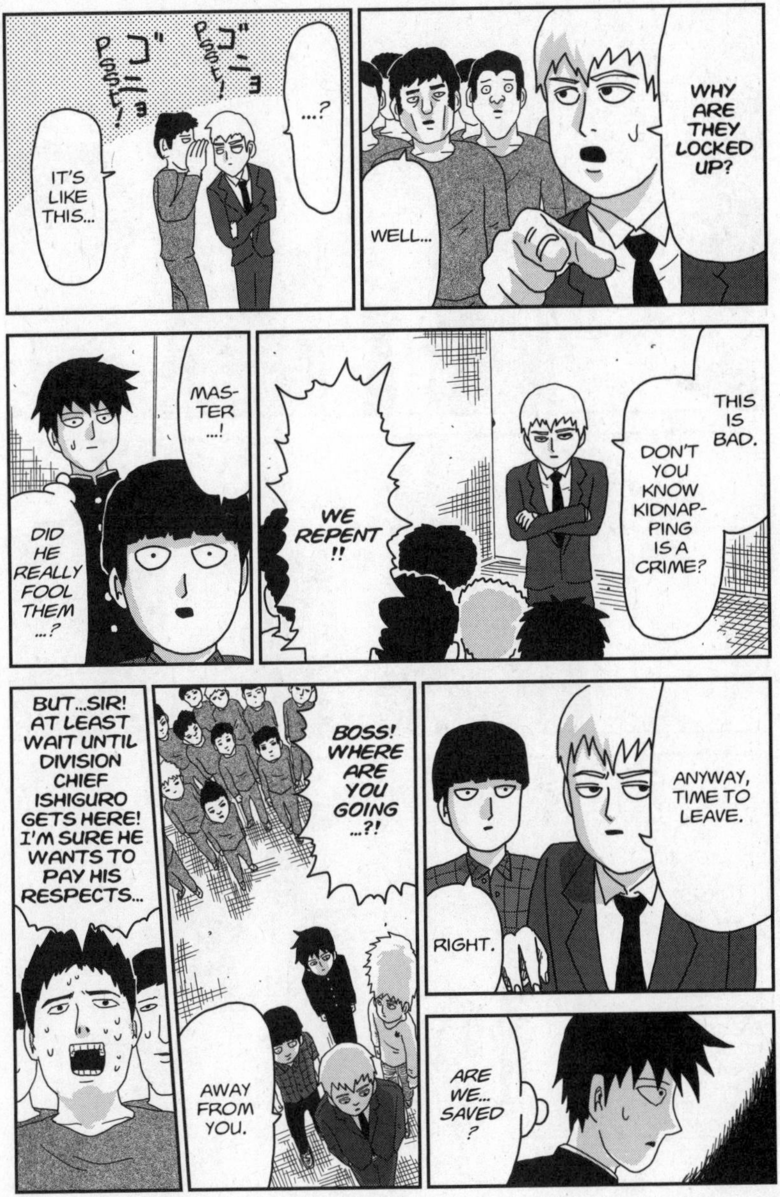
WHY ARE THEY LOCKED UP?
WELL...
...?
PSSST!
ゴニョ
PSSST!
ゴニョ
IT'S LIKE THIS...
THIS IS BAD.
DON'T YOU KNOW KIDNAP-PING IS A CRIME?
WE REPENT!!
MAS-TER...!
DID HE REALLY FOOL THEM...?
ANYWAY, TIME TO LEAVE.
RIGHT.
ARE WE... SAVED?
BOSS! WHERE ARE YOU GOING...?!
AWAY FROM YOU.
BUT...SIR! AT LEAST WAIT UNTIL DIVISION CHIEF ISHIGURO GETS HERE! I'M SURE HE WANTS TO PAY HIS RESPECTS...

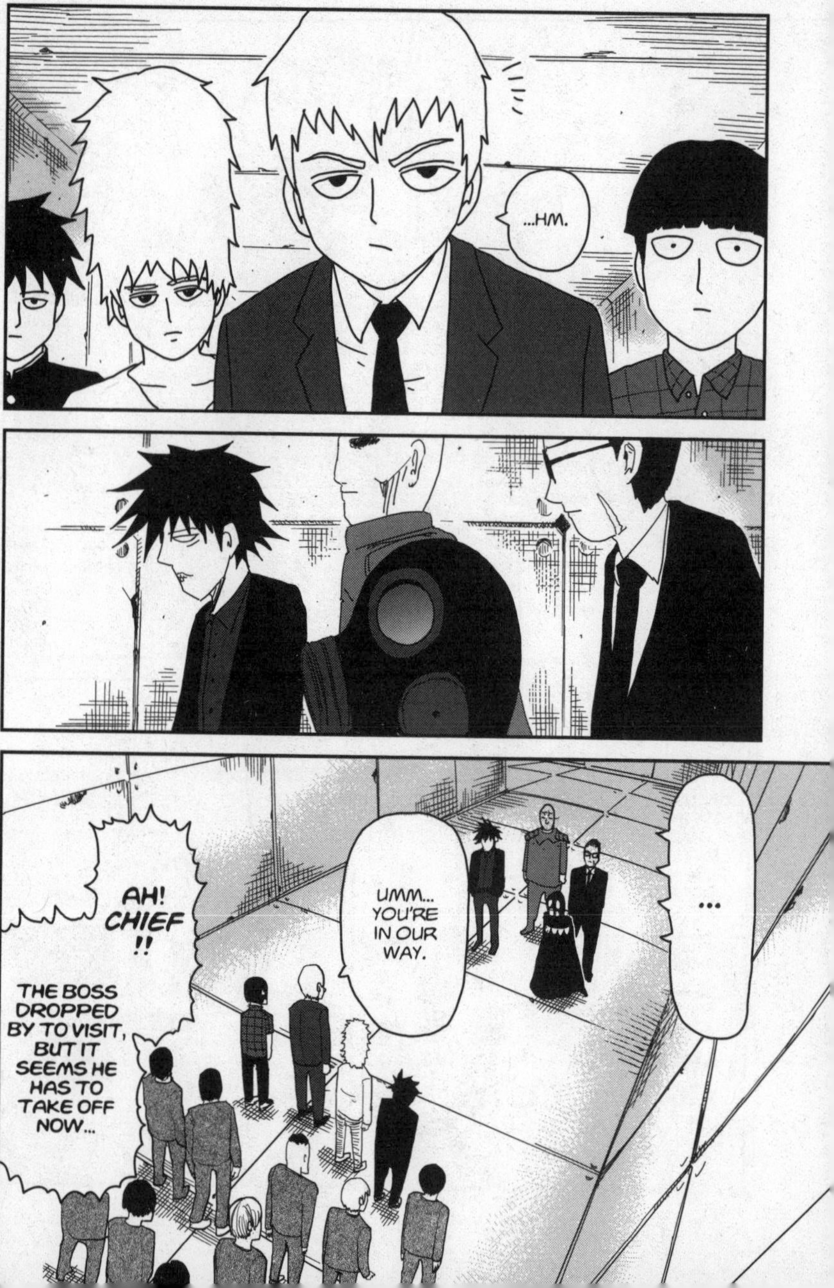
...HM.
...
UMM... YOU'RE IN OUR WAY.
AH! CHIEF!!
THE BOSS DROPPED BY TO VISIT, BUT IT SEEMS HE HAS TO TAKE OFF NOW...

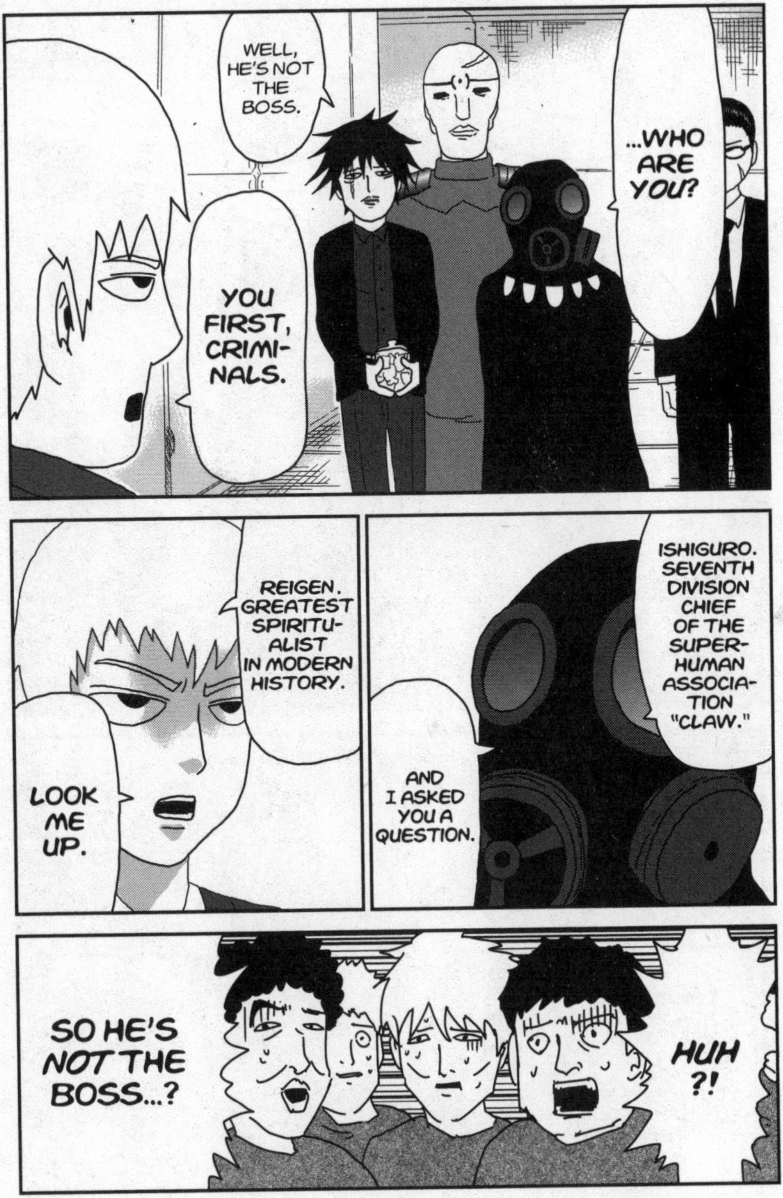
...WHO ARE YOU?
WELL, HE'S NOT THE BOSS.
YOU FIRST, CRIMINALS.
ISHIGURO. SEVENTH DIVISION CHIEF OF THE SUPER-HUMAN ASSOCIATION "CLAW."
AND I ASKED YOU A QUESTION.
REIGEN. GREATEST SPIRITUALIST IN MODERN HISTORY.
LOOK ME UP.
HUH?!
SO HE'S NOT THE BOSS...?

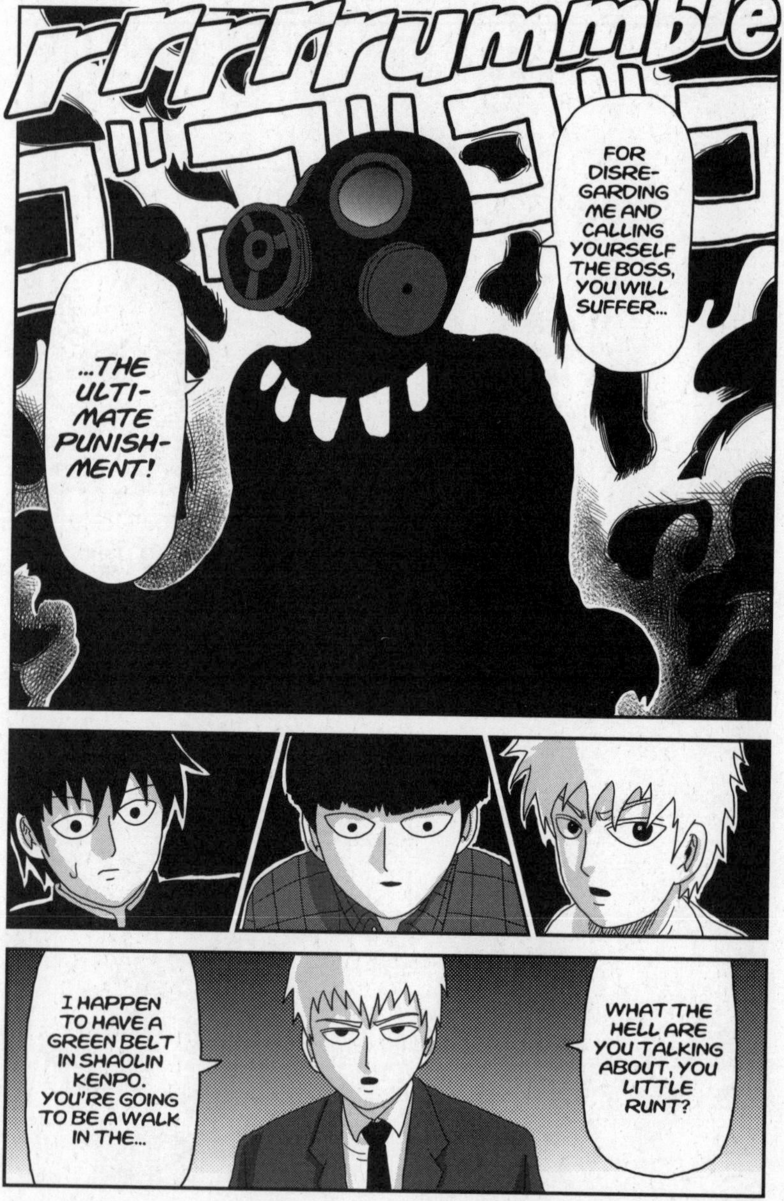
rrrrrummble
FOR DISREGARDING ME AND CALLING YOURSELF THE BOSS, YOU WILL SUFFER...
...THE ULTIMATE PUNISHMENT!
WHAT THE HELL ARE YOU TALKING ABOUT, YOU LITTLE RUNT?
I HAPPEN TO HAVE A GREEN BELT IN SHAOLIN KENPO. YOU'RE GOING TO BE A WALK IN THE...

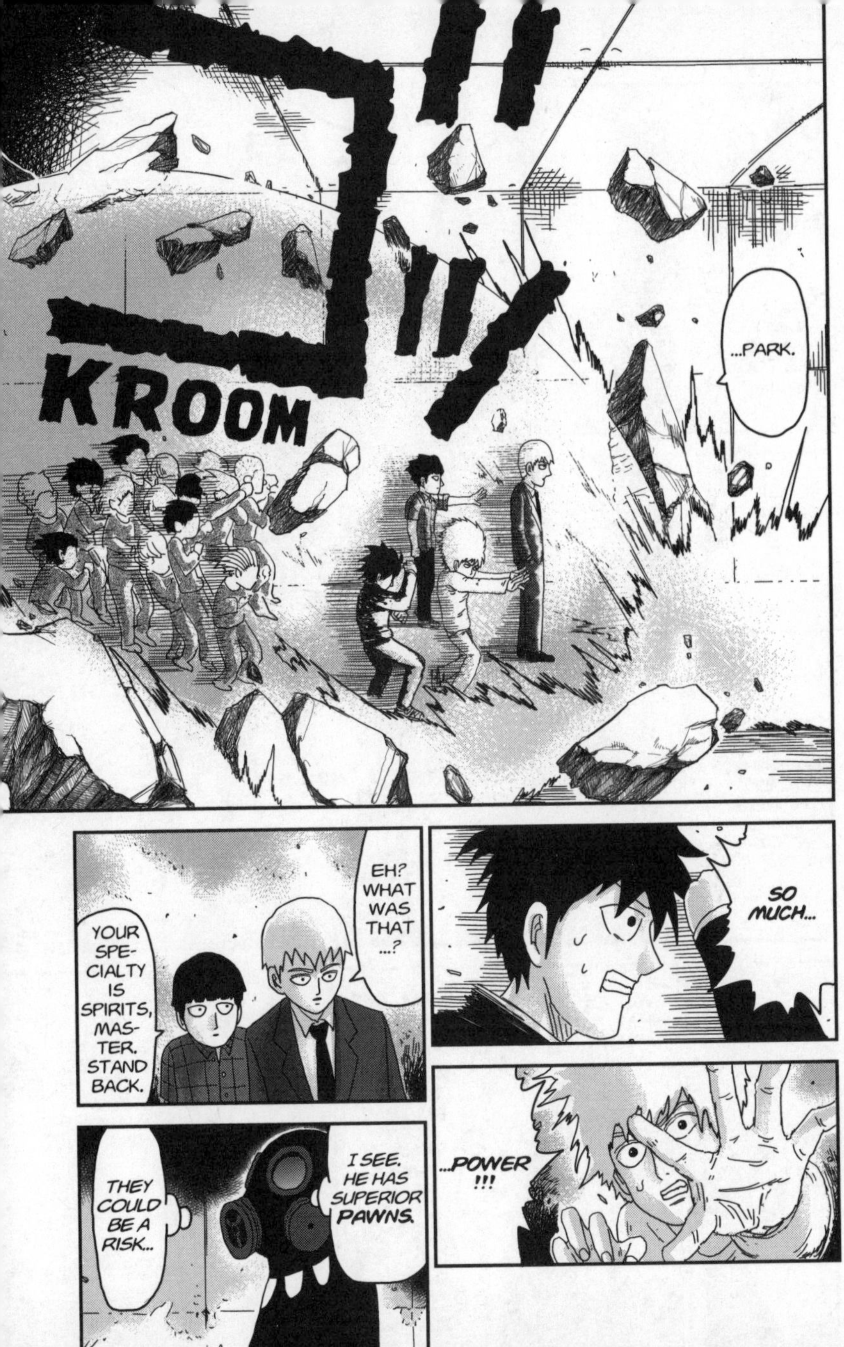
...PARK.
KROOM
SO MUCH...
EH? WHAT WAS THAT ...?
YOUR SPE-CIALTY IS SPIRITS, MAS-TER. STAND BACK.
...POWER !!!
I SEE. HE HAS SUPERIOR PAWNS.
THEY COULD BE A RISK...

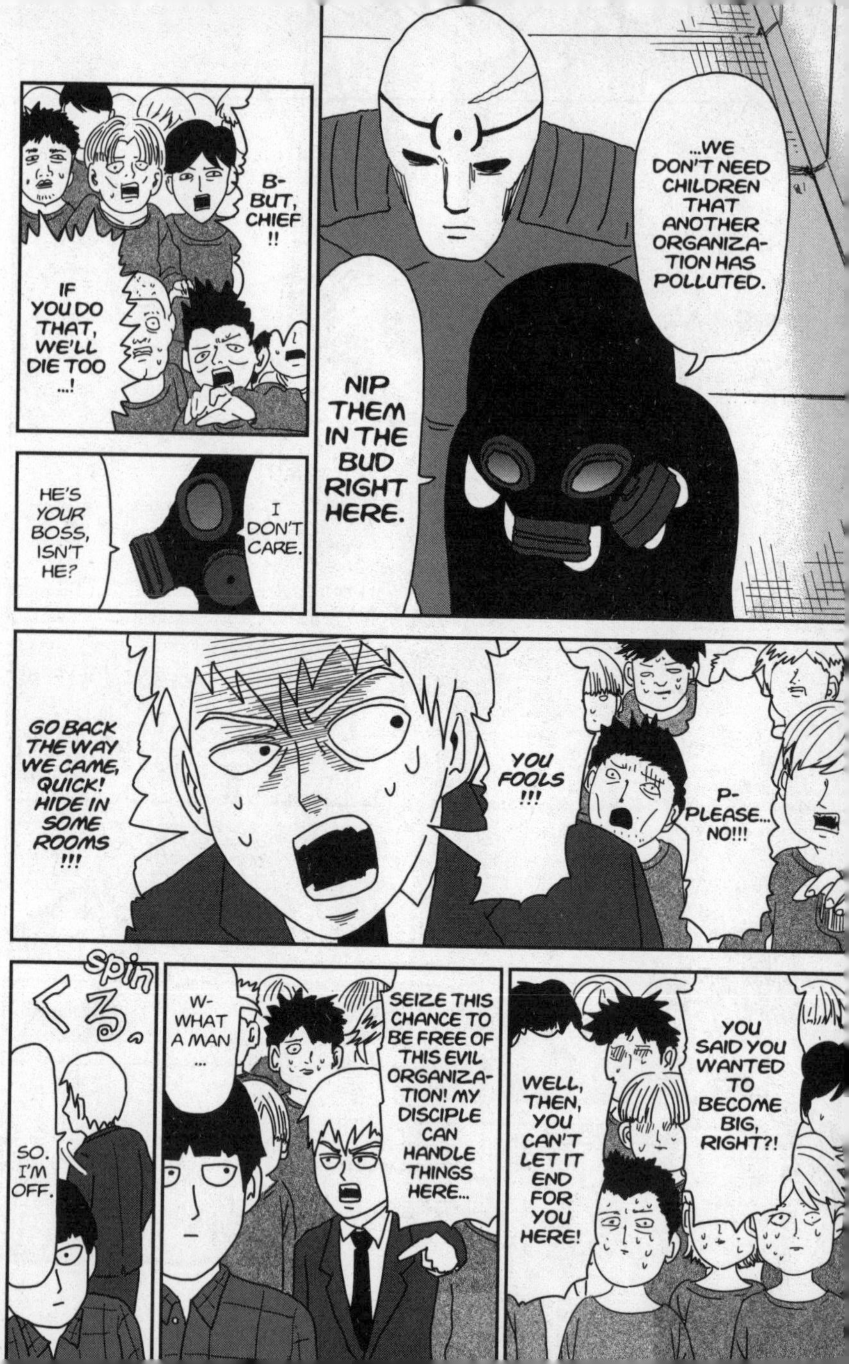
...WE DON'T NEED CHILDREN THAT ANOTHER ORGANIZA-TION HAS POLLUTED.
NIP THEM IN THE BUD RIGHT HERE.
B-BUT, CHIEF!!
IF YOU DO THAT, WE'LL DIE TOO ...!
I DON'T CARE.
HE'S YOUR BOSS, ISN'T HE?
P-PLEASE... NO!!!
YOU FOOLS!!!
GO BACK THE WAY WE CAME, QUICK! HIDE IN SOME ROOMS!!!
YOU SAID YOU WANTED TO BECOME BIG, RIGHT?!
WELL, THEN, YOU CAN'T LET IT END FOR YOU HERE!
SEIZE THIS CHANCE TO BE FREE OF THIS EVIL ORGANIZA-TION! MY DISCIPLE CAN HANDLE THINGS HERE...
W-WHAT A MAN ...
spin
くる。
SO. I'M OFF.

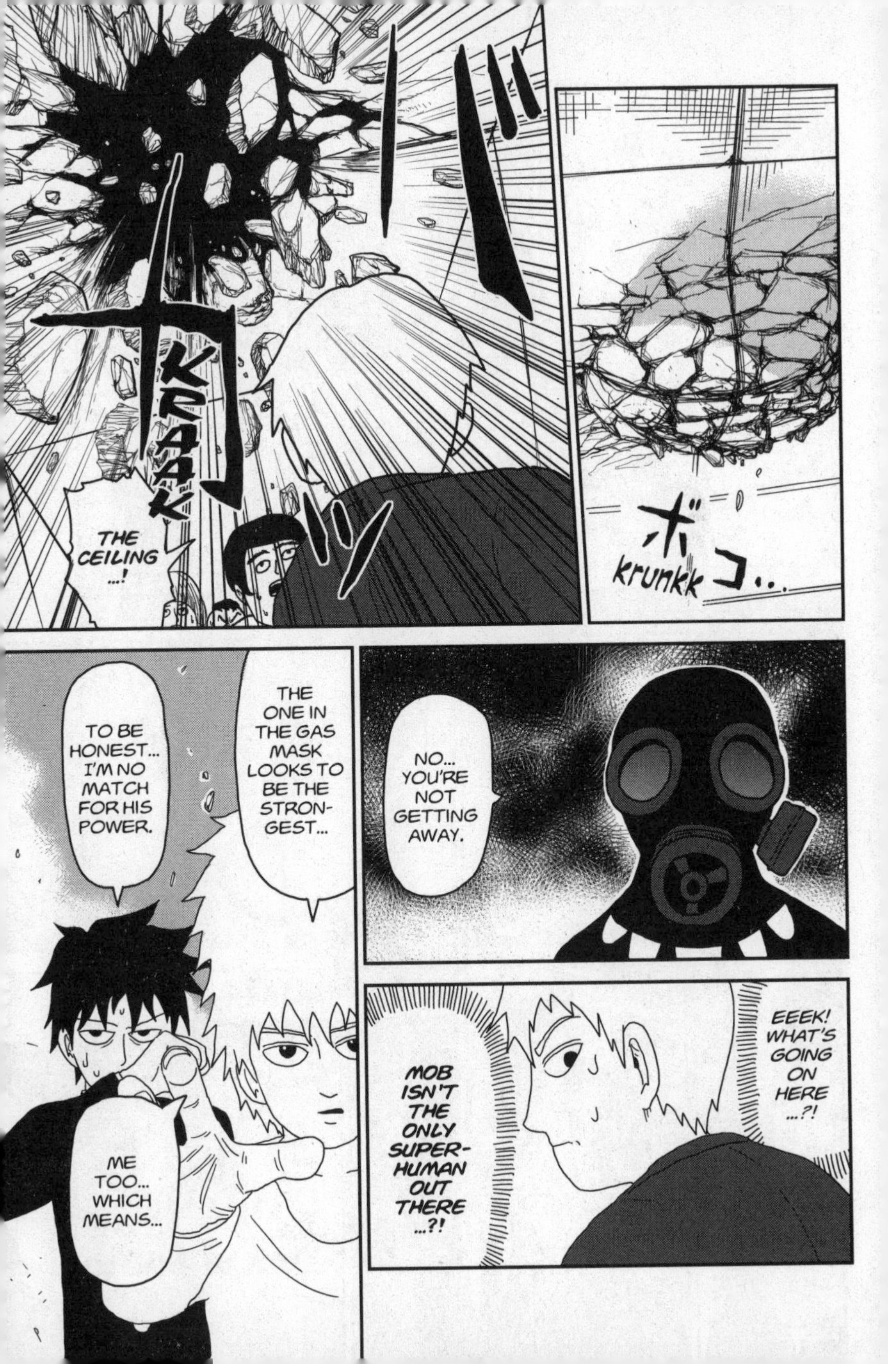
krunkk ボコ...
KRAAK
THE CEILING...!
NO... YOU'RE NOT GETTING AWAY.
EEEK! WHAT'S GOING ON HERE...?!
MOB ISN'T THE ONLY SUPER-HUMAN OUT THERE...?!
THE ONE IN THE GAS MASK LOOKS TO BE THE STRONGEST...
TO BE HONEST... I'M NO MATCH FOR HIS POWER.
ME TOO... WHICH MEANS...

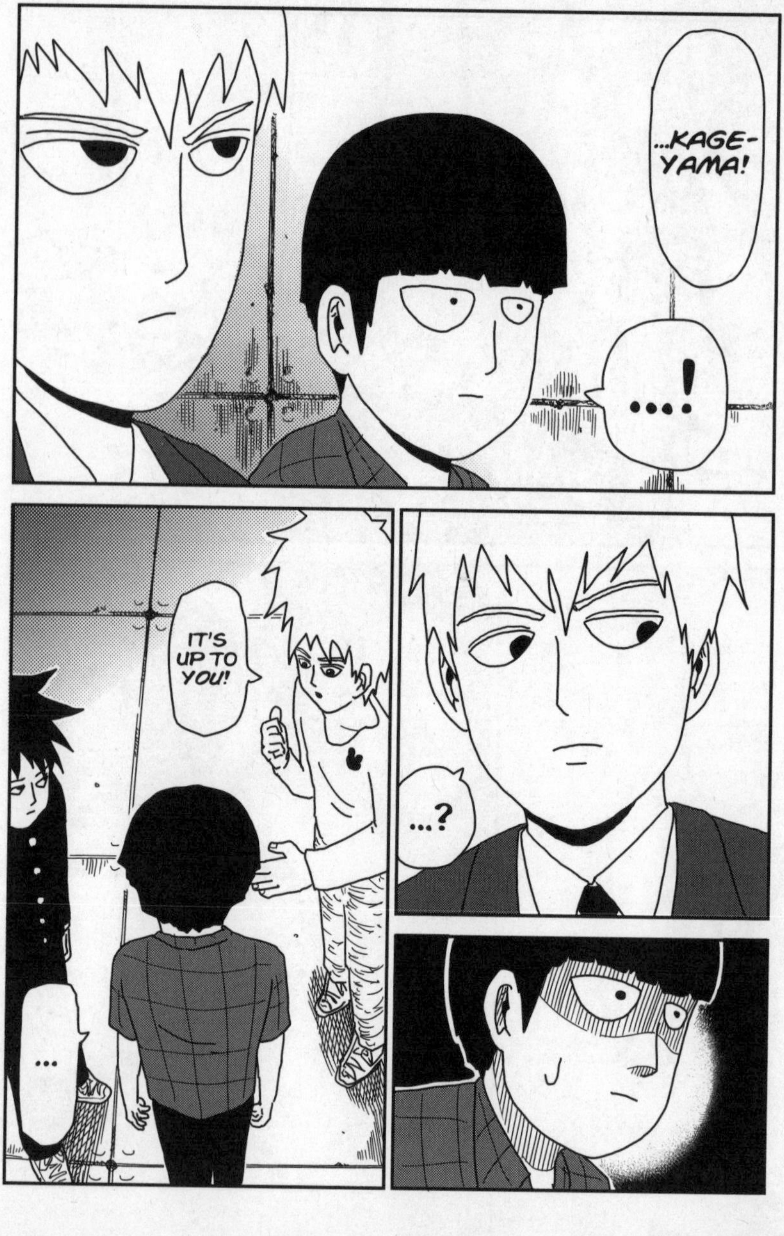
...KAGE-YAMA!
...!
...?
IT'S UP TO YOU!
...

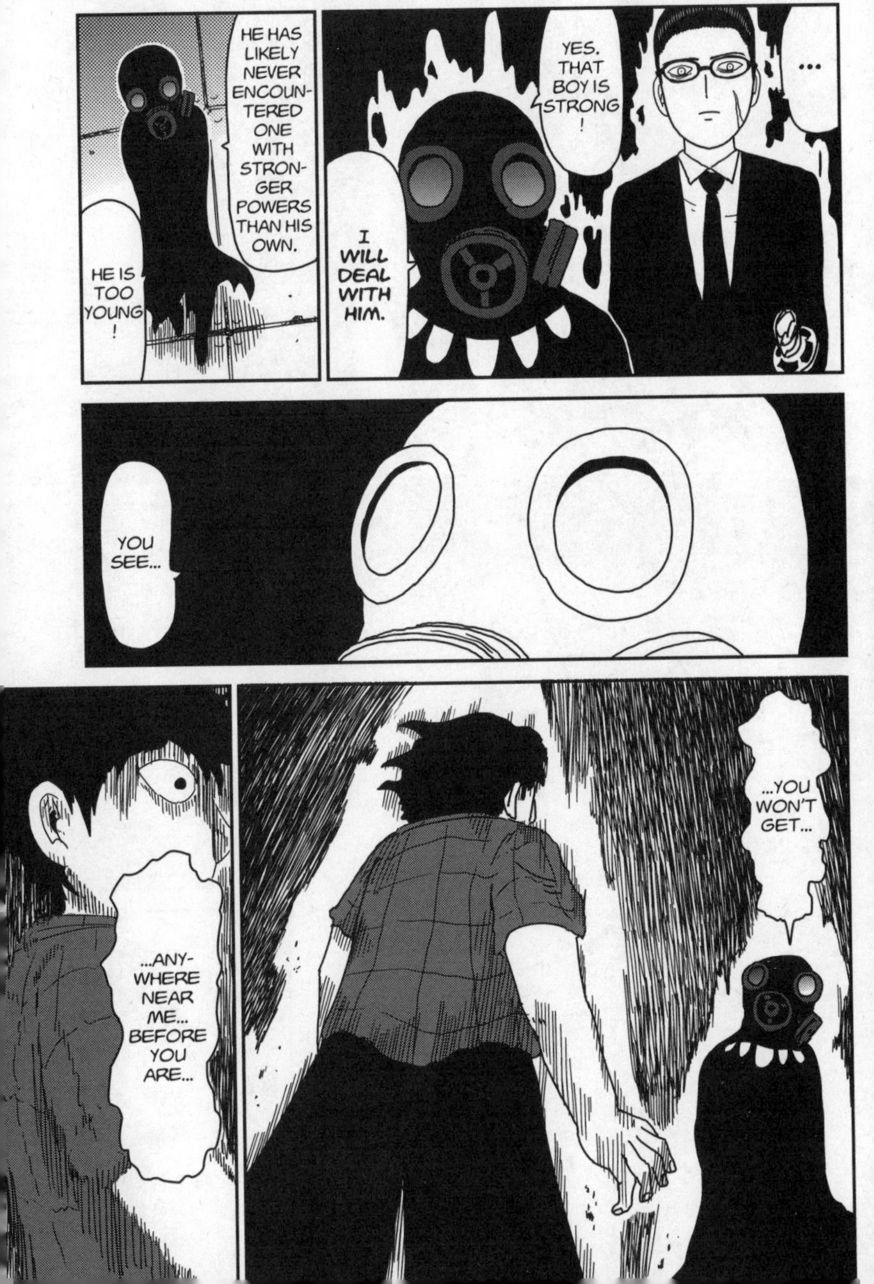
...
YES. THAT BOY IS STRONG!
I WILL DEAL WITH HIM.
HE HAS LIKELY NEVER ENCOUNTERED ONE WITH STRONGER POWERS THAN HIS OWN.
HE IS TOO YOUNG!
YOU SEE...
...YOU WON'T GET...
...ANYWHERE NEAR ME... BEFORE YOU ARE...

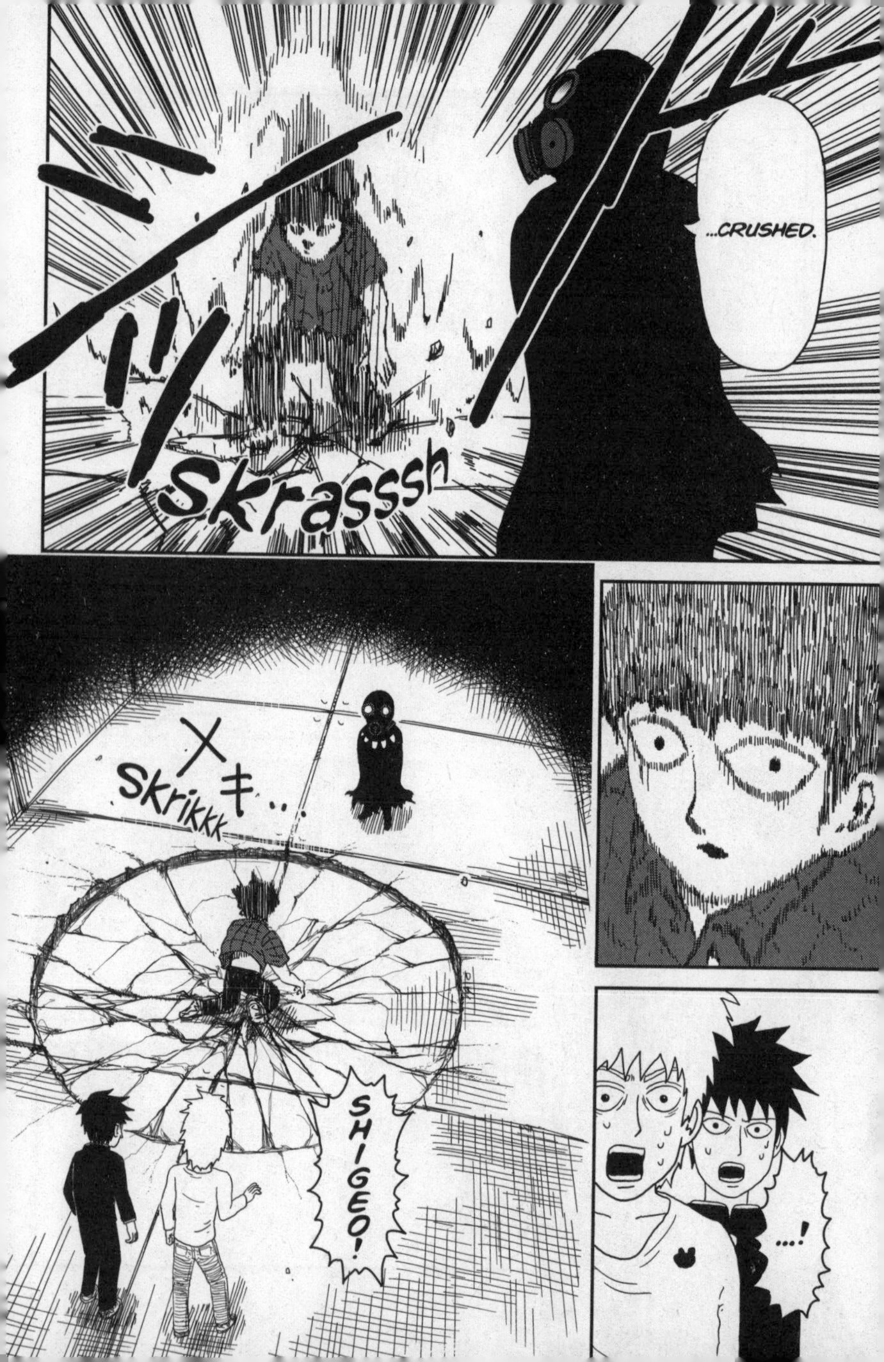
...CRUSHED.
Skrasssh
...!
メキ...
Skrikkk
SHIGEO!

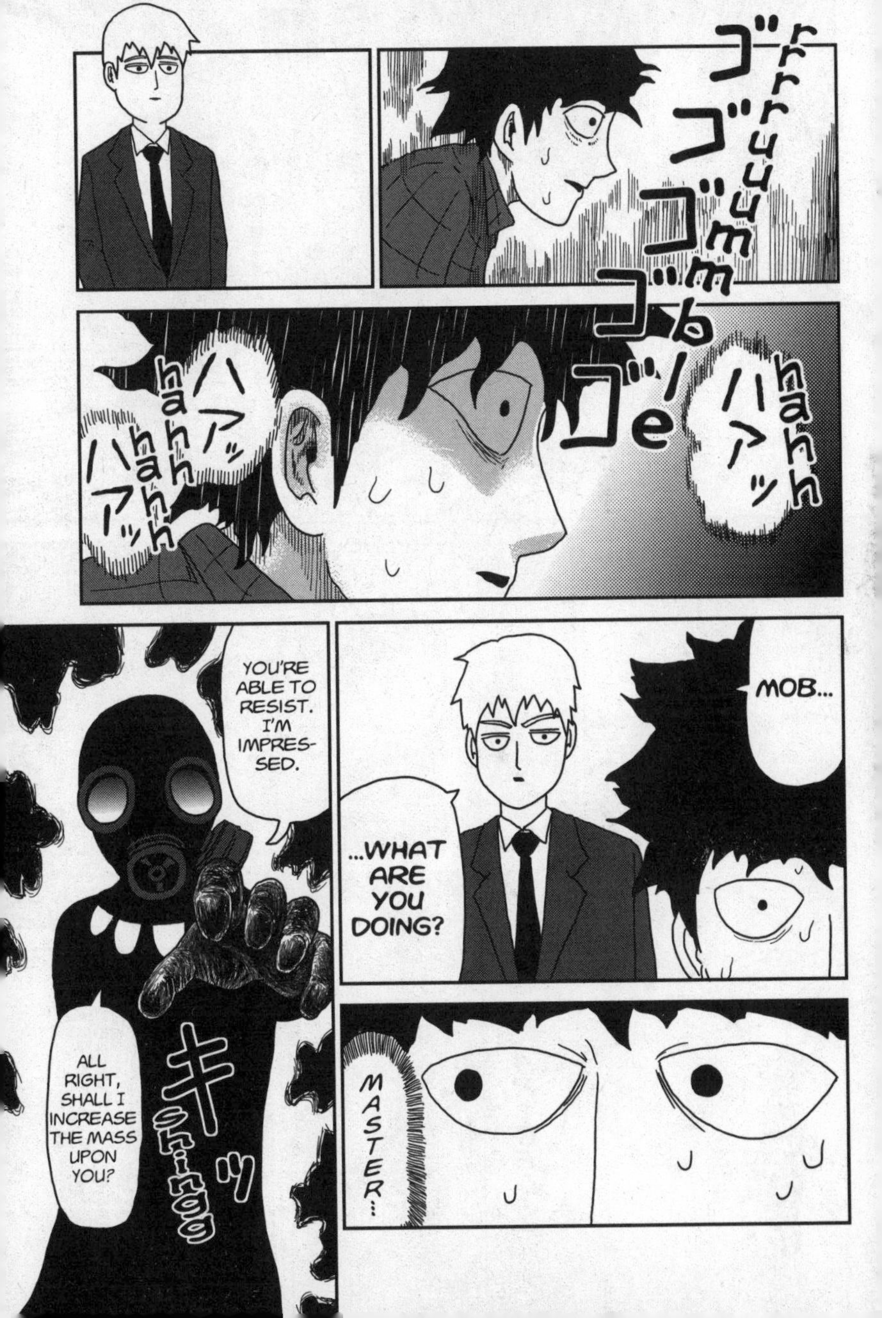
ゴゴゴゴ
rrrruuummmble
ハアッ
hahh
ハアッ
hahh
ハアッ
hahh
MOB...
...WHAT ARE YOU DOING?
MASTER...
YOU'RE ABLE TO RESIST. I'M IMPRES-SED.
キッ
shingg
ALL RIGHT, SHALL I INCREASE THE MASS UPON YOU?

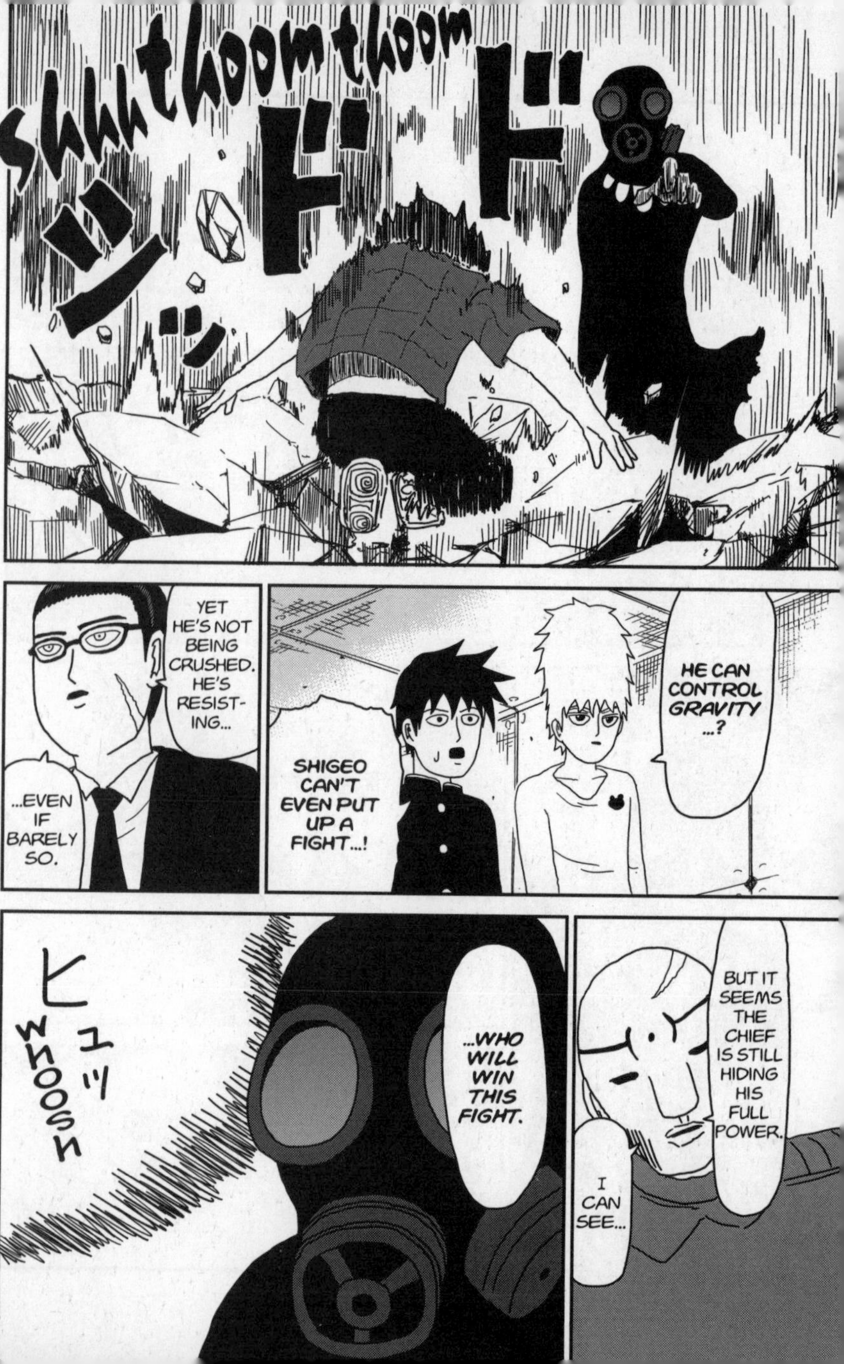
shhh thoom thoom
ドドド
HE CAN CONTROL GRAVITY ...?
SHIGEO CAN'T EVEN PUT UP A FIGHT...!
YET HE'S NOT BEING CRUSHED. HE'S RESIST-ING...
...EVEN IF BARELY SO.
BUT IT SEEMS THE CHIEF IS STILL HIDING HIS FULL POWER.
I CAN SEE...
...WHO WILL WIN THIS FIGHT.
ヒュッ
WHOOSH

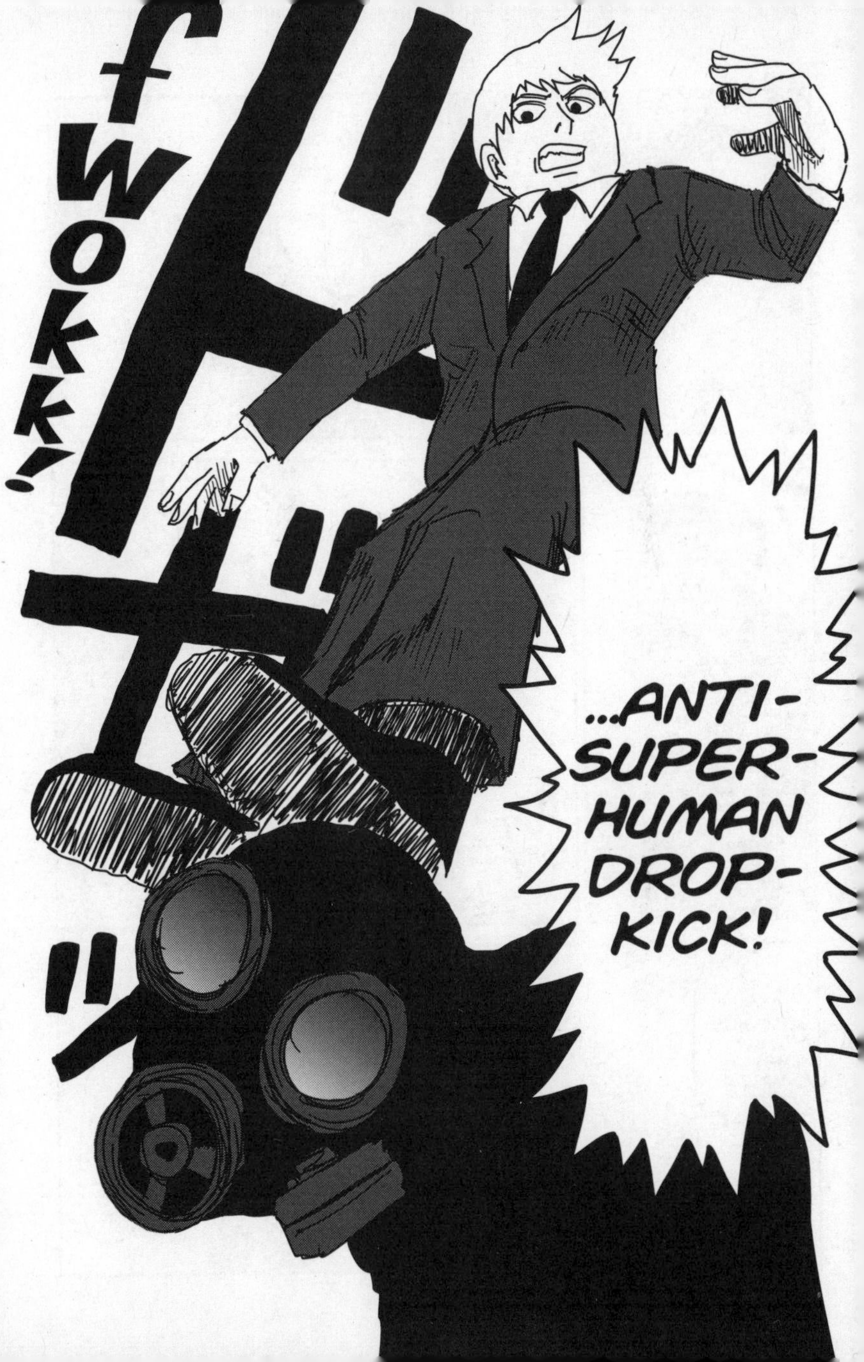

...ANTI-SUPER-HUMAN DROP-KICK!
fwokk!

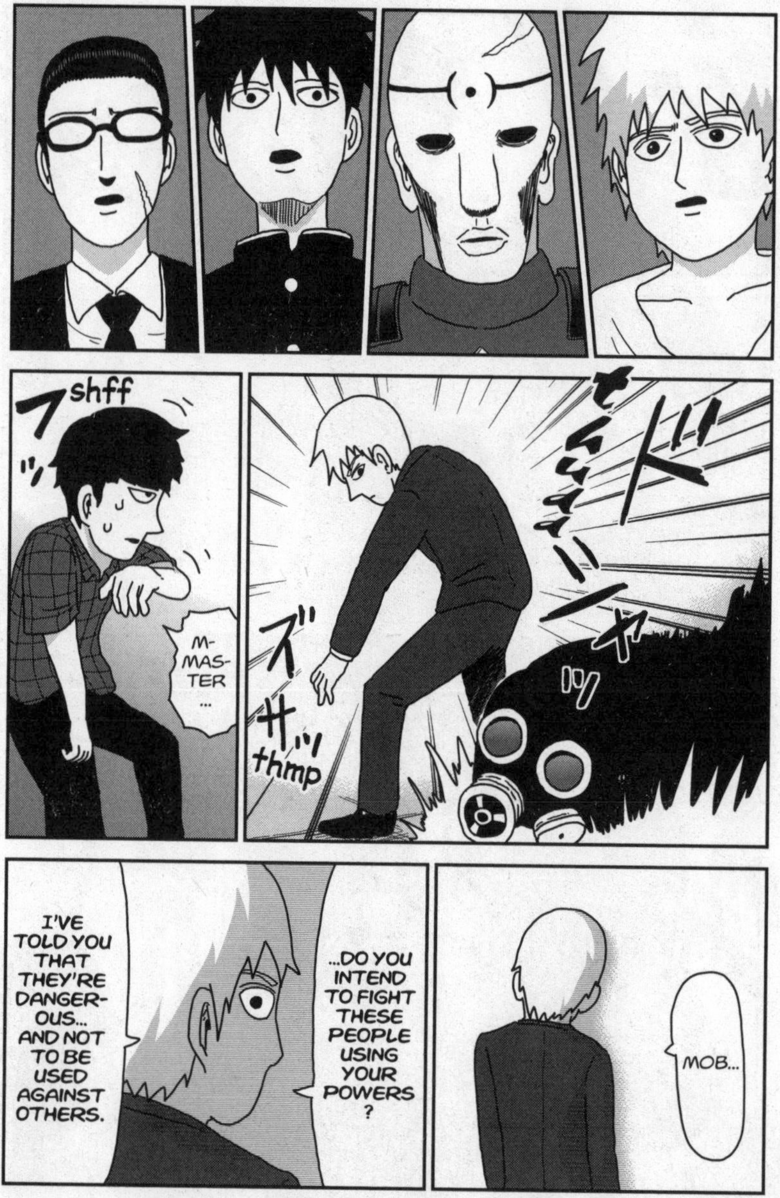
thmp
shff
M-MASTER...
MOB...
...DO YOU INTEND TO FIGHT THESE PEOPLE USING YOUR POWERS?
I'VE TOLD YOU THAT THEY'RE DANGEROUS... AND NOT TO BE USED AGAINST OTHERS.

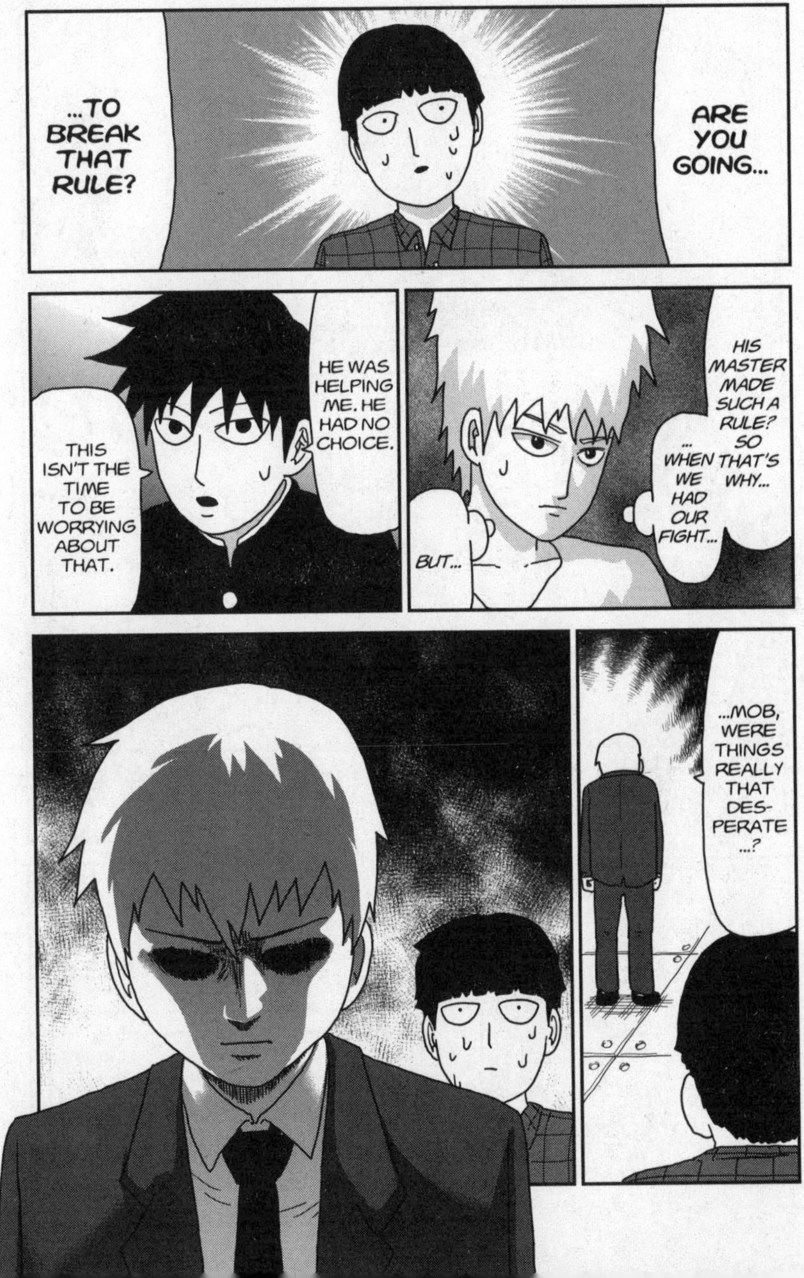
ARE YOU GOING...
...TO BREAK THAT RULE?
HIS MASTER MADE SUCH A RULE? SO THAT'S WHY...
... WHEN WE HAD OUR FIGHT...
BUT...
HE WAS HELPING ME. HE HAD NO CHOICE.
THIS ISN'T THE TIME TO BE WORRYING ABOUT THAT.
...MOB, WERE THINGS REALLY THAT DES-PERATE ...?

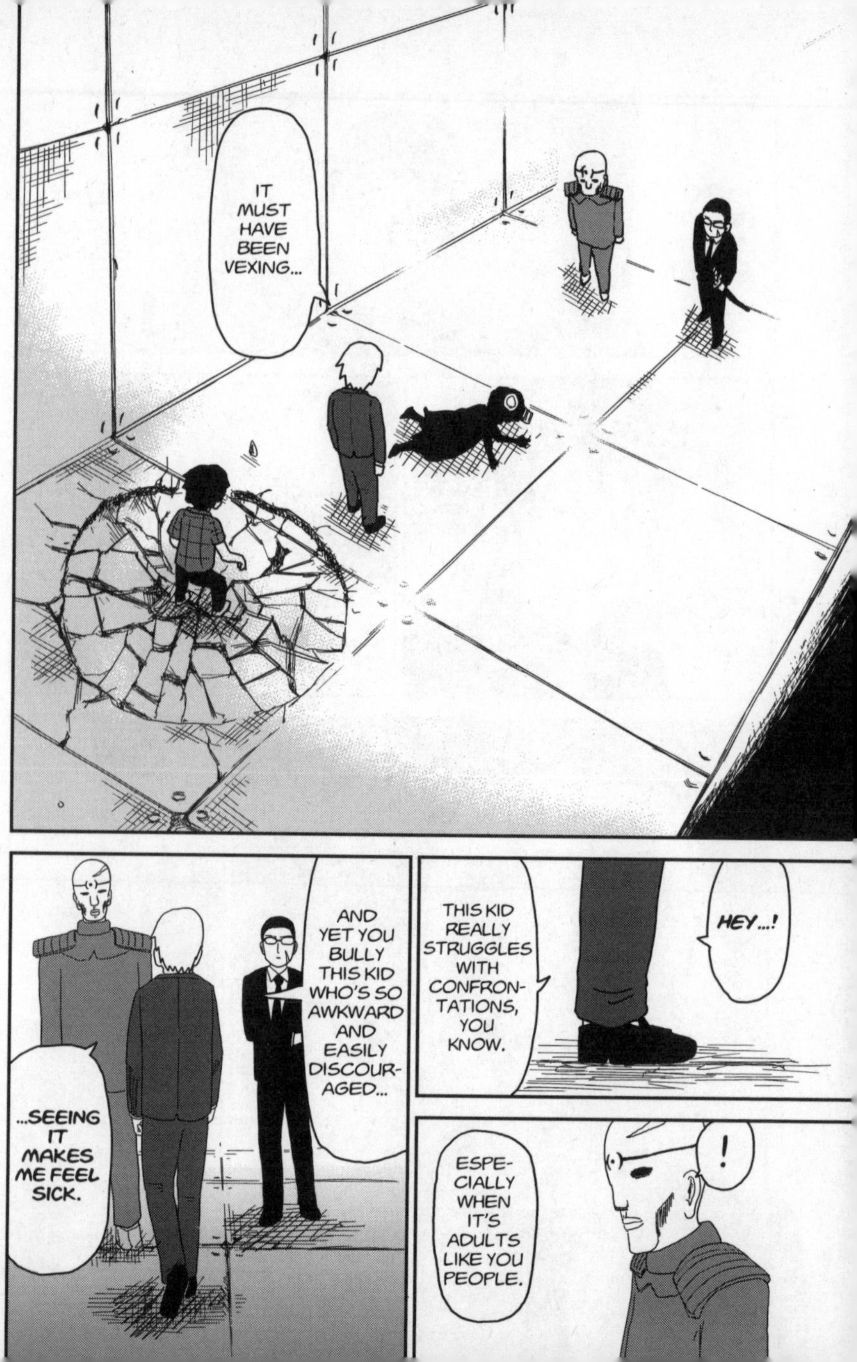
IT MUST HAVE BEEN VEXING...
HEY...!
THIS KID REALLY STRUGGLES WITH CONFRON-TATIONS, YOU KNOW.
!
ESPE-CIALLY WHEN IT'S ADULTS LIKE YOU PEOPLE.
AND YET YOU BULLY THIS KID WHO'S SO AWKWARD AND EASILY DISCOUR-AGED...
...SEEING IT MAKES ME FEEL SICK.

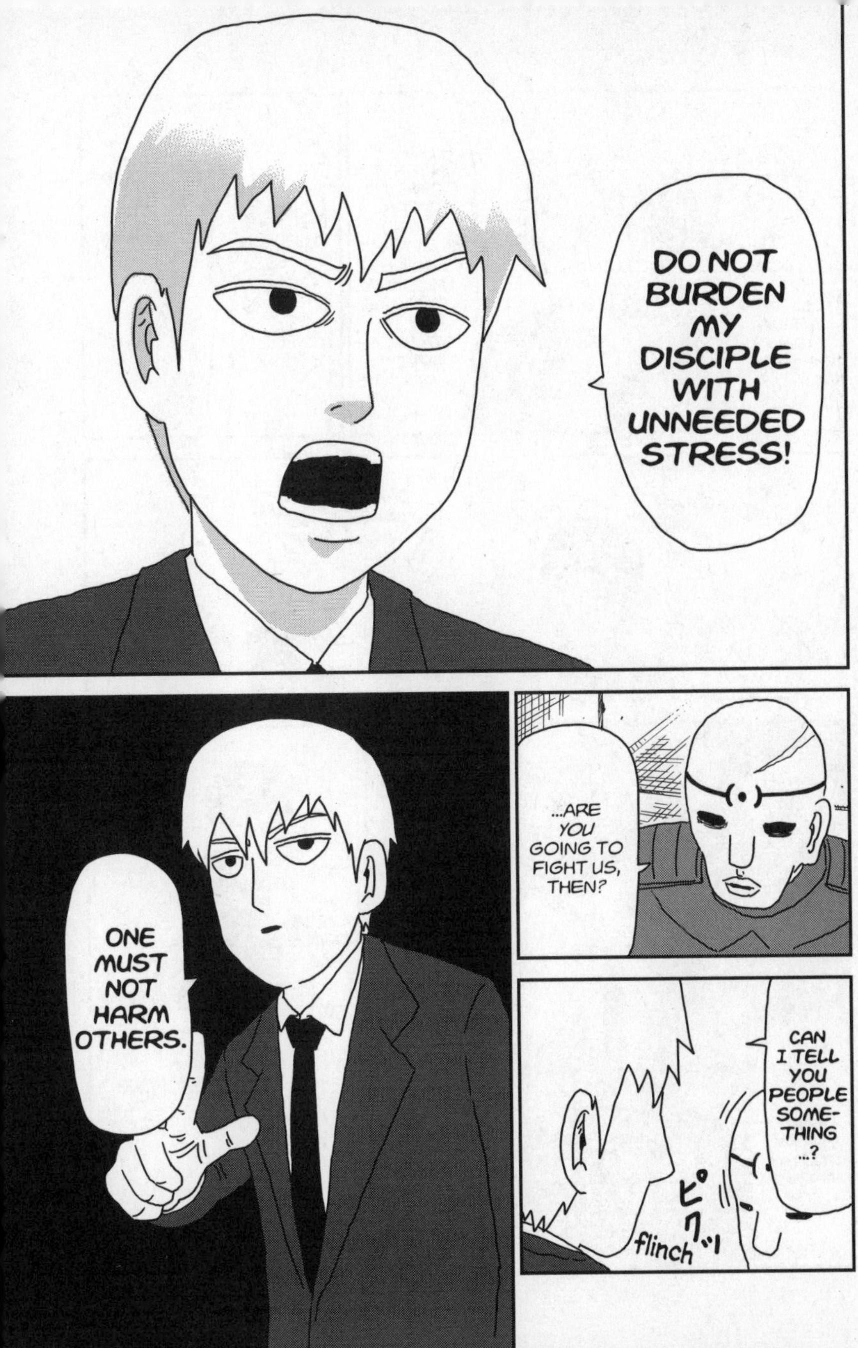
DO NOT BURDEN MY DISCIPLE WITH UNNEEDED STRESS!
...ARE YOU GOING TO FIGHT US, THEN?
CAN I TELL YOU PEOPLE SOME-THING ...?
ピクッ
flinch
ONE MUST NOT HARM OTHERS.

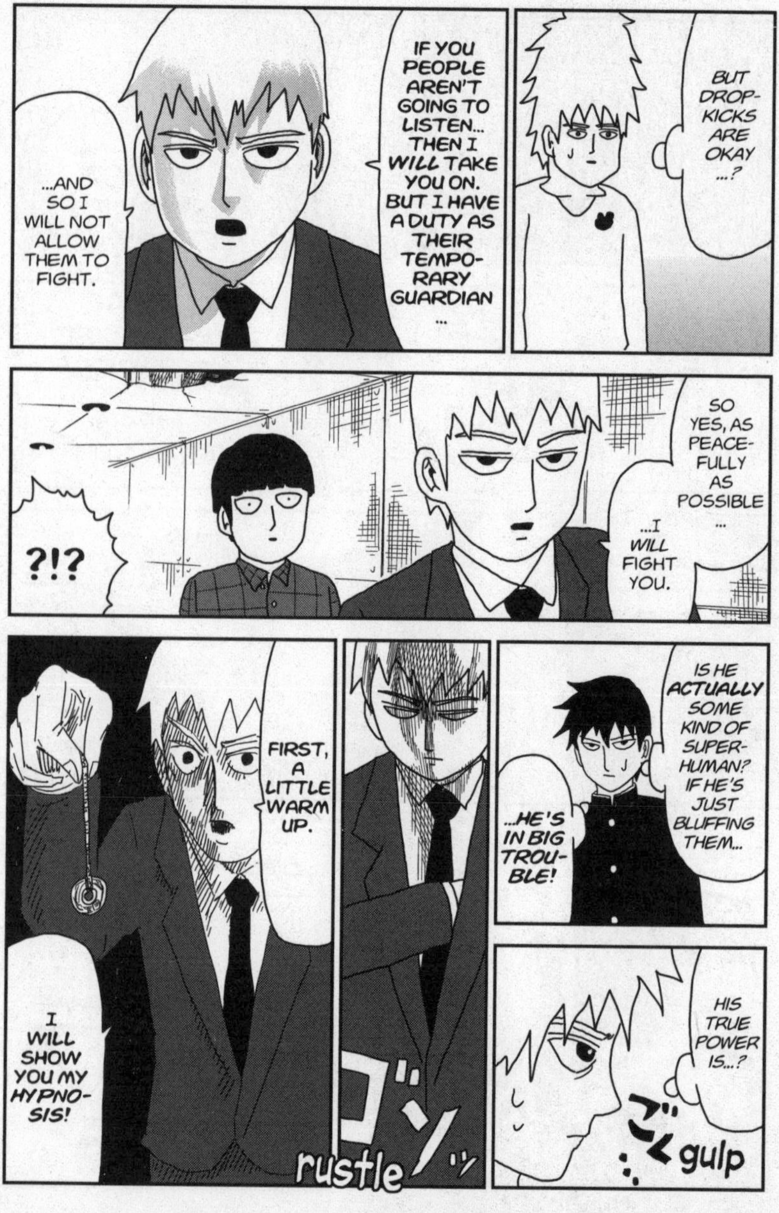
BUT DROP-KICKS ARE OKAY ...?
IF YOU PEOPLE AREN'T GOING TO LISTEN... THEN I WILL TAKE YOU ON. BUT I HAVE A DUTY AS THEIR TEMPORARY GUARDIAN ...
...AND SO I WILL NOT ALLOW THEM TO FIGHT.
SO YES, AS PEACEFULLY AS POSSIBLE ...
...I WILL FIGHT YOU.
?!?
IS HE ACTUALLY SOME KIND OF SUPERHUMAN? IF HE'S JUST BLUFFING THEM...
...HE'S IN BIG TROUBLE!
HIS TRUE POWER IS...?
ごく gulp
ゴソッ rustle
FIRST, A LITTLE WARM UP.
I WILL SHOW YOU MY HYPNOSIS!

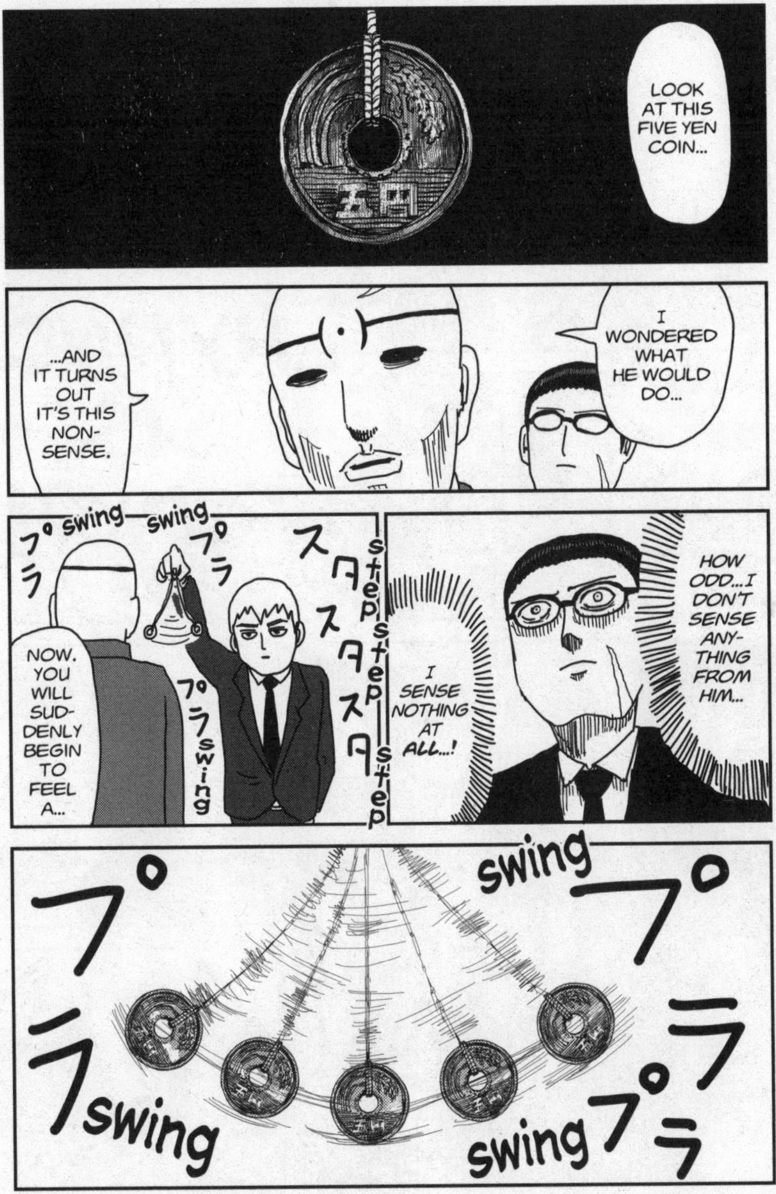
LOOK AT THIS FIVE YEN COIN...
五円
I WONDERED WHAT HE WOULD DO...
...AND IT TURNS OUT IT'S THIS NONSENSE.
HOW ODD...I DON'T SENSE ANYTHING FROM HIM...
I SENSE NOTHING AT ALL...!
スタスタ step step step
プラ swing
プラ swing
プラ swing
NOW. YOU WILL SUDDENLY BEGIN TO FEEL A...
プラ swing
プラ swing
プラ swing

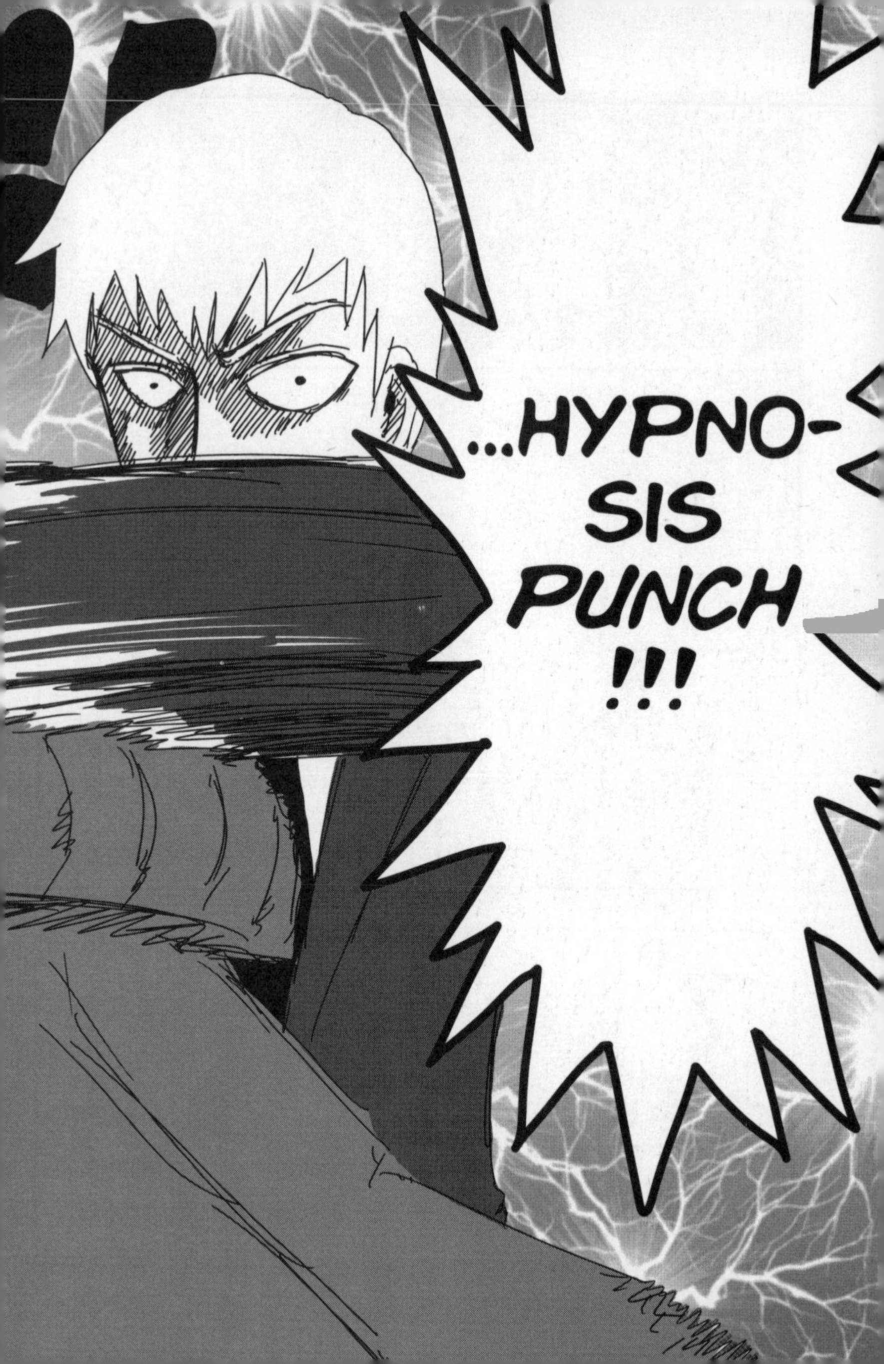
...HYPNO-SIS PUNCH !!!

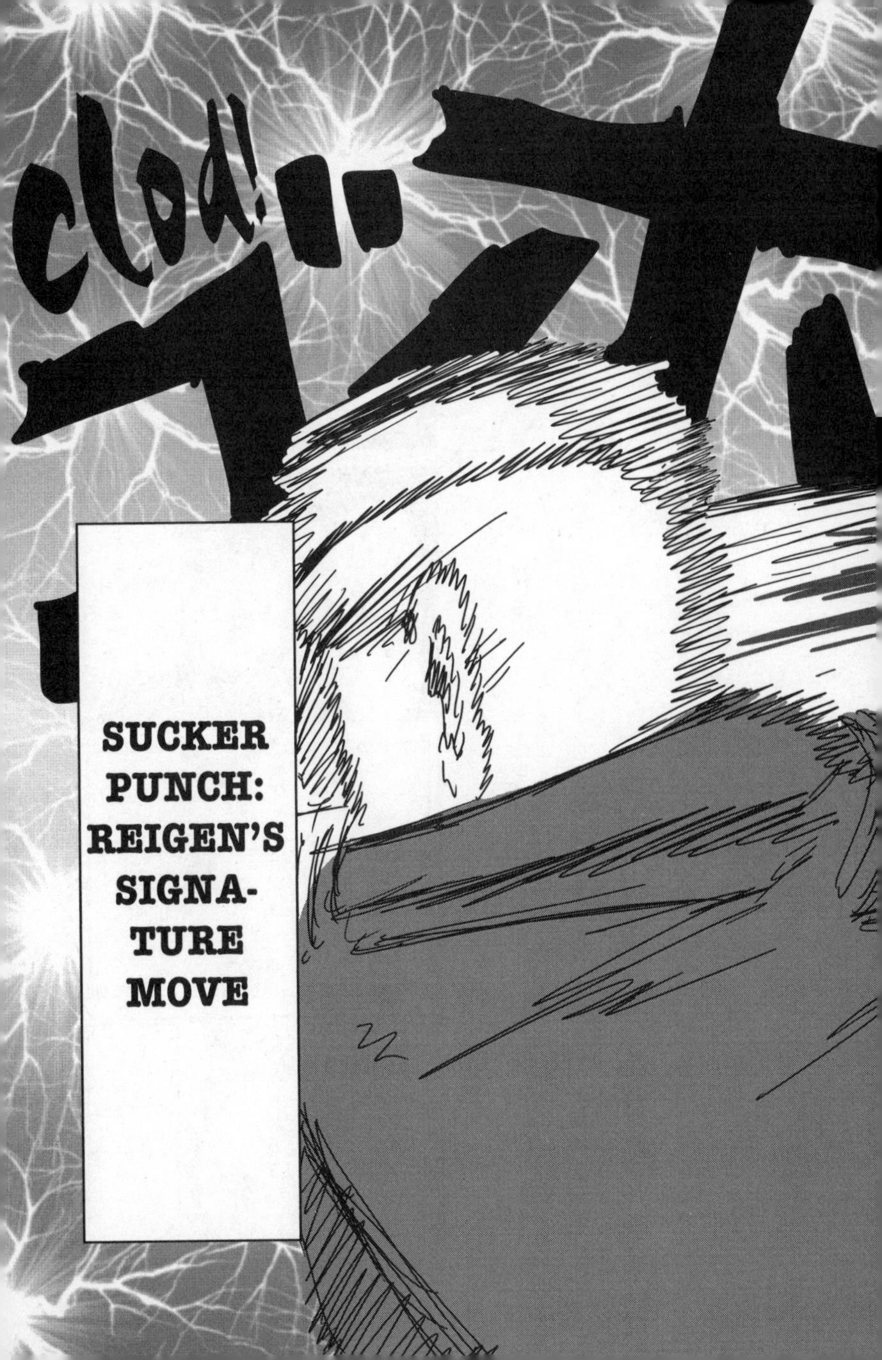
CLOD!!
SUCKER PUNCH: REIGEN'S SIGNATURE MOVE

Matsuo's Evil Spirit Observation Log (#2)

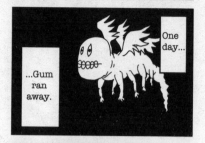

One day...
...Gum ran away.
I was so worried, I walked around night after night looking for him.
GUM! COME BACK!
I found him at last, being harassed by some crows.
I sent out my spiritual power to him.
Thus recharged, he murdered those crows.
Although they were a murder already.

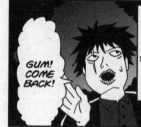

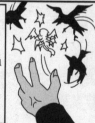

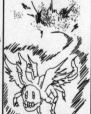

CHAPTER 46: MASTER

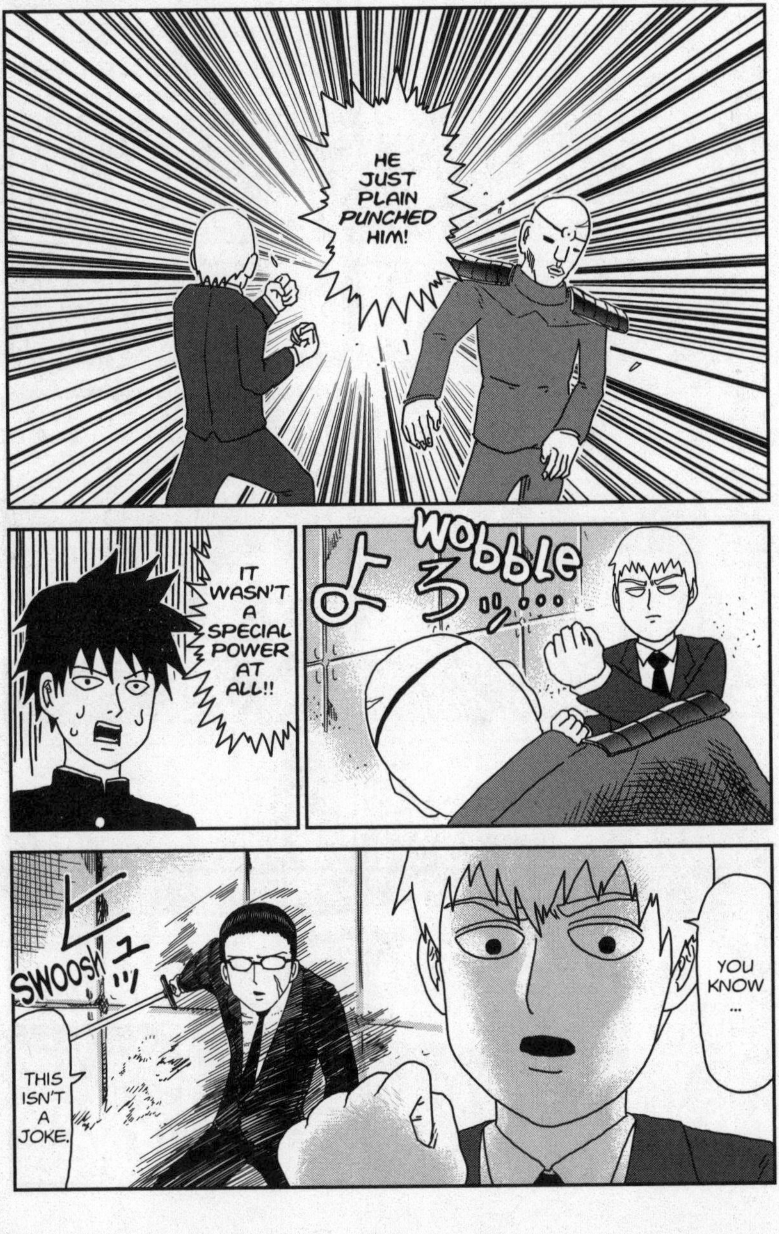
HE JUST PLAIN PUNCHED HIM!
wobble
よろッ...
IT WASN'T A SPECIAL POWER AT ALL!!
YOU KNOW ...
SWOOSH
ヒュッ
THIS ISN'T A JOKE.

LOOK OUT!

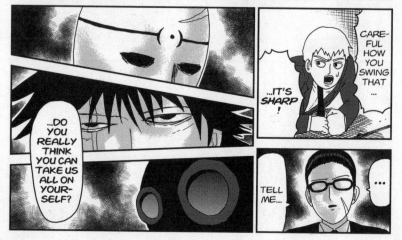

CAREFUL HOW YOU SWING THAT...

...IT'S SHARP!

...DO YOU REALLY THINK YOU CAN TAKE US ALL ON YOURSELF?

TELL ME...

...

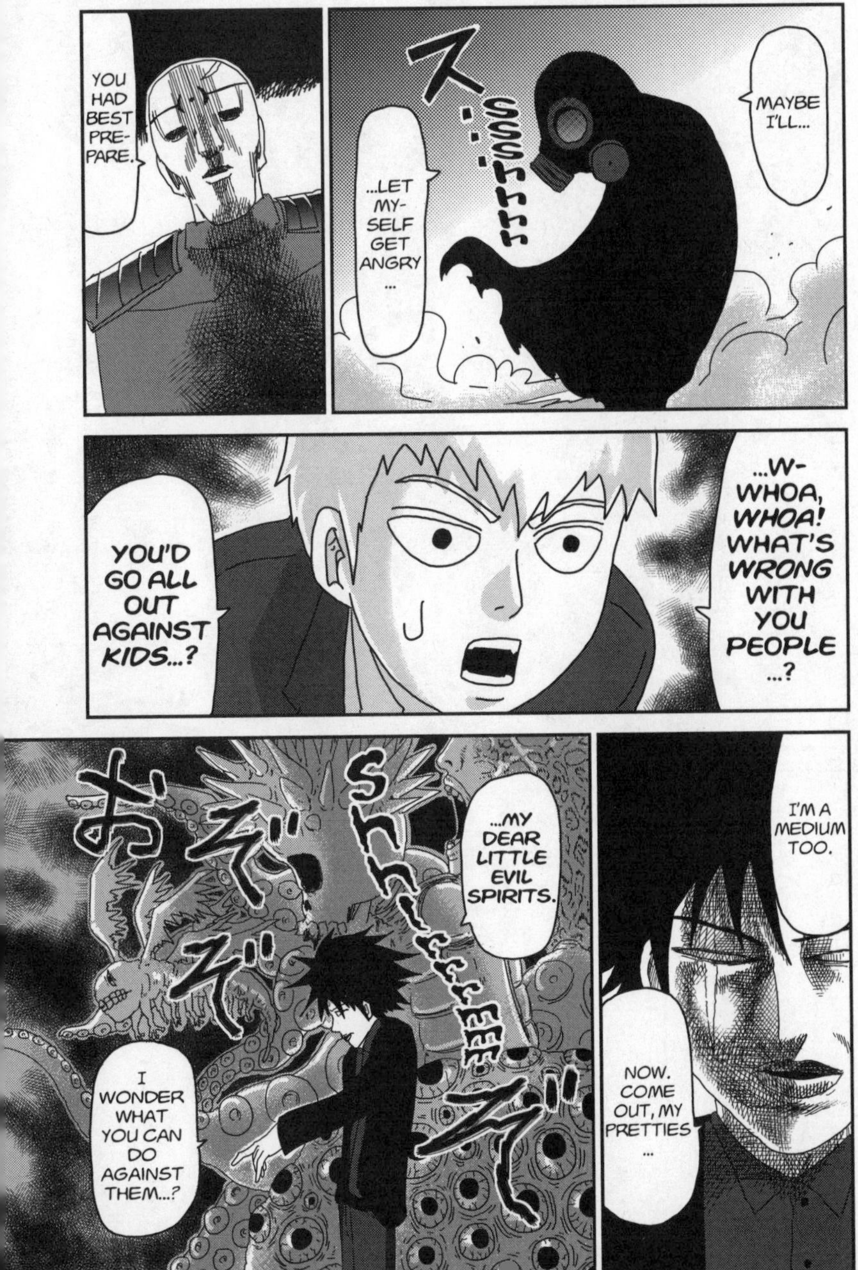
MAYBE I'LL...
ス
SSShhhh
...LET MY-SELF GET ANGRY ...
YOU HAD BEST PRE-PARE.
...W-WHOA, WHOA! WHAT'S WRONG WITH YOU PEOPLE ...?
YOU'D GO ALL OUT AGAINST KIDS...?
I'M A MEDIUM TOO.
NOW. COME OUT, MY PRETTIES ...
...MY DEAR LITTLE EVIL SPIRITS.
おぞぞ
I WONDER WHAT YOU CAN DO AGAINST THEM...?

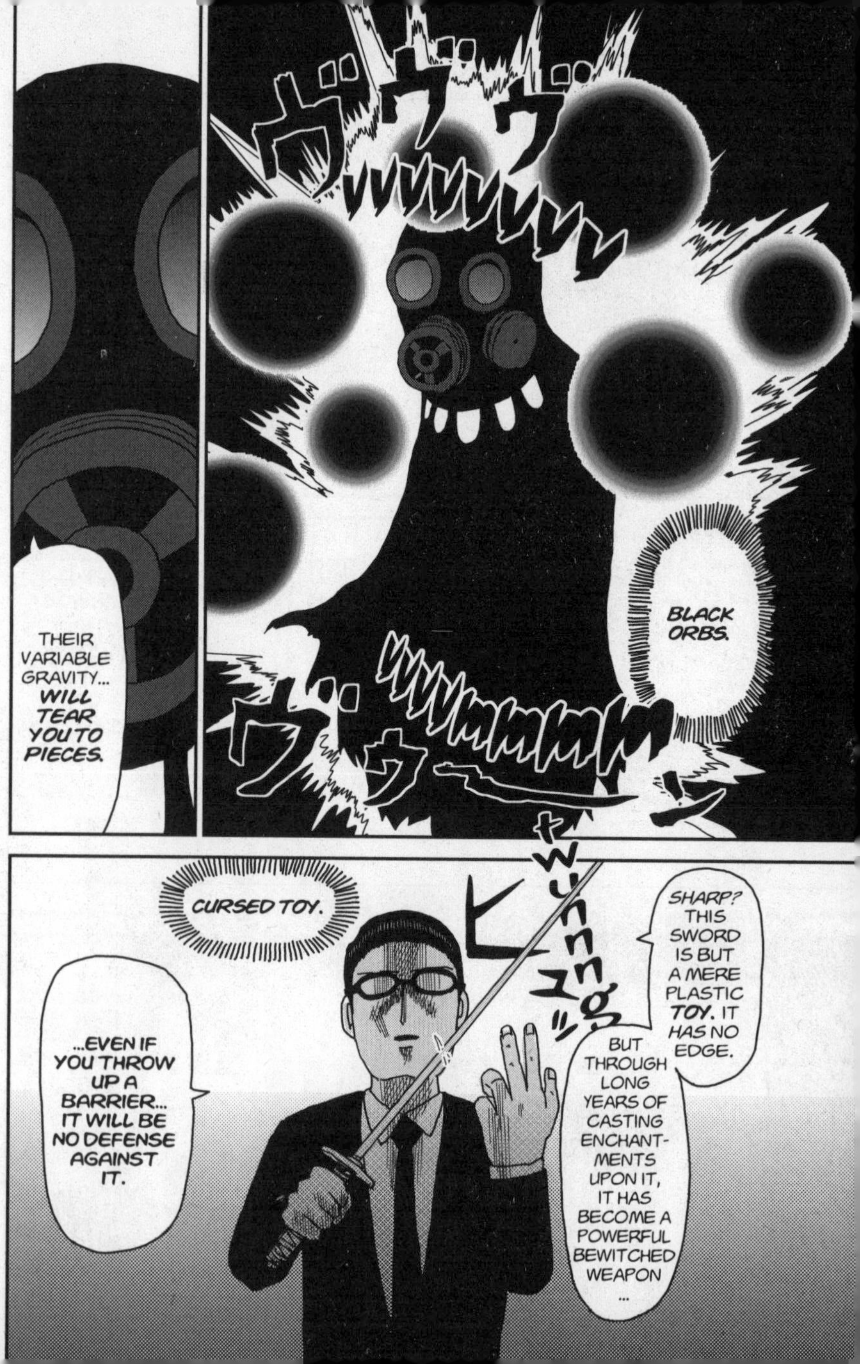
BLACK ORBS.
THEIR VARIABLE GRAVITY... WILL TEAR YOU TO PIECES.
twunnng
CURSED TOY.
SHARP? THIS SWORD IS BUT A MERE PLASTIC TOY. IT HAS NO EDGE.
BUT THROUGH LONG YEARS OF CASTING ENCHANT-MENTS UPON IT, IT HAS BECOME A POWERFUL BEWITCHED WEAPON ...
...EVEN IF YOU THROW UP A BARRIER... IT WILL BE NO DEFENSE AGAINST IT.

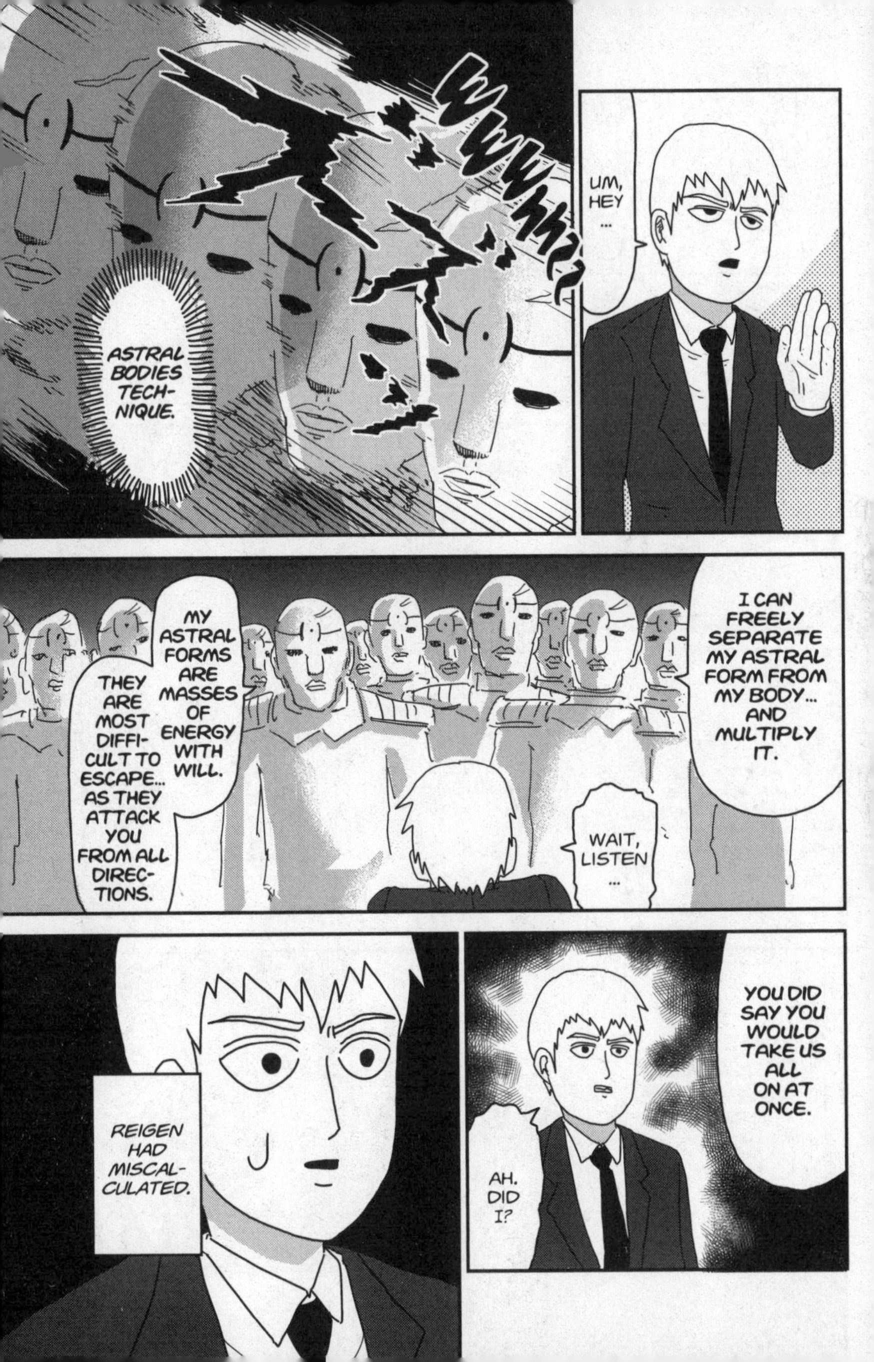
UM, HEY ...
ASTRAL BODIES TECH-NIQUE.
I CAN FREELY SEPARATE MY ASTRAL FORM FROM MY BODY... AND MULTIPLY IT.
WAIT, LISTEN ...
MY ASTRAL FORMS ARE MASSES OF ENERGY WITH WILL.
THEY ARE MOST DIFFI-CULT TO ESCAPE... AS THEY ATTACK YOU FROM ALL DIREC-TIONS.
YOU DID SAY YOU WOULD TAKE US ALL ON AT ONCE.
AH. DID I?
REIGEN HAD MISCAL-CULATED.

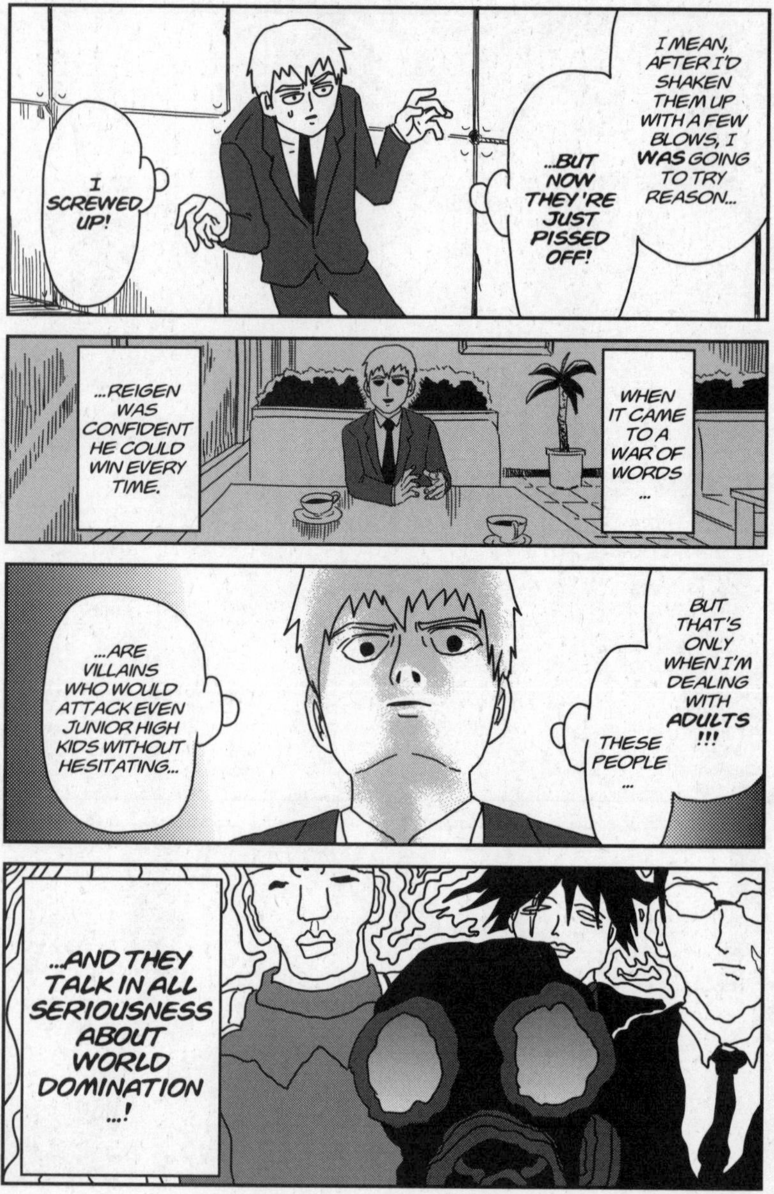
I MEAN, AFTER I'D SHAKEN THEM UP WITH A FEW BLOWS, I WAS GOING TO TRY REASON...
...BUT NOW THEY'RE JUST PISSED OFF!
I SCREWED UP!
WHEN IT CAME TO A WAR OF WORDS...
...REIGEN WAS CONFIDENT HE COULD WIN EVERY TIME.
BUT THAT'S ONLY WHEN I'M DEALING WITH ADULTS!!!
THESE PEOPLE...
...ARE VILLAINS WHO WOULD ATTACK EVEN JUNIOR HIGH KIDS WITHOUT HESITATING...
...AND THEY TALK IN ALL SERIOUSNESS ABOUT WORLD DOMINATION...!

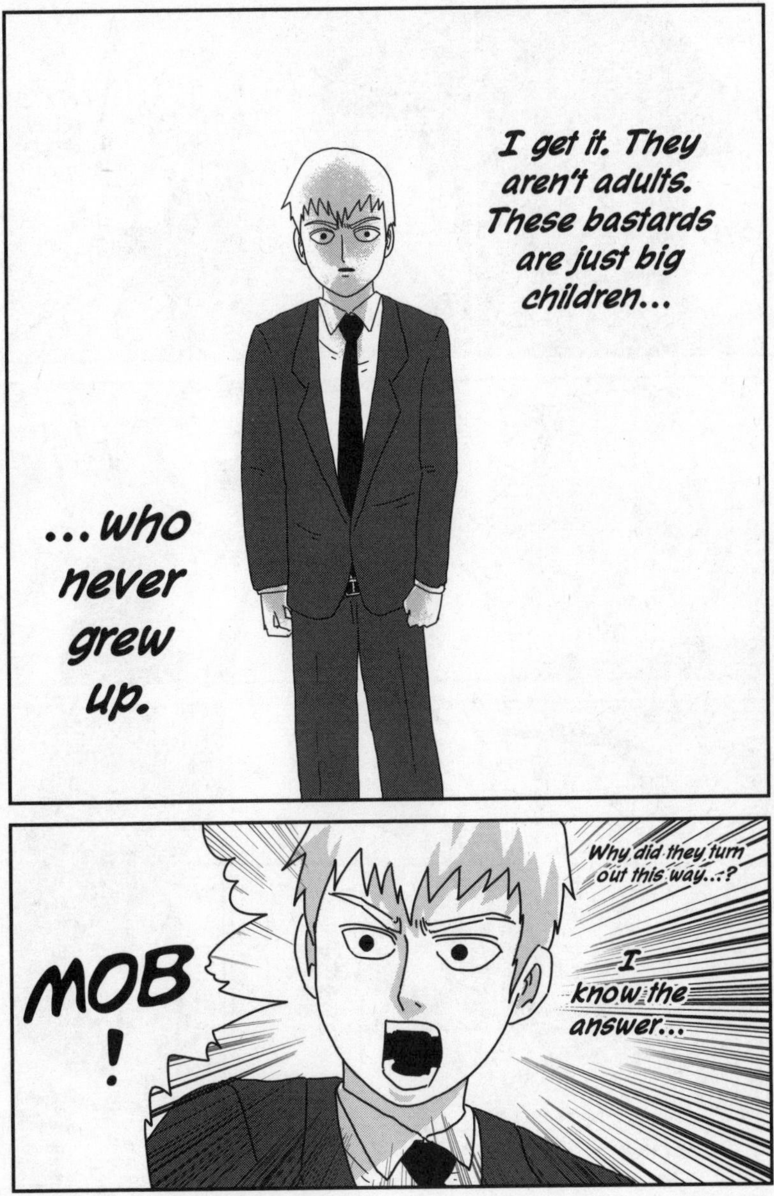
I get it. They aren't adults. These bastards are just big children...
...who never grew up.
Why did they turn out this way...?
I know the answer...
MOB!

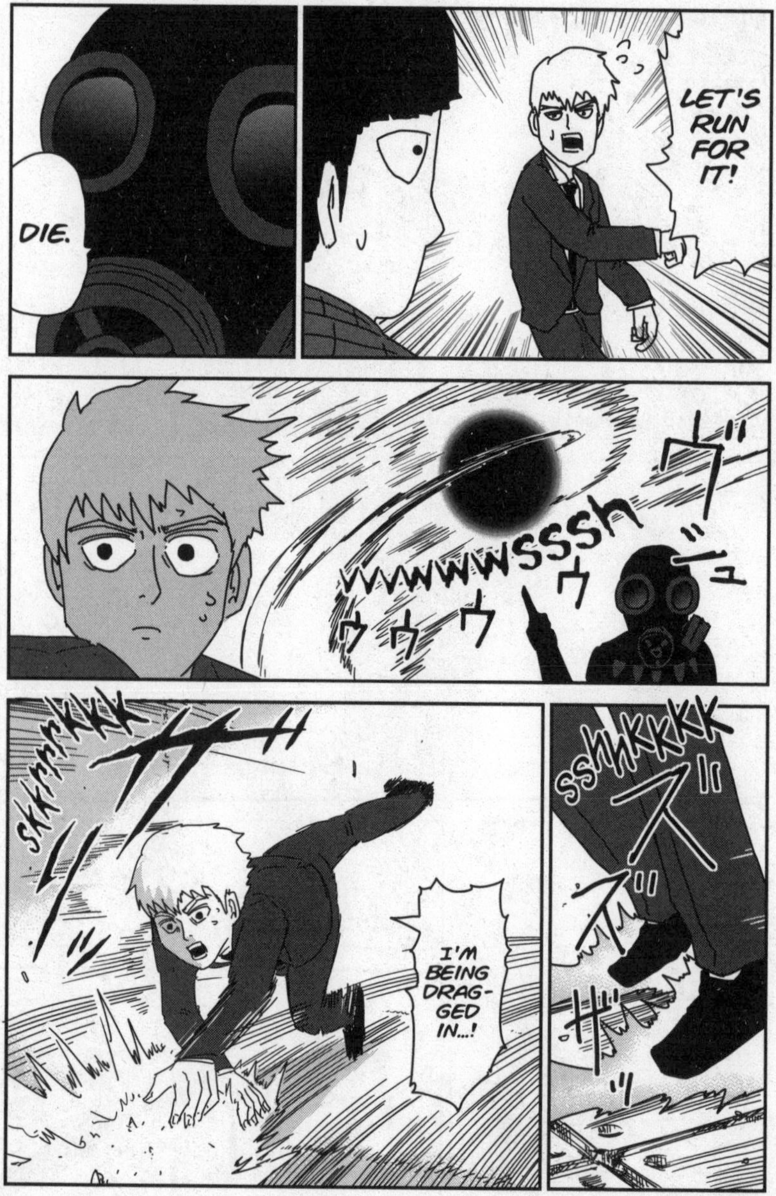
LET'S RUN FOR IT!
DIE.
VVVWWWSSSh
sshhkkkk
skrrrkkkk
I'M BEING DRAG-GED IN...!

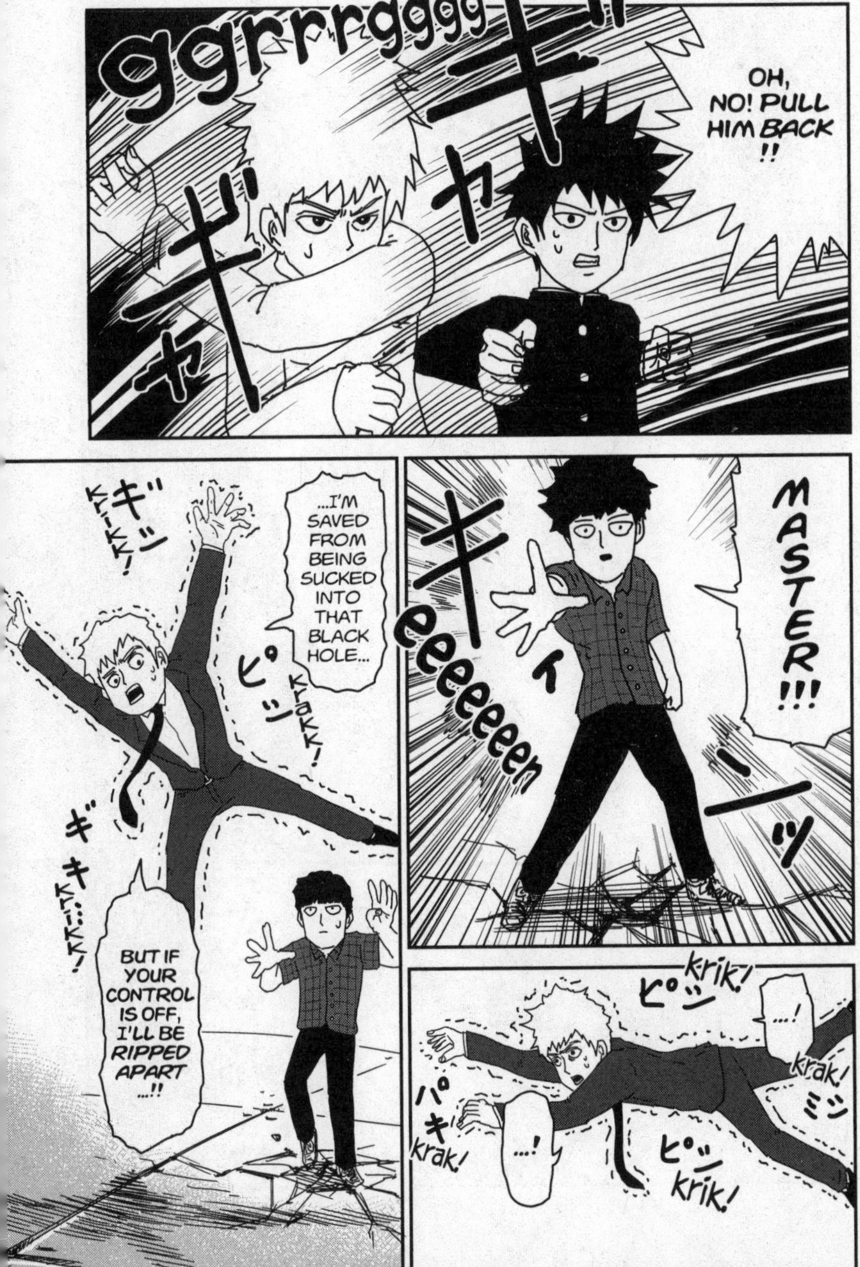
ggrrrgggg
OH, NO! PULL HIM BACK!!
MASTER!!!
eeeeeeeen
krik!
...!
krak!
krak!
...!
krik!
...I'M SAVED FROM BEING SUCKED INTO THAT BLACK HOLE...
krakk!
krakk!
krakk!
BUT IF YOUR CONTROL IS OFF, I'LL BE RIPPED APART ...!!

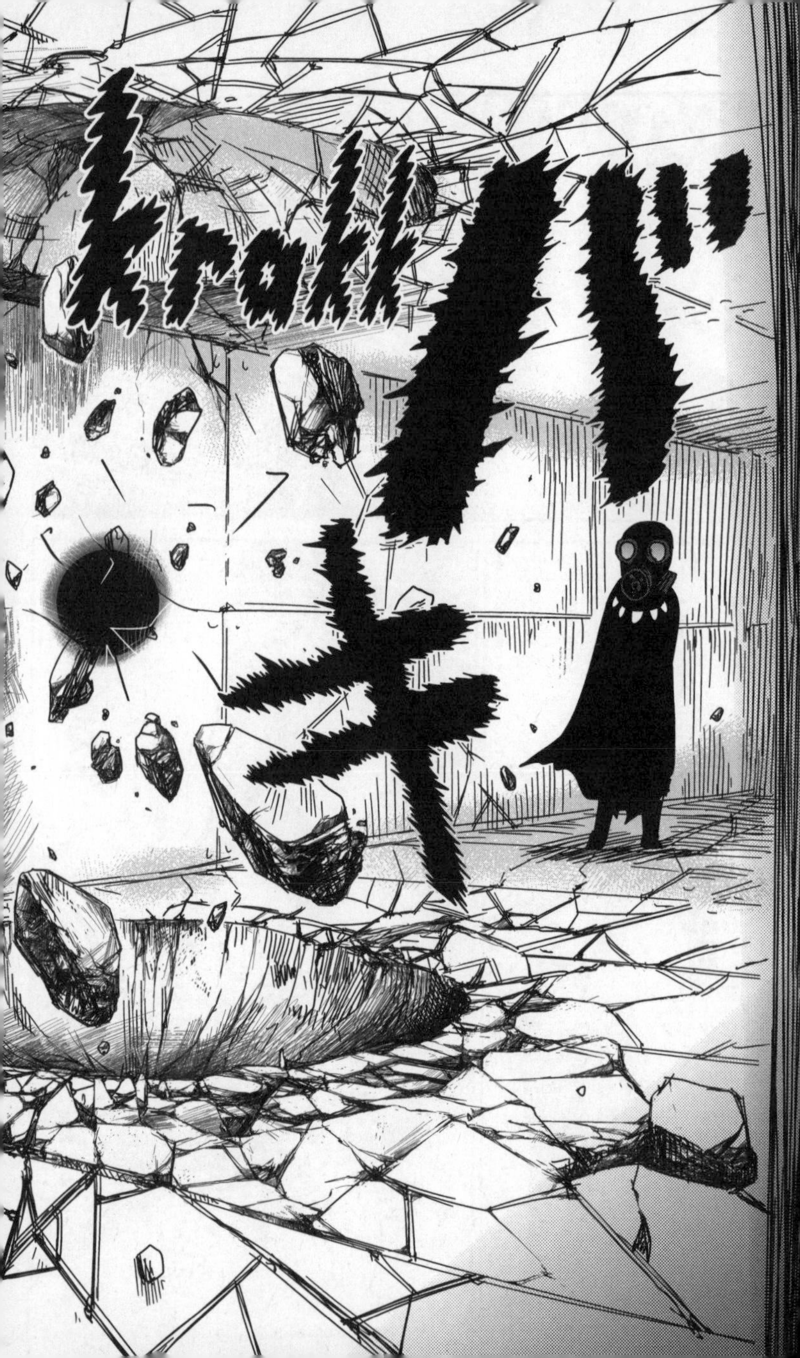
krakk
バキ

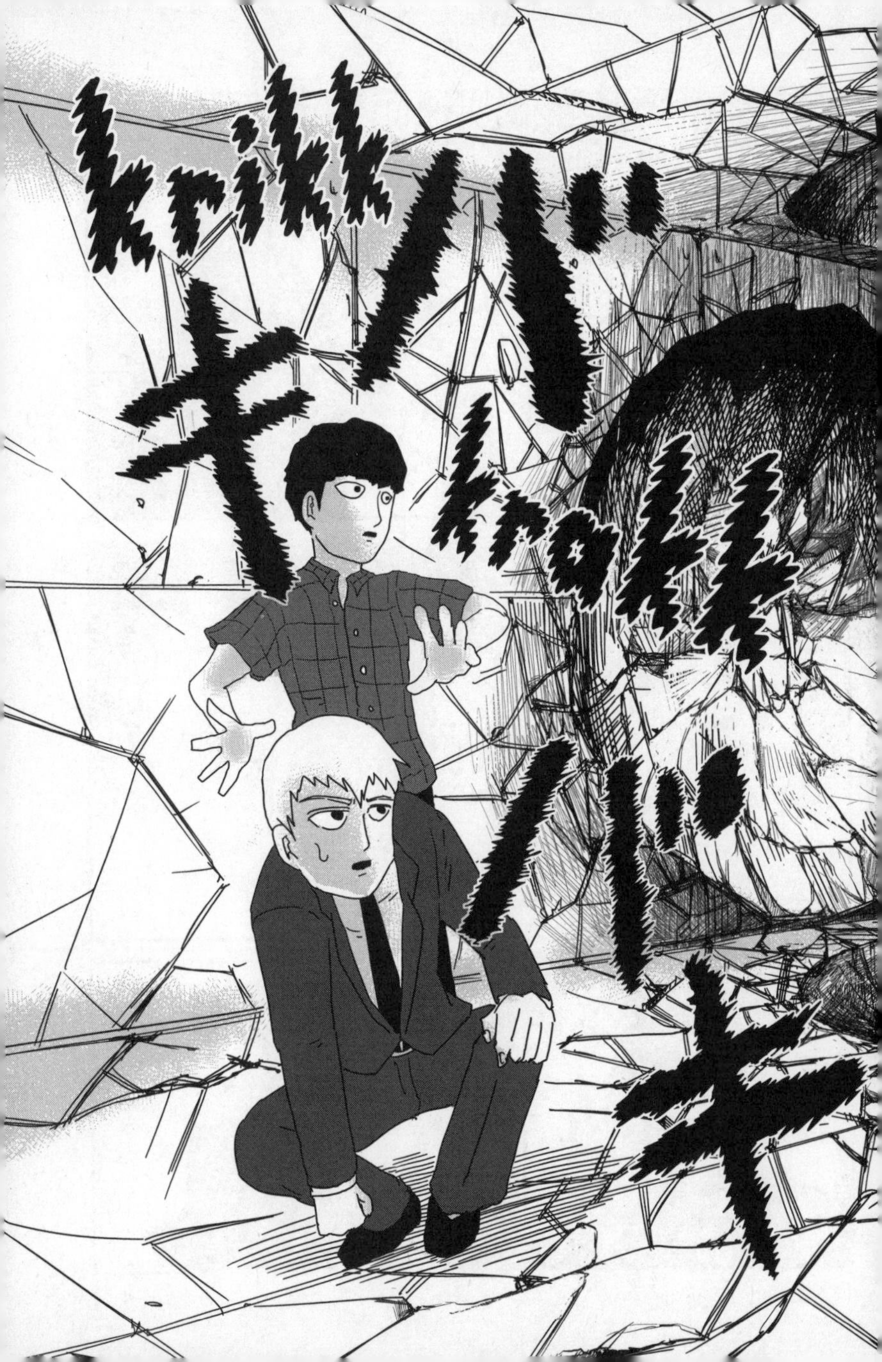
krikk
krakk

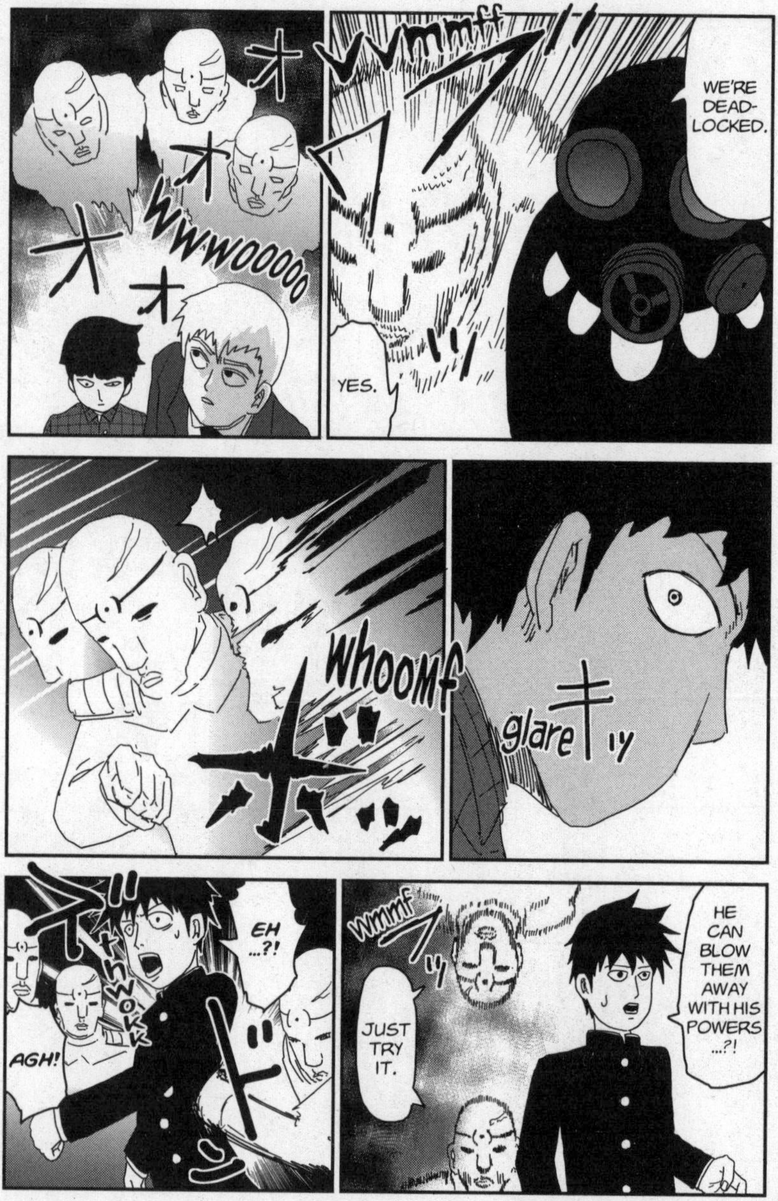
vvmmff
WE'RE DEAD-LOCKED.
YES.
WWWOOOOOO
glare
whoomf
HE CAN BLOW THEM AWAY WITH HIS POWERS ...?!
wmmf
JUST TRY IT.
EH ...?!
thwokk
AGH!

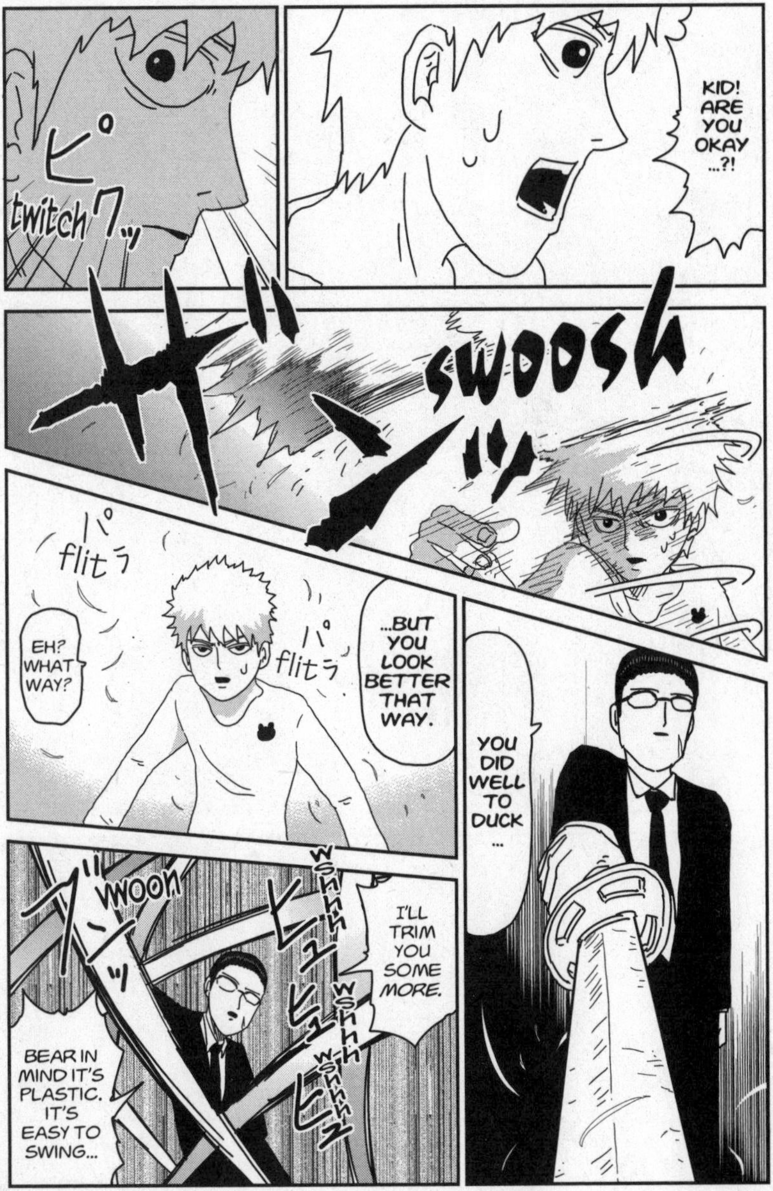
KID! ARE YOU OKAY ...?!
twitch
swoosh
YOU DID WELL TO DUCK ...
...BUT YOU LOOK BETTER THAT WAY.
flit
flit
EH? WHAT WAY?
I'LL TRIM YOU SOME MORE.
wshhh
wshhh
wshhh
wwoon
BEAR IN MIND IT'S PLASTIC. IT'S EASY TO SWING...

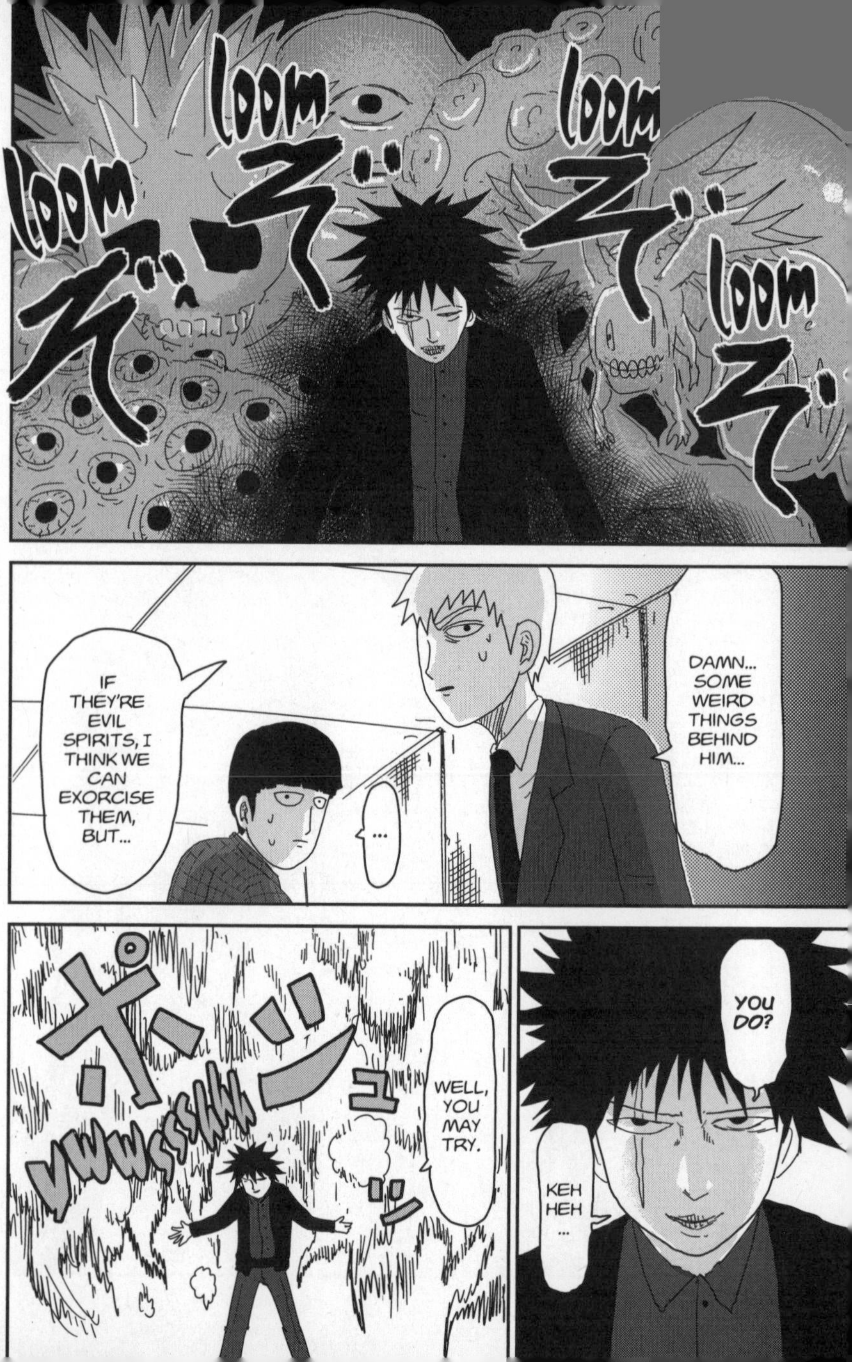

loom
loom
loom
loom
loom
DAMN... SOME WEIRD THINGS BEHIND HIM...
...
IF THEY'RE EVIL SPIRITS, I THINK WE CAN EXORCISE THEM, BUT...
YOU DO?
KEH HEH ...
WELL, YOU MAY TRY.
VWWSSSHHH

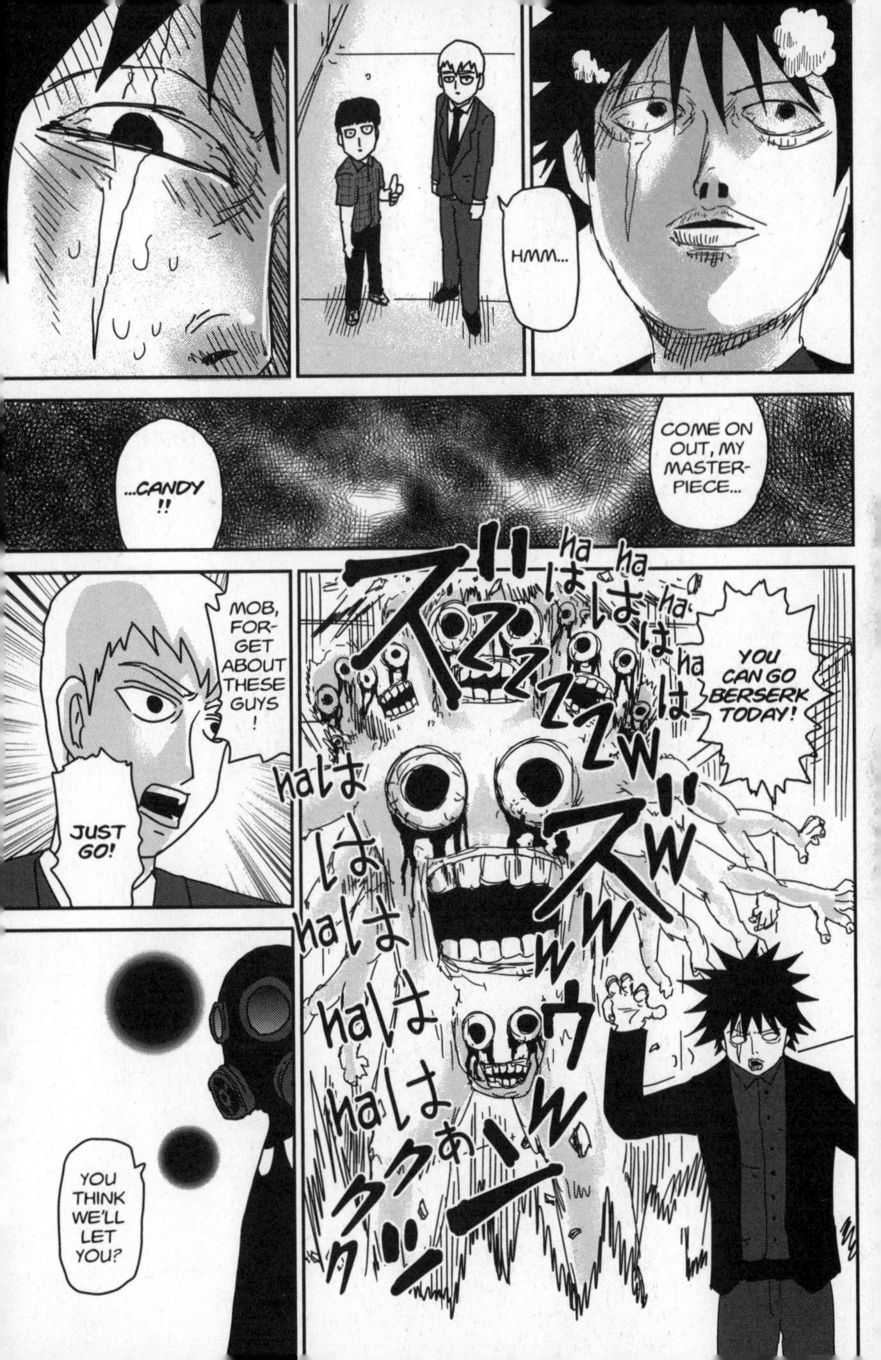
HMM...
COME ON OUT, MY MASTER-PIECE...
...CANDY !!
YOU CAN GO BERSERK TODAY!
MOB, FOR-GET ABOUT THESE GUYS!
JUST GO!
YOU THINK WE'LL LET YOU?

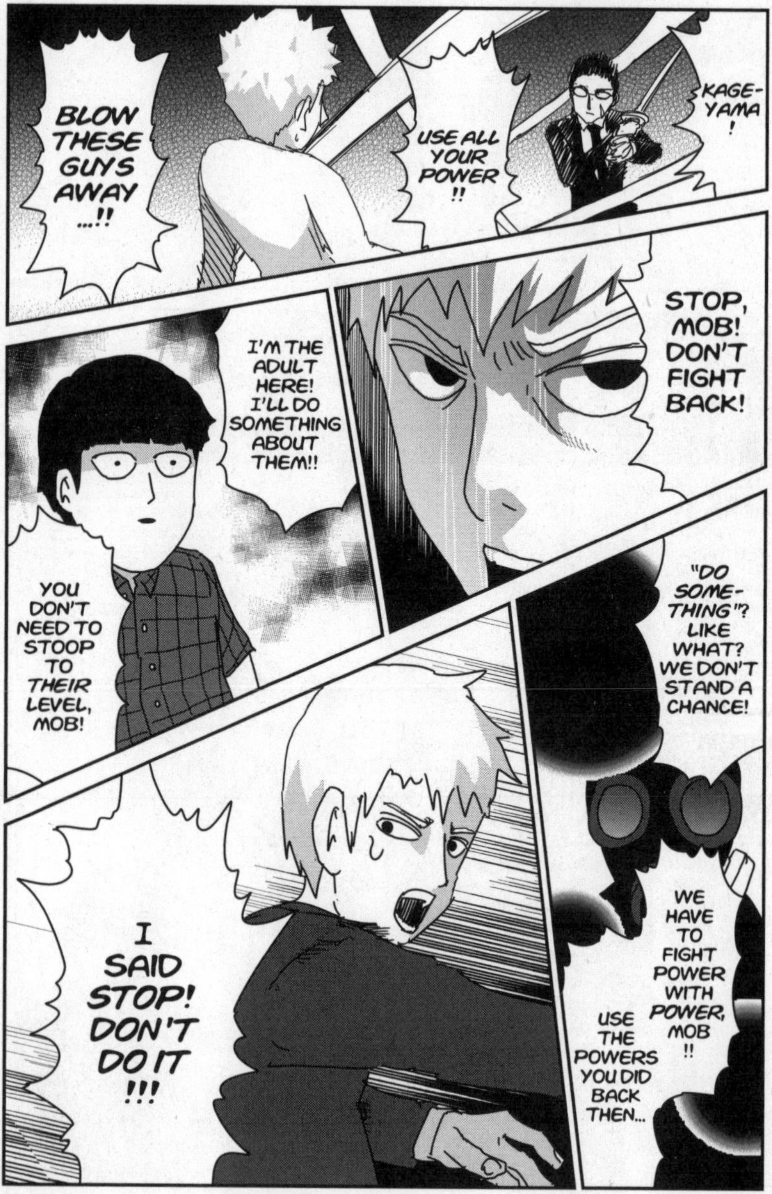
KAGE-YAMA!
USE ALL YOUR POWER!!
BLOW THESE GUYS AWAY ...!!
STOP, MOB! DON'T FIGHT BACK!
I'M THE ADULT HERE! I'LL DO SOMETHING ABOUT THEM!!
YOU DON'T NEED TO STOOP TO THEIR LEVEL, MOB!
"DO SOMETHING"? LIKE WHAT? WE DON'T STAND A CHANCE!
WE HAVE TO FIGHT POWER WITH POWER, MOB!!
USE THE POWERS YOU DID BACK THEN...
I SAID STOP! DON'T DO IT!!!

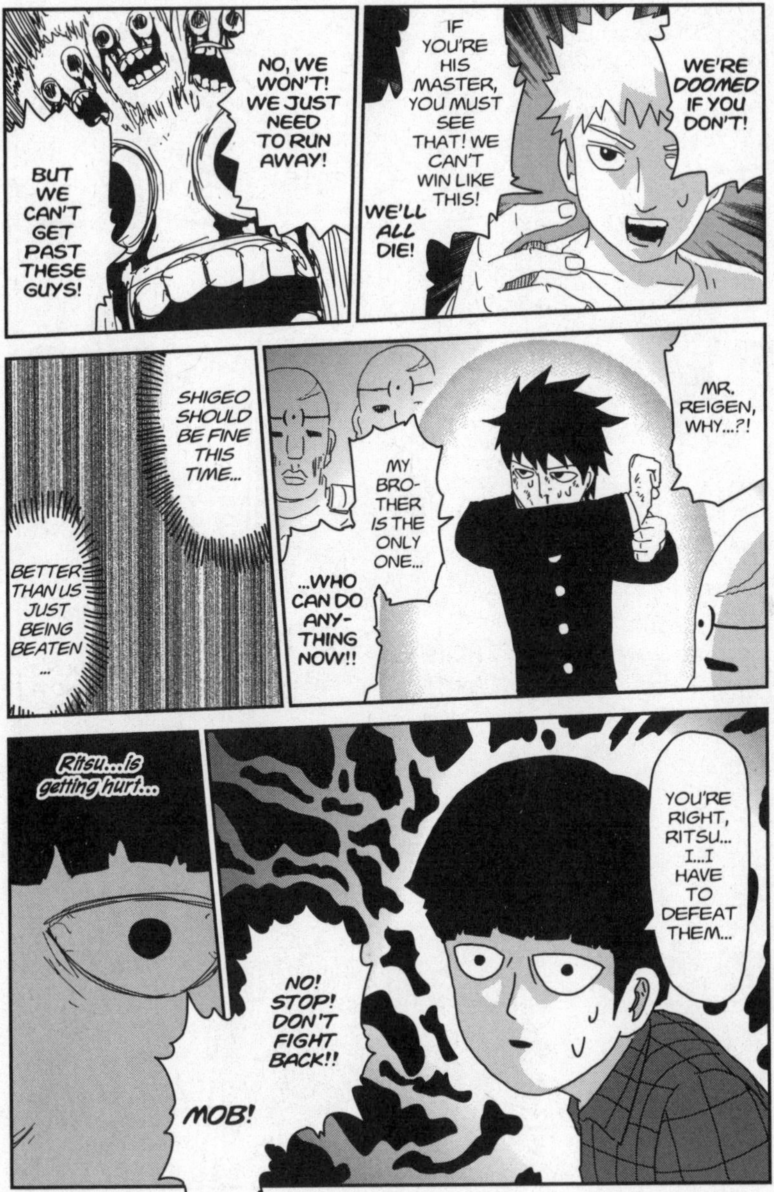
WE'RE DOOMED IF YOU DON'T!
IF YOU'RE HIS MASTER, YOU MUST SEE THAT! WE CAN'T WIN LIKE THIS!
WE'LL ALL DIE!
NO, WE WON'T! WE JUST NEED TO RUN AWAY!
BUT WE CAN'T GET PAST THESE GUYS!
MR. REIGEN, WHY...?!
MY BROTHER IS THE ONLY ONE...
...WHO CAN DO ANYTHING NOW!!
SHIGEO SHOULD BE FINE THIS TIME...
BETTER THAN US JUST BEING BEATEN ...
YOU'RE RIGHT, RITSU... I...I HAVE TO DEFEAT THEM...
NO! STOP! DON'T FIGHT BACK!!
MOB!
Ritsu...is getting hurt...

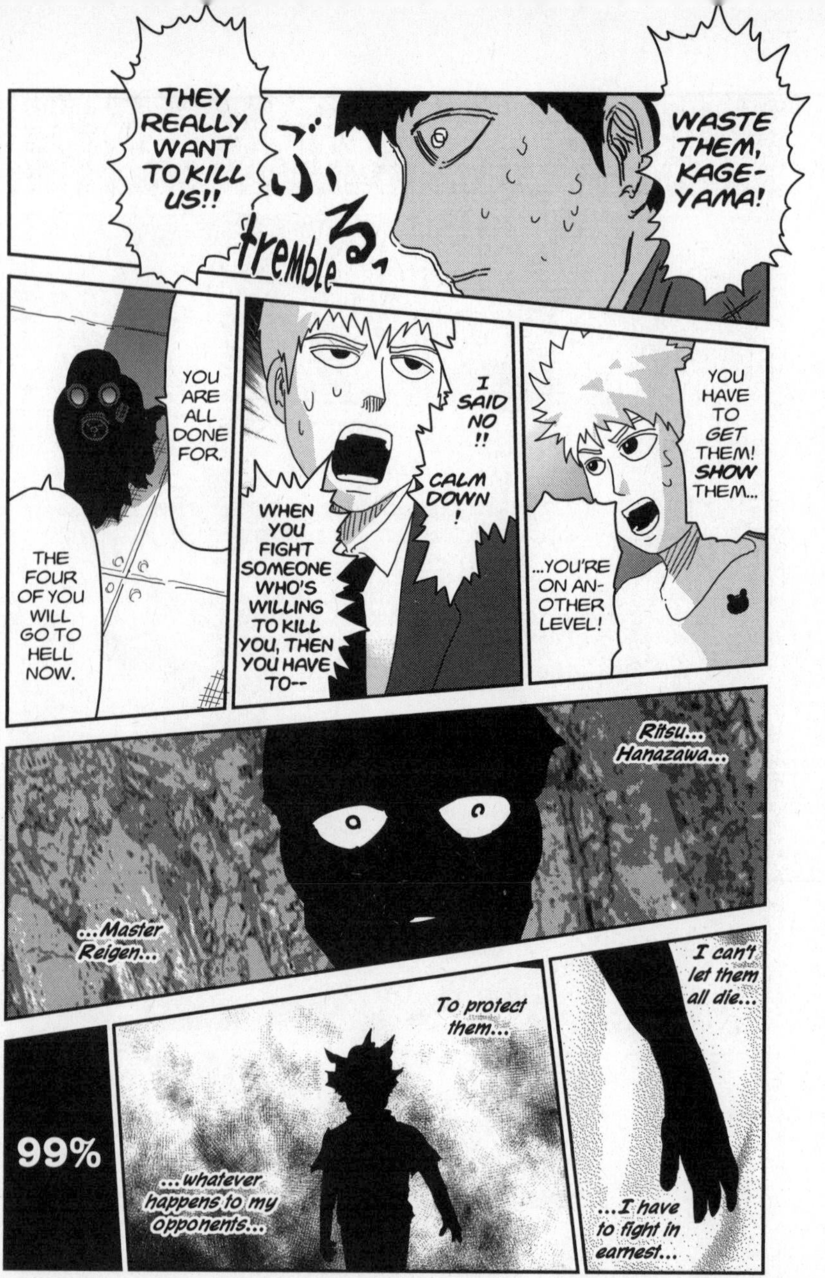
WASTE THEM, KAGE-YAMA!
THEY REALLY WANT TO KILL US!!
ぶる
tremble
YOU HAVE TO GET THEM! SHOW THEM...
...YOU'RE ON AN-OTHER LEVEL!
I SAID NO!!
CALM DOWN!
WHEN YOU FIGHT SOMEONE WHO'S WILLING TO KILL YOU, THEN YOU HAVE TO--
YOU ARE ALL DONE FOR.
THE FOUR OF YOU WILL GO TO HELL NOW.
Ritsu... Hanazawa...
...Master Reigen...
I can't let them all die...
...I have to fight in earnest...
To protect them...
...whatever happens to my opponents...
99%

MURDEROUS INTENT

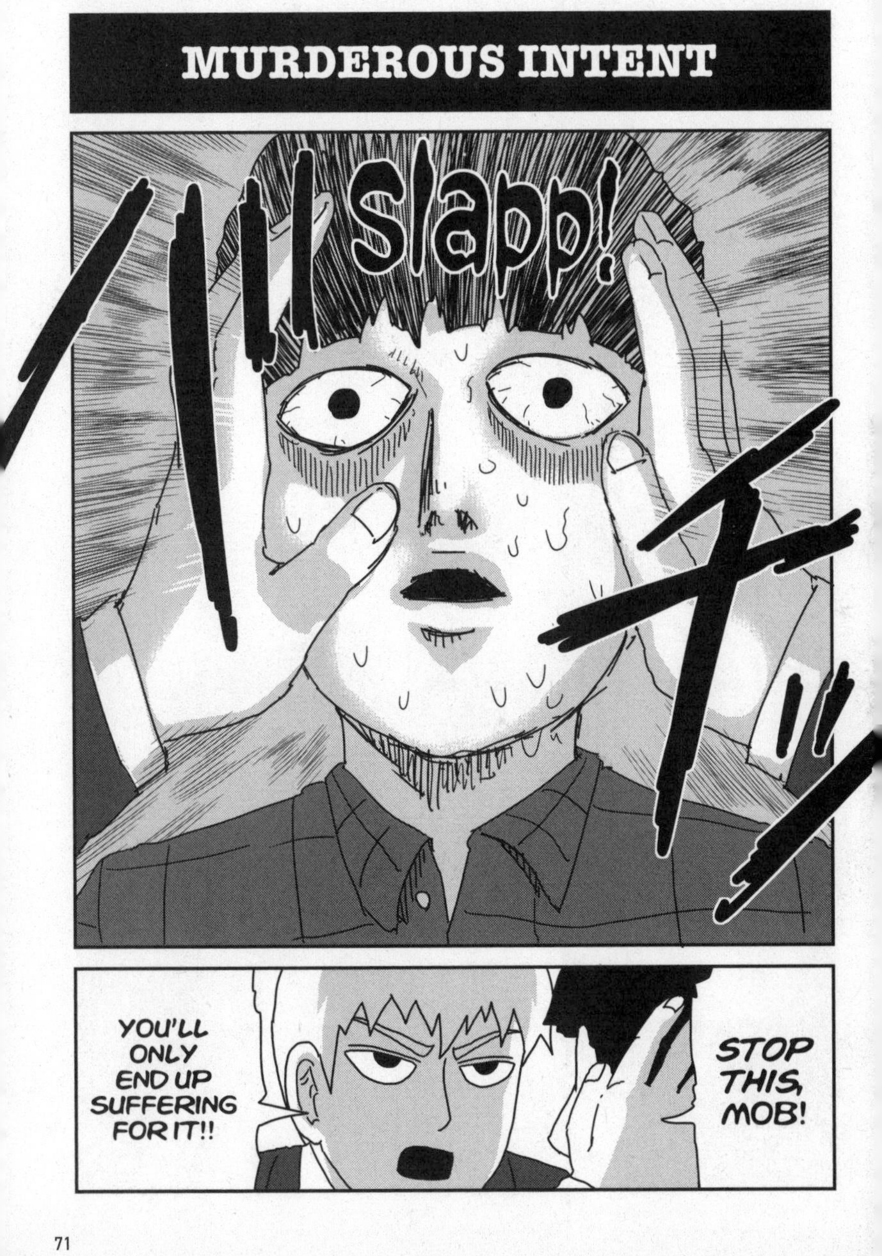
slapp!
STOP THIS, MOB!
YOU'LL ONLY END UP SUFFERING FOR IT!!

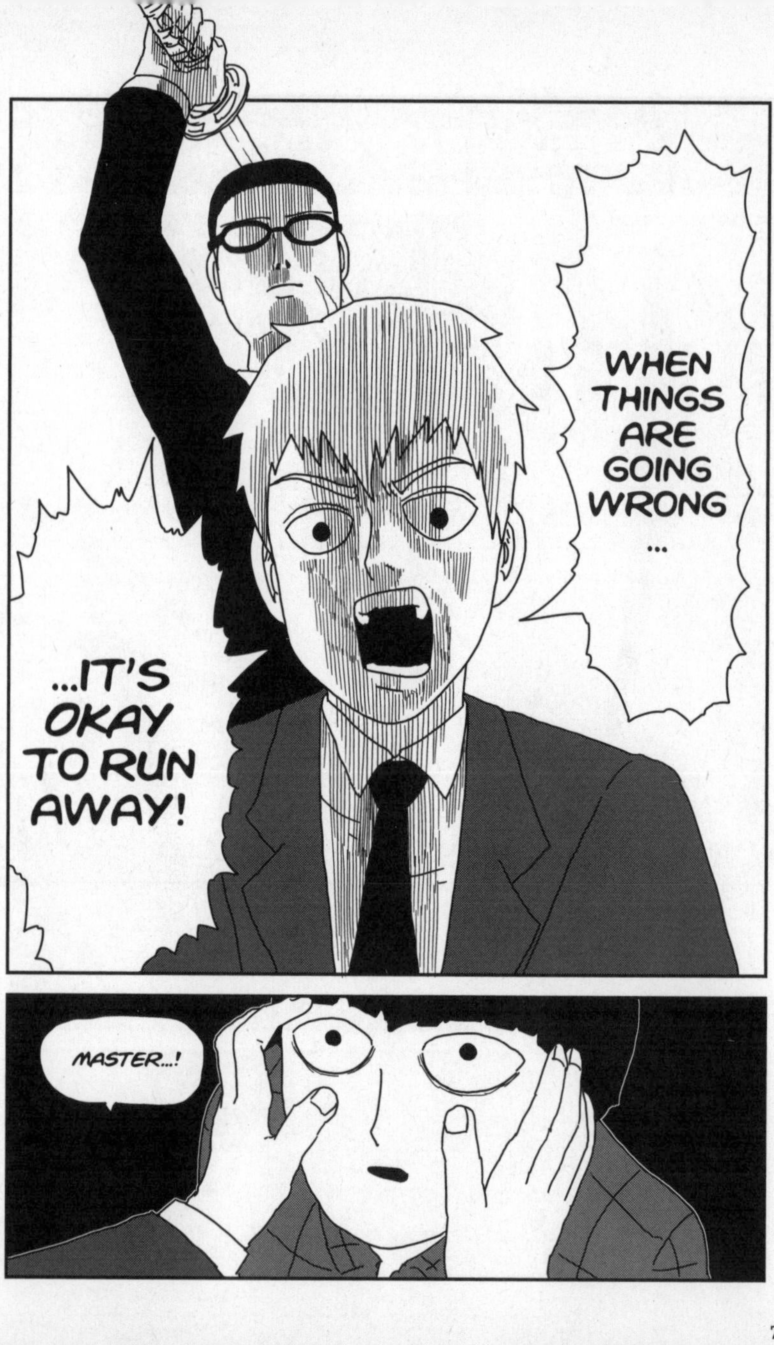
WHEN THINGS ARE GOING WRONG...
...IT'S OKAY TO RUN AWAY!
MASTER...!

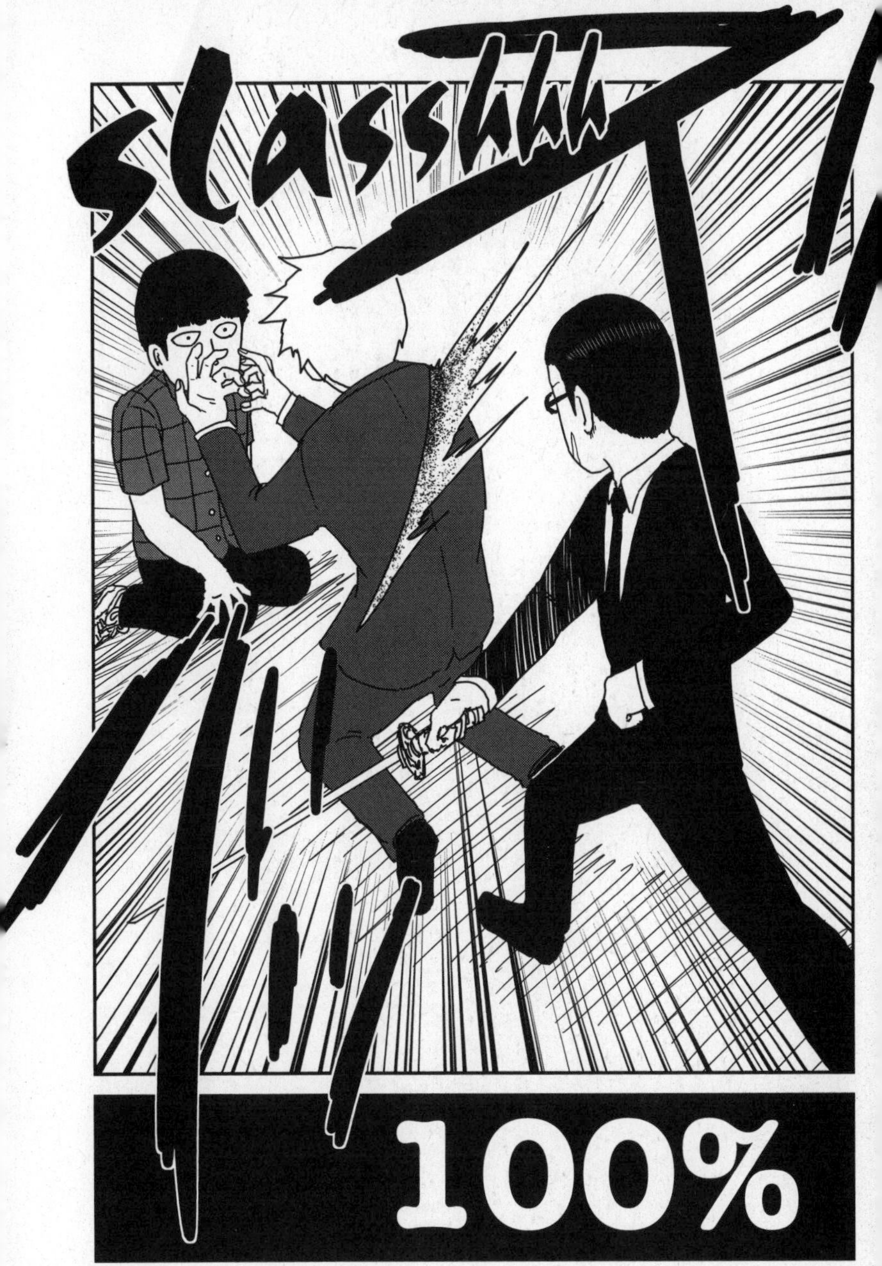
slasshhh
100%

Matsuo's Evil Spirit Observation Log (#3)

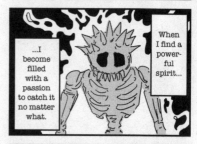

When I find a powerful spirit...
...I become filled with a passion to catch it no matter what.
COOKIE! GUM!
HIT IT HARD!
NOW! GHOST CAPSULE!!
Once sealed inside my hermetic container, infused with my spiritual presence...
...they obey the name I bind them by.
O DARK AND EVIL SPIRIT! I SHALL CALL YOU... CARAMEL!

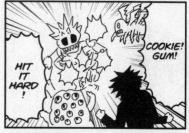

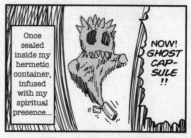

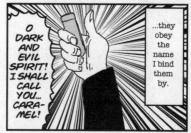

CHAPTER 47: RENTAL

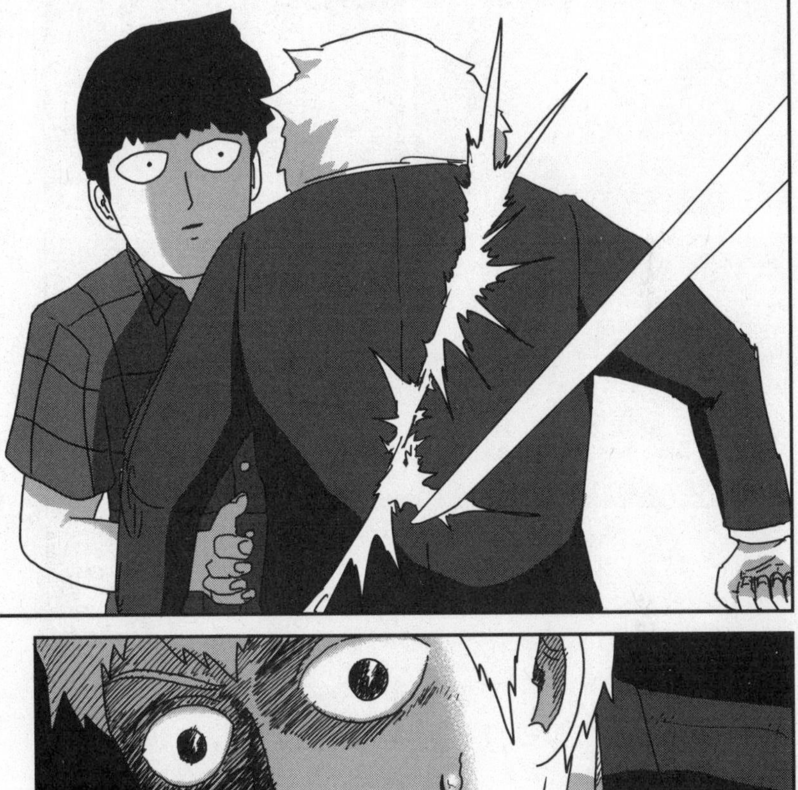

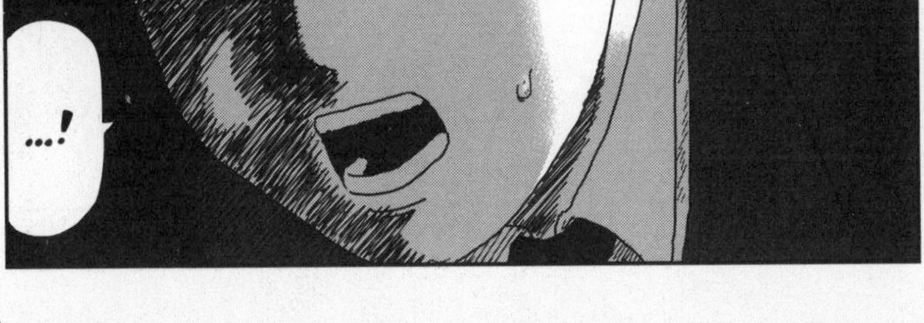
...!

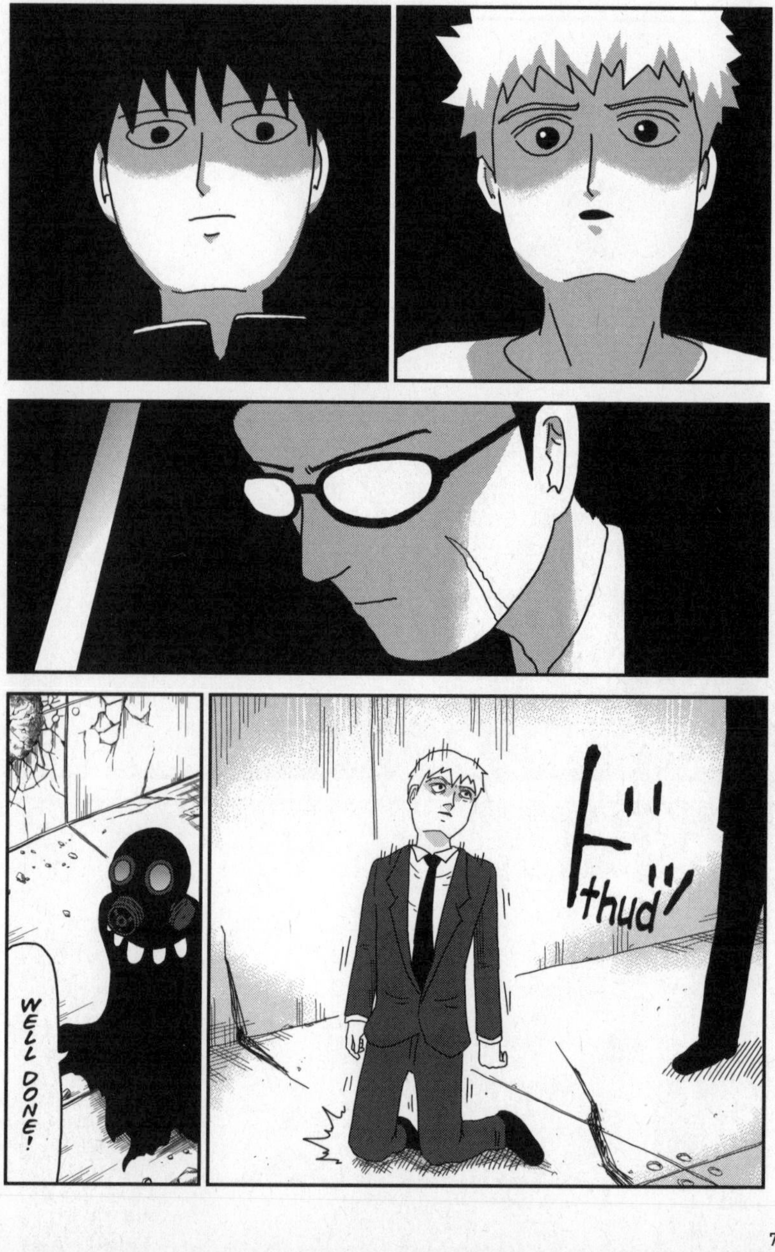
thud
WELL DONE!

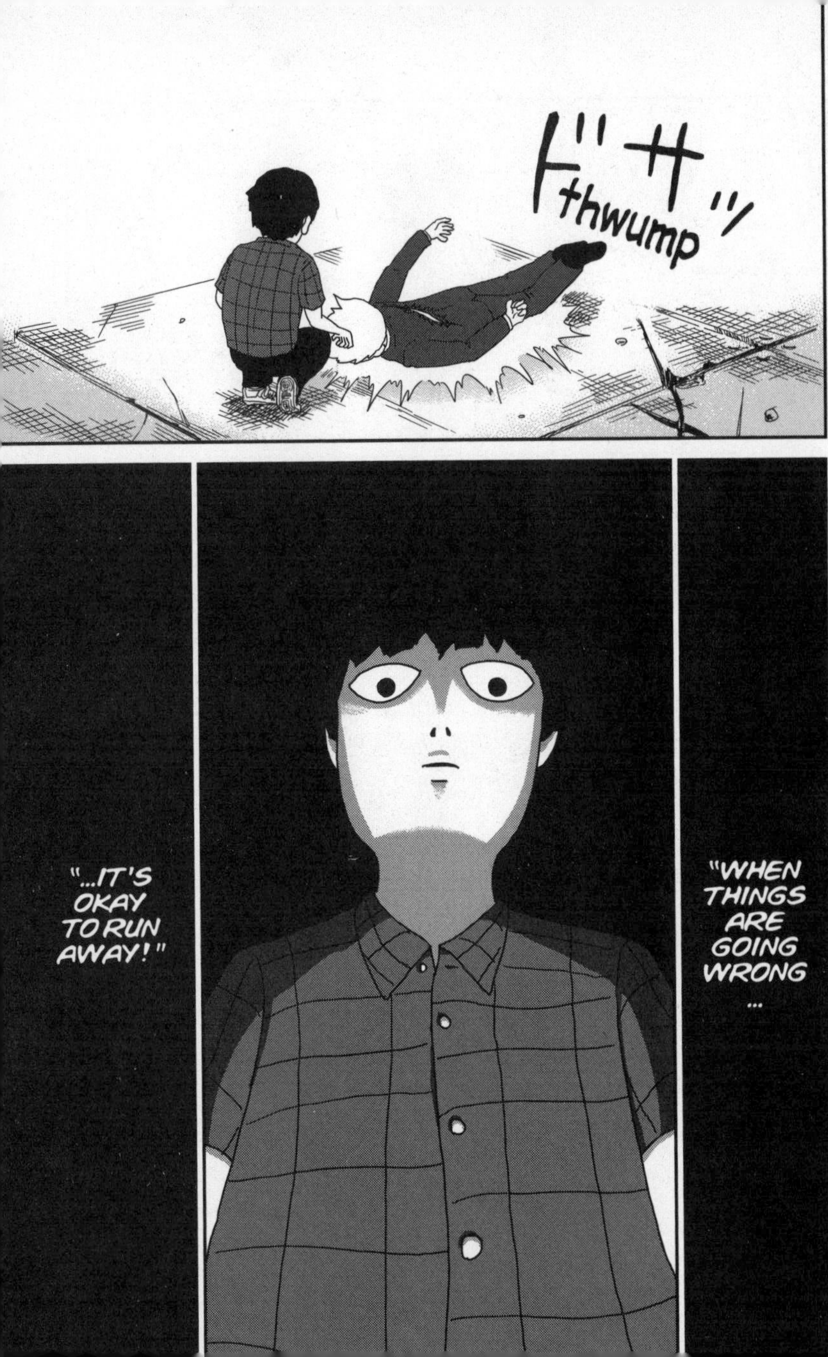
ドサッ
thwump
"WHEN THINGS ARE GOING WRONG ...
"...IT'S OKAY TO RUN AWAY!"

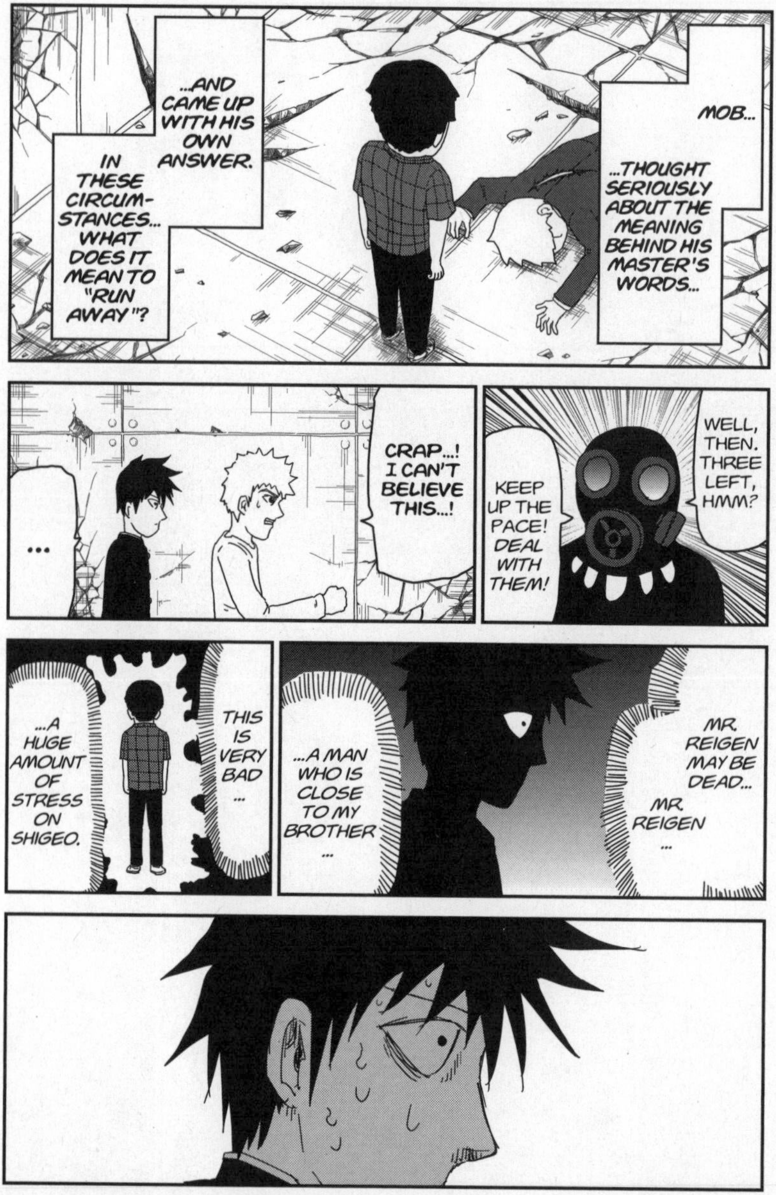
MOB...
...THOUGHT SERIOUSLY ABOUT THE MEANING BEHIND HIS MASTER'S WORDS...
...AND CAME UP WITH HIS OWN ANSWER.
IN THESE CIRCUM-STANCES... WHAT DOES IT MEAN TO "RUN AWAY"?
WELL, THEN. THREE LEFT, HMM?
KEEP UP THE PACE! DEAL WITH THEM!
CRAP...! I CAN'T BELIEVE THIS...!
...
MR. REIGEN MAY BE DEAD...
MR. REIGEN ...
...A MAN WHO IS CLOSE TO MY BROTHER ...
THIS IS VERY BAD ...
...A HUGE AMOUNT OF STRESS ON SHIGEO.

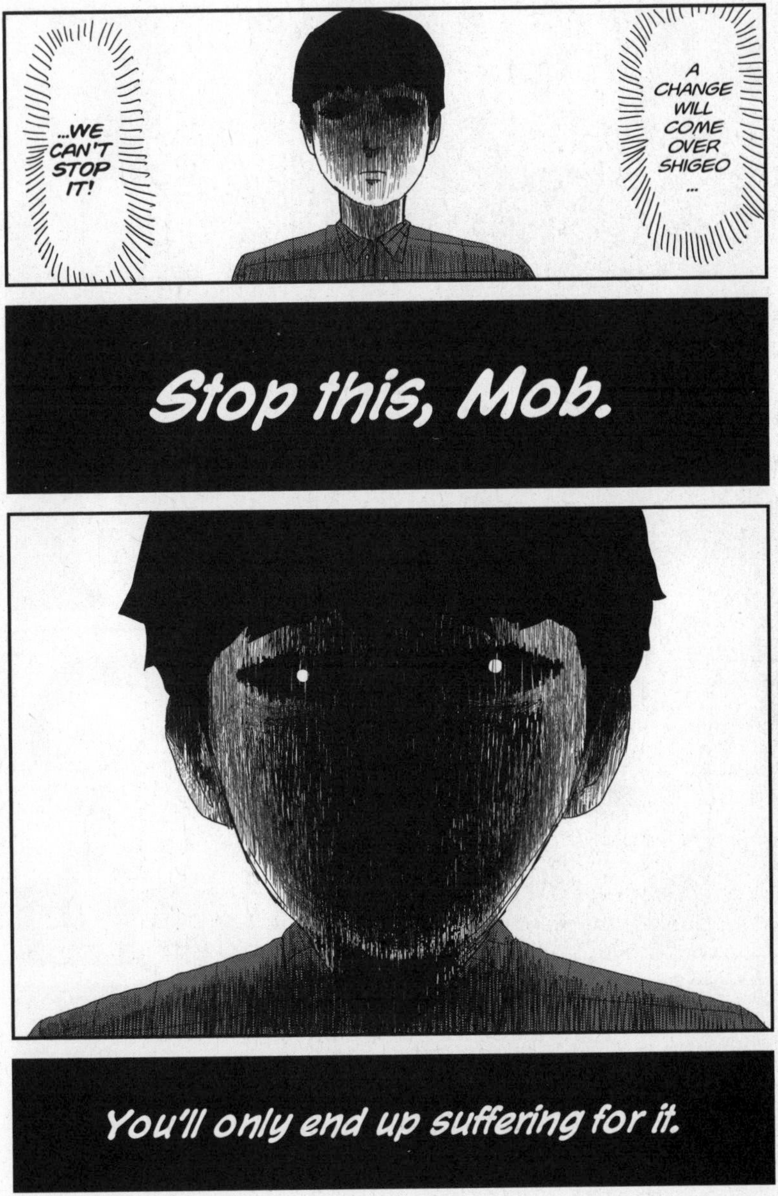
A CHANGE WILL COME OVER SHIGEO ...
...WE CAN'T STOP IT!
Stop this, Mob.
You'll only end up suffering for it.

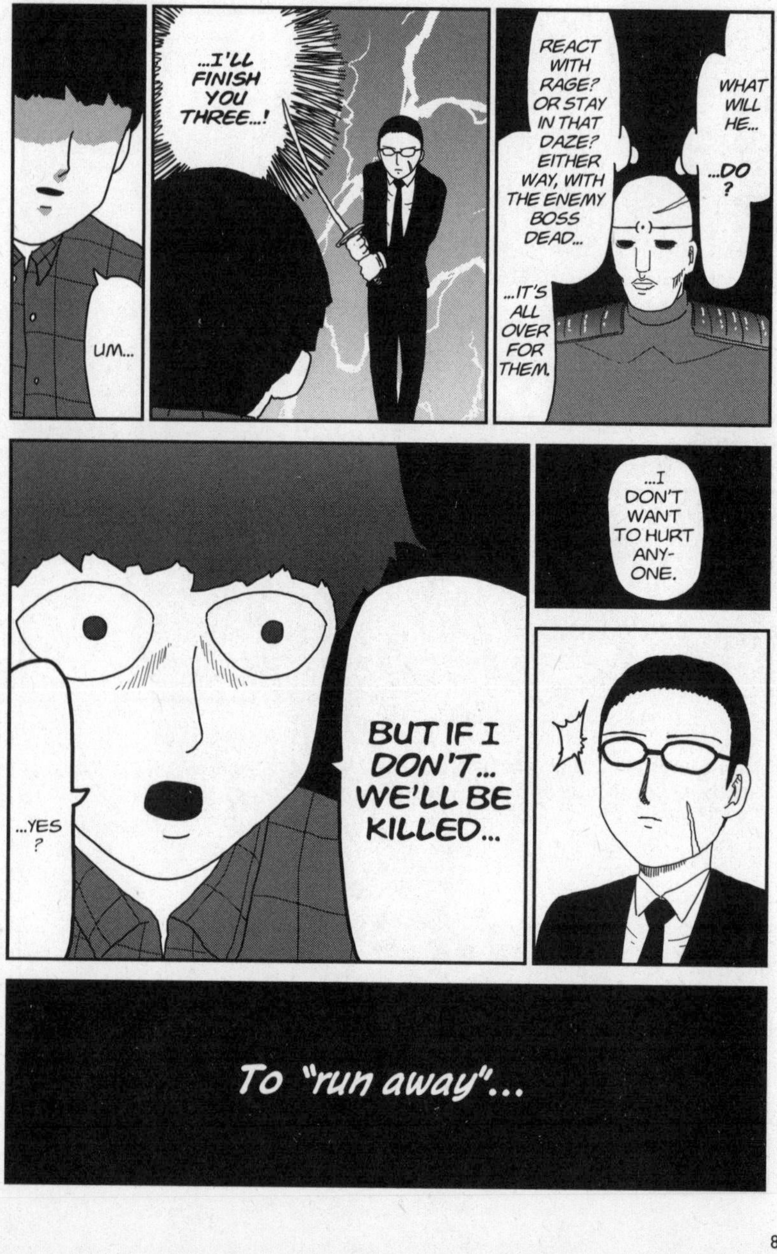
WHAT WILL HE...
...DO?
REACT WITH RAGE? OR STAY IN THAT DAZE? EITHER WAY, WITH THE ENEMY BOSS DEAD...
...IT'S ALL OVER FOR THEM.
...I'LL FINISH YOU THREE...!
UM...
...I DON'T WANT TO HURT ANY-ONE.
BUT IF I DON'T... WE'LL BE KILLED...
...YES?
To "run away"...

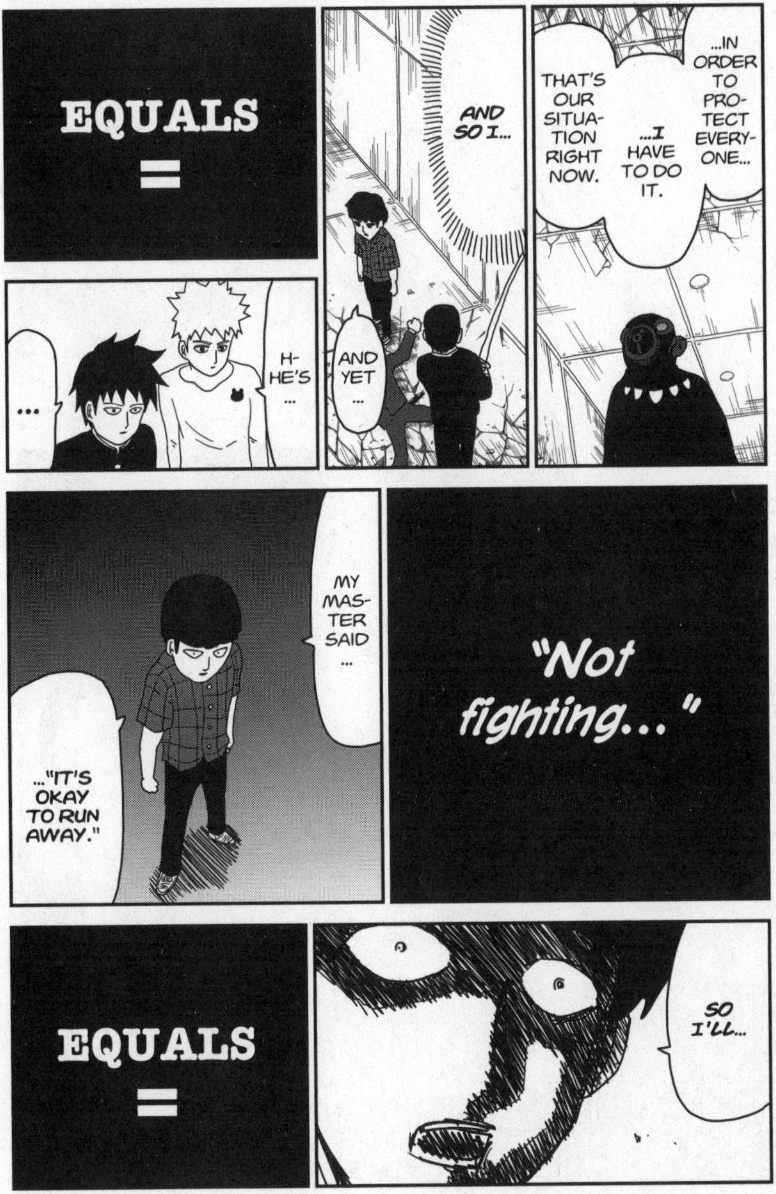
...IN ORDER TO PROTECT EVERYONE...
...I HAVE TO DO IT.
THAT'S OUR SITUATION RIGHT NOW.
AND SO I...
AND YET...
EQUALS
=
H-HE'S...
...
"Not fighting..."
MY MASTER SAID...
..."IT'S OKAY TO RUN AWAY."
SO I'LL...
EQUALS
=

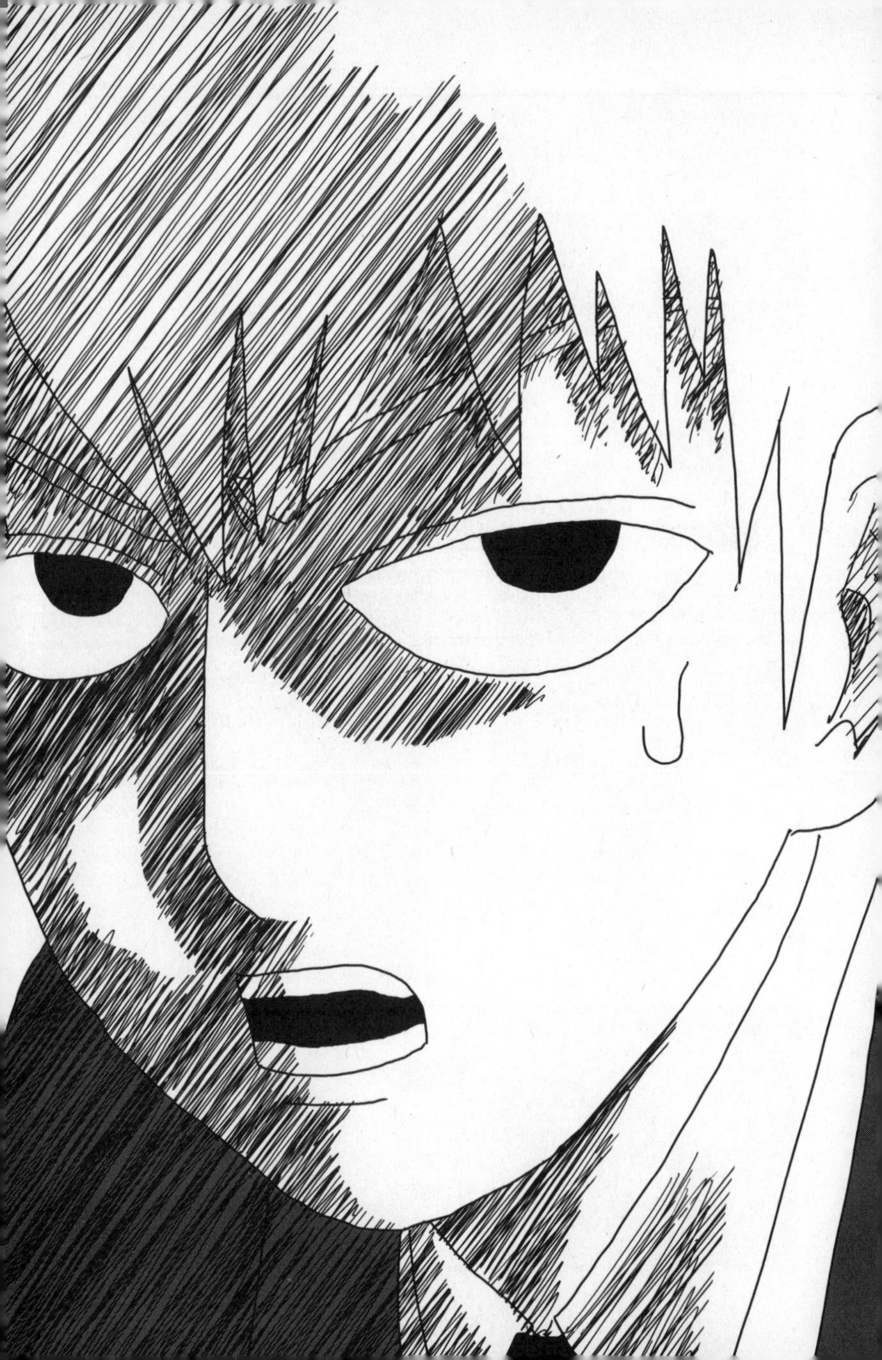

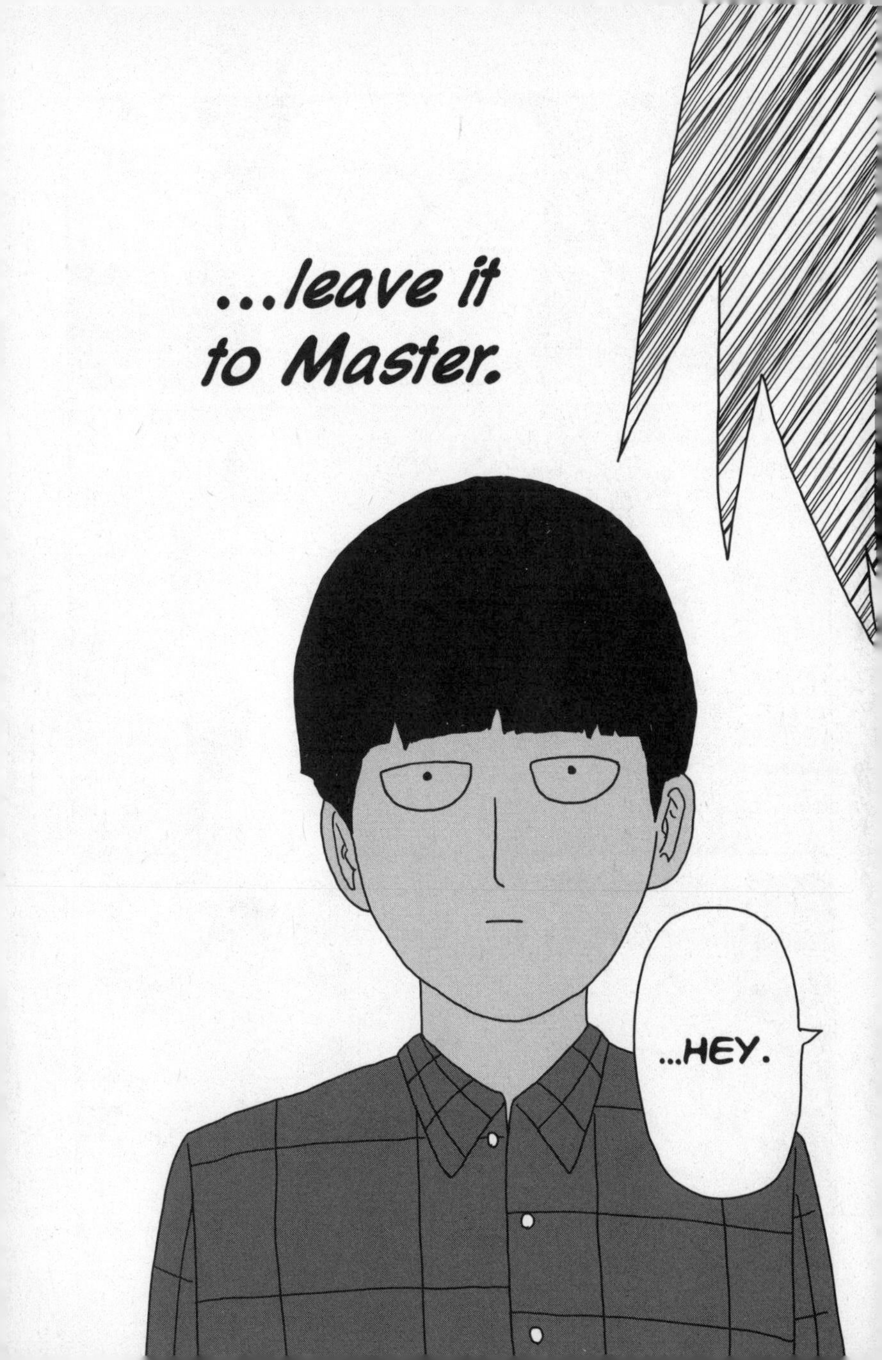
...leave it to Master.
...HEY.

Impossible...!

...?!

YOU'RE... UNHURT ?!

BUT THAT CAN'T BE...!

DON'T HIT ME LIKE THAT, OKAY ...?

FOR A MINUTE THERE, I WAS SCARED YOU'D ACTU- ALLY CUT ME.

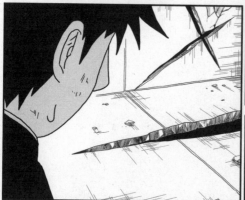

...Did he swing and miss...?

No...

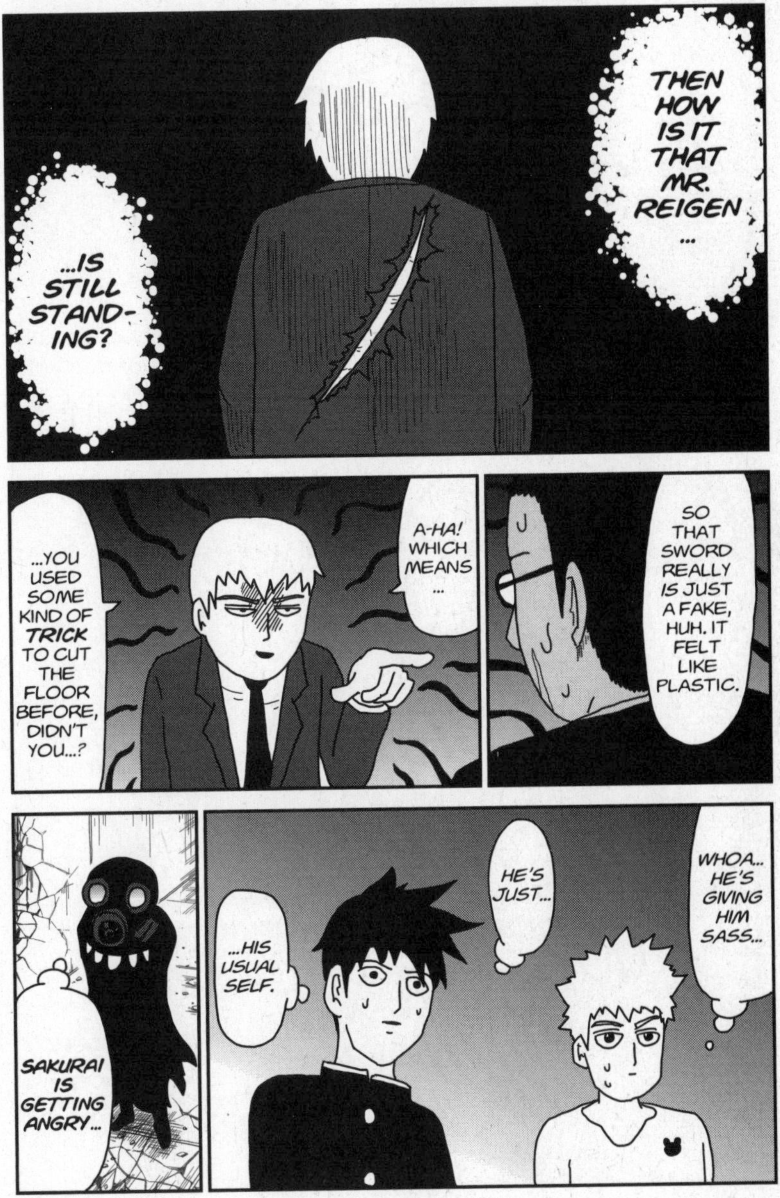
THEN HOW IS IT THAT MR. REIGEN...
...IS STILL STAND-ING?
SO THAT SWORD REALLY IS JUST A FAKE, HUH. IT FELT LIKE PLASTIC.
A-HA! WHICH MEANS...
...YOU USED SOME KIND OF TRICK TO CUT THE FLOOR BEFORE, DIDN'T YOU...?
WHOA... HE'S GIVING HIM SASS...
HE'S JUST...
...HIS USUAL SELF.
SAKURAI IS GETTING ANGRY...

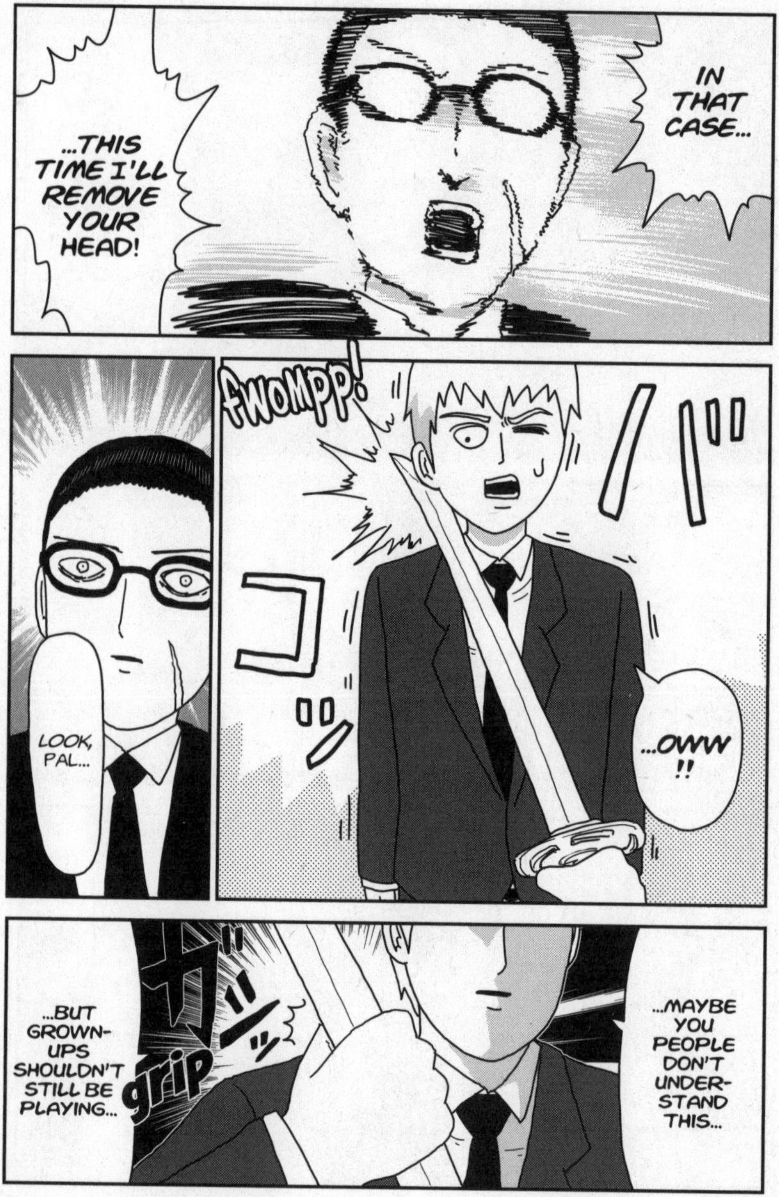

IN THAT CASE...
...THIS TIME I'LL REMOVE YOUR HEAD!
fwompp!
...OWW!!
LOOK, PAL...
...MAYBE YOU PEOPLE DON'T UNDER-STAND THIS...
grip
...BUT GROWN-UPS SHOULDN'T STILL BE PLAYING...

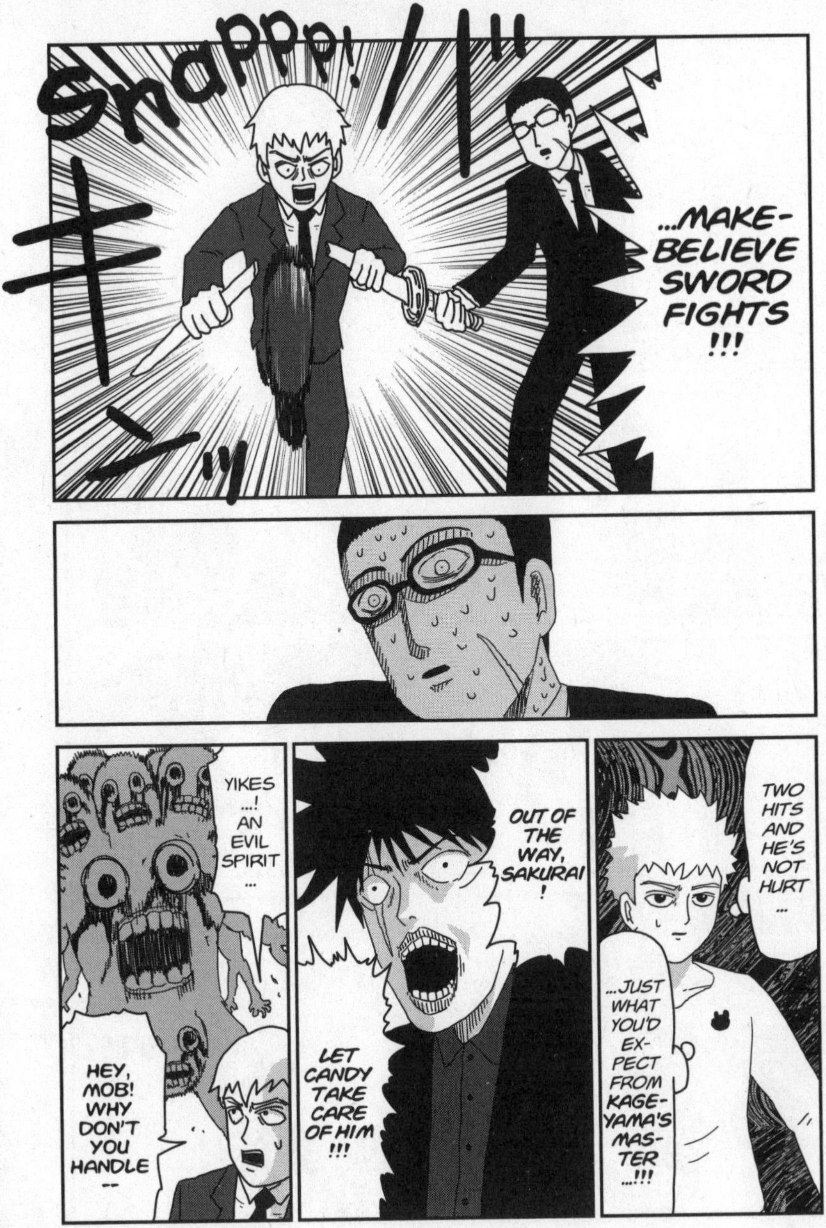
...MAKE-BELIEVE SWORD FIGHTS!!!
SNAPPP!!!
TWO HITS AND HE'S NOT HURT...
...JUST WHAT YOU'D EXPECT FROM KAGEYAMA'S MASTER...!!!
OUT OF THE WAY, SAKURAI!
LET CANDY TAKE CARE OF HIM!!!
YIKES...! AN EVIL SPIRIT...
HEY, MOB! WHY DON'T YOU HANDLE --

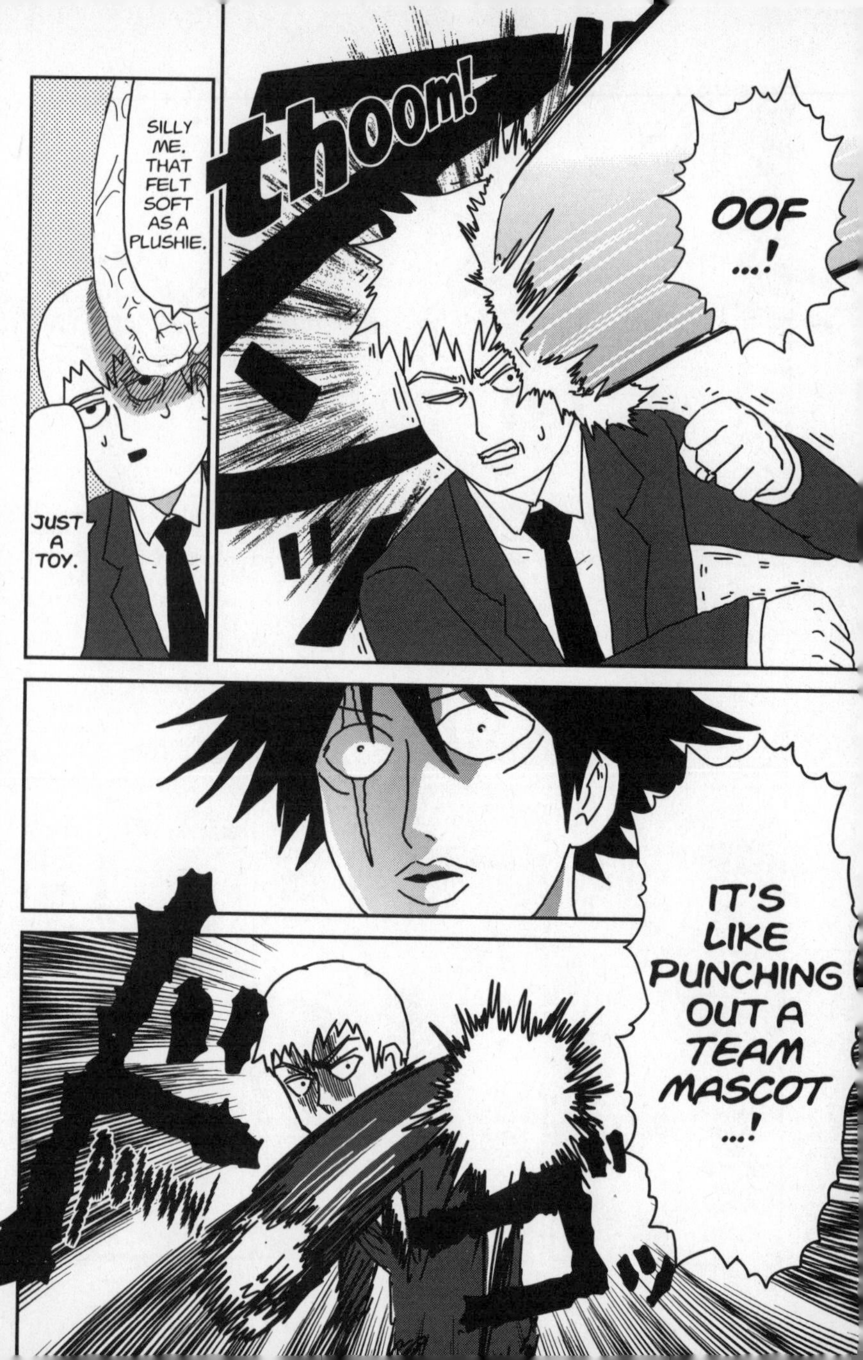
thoom!
OOF ...!
SILLY ME. THAT FELT SOFT AS A PLUSHIE.
JUST A TOY.
IT'S LIKE PUNCHING OUT A TEAM MASCOT ...!
Powww!

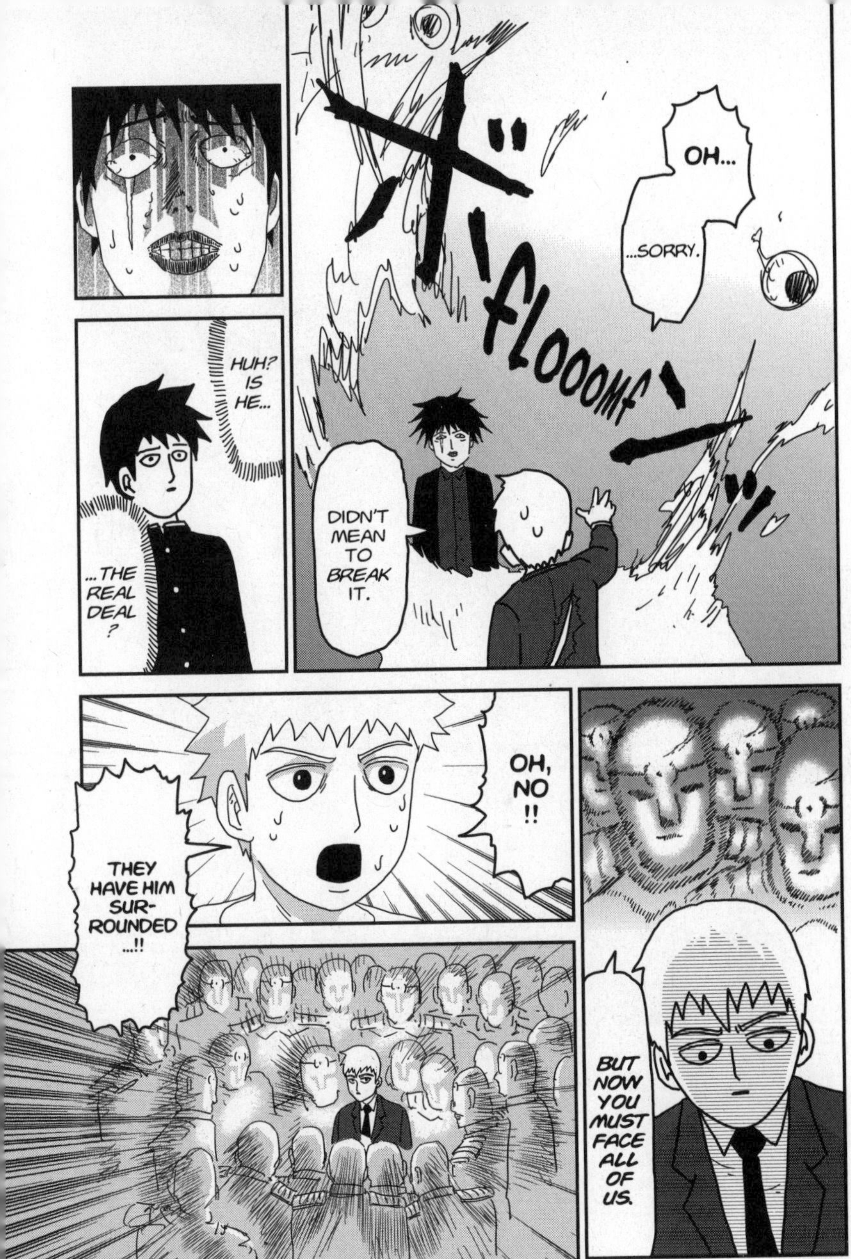
OH...
...SORRY.
FLOOOMF
DIDN'T MEAN TO BREAK IT.
HUH? IS HE...
...THE REAL DEAL?
BUT NOW YOU MUST FACE ALL OF US.
OH, NO!!
THEY HAVE HIM SUR-ROUNDED...!!

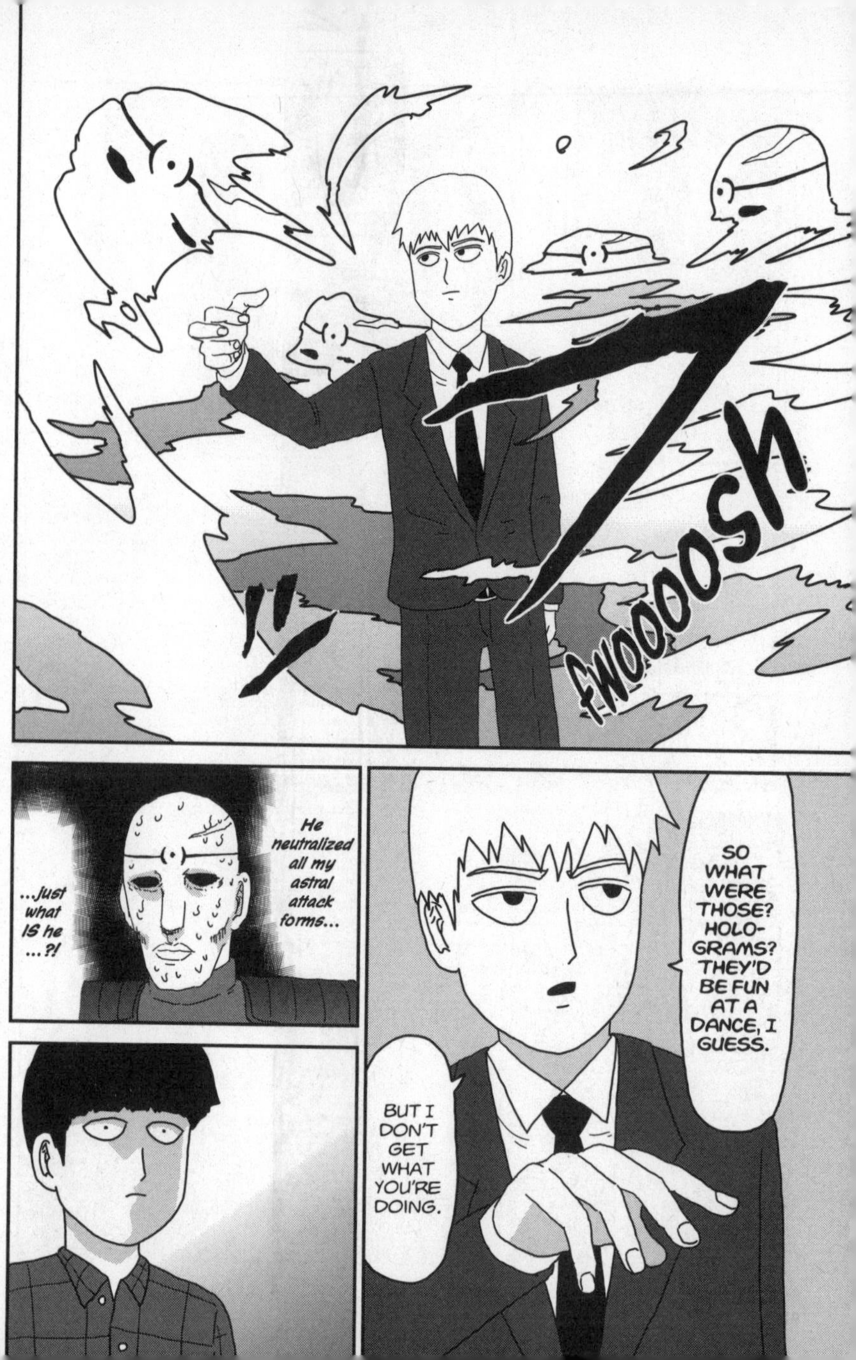
FWOOOOSH
SO WHAT WERE THOSE? HOLO-GRAMS? THEY'D BE FUN AT A DANCE, I GUESS.
BUT I DON'T GET WHAT YOU'RE DOING.
He neutralized all my astral attack forms...
...just what IS he ...?!

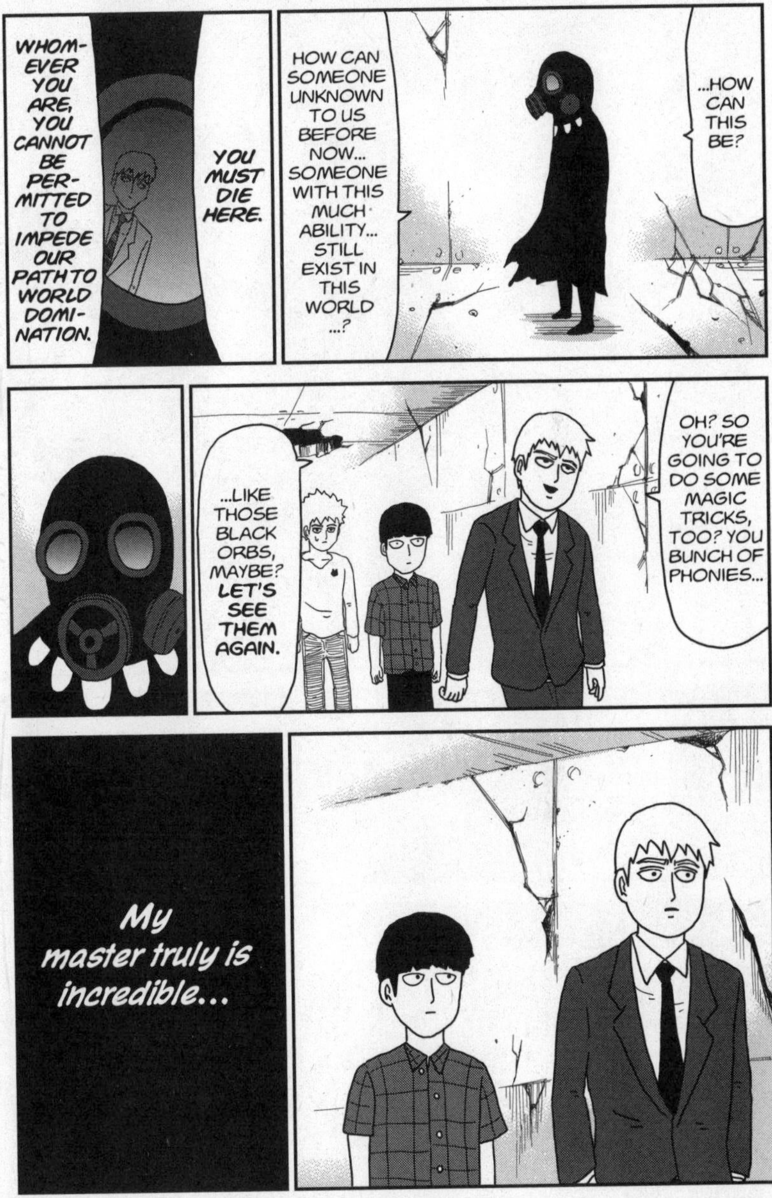
...HOW CAN THIS BE?
HOW CAN SOMEONE UNKNOWN TO US BEFORE NOW... SOMEONE WITH THIS MUCH ABILITY... STILL EXIST IN THIS WORLD ...?
YOU MUST DIE HERE.
WHOMEVER YOU ARE, YOU CANNOT BE PERMITTED TO IMPEDE OUR PATH TO WORLD DOMINATION.
OH? SO YOU'RE GOING TO DO SOME MAGIC TRICKS, TOO? YOU BUNCH OF PHONIES...
...LIKE THOSE BLACK ORBS, MAYBE? LET'S SEE THEM AGAIN.
My master truly is incredible...

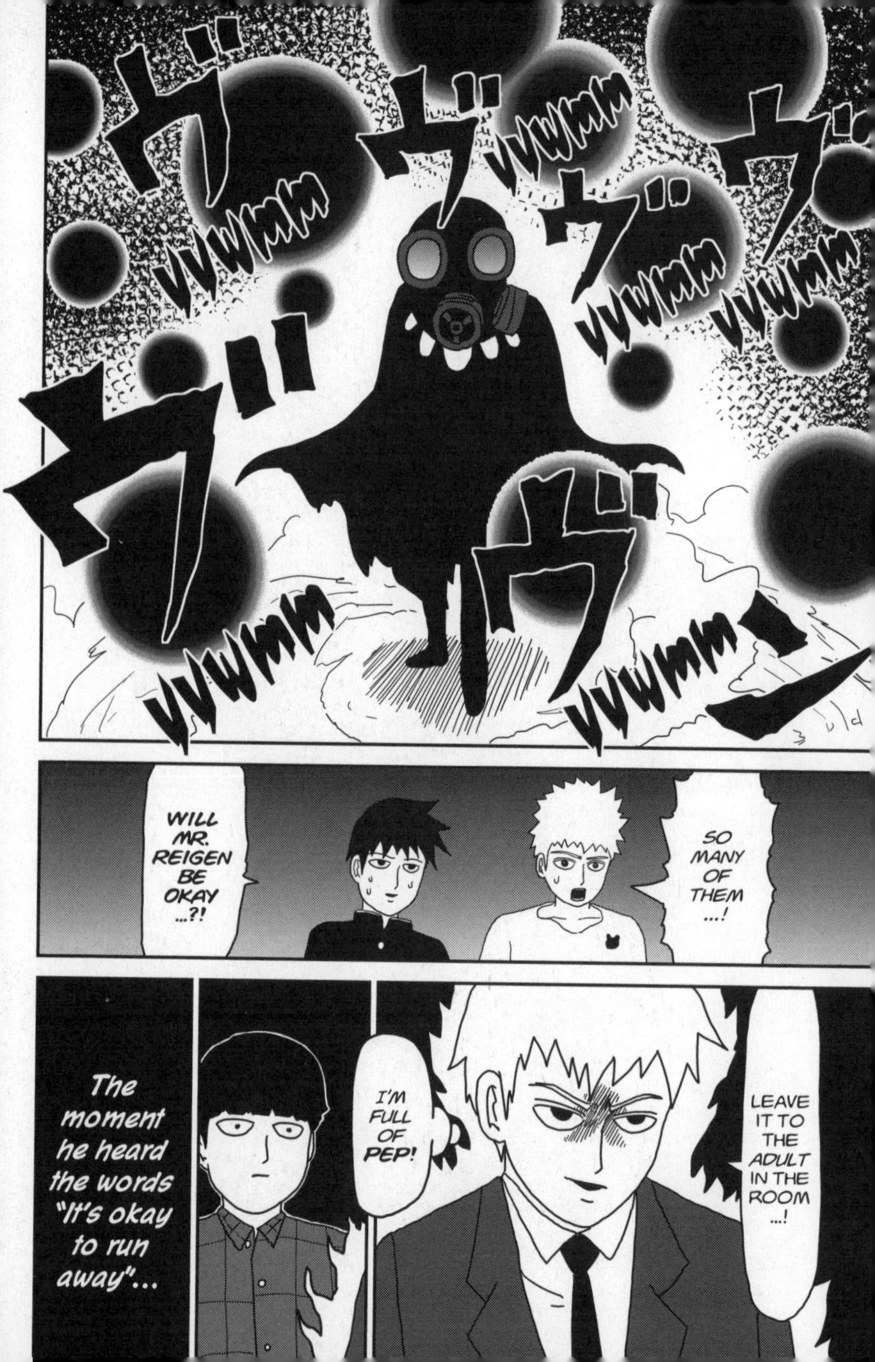

ヴ
VVWMM
ヴ
VVWMM
ヴ
VVWMM
ヴ
VVWMM
ヴ
VVWMM
ヴ
VVWMM
ヴ
VVWMM
SO MANY OF THEM ...!
WILL MR. REIGEN BE OKAY ...?!
LEAVE IT TO THE ADULT IN THE ROOM ...!
I'M FULL OF PEP!
The moment he heard the words "It's okay to run away"...

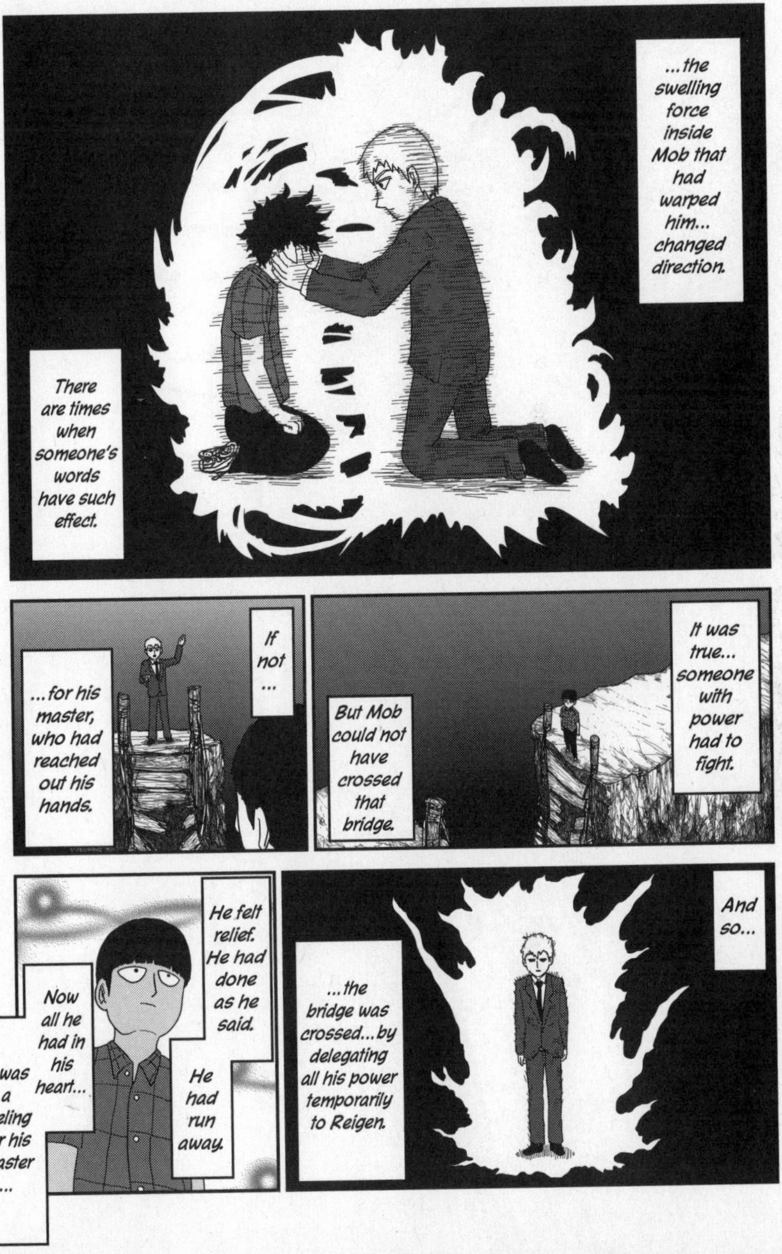
...the swelling force inside Mob that had warped him... changed direction.
There are times when someone's words have such effect.
It was true... someone with power had to fight.
But Mob could not have crossed that bridge.
If not ...
...for his master, who had reached out his hands.
And so...
...the bridge was crossed...by delegating all his power temporarily to Reigen.
He felt relief. He had done as he said.
He had run away.
Now all he had in his heart...
...was a feeling for his master ...

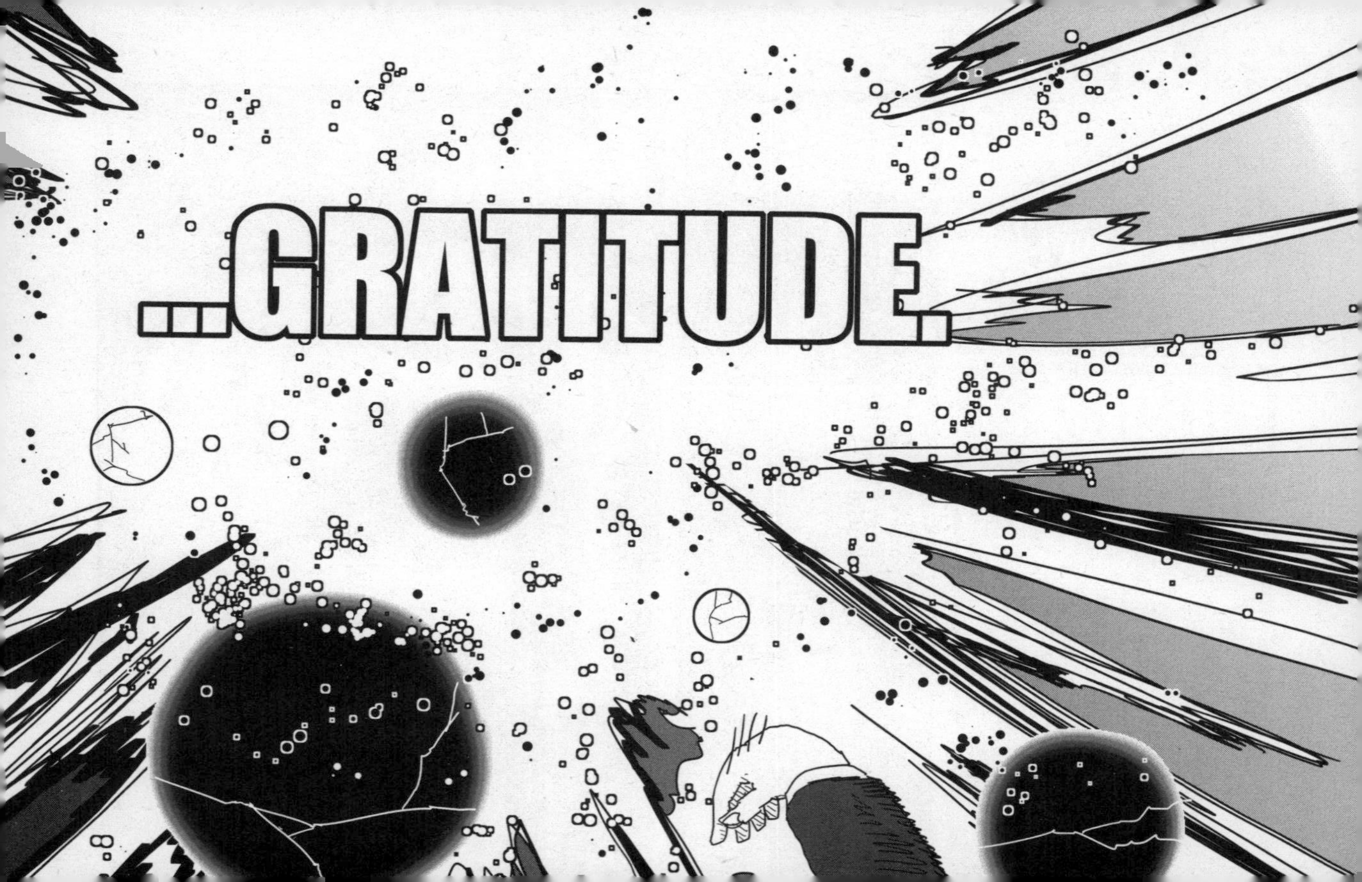
...GRATITUDE.

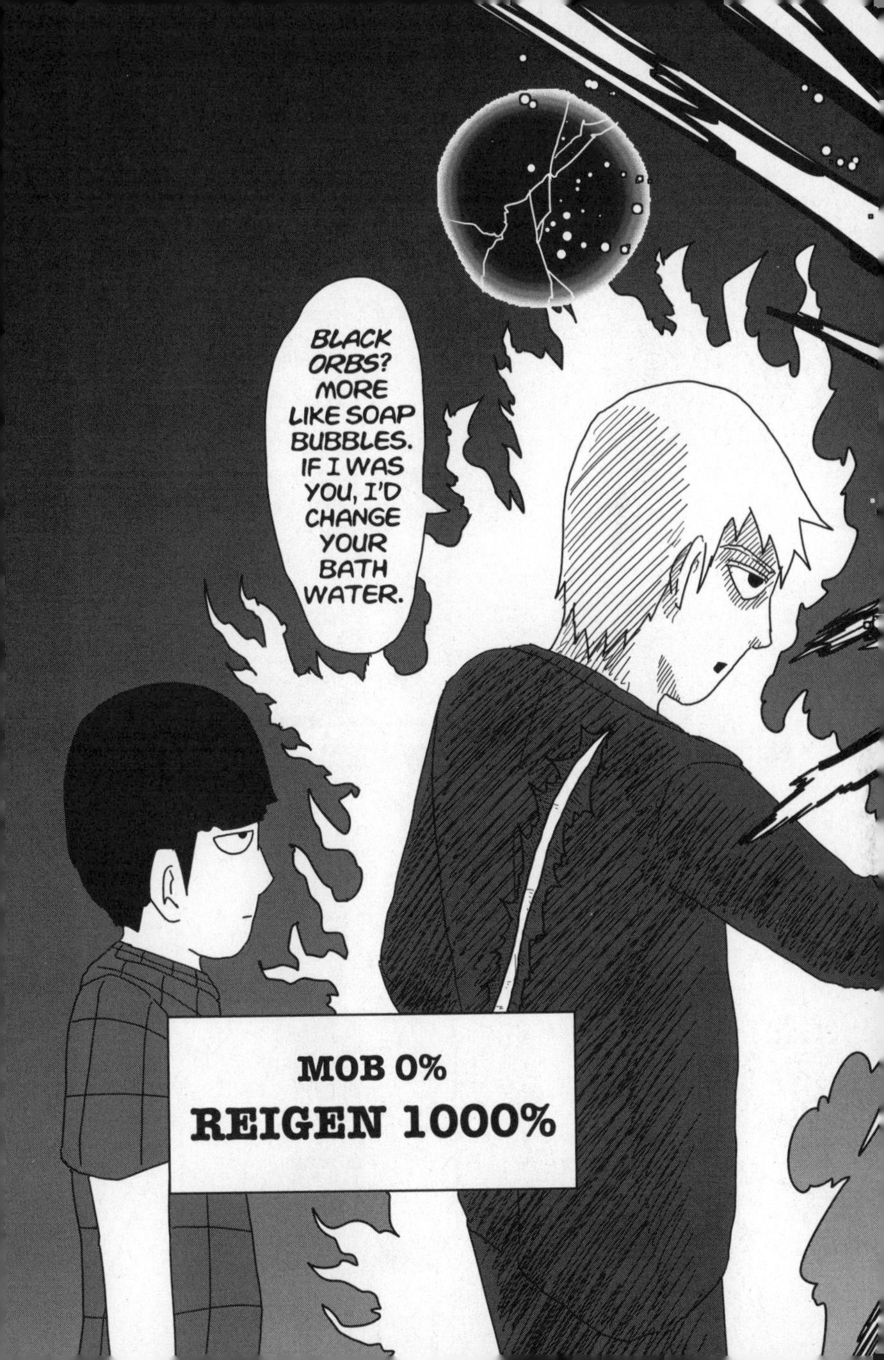
BLACK ORBS? MORE LIKE SOAP BUBBLES. IF I WAS YOU, I'D CHANGE YOUR BATH WATER.
MOB 0%
REIGEN 1000%

Matsuo's Evil Spirit Observation Log (#4)

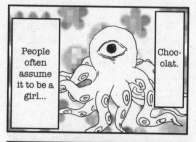

Choc-olat.
People often assume it to be a girl...
...just because of the way Chocolat clings to a nice-looking guy's back...
HM? I FEEL SO HEAVY ALL OF A SUDDEN ...
...and drains his vitality until he's near dead...
GHH ...
WHAT'S WRONG? YOU DON'T LOOK GOOD!
...and comes back with such a happy look.
OH, YOU NAUGHTY CHILD.

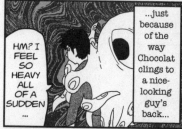

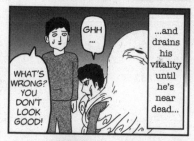

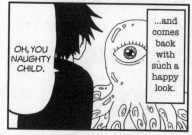

CHAPTER 48: OVERWHELM

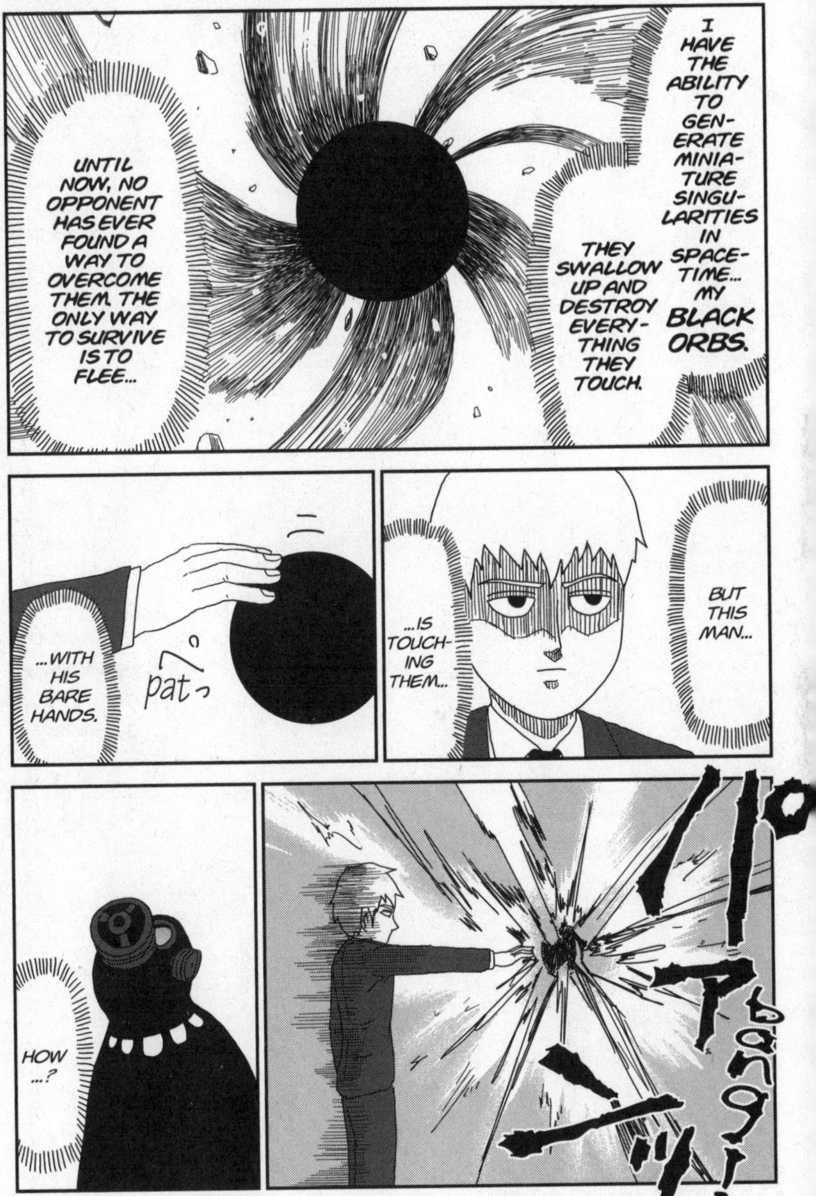
I HAVE THE ABILITY TO GENERATE MINIATURE SINGULARITIES IN SPACE-TIME... MY BLACK ORBS.
THEY SWALLOW UP AND DESTROY EVERYTHING THEY TOUCH.
UNTIL NOW, NO OPPONENT HAS EVER FOUND A WAY TO OVERCOME THEM. THE ONLY WAY TO SURVIVE IS TO FLEE...
BUT THIS MAN...
...IS TOUCHING THEM...
...WITH HIS BARE HANDS.
pat
HOW ...?

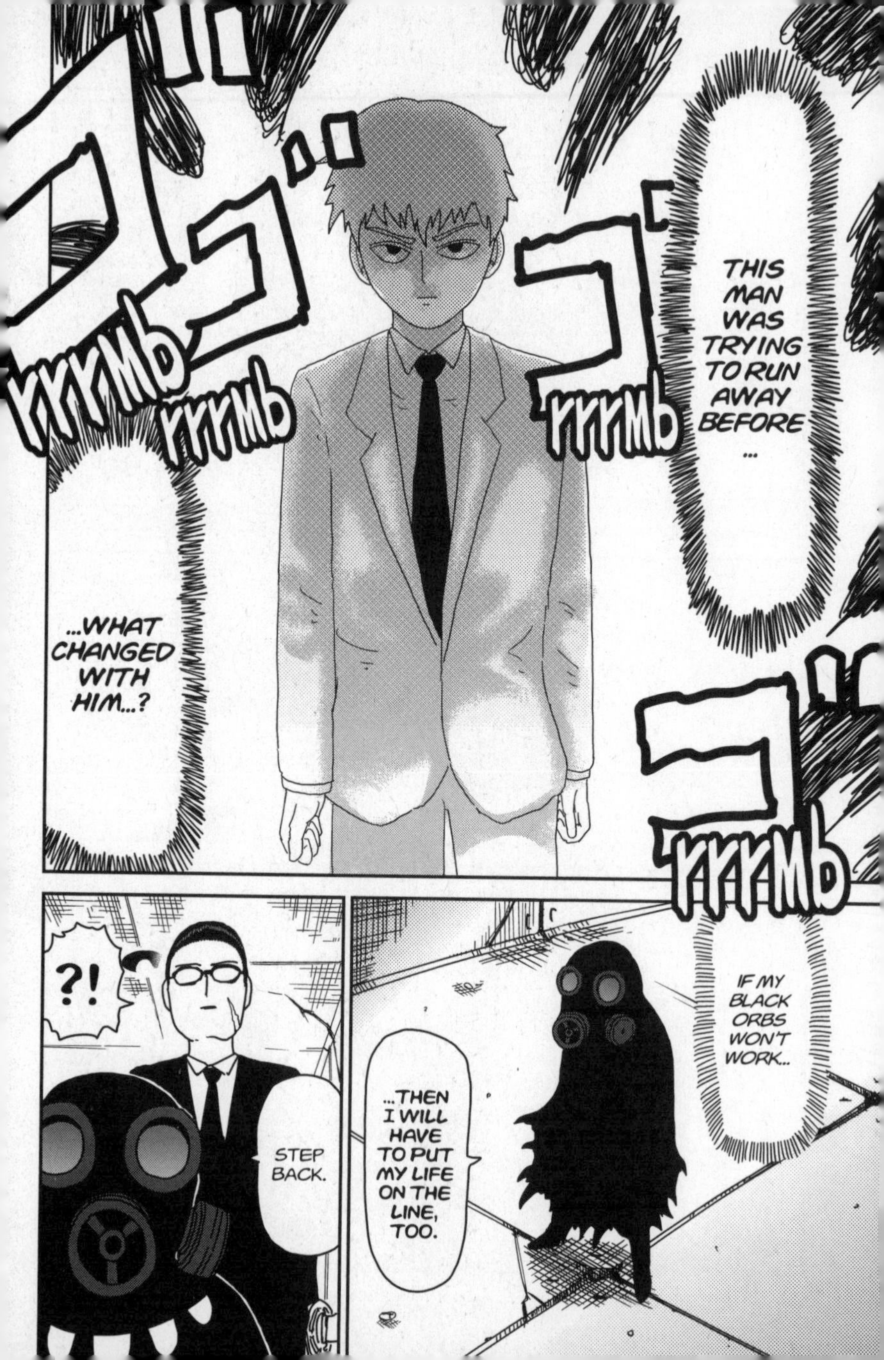
rrrmb
THIS MAN WAS TRYING TO RUN AWAY BEFORE ...
rrrmb
rrrmb
...WHAT CHANGED WITH HIM...?
rrrmb
IF MY BLACK ORBS WON'T WORK...
...THEN I WILL HAVE TO PUT MY LIFE ON THE LINE, TOO.
?!
STEP BACK.

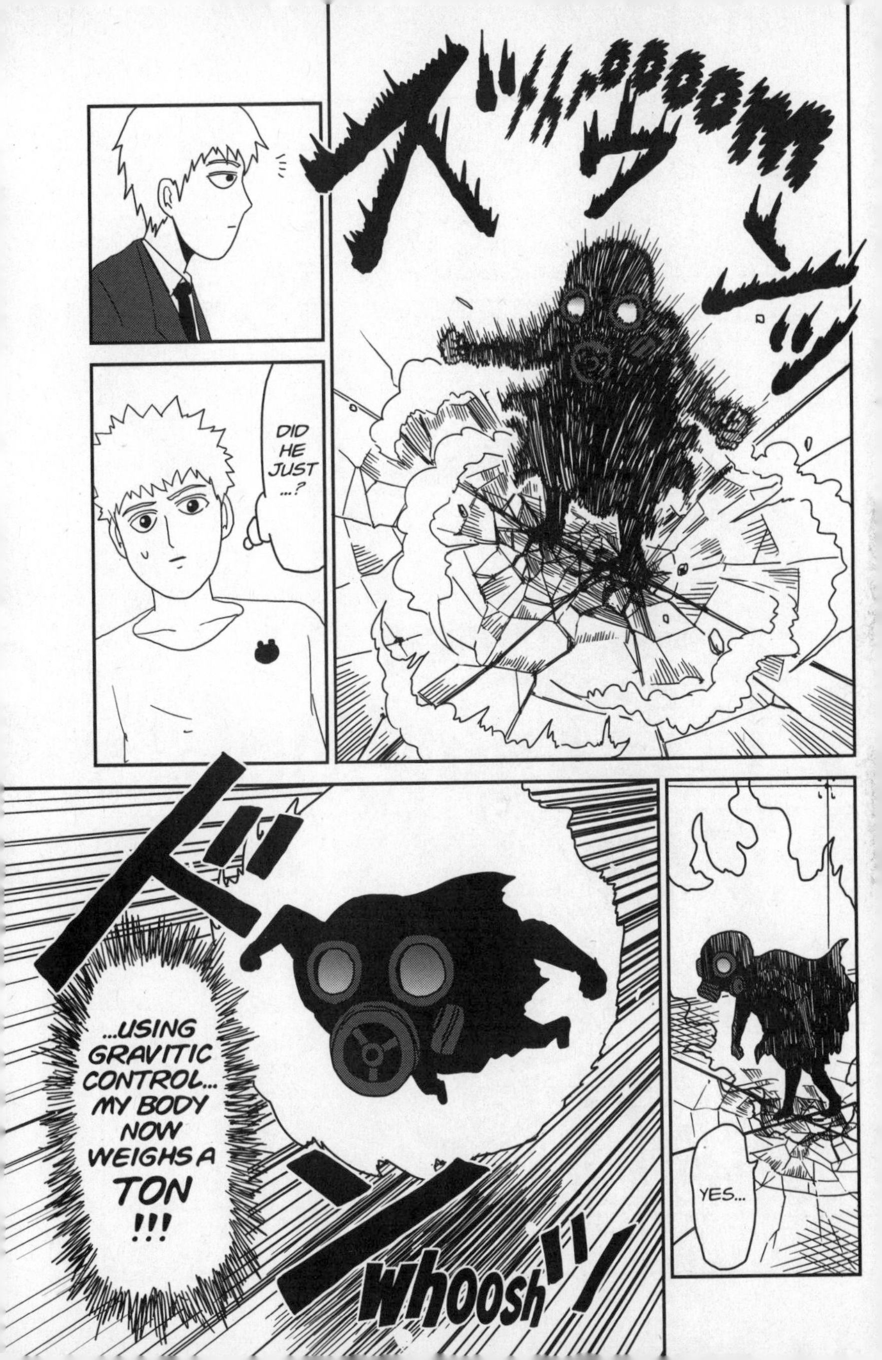
BOOOM
DID HE JUST ...?
YES...
...USING GRAVITIC CONTROL... MY BODY NOW WEIGHS A TON !!!
whoosh

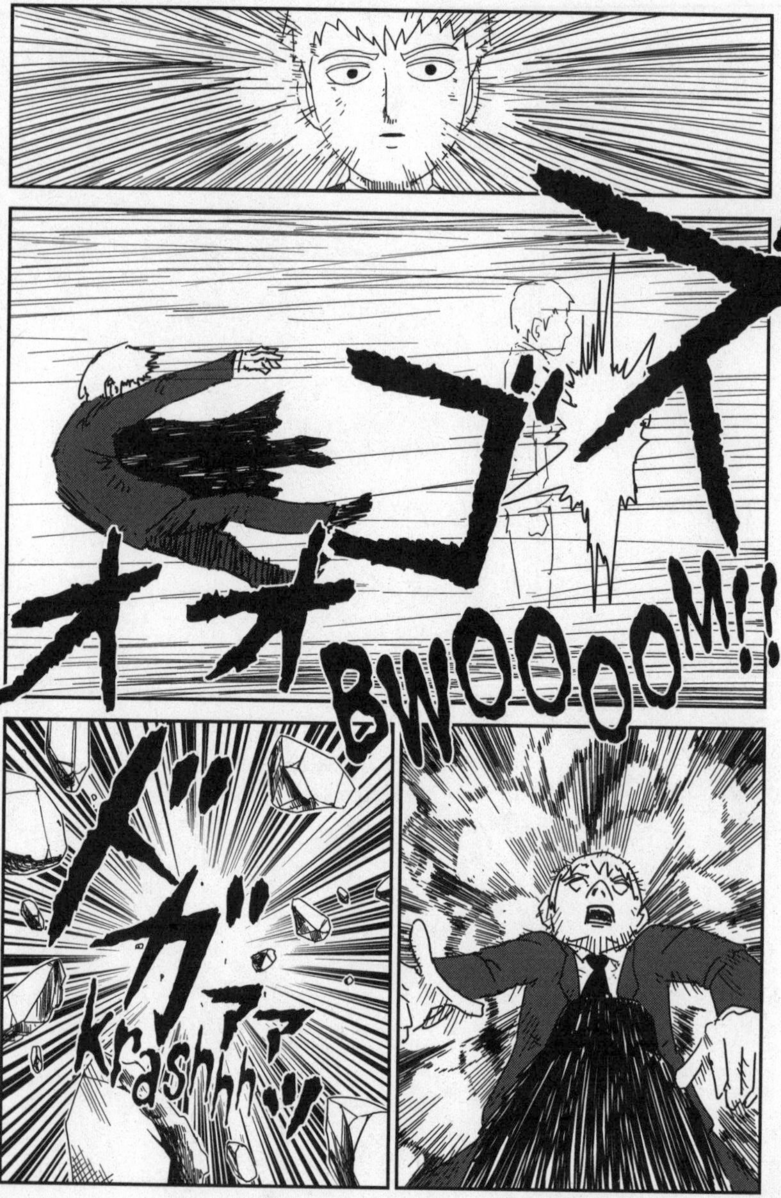
BWOOOOM!!
krashh..!

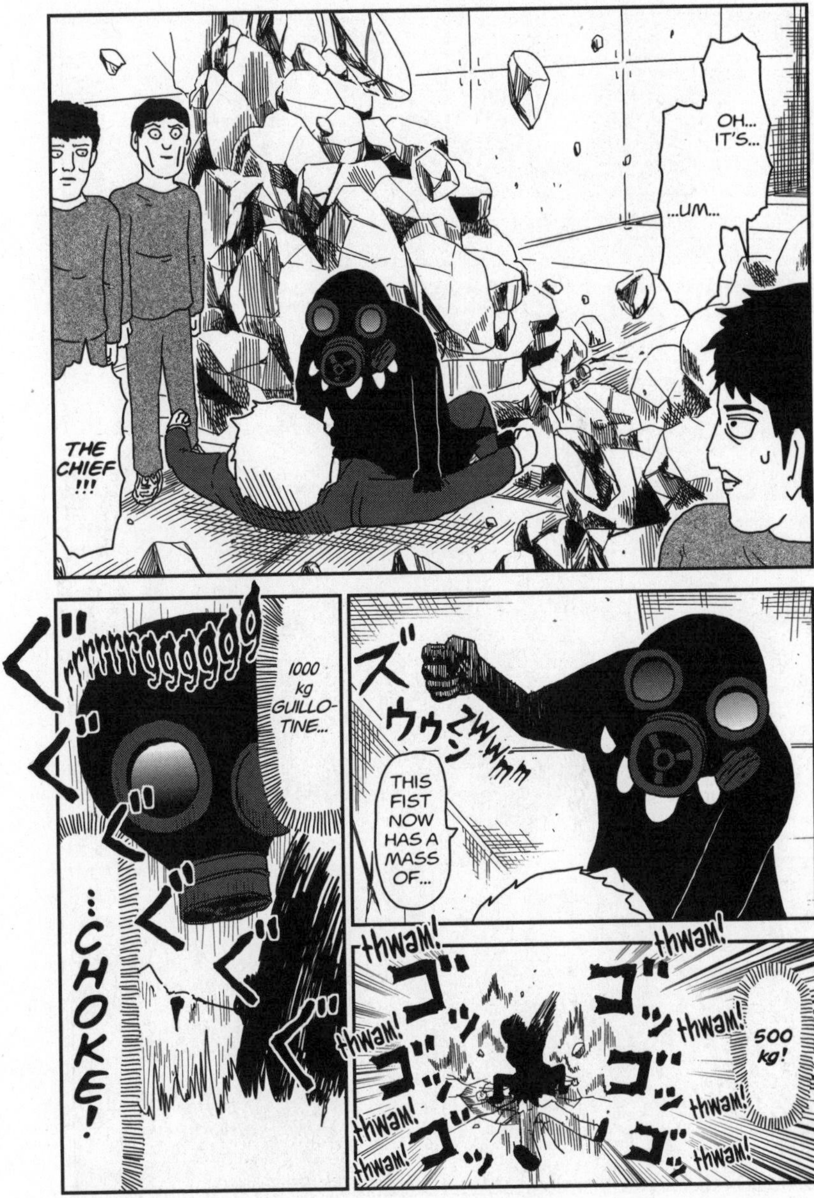

OH... IT'S...
...UM...
THE CHIEF!!!
ズウゥン
zwwmm
THIS FIST NOW HAS A MASS OF...
thwam! thwam! thwam! thwam! thwam! thwam! thwam!
ゴッ ゴッ ゴッ ゴッ ゴッ ゴッ
500 kg!
1000 kg GUILLOTINE...
rrrrrrgggggg
ぐぐぐぐぐぐ
...CHOKE!

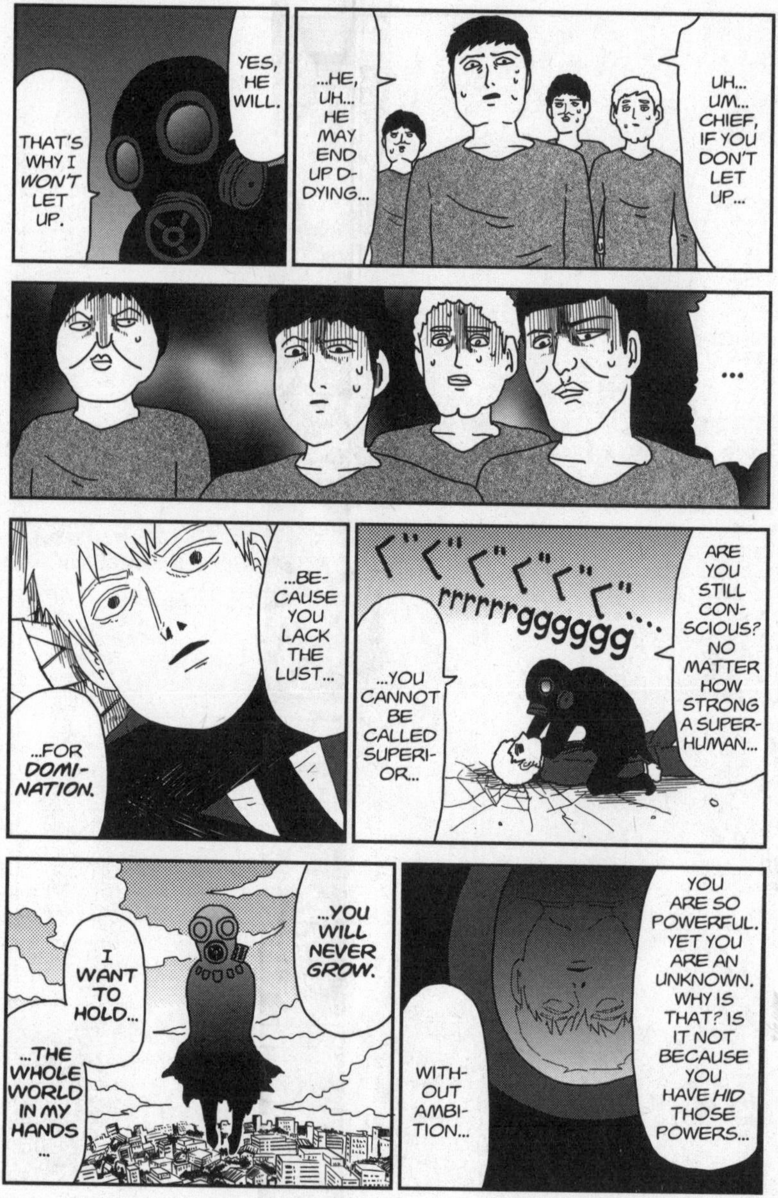
UH... UM... CHIEF, IF YOU DON'T LET UP...
...HE, UH... HE MAY END UP D-DYING...
YES, HE WILL.
THAT'S WHY I *WON'T* LET UP.
...
ARE YOU STILL CONSCIOUS? NO MATTER HOW STRONG A SUPERHUMAN...
ぐぐぐぐぐぐ
rrrrrrgggggg...
...YOU CANNOT BE CALLED SUPERIOR...
...BECAUSE YOU LACK THE LUST...
...FOR *DOMINATION*.
YOU ARE SO POWERFUL. YET YOU ARE AN UNKNOWN. WHY IS THAT? IS IT NOT BECAUSE YOU HAVE *HID* THOSE POWERS...
WITHOUT AMBITION...
...YOU WILL NEVER *GROW*.
I WANT TO HOLD...
...THE WHOLE WORLD IN MY HANDS...

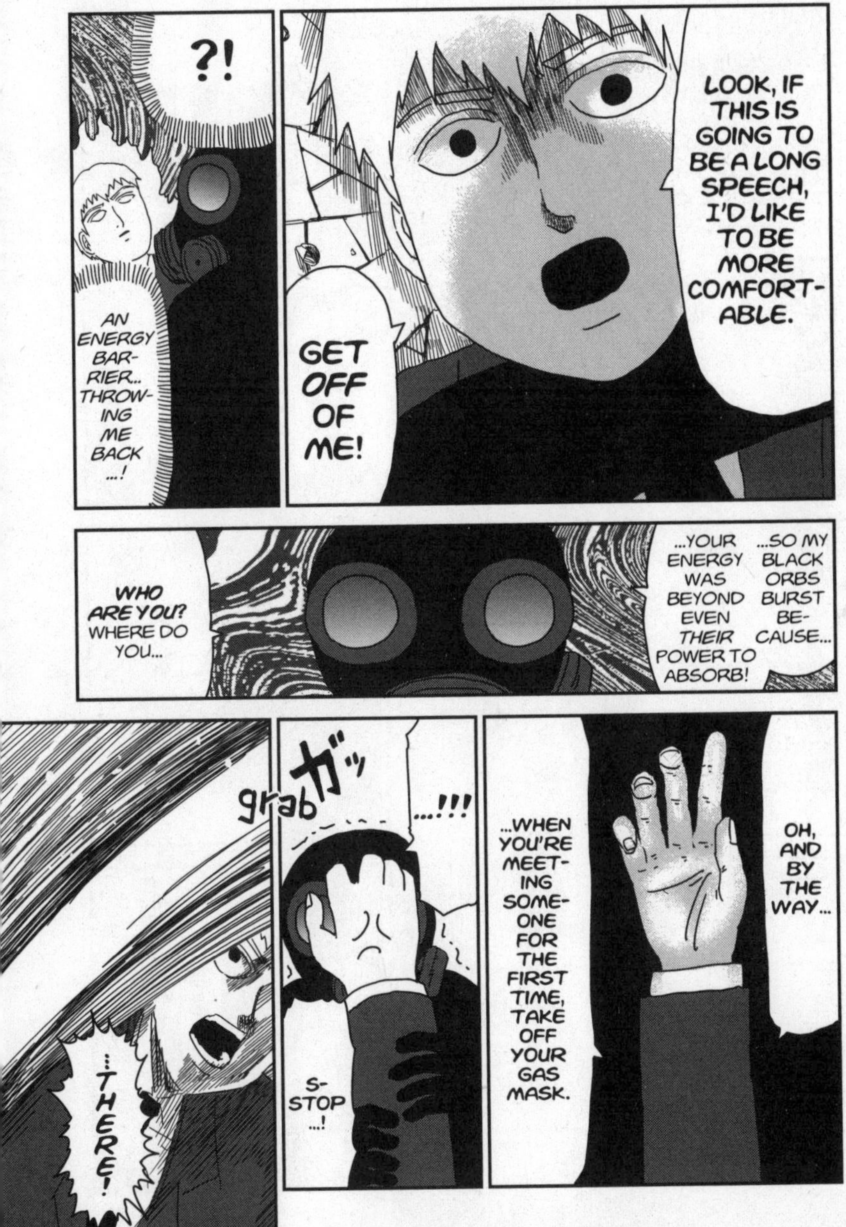
LOOK, IF THIS IS GOING TO BE A LONG SPEECH, I'D LIKE TO BE MORE COMFORTABLE.
GET OFF OF ME!
?!
AN ENERGY BARRIER... THROWING ME BACK...!
...SO MY BLACK ORBS BURST BECAUSE...
...YOUR ENERGY WAS BEYOND EVEN THEIR POWER TO ABSORB!
WHO ARE YOU? WHERE DO YOU...
OH, AND BY THE WAY...
...WHEN YOU'RE MEETING SOMEONE FOR THE FIRST TIME, TAKE OFF YOUR GAS MASK.
grab ガッ
...!!!
S-STOP...!
...THERE!

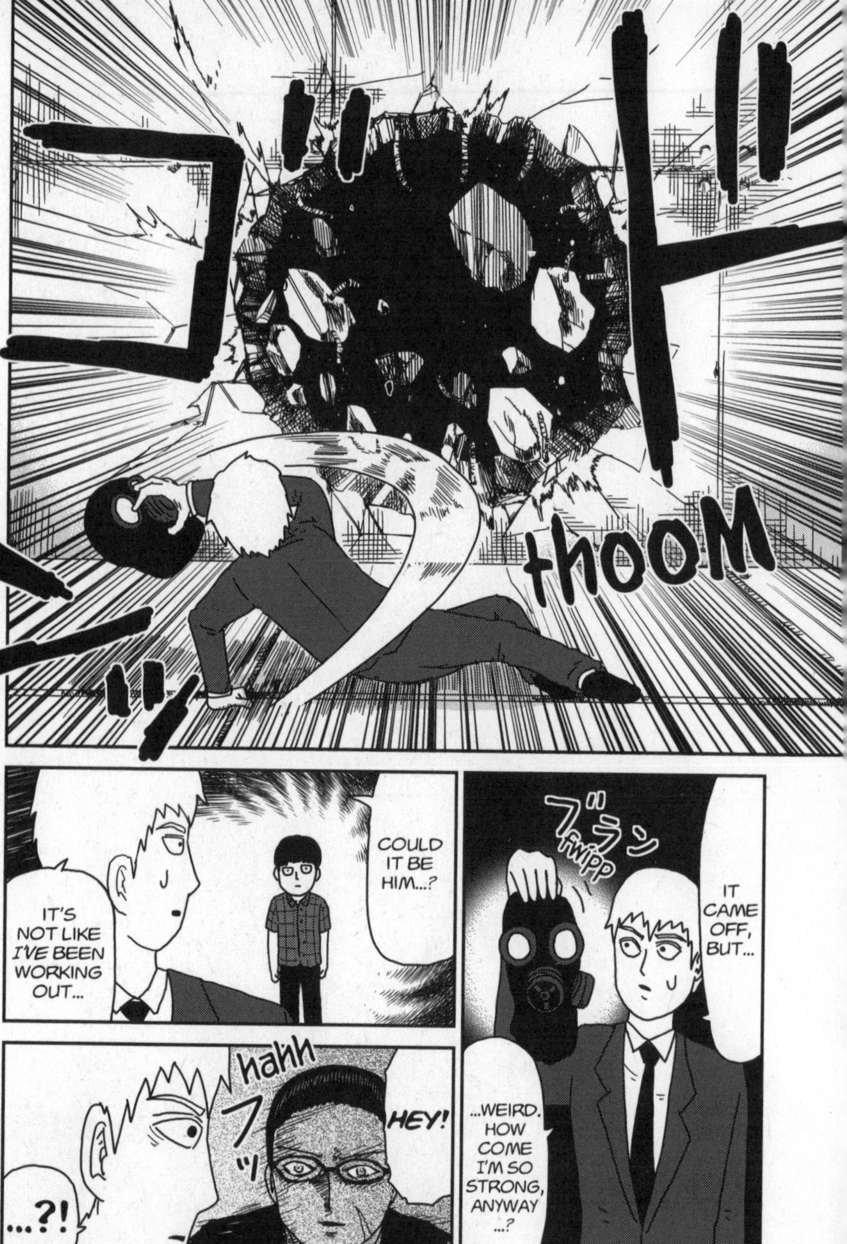
thoOM
ブラン
fwipp
IT CAME OFF, BUT...
...WEIRD. HOW COME I'M SO STRONG, ANYWAY...?
COULD IT BE HIM...?
IT'S NOT LIKE *I'VE* BEEN WORKING OUT...
hahh
フッ
HEY!
...?!

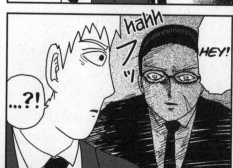

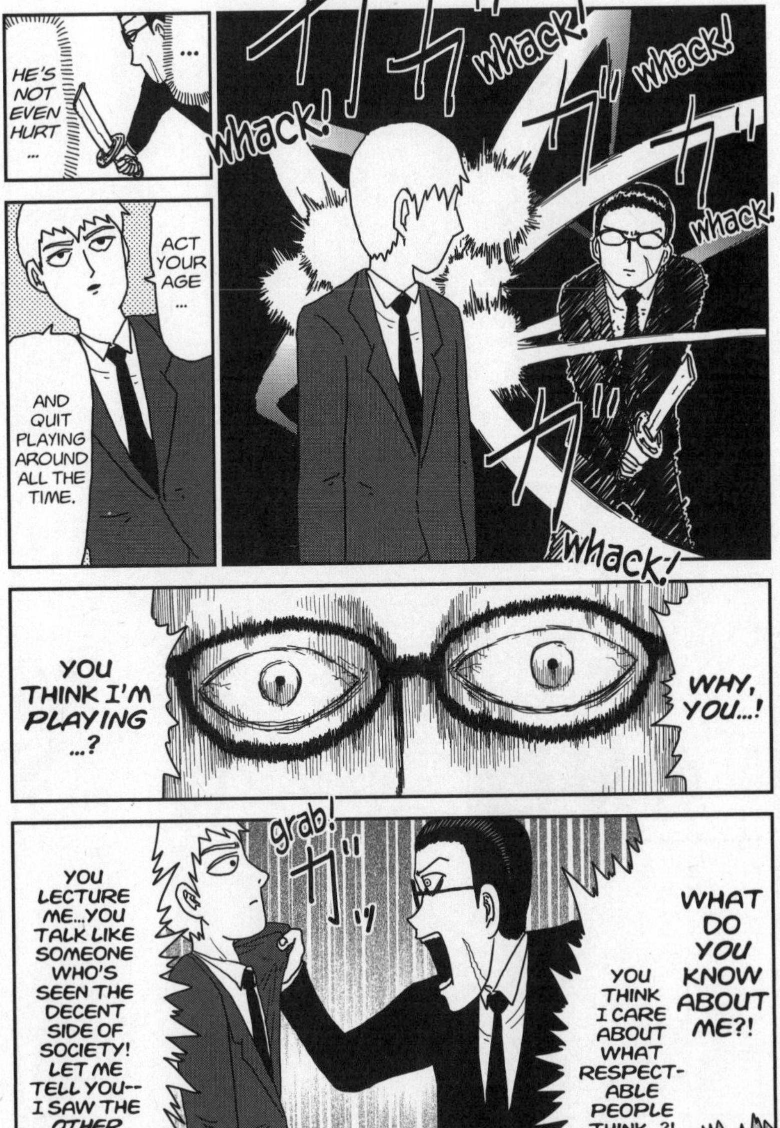
whack!
whack!
whack!
whack!
whack!
...
HE'S NOT EVEN HURT ...
ACT YOUR AGE ...
AND QUIT PLAYING AROUND ALL THE TIME.
WHY, YOU...!
YOU THINK I'M PLAYING ...?
WHAT DO YOU KNOW ABOUT ME?!
YOU THINK I CARE ABOUT WHAT RESPECT-ABLE PEOPLE THINK...?!
grab!
YOU LECTURE ME...YOU TALK LIKE SOMEONE WHO'S SEEN THE DECENT SIDE OF SOCIETY! LET ME TELL YOU-- I SAW THE OTHER SIDE...!

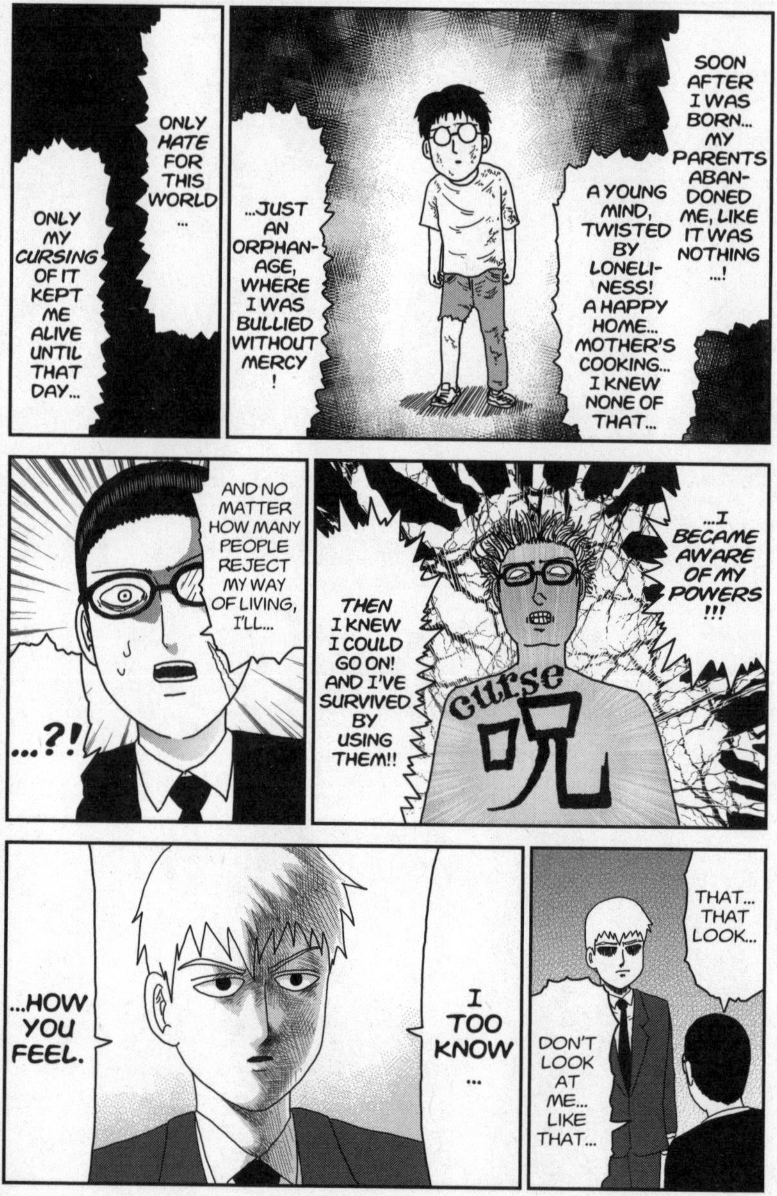

SOON AFTER I WAS BORN... MY PARENTS ABANDONED ME, LIKE IT WAS NOTHING...!
A YOUNG MIND, TWISTED BY LONELINESS! A HAPPY HOME... MOTHER'S COOKING... I KNEW NONE OF THAT...
...JUST AN ORPHANAGE, WHERE I WAS BULLIED WITHOUT MERCY!
ONLY HATE FOR THIS WORLD...
ONLY MY CURSING OF IT KEPT ME ALIVE UNTIL THAT DAY...
...I BECAME AWARE OF MY POWERS!!!
curse
呪
THEN I KNEW I COULD GO ON! AND I'VE SURVIVED BY USING THEM!!
AND NO MATTER HOW MANY PEOPLE REJECT MY WAY OF LIVING, I'LL...
...?!
THAT... THAT LOOK...
DON'T LOOK AT ME... LIKE THAT...
I TOO KNOW...
...HOW YOU FEEL.

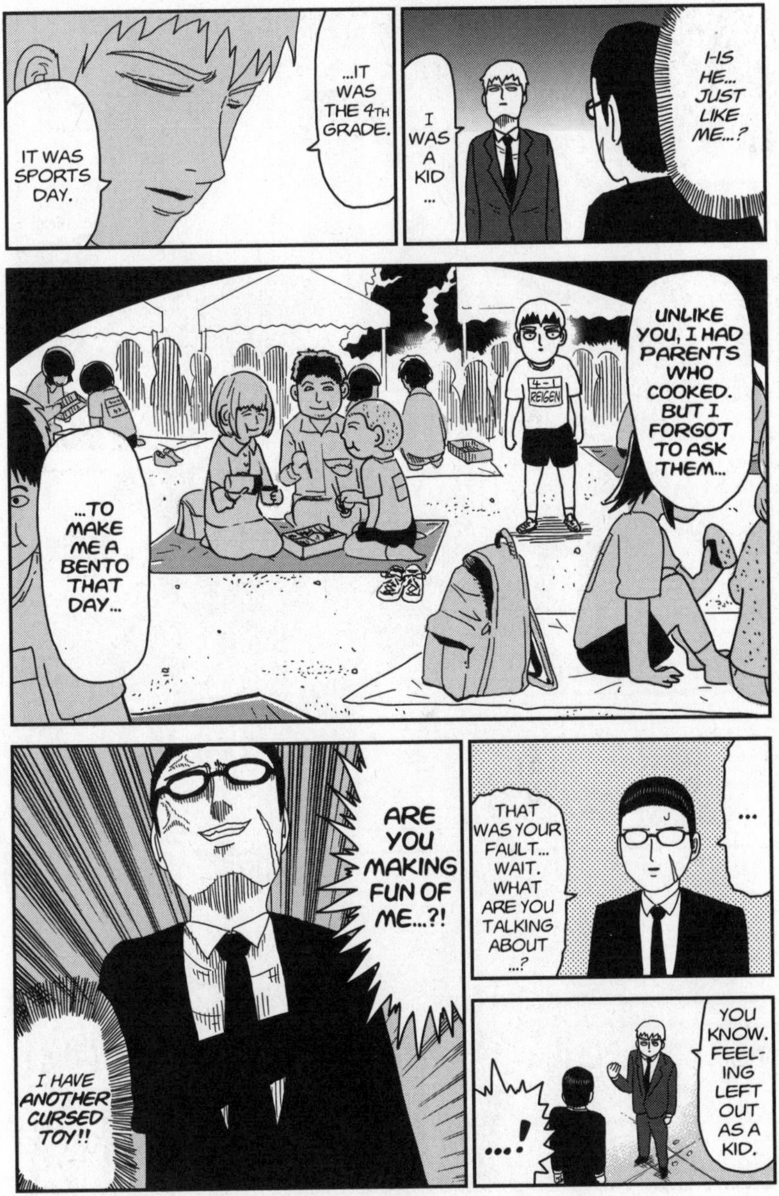

I-IS HE... JUST LIKE ME...?
I WAS A KID ...
...IT WAS THE 4TH GRADE.
IT WAS SPORTS DAY.
UNLIKE YOU, I HAD PARENTS WHO COOKED. BUT I FORGOT TO ASK THEM...
4-1 REIGEN
...TO MAKE ME A BENTO THAT DAY...
...
THAT WAS YOUR FAULT... WAIT. WHAT ARE YOU TALKING ABOUT ...?
YOU KNOW. FEELING LEFT OUT AS A KID.
...!
ARE YOU MAKING FUN OF ME...?!
I HAVE ANOTHER CURSED TOY!!

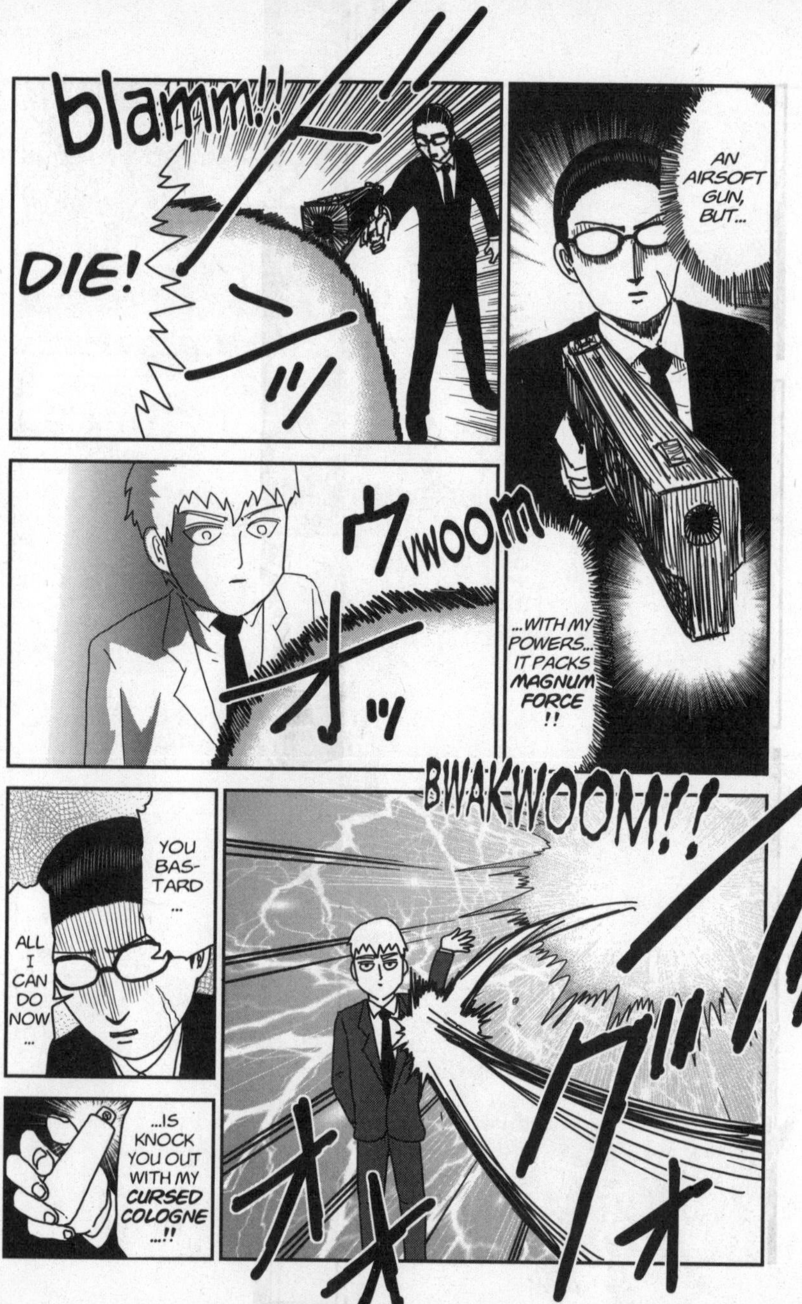

AN AIRSOFT GUN, BUT...
...WITH MY POWERS... IT PACKS MAGNUM FORCE!!
blamm!!
DIE!
VWOOM
BWAKWOOM!!
YOU BASTARD...
ALL I CAN DO NOW...
...IS KNOCK YOU OUT WITH MY CURSED COLOGNE...!!

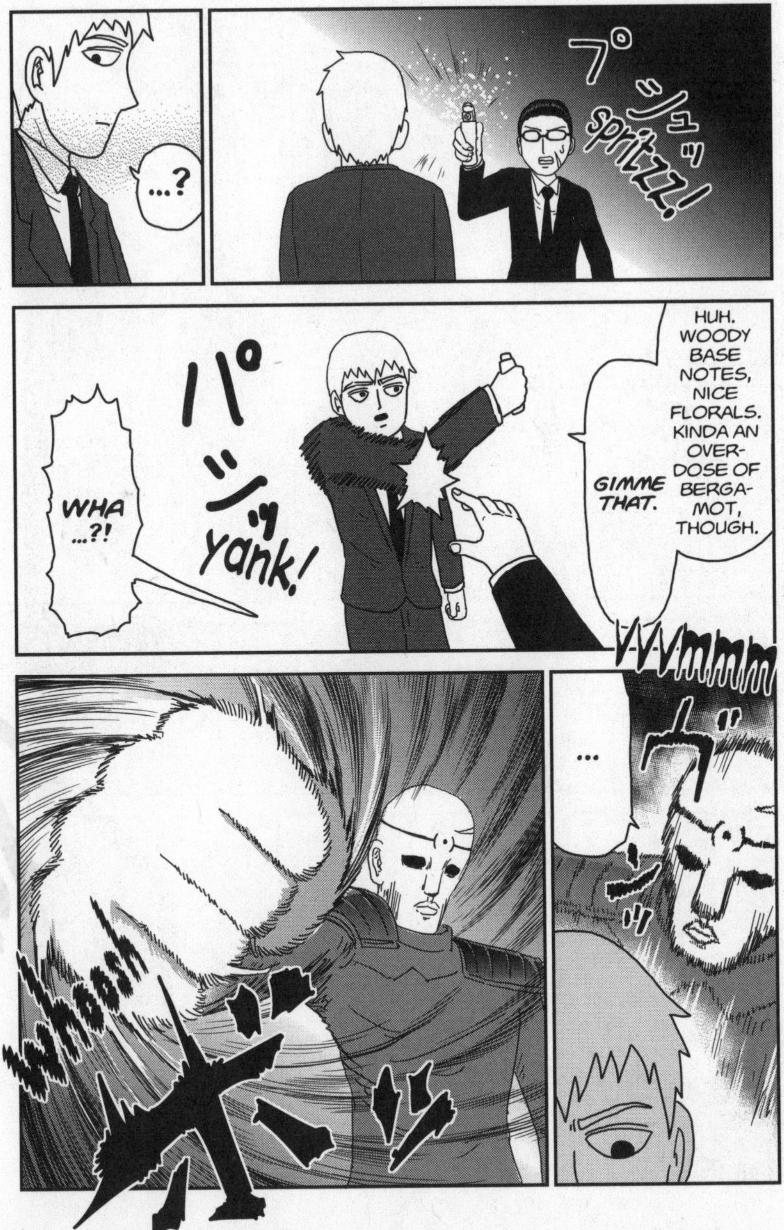
プシュッ
spritzzz!
...?
HUH. WOODY BASE NOTES, NICE FLORALS. KINDA AN OVER-DOSE OF BERGA-MOT, THOUGH.
GIMME THAT.
パシッ
yank!
WHA ...?!
VVVmmm
...
whoosh

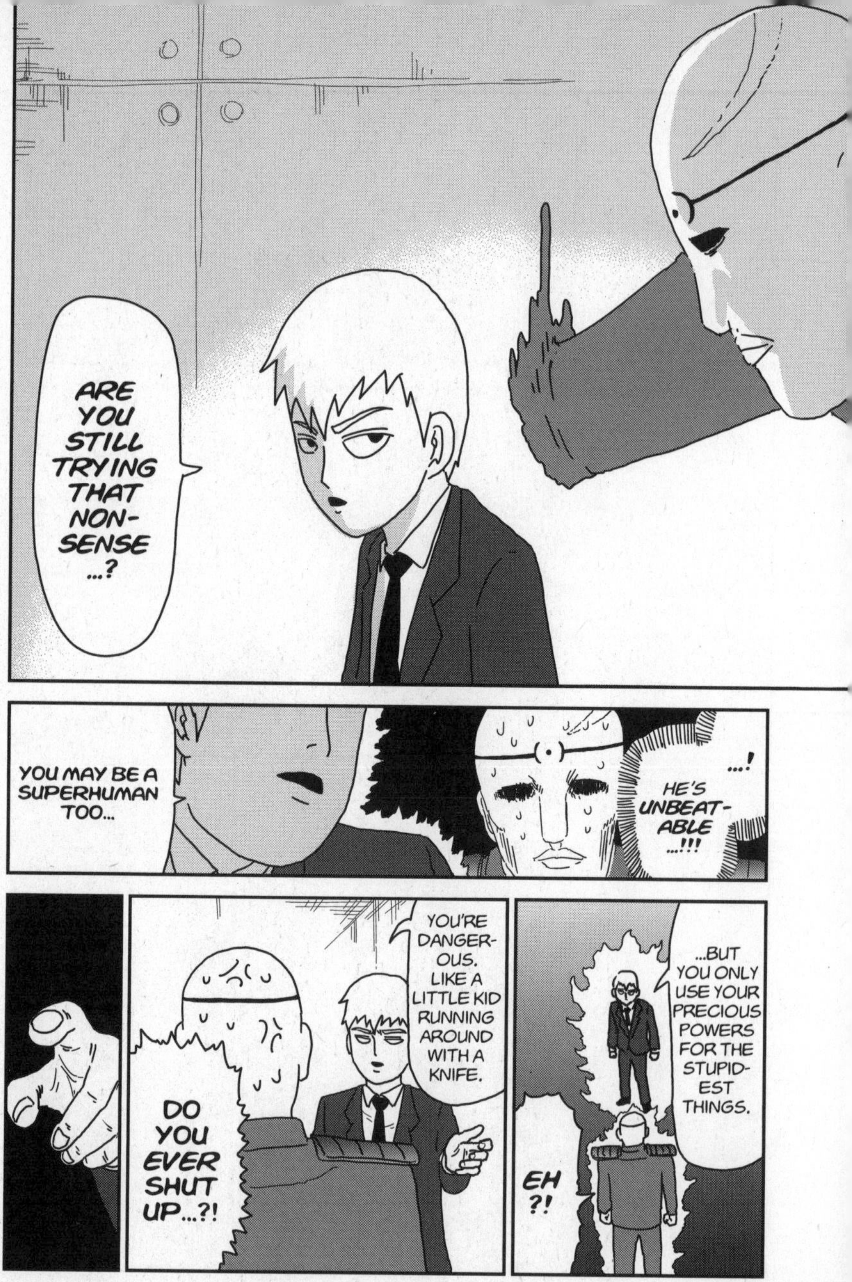
ARE YOU STILL TRYING THAT NONSENSE ...?
...!
HE'S UNBEATABLE ...!!!
YOU MAY BE A SUPERHUMAN TOO...
...BUT YOU ONLY USE YOUR PRECIOUS POWERS FOR THE STUPIDEST THINGS.
EH ?!
YOU'RE DANGEROUS. LIKE A LITTLE KID RUNNING AROUND WITH A KNIFE.
DO YOU EVER SHUT UP...?!

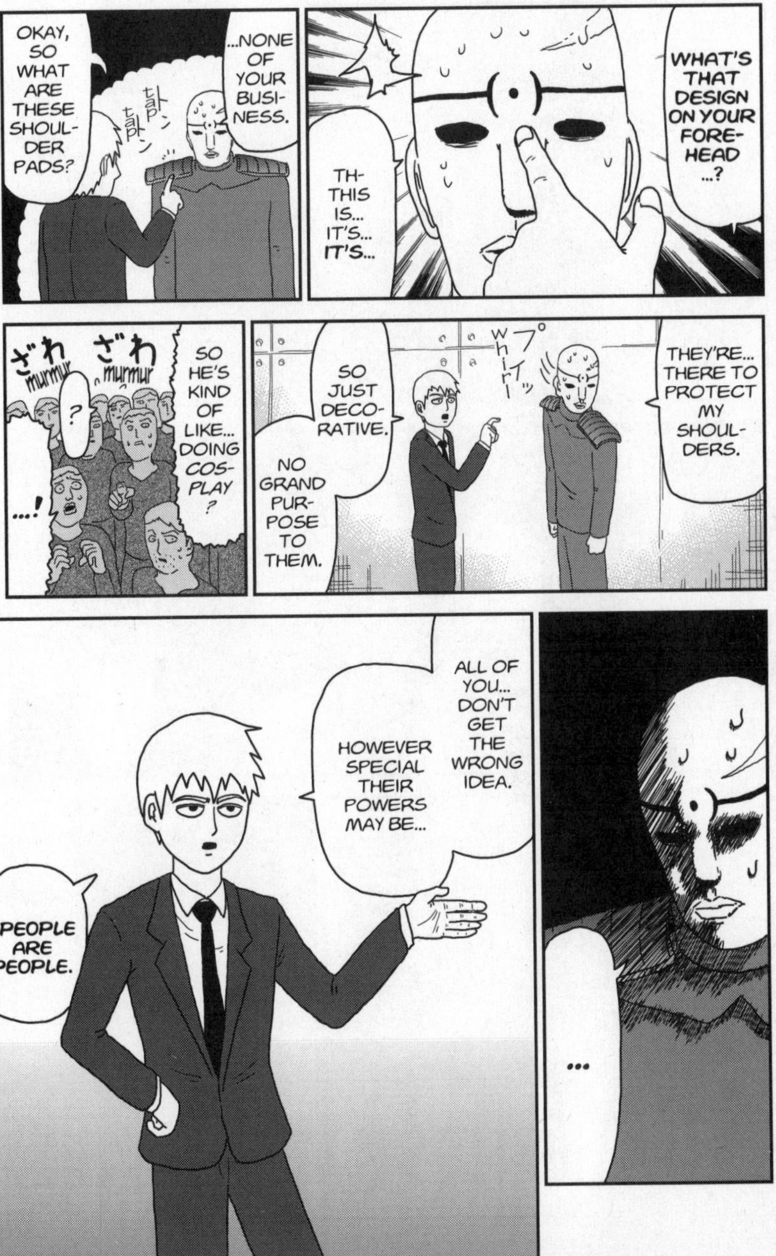
WHAT'S THAT DESIGN ON YOUR FOREHEAD ...?
TH-THIS IS... IT'S... IT'S...
OKAY, SO WHAT ARE THESE SHOULDER PADS?
tap tap
...NONE OF YOUR BUSINESS.
THEY'RE... THERE TO PROTECT MY SHOULDERS.
whirl
SO JUST DECORATIVE.
NO GRAND PURPOSE TO THEM.
SO HE'S KIND OF LIKE... DOING COSPLAY?
ざわ murmur ざわ murmur
?
...!
...
ALL OF YOU... DON'T GET THE WRONG IDEA.
HOWEVER SPECIAL THEIR POWERS MAY BE...
...PEOPLE ARE PEOPLE.

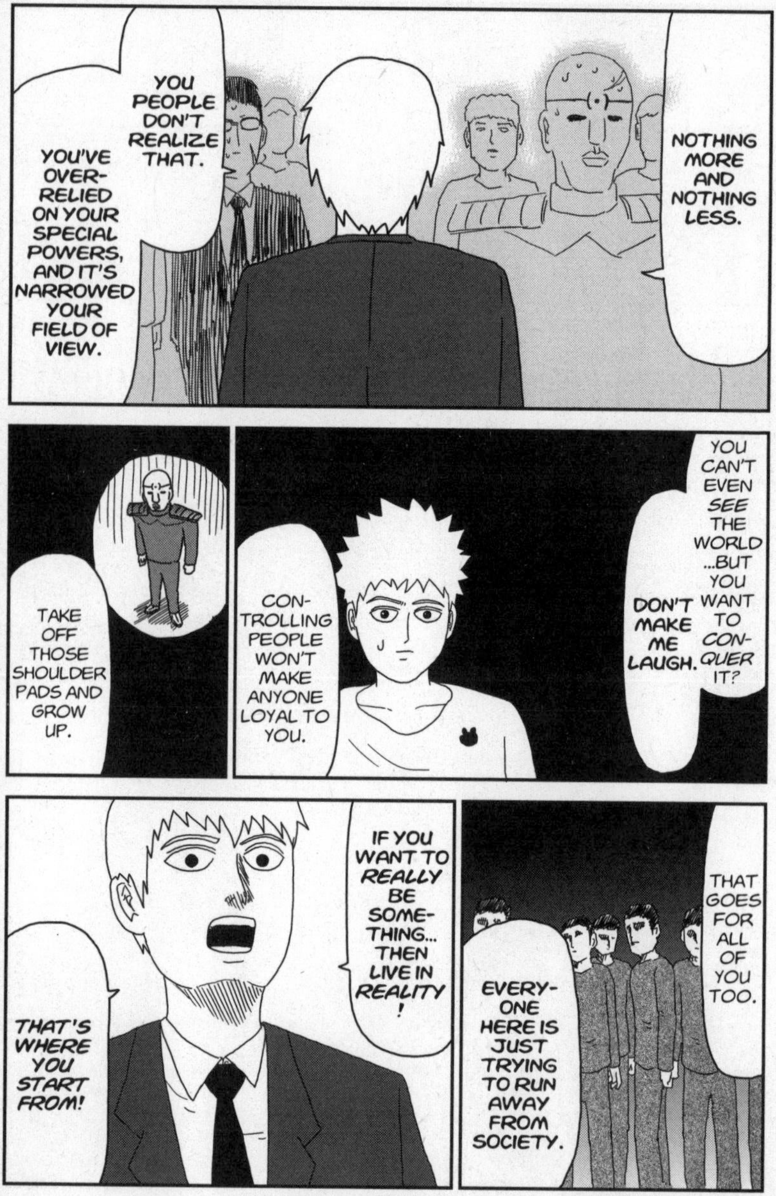
NOTHING MORE AND NOTHING LESS.
YOU PEOPLE DON'T REALIZE THAT.
YOU'VE OVER-RELIED ON YOUR SPECIAL POWERS, AND IT'S NARROWED YOUR FIELD OF VIEW.
YOU CAN'T EVEN *SEE* THE WORLD ...BUT YOU WANT TO *CONQUER* IT?
DON'T MAKE ME LAUGH.
CONTROLLING PEOPLE WON'T MAKE ANYONE LOYAL TO YOU.
TAKE OFF THOSE SHOULDER PADS AND GROW UP.
THAT GOES FOR ALL OF YOU TOO.
EVERYONE HERE IS JUST TRYING TO RUN AWAY FROM SOCIETY.
IF YOU WANT TO *REALLY* BE SOMETHING... THEN *LIVE IN REALITY*!
THAT'S WHERE YOU START FROM!

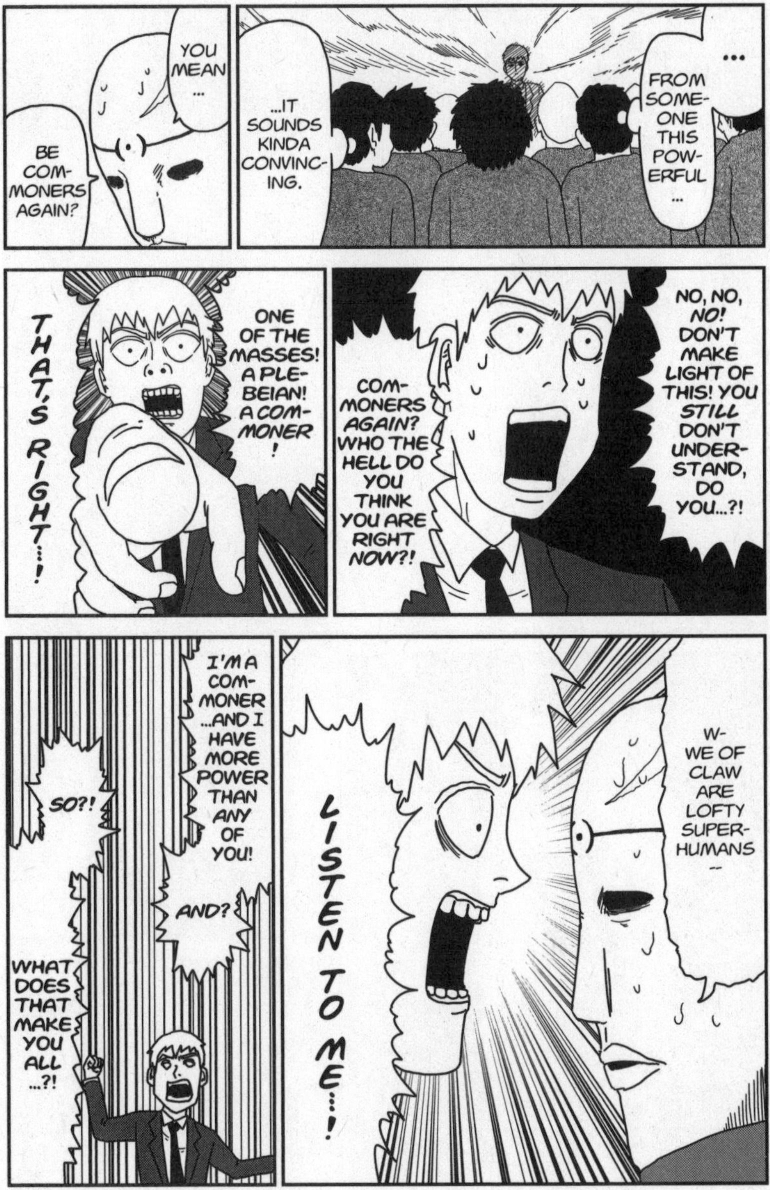
... FROM SOMEONE THIS POWERFUL ...
...IT SOUNDS KINDA CONVINCING.
YOU MEAN ...
BE COMMONERS AGAIN?
NO, NO, NO! DON'T MAKE LIGHT OF THIS! YOU STILL DON'T UNDERSTAND, DO YOU...?!
COMMONERS AGAIN? WHO THE HELL DO YOU THINK YOU ARE RIGHT NOW?!
ONE OF THE MASSES! A PLEBEIAN! A COMMONER!
THAT'S RIGHT...!
W-WE OF CLAW ARE LOFTY SUPERHUMANS --
LISTEN TO ME...!
I'M A COMMONER ...AND I HAVE MORE POWER THAN ANY OF YOU!
SO?!
AND?
WHAT DOES THAT MAKE YOU ALL ...?!

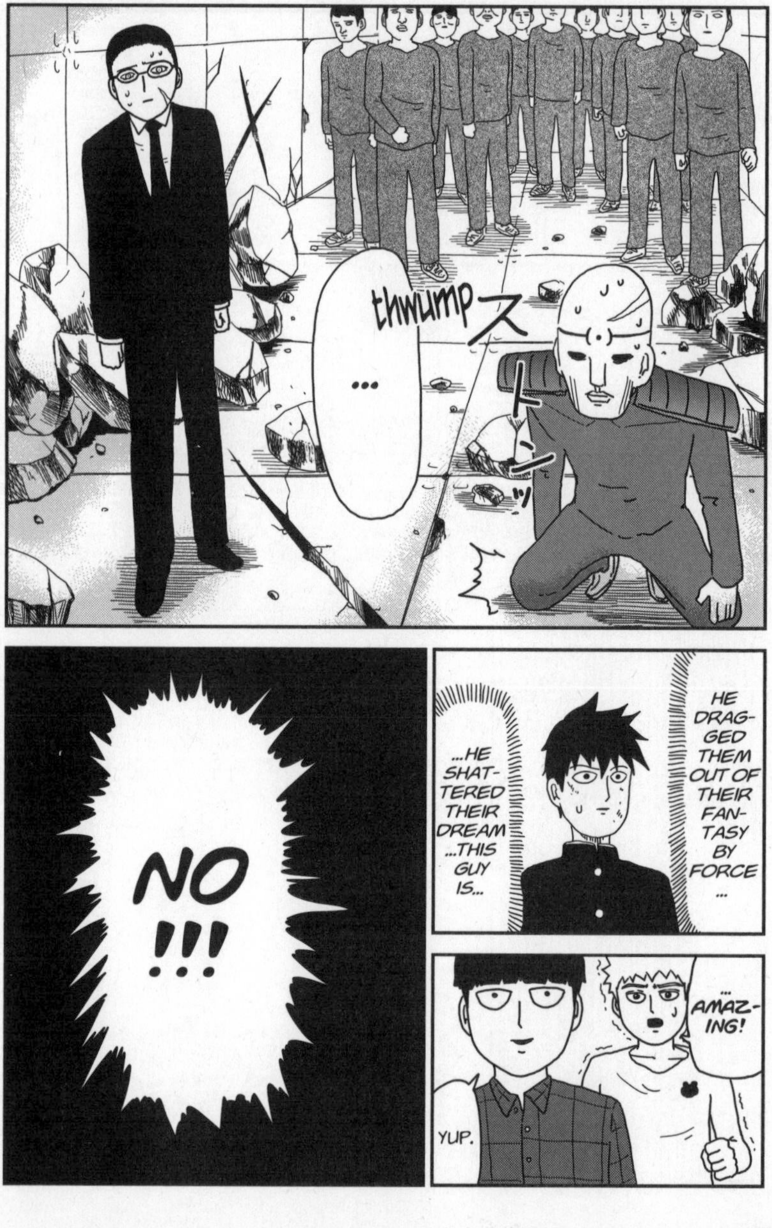
thwump
ストーンッ
...
HE DRAGGED THEM OUT OF THEIR FANTASY BY FORCE...
...HE SHATTERED THEIR DREAM ...THIS GUY IS...
...AMAZING!
YUP.
NO!!!

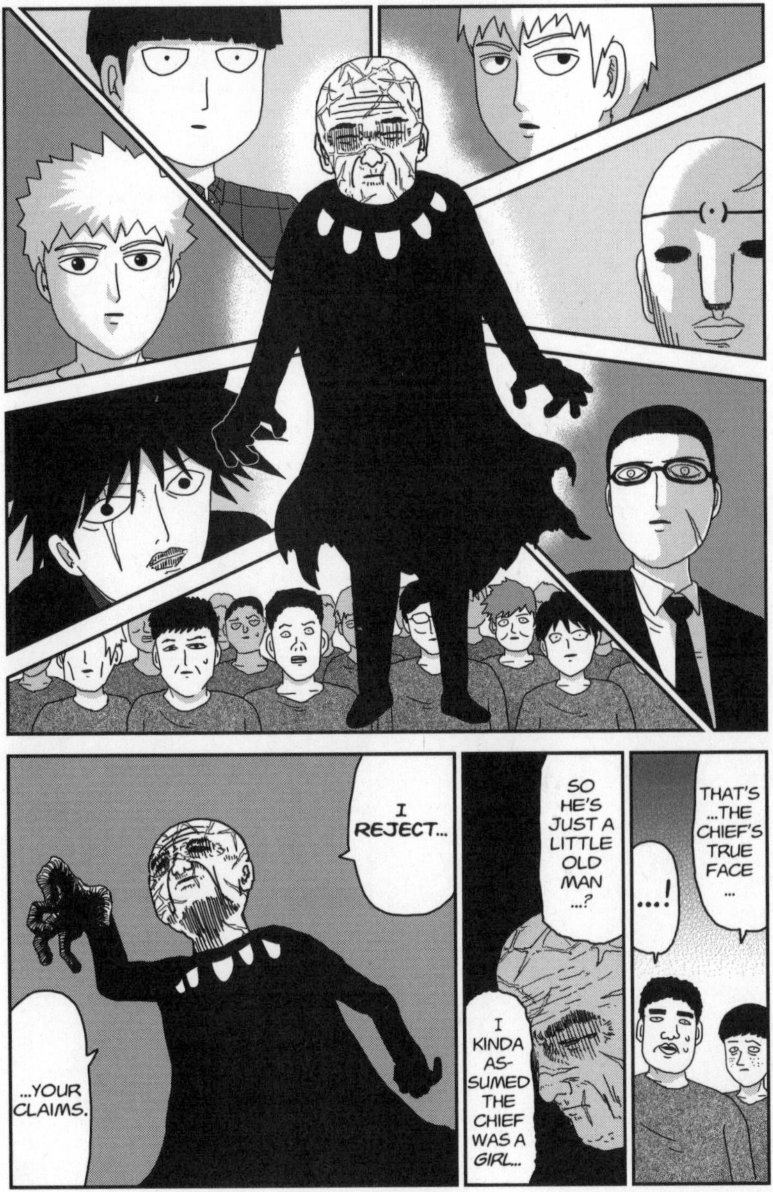
THAT'S ...THE CHIEF'S TRUE FACE ...
...!
SO HE'S JUST A LITTLE OLD MAN ...?
I KINDA AS-SUMED THE CHIEF WAS A GIRL...
I REJECT...
...YOUR CLAIMS.

Matsuo's Evil Spirit Observation Log (#5)

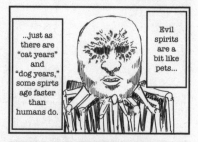

Evil spirits are a bit like pets...
...just as there are "cat years" and "dog years," some spirts age faster than humans do.
COME FORTH, YOUNG WHIP!
LASH AND FLOG THE MIND OF OUR ENEMY !!
Whip was a kid just a week ago.

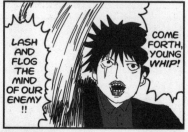

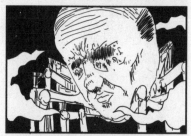

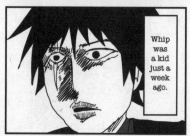

CHAPTER 49: AN END

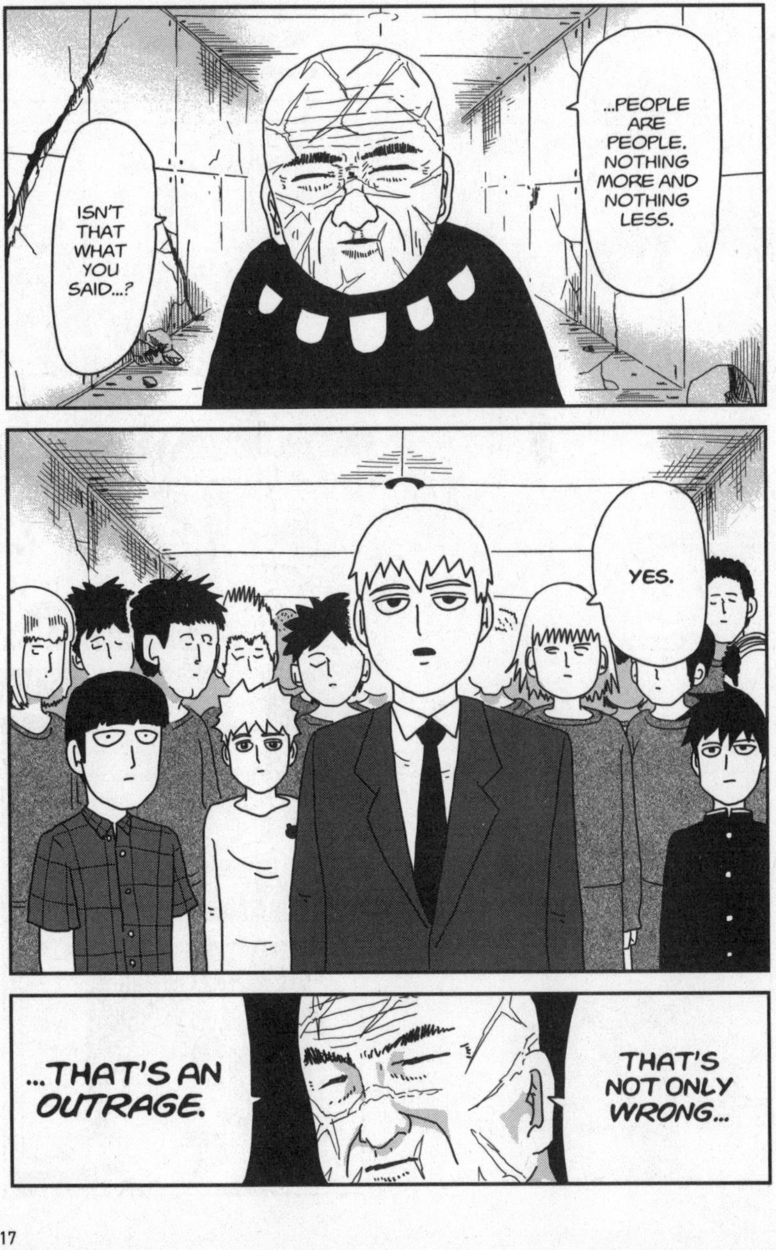

...PEOPLE ARE PEOPLE. NOTHING MORE AND NOTHING LESS.
ISN'T THAT WHAT YOU SAID...?
YES.
THAT'S NOT ONLY WRONG...
...THAT'S AN *OUTRAGE.*

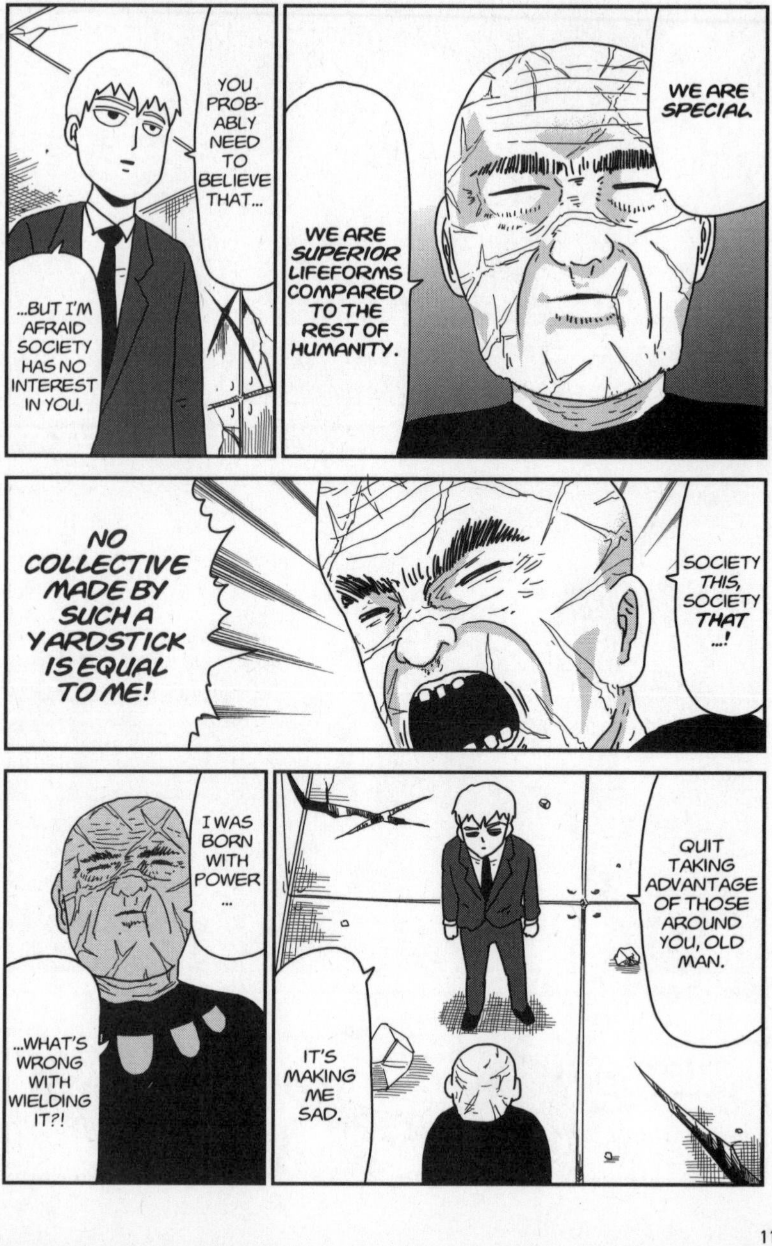
WE ARE SPECIAL.
WE ARE SUPERIOR LIFEFORMS COMPARED TO THE REST OF HUMANITY.
YOU PROBABLY NEED TO BELIEVE THAT...
...BUT I'M AFRAID SOCIETY HAS NO INTEREST IN YOU.
SOCIETY THIS, SOCIETY THAT...!
NO COLLECTIVE MADE BY SUCH A YARDSTICK IS EQUAL TO ME!
QUIT TAKING ADVANTAGE OF THOSE AROUND YOU, OLD MAN.
IT'S MAKING ME SAD.
I WAS BORN WITH POWER...
...WHAT'S WRONG WITH WIELDING IT?!

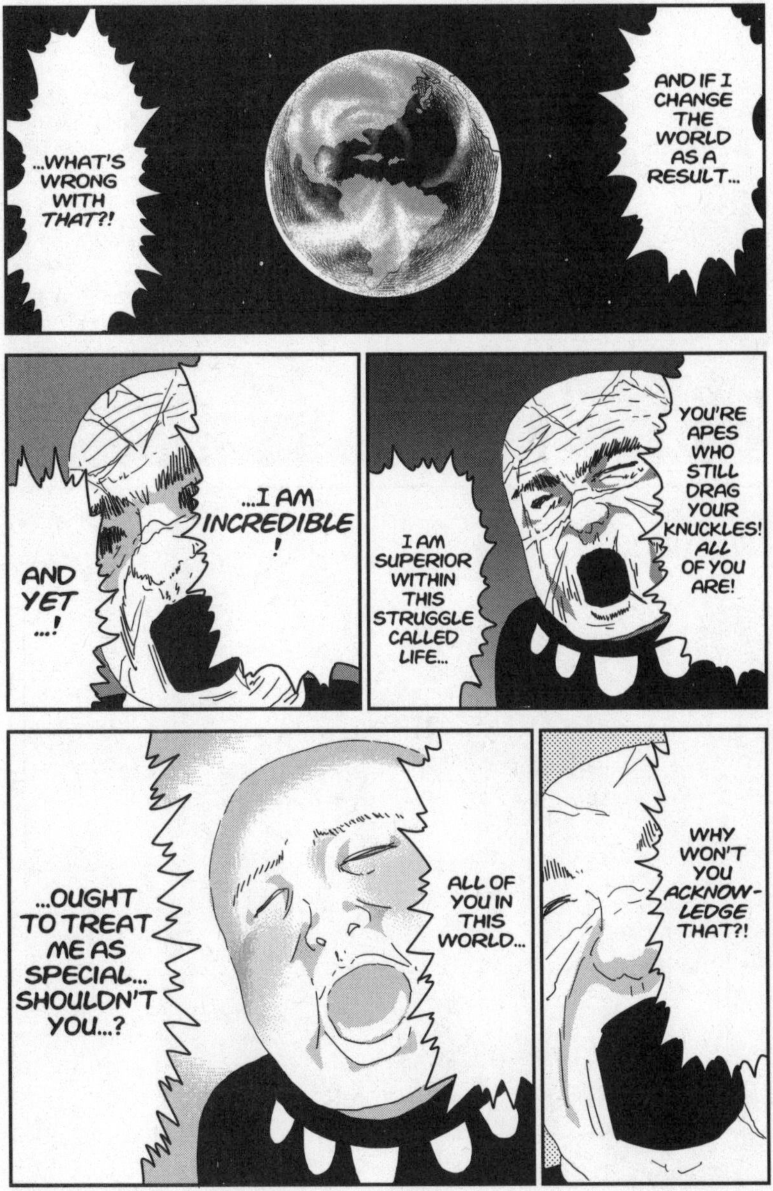
AND IF I CHANGE THE WORLD AS A RESULT...
...WHAT'S WRONG WITH THAT?!
YOU'RE APES WHO STILL DRAG YOUR KNUCKLES! ALL OF YOU ARE!
I AM SUPERIOR WITHIN THIS STRUGGLE CALLED LIFE...
...I AM INCREDIBLE!
AND YET...!
WHY WON'T YOU ACKNOWLEDGE THAT?!
ALL OF YOU IN THIS WORLD...
...OUGHT TO TREAT ME AS SPECIAL... SHOULDN'T YOU...?

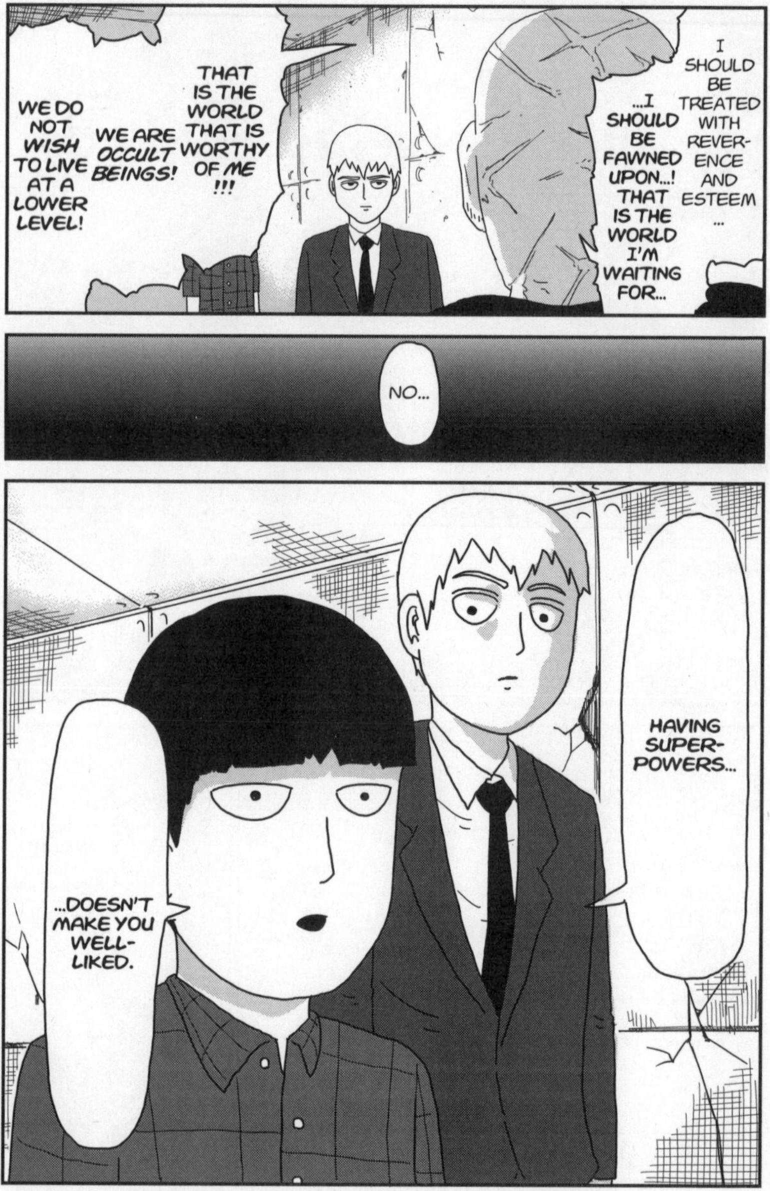
I SHOULD BE TREATED WITH REVERENCE AND ESTEEM...
...I SHOULD BE FAWNED UPON...! THAT IS THE WORLD I'M WAITING FOR...
THAT IS THE WORLD THAT IS WORTHY OF ME!!!
WE ARE OCCULT BEINGS!
WE DO NOT WISH TO LIVE AT A LOWER LEVEL!
NO...
HAVING SUPER-POWERS...
...DOESN'T MAKE YOU WELL-LIKED.

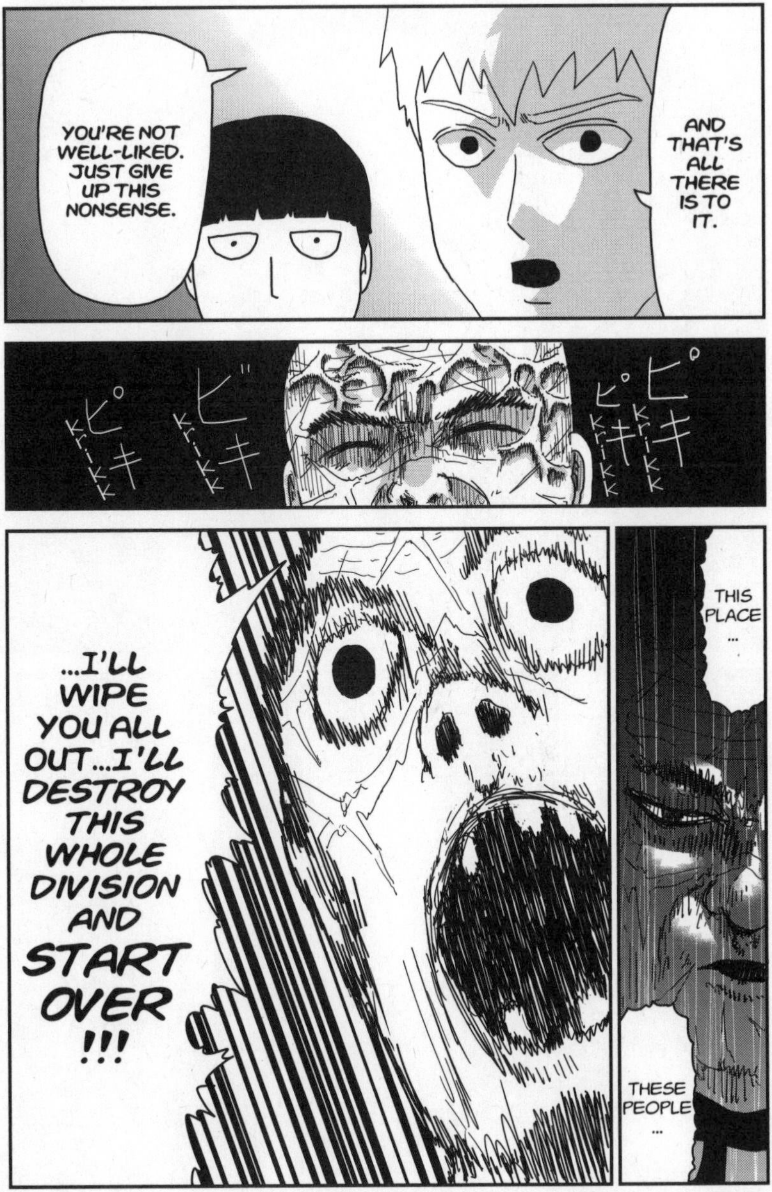
YOU'RE NOT WELL-LIKED. JUST GIVE UP THIS NONSENSE.
AND THAT'S ALL THERE IS TO IT.
ピキ
krikk
ピキ
krikk
ビキ
krikk
ピキ
krikk
THIS PLACE ...
THESE PEOPLE ...
...I'LL WIPE YOU ALL OUT...I'LL DESTROY THIS WHOLE DIVISION AND START OVER!!!

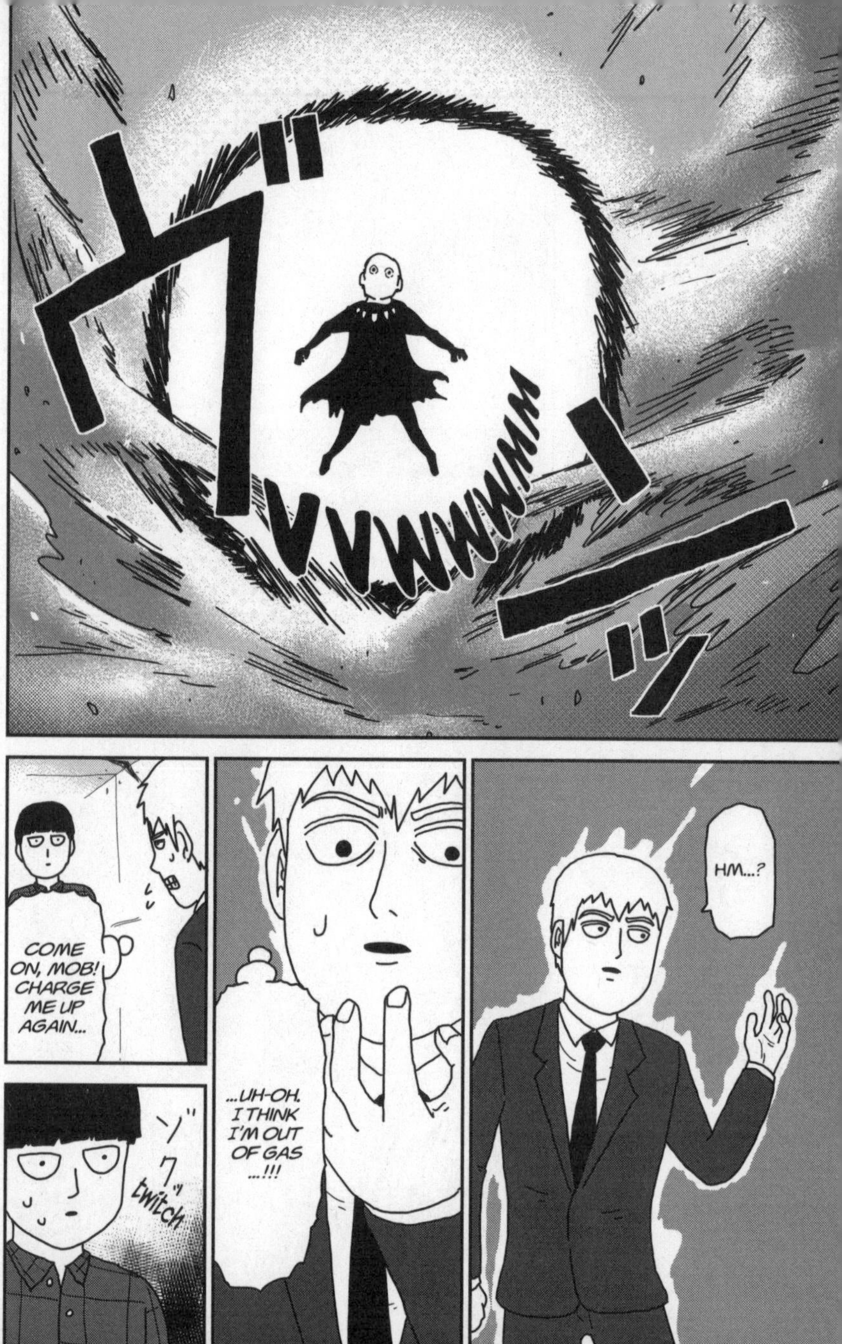
VVWWWMM
HM...?
...UH-OH. I THINK I'M OUT OF GAS ...!!!
COME ON, MOB! CHARGE ME UP AGAIN...
twitch

...?!

?!!

...ACTU-ALLY, I'M OUT OF--

umm...

NOW HE'S A BLACK HOLE ...!

OH, CRAP ...!!

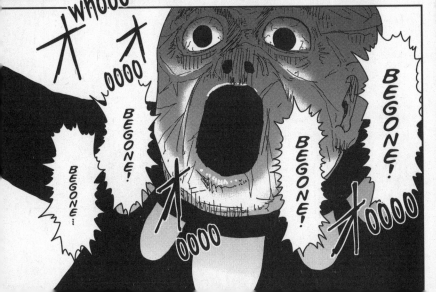

WHOOO

OOOO

BEGONE!

BEGONE!

BEGONE!

BEGONE!

BEGONE!

BEGONE!

OOOO

OOOO

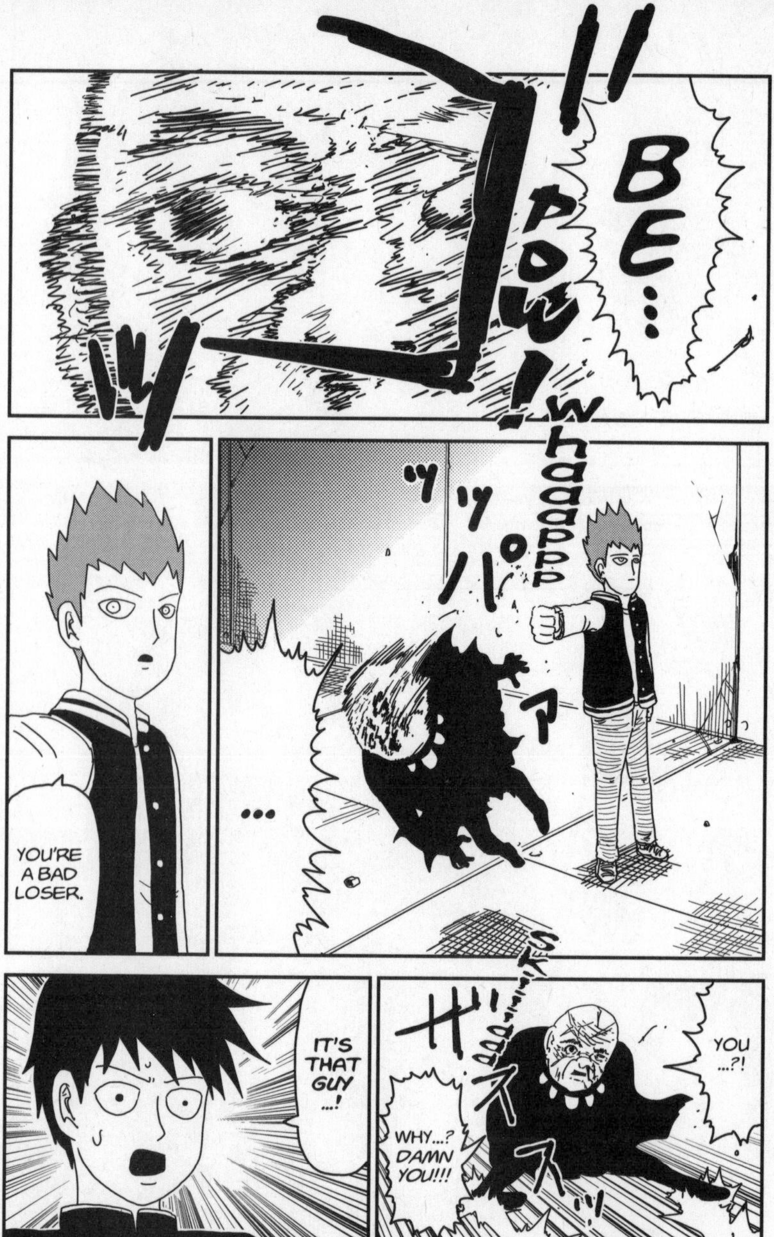
BE...
POW!
whaaapp
...
YOU'RE A BAD LOSER.
YOU ...?!
SKiiiiiiddd
WHY...? DAMN YOU!!!
IT'S THAT GUY ...!

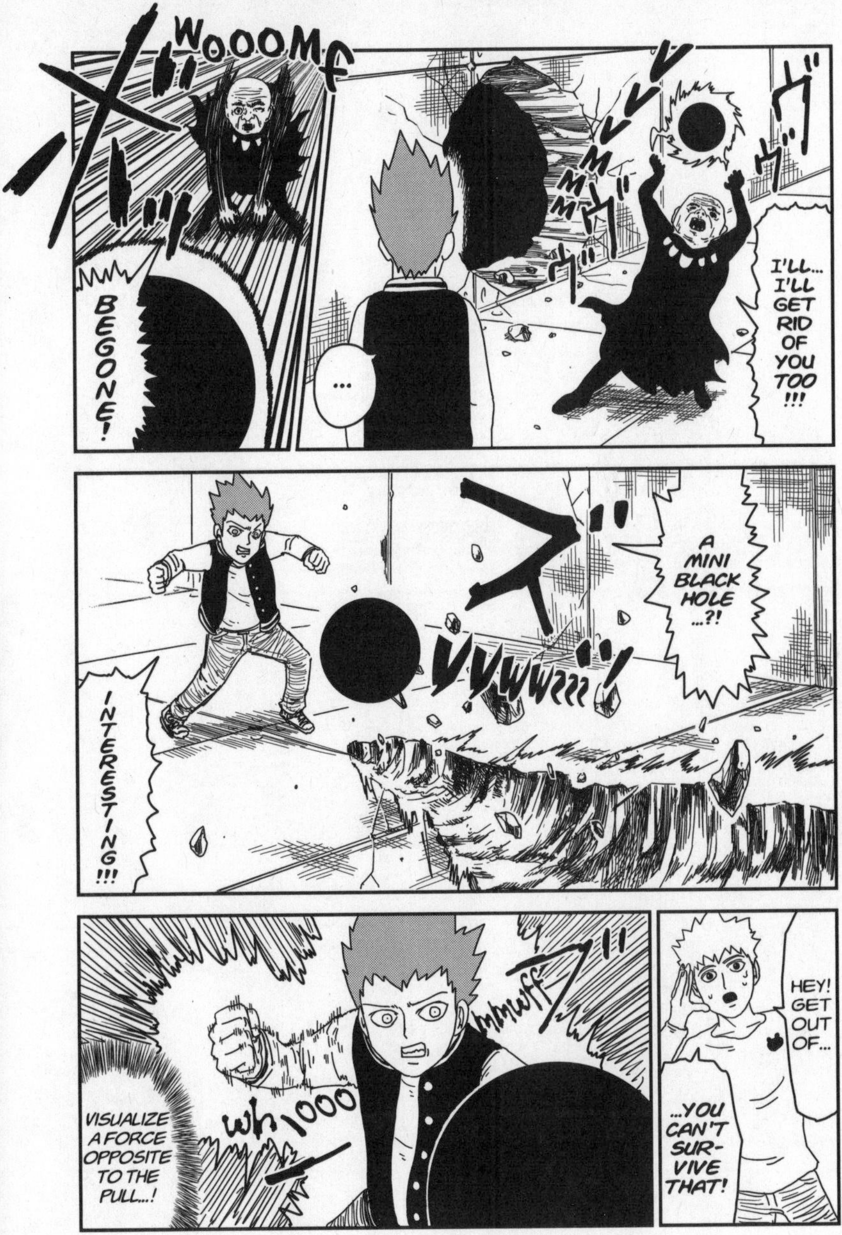

I'LL... I'LL GET RID OF YOU TOO!!!
...
WOOOMF
BEGONE!
A MINI BLACK HOLE ...?!
VVWZZZ!
INTERESTING!!!
HEY! GET OUT OF...
...YOU CAN'T SURVIVE THAT!
MMWFF
WHOOO
VISUALIZE A FORCE OPPOSITE TO THE PULL...!

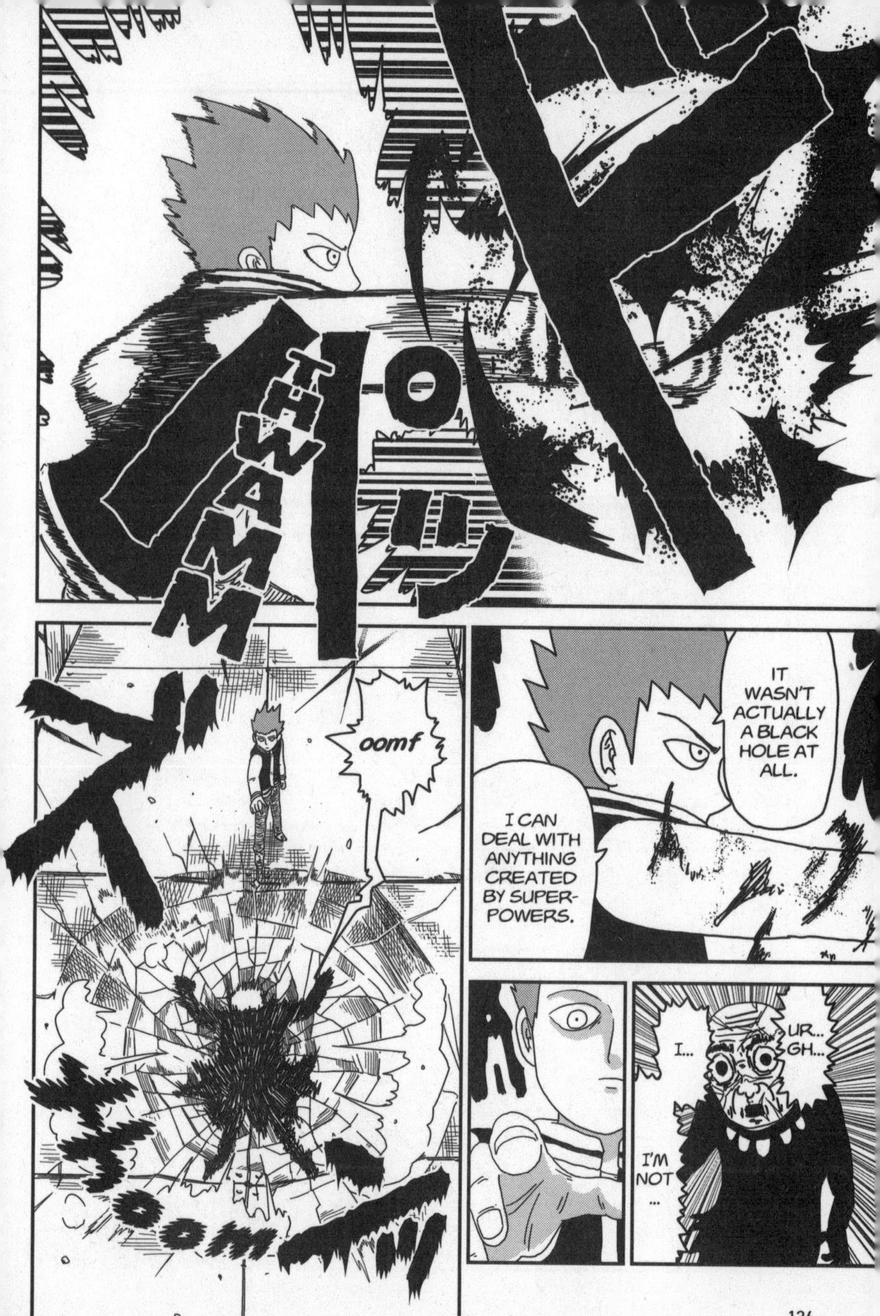
THWAMM
IT WASN'T ACTUALLY A BLACK HOLE AT ALL.
I CAN DEAL WITH ANYTHING CREATED BY SUPER-POWERS.
UR... GH...
I...
I'M NOT ...
oomf

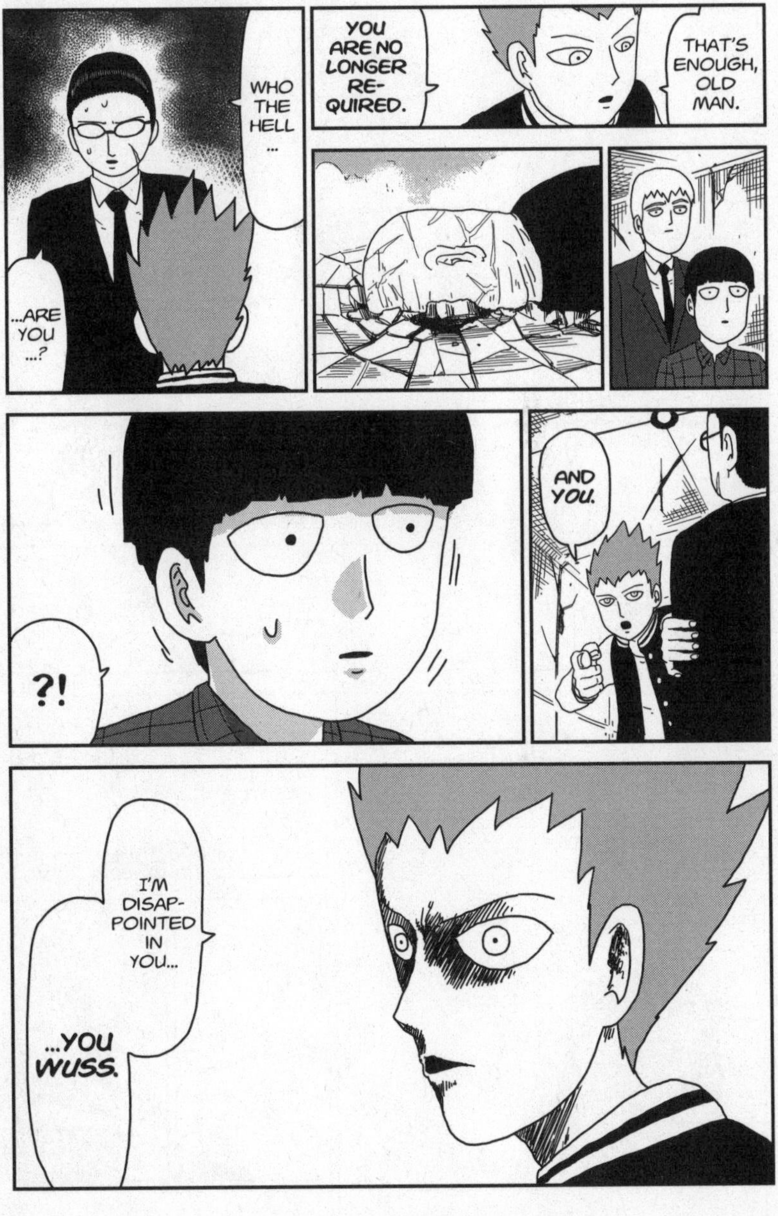
THAT'S ENOUGH, OLD MAN.
YOU ARE NO LONGER RE-QUIRED.
WHO THE HELL ...
...ARE YOU ...?
AND YOU.
?!
I'M DISAP-POINTED IN YOU...
...YOU WUSS.

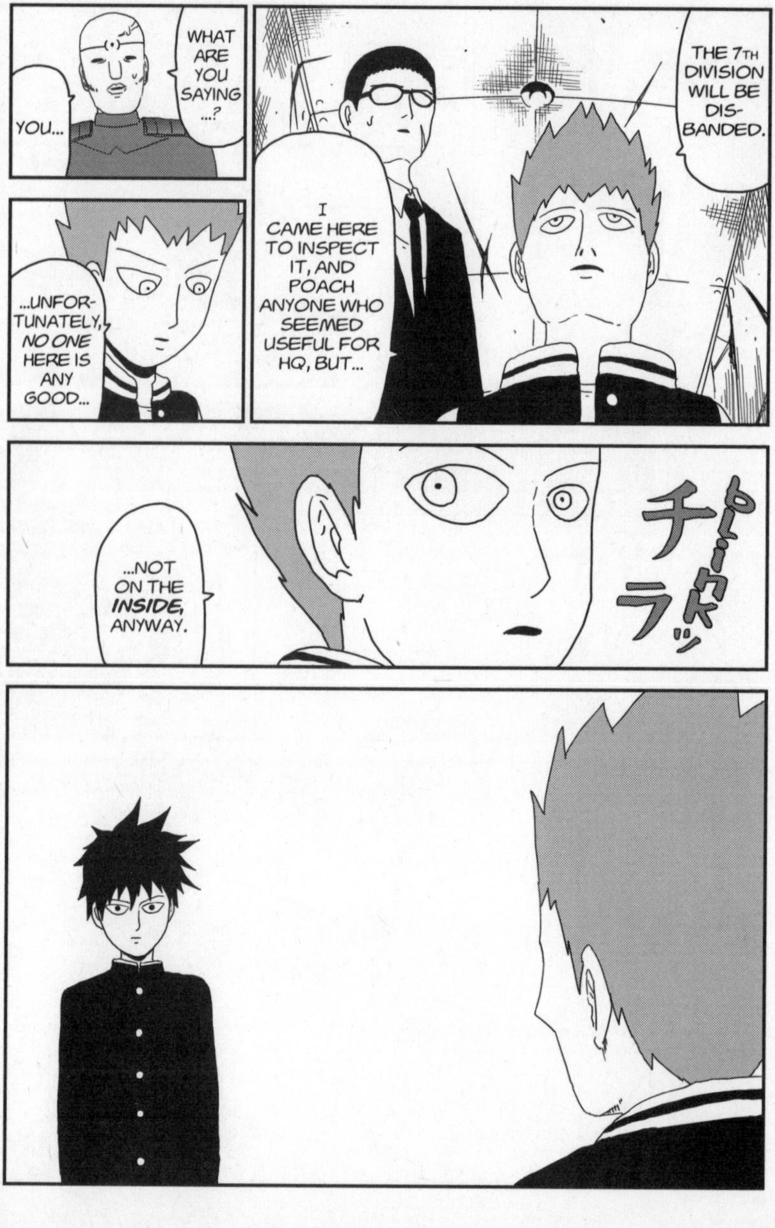
THE 7TH DIVISION WILL BE DIS-BANDED.
I CAME HERE TO INSPECT IT, AND POACH ANYONE WHO SEEMED USEFUL FOR HQ, BUT...
WHAT ARE YOU SAYING ...?
YOU...
...UNFORTUNATELY, *NO ONE* HERE IS ANY GOOD...
チラッ
...NOT ON THE ***INSIDE,*** ANYWAY.

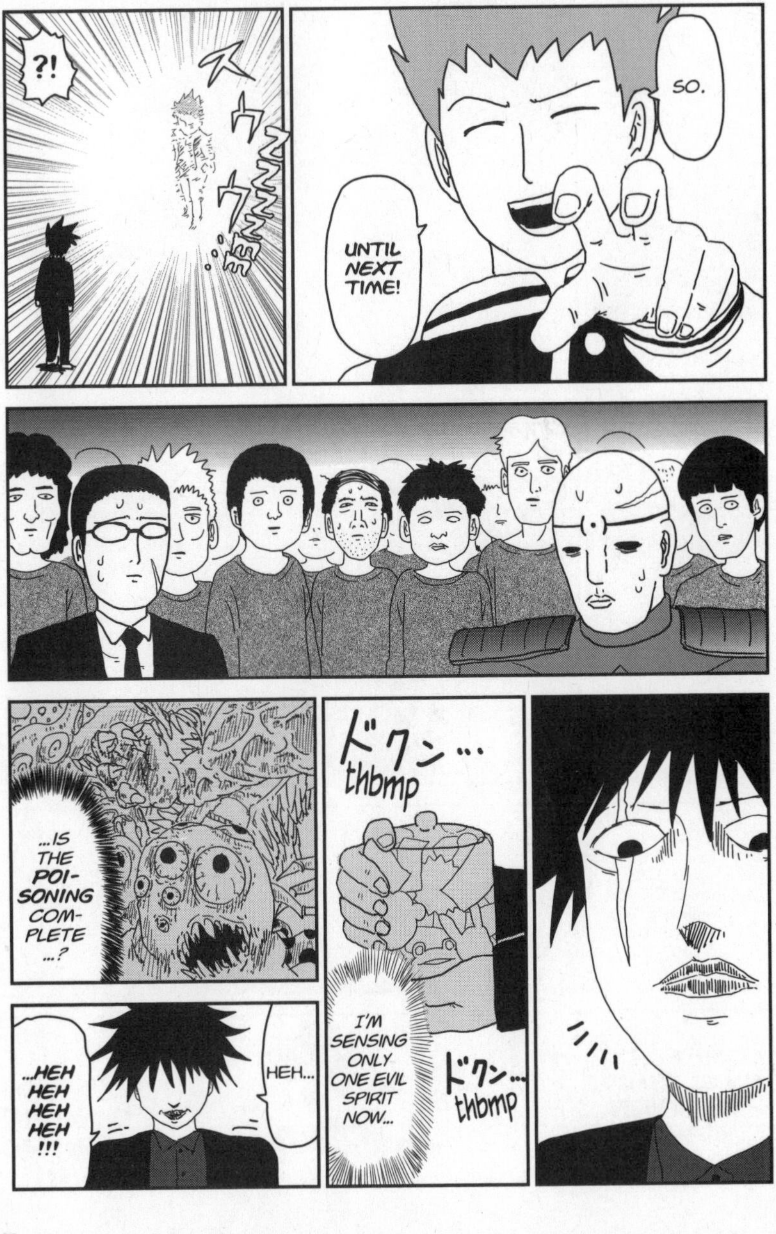

SO.
UNTIL NEXT TIME!
?!
ドクン…
thbmp
I'M SENSING ONLY ONE EVIL SPIRIT NOW...
ドクン…
thbmp
...IS THE POI-SONING COM-PLETE ...?
HEH...
...HEH HEH HEH HEH !!!

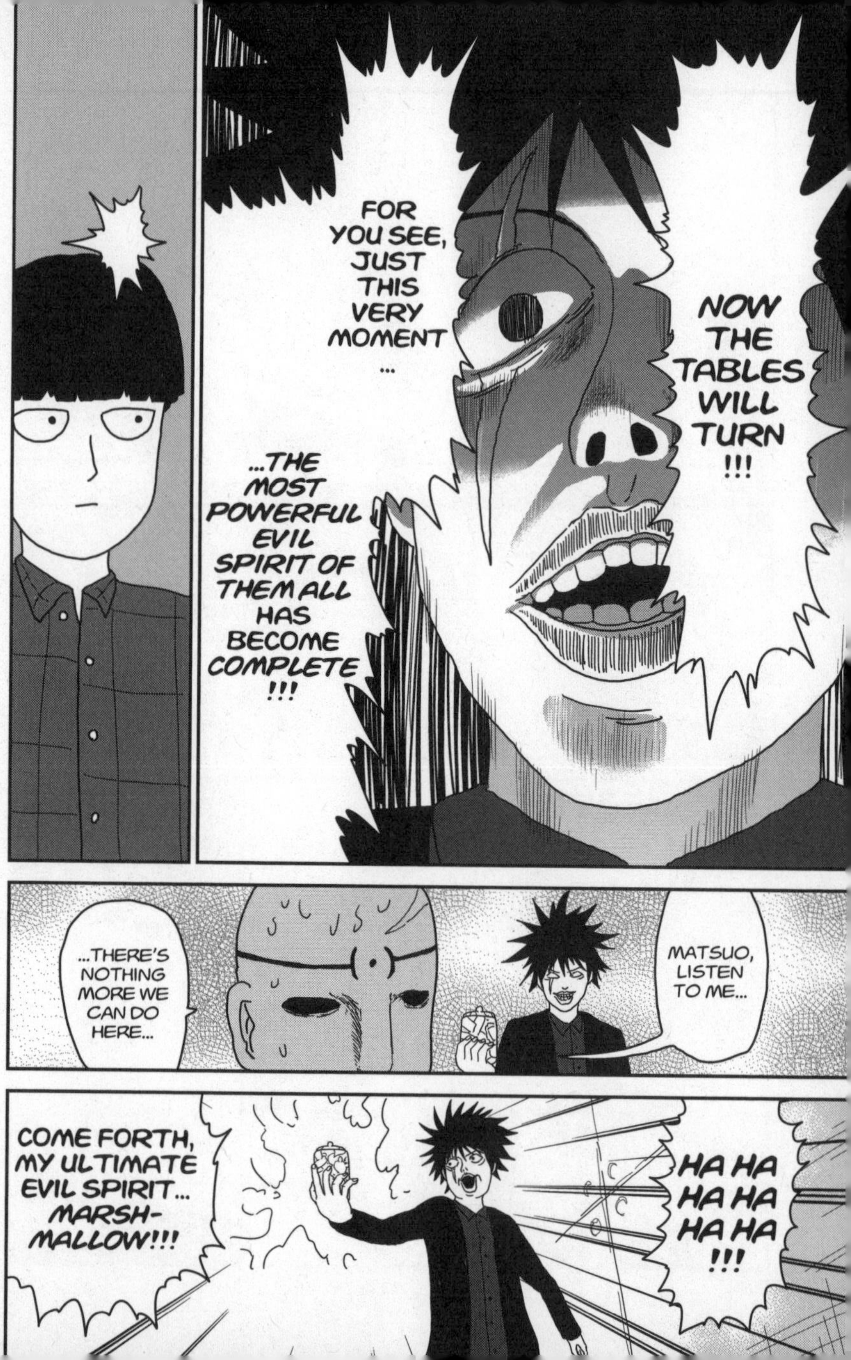
NOW THE TABLES WILL TURN!!!
FOR YOU SEE, JUST THIS VERY MOMENT...
...THE MOST POWERFUL EVIL SPIRIT OF THEM ALL HAS BECOME COMPLETE!!!
MATSUO, LISTEN TO ME...
...THERE'S NOTHING MORE WE CAN DO HERE...
HA HA HA HA HA HA!!!
COME FORTH, MY ULTIMATE EVIL SPIRIT... MARSH-MALLOW!!!

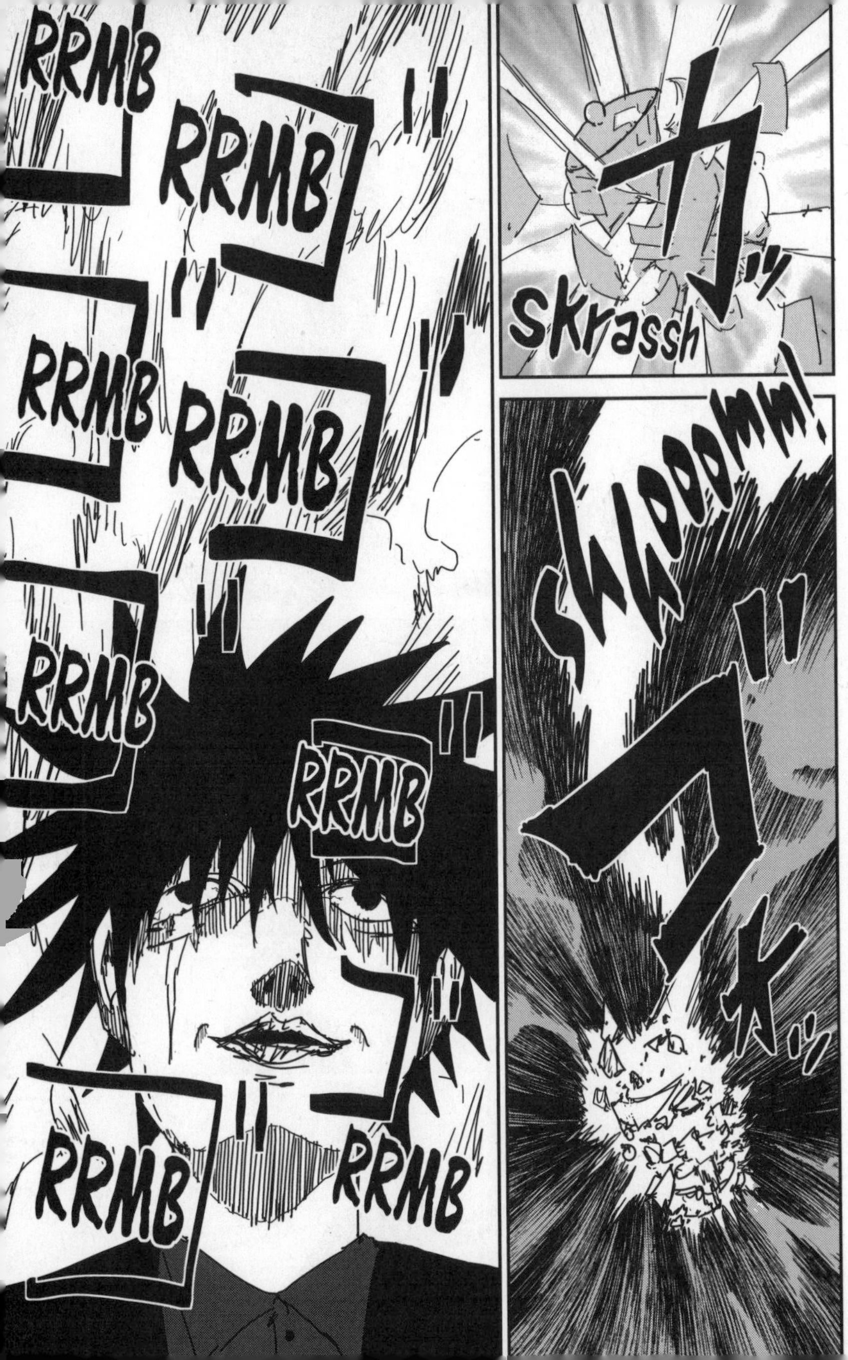
Skrassh
SHHOOOMM!
RRMB
RRMB
RRMB
RRMB
RRMB
RRMB
RRMB
RRMB

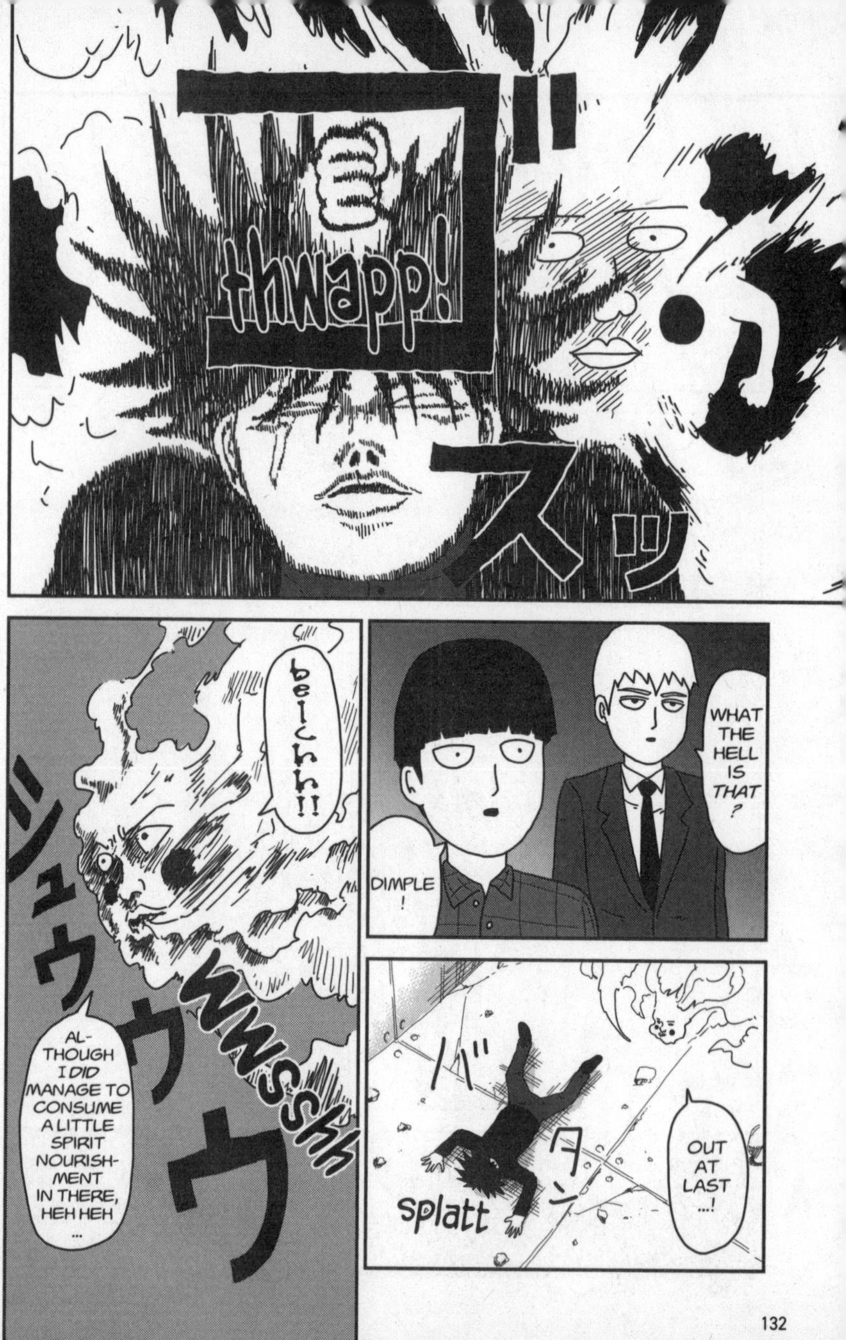
thwapp!
スッ
WHAT THE HELL IS THAT?
DIMPLE!
バタン
splatt
OUT AT LAST ...!
belchhh!!
シュウウウ
WWSSHH
AL-THOUGH I DID MANAGE TO CONSUME A LITTLE SPIRIT NOURISH-MENT IN THERE, HEH HEH ...

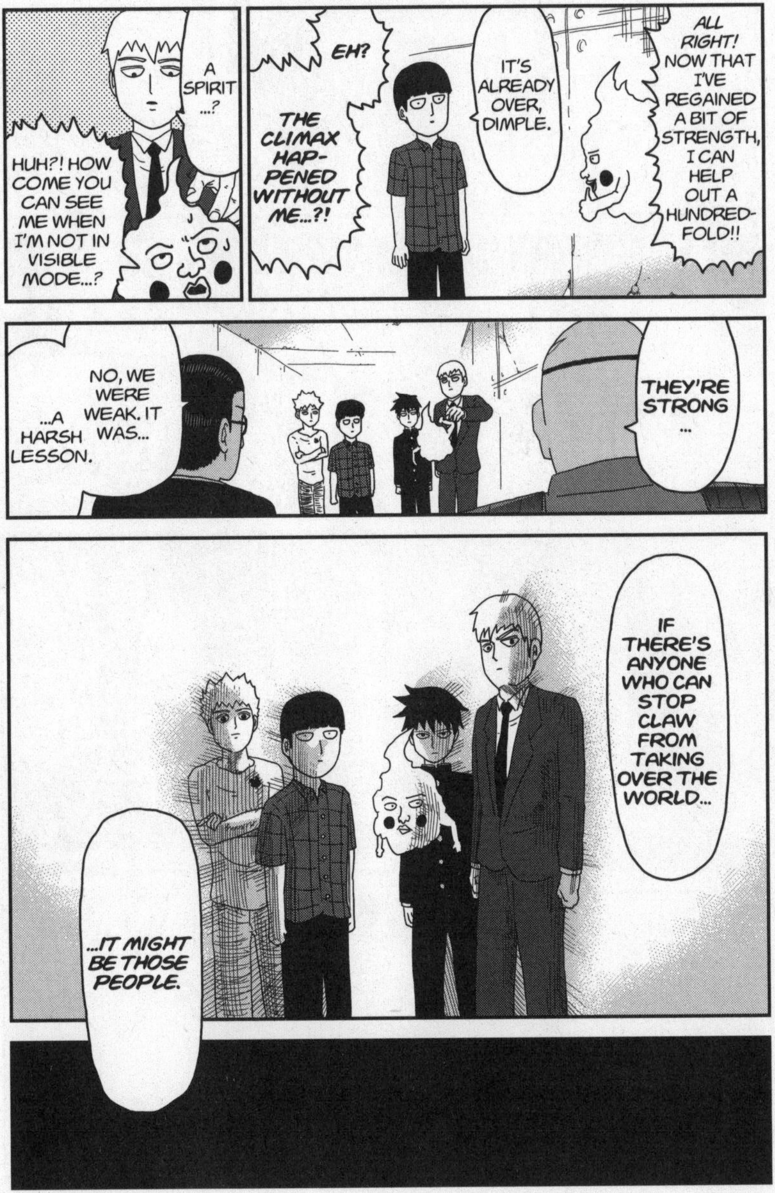
ALL RIGHT! NOW THAT I'VE REGAINED A BIT OF STRENGTH, I CAN HELP OUT A HUNDRED-FOLD!!
IT'S ALREADY OVER, DIMPLE.
EH?
THE CLIMAX HAP-PENED WITHOUT ME...?!
A SPIRIT ...?
HUH?! HOW COME YOU CAN SEE ME WHEN I'M NOT IN VISIBLE MODE...?
THEY'RE STRONG ...
NO, WE WERE WEAK. IT WAS...
...A HARSH LESSON.
IF THERE'S ANYONE WHO CAN STOP CLAW FROM TAKING OVER THE WORLD...
...IT MIGHT BE THOSE PEOPLE.

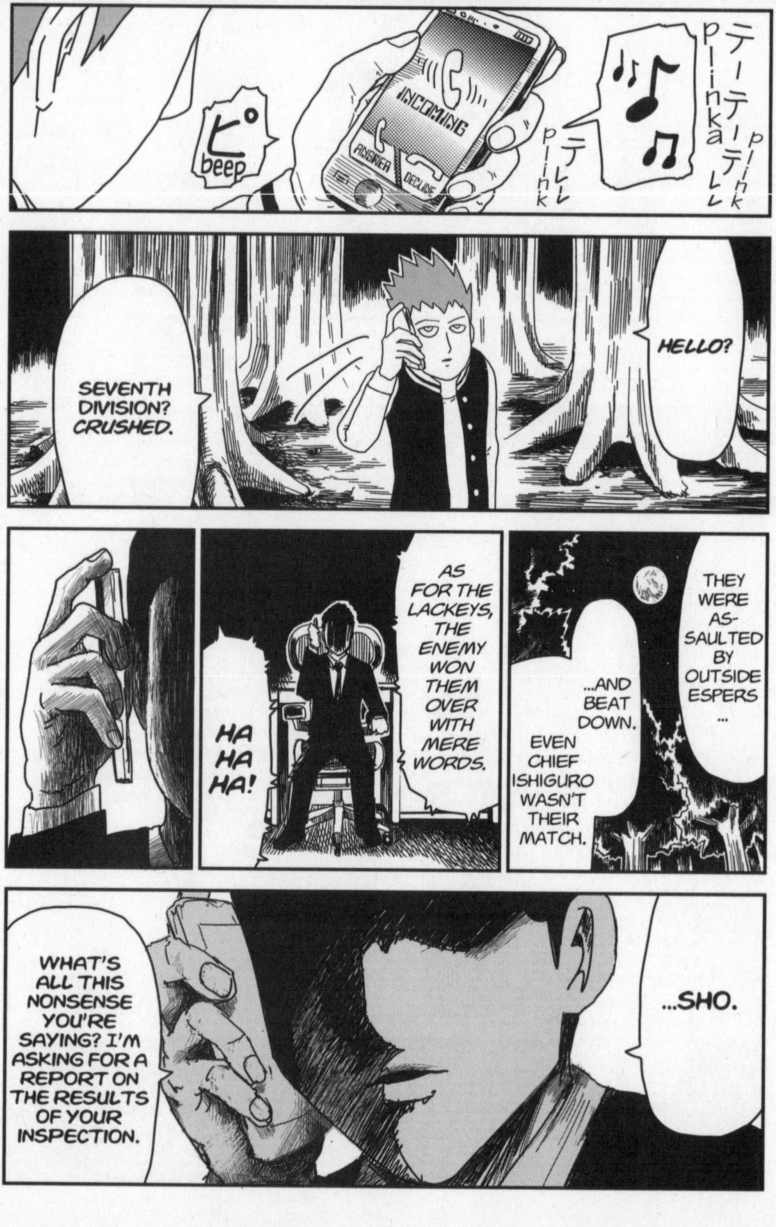

テーテーテレレ
plinka plink
テレレ
plink
INCOMING
ANSWER
DECLINE
ピ
beep
HELLO?
SEVENTH DIVISION? CRUSHED.
THEY WERE AS-SAULTED BY OUTSIDE ESPERS...
...AND BEAT DOWN.
EVEN CHIEF ISHIGURO WASN'T THEIR MATCH.
AS FOR THE LACKEYS, THE ENEMY WON THEM OVER WITH MERE WORDS.
HA HA HA!
...SHO.
WHAT'S ALL THIS NONSENSE YOU'RE SAYING? I'M ASKING FOR A REPORT ON THE RESULTS OF YOUR INSPECTION.

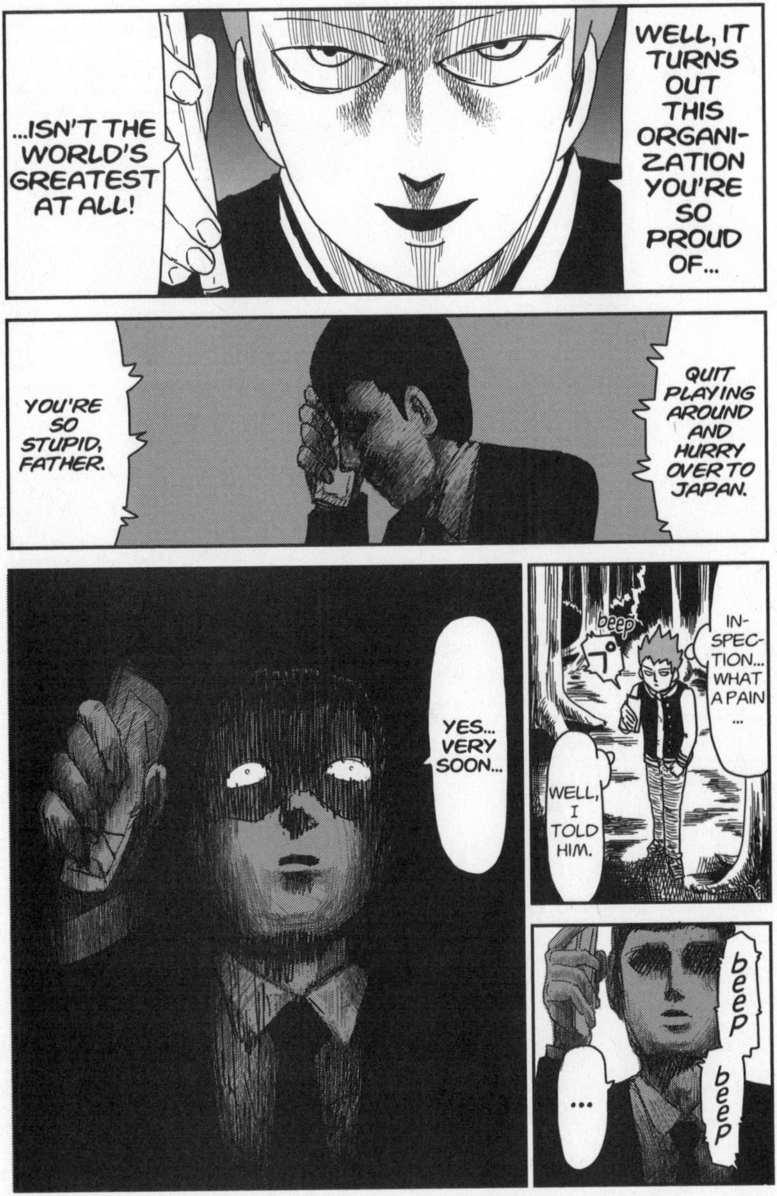
WELL, IT TURNS OUT THIS ORGANIZATION YOU'RE SO PROUD OF...
...ISN'T THE WORLD'S GREATEST AT ALL!
QUIT PLAYING AROUND AND HURRY OVER TO JAPAN.
YOU'RE SO STUPID, FATHER.
beep
INSPECTION... WHAT A PAIN ...
WELL, I TOLD HIM.
beep beep
...
YES... VERY SOON...

Matsuo's Evil Spirit Observation Log (#6)

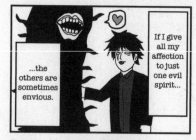

If I give all my affection to just one evil spirit...
...the others are sometimes envious.
HEY, HEY! STOP FIGHTING!
I SAID STOP IT, YOU TWO ...!
GAH!! YOU ATE HER ...?!
OF ALL THE ...!
YOU HOPELESS CHILD...
Might makes right.

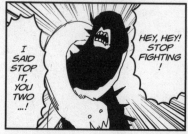

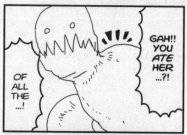

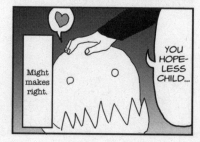

CHAPTER 50: NO CHANGE

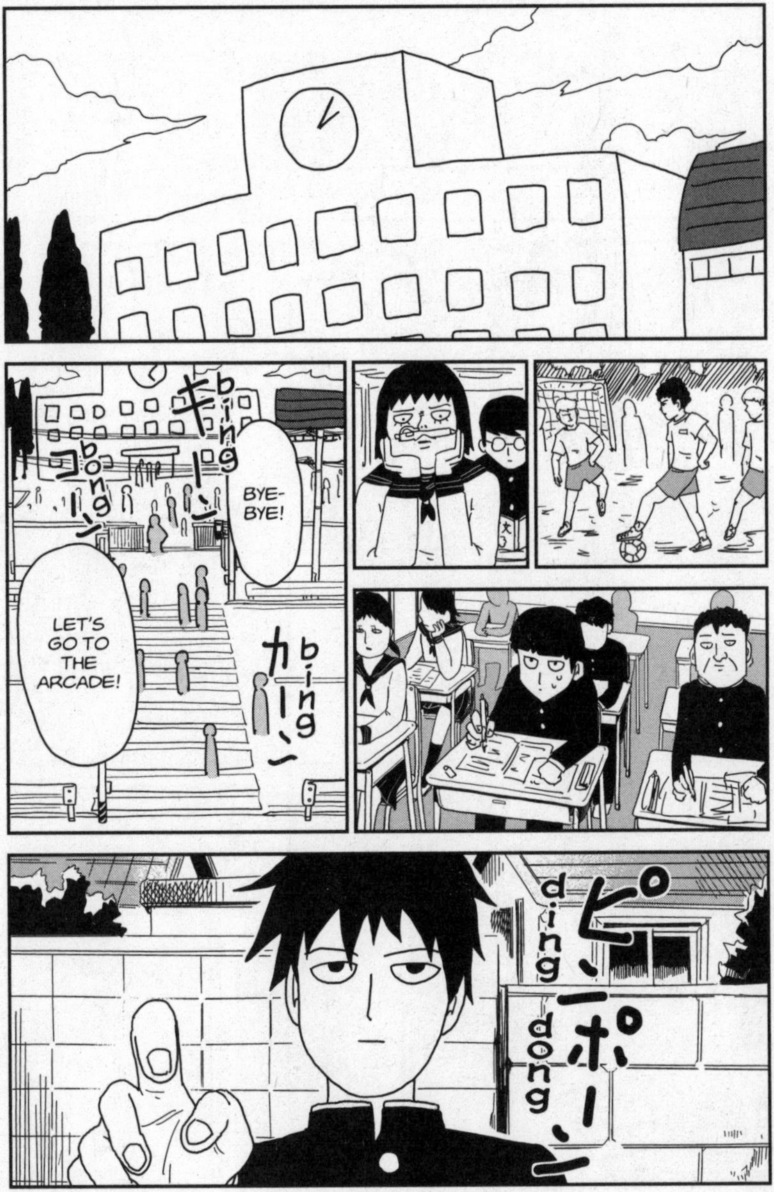
bing
bong
BYE-BYE!
LET'S GO TO THE ARCADE!
bing
ding dong

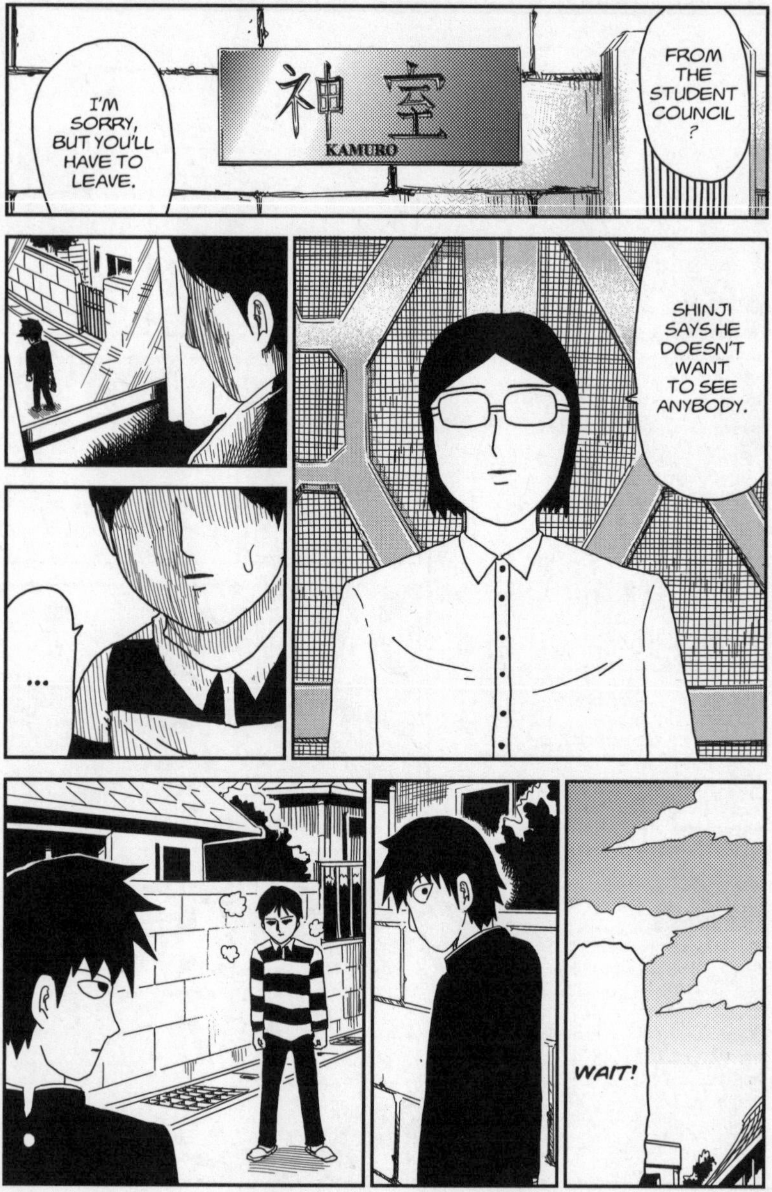
FROM THE STUDENT COUNCIL ?
神 室
KAMURO
I'M SORRY, BUT YOU'LL HAVE TO LEAVE.
SHINJI SAYS HE DOESN'T WANT TO SEE ANYBODY.
...
WAIT!

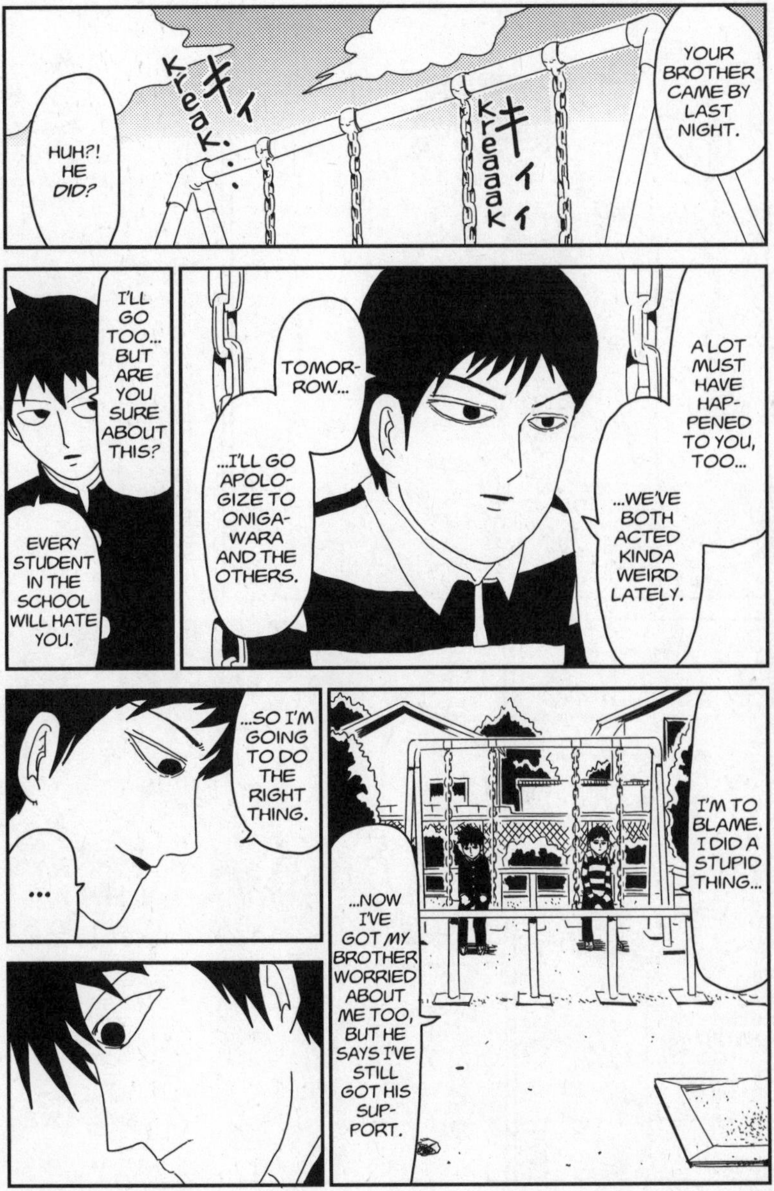
YOUR BROTHER CAME BY LAST NIGHT.
キィィ
KREAAAK
キィ
KREAK!
HUH?! HE DID?
A LOT MUST HAVE HAPPENED TO YOU, TOO...
...WE'VE BOTH ACTED KINDA WEIRD LATELY.
TOMORROW...
...I'LL GO APOLOGIZE TO ONIGAWARA AND THE OTHERS.
I'LL GO TOO... BUT ARE YOU SURE ABOUT THIS?
EVERY STUDENT IN THE SCHOOL WILL HATE YOU.
I'M TO BLAME. I DID A STUPID THING...
...NOW I'VE GOT MY BROTHER WORRIED ABOUT ME TOO, BUT HE SAYS I'VE STILL GOT HIS SUPPORT.
...SO I'M GOING TO DO THE RIGHT THING.
...

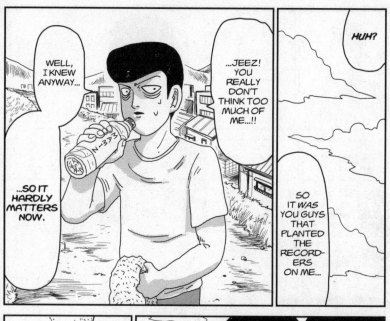

HUH?
SO IT WAS YOU GUYS THAT PLANTED THE RECORDERS ON ME...
...JEEZ! YOU REALLY DON'T THINK TOO MUCH OF ME...!!
WELL, I KNEW ANYWAY...
...SO IT HARDLY MATTERS NOW.
EH?
WHAT DO YOU MEAN?
WHETHER I WAS THE CULPRIT OR NOT MAKES NO DIFFERENCE.
IT WAS IN THE AIR. AS SOON AS THEY HAD AN EXCUSE, THEY WERE ALL GONNA USE IT TO KICK ME OUT...
THE REAL PROBLEM WAS...
...THAT EVERYONE HATED ME TO DEATH IN THE FIRST PLACE.

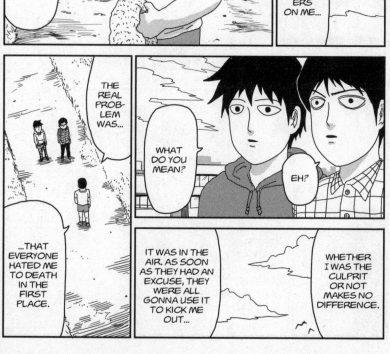

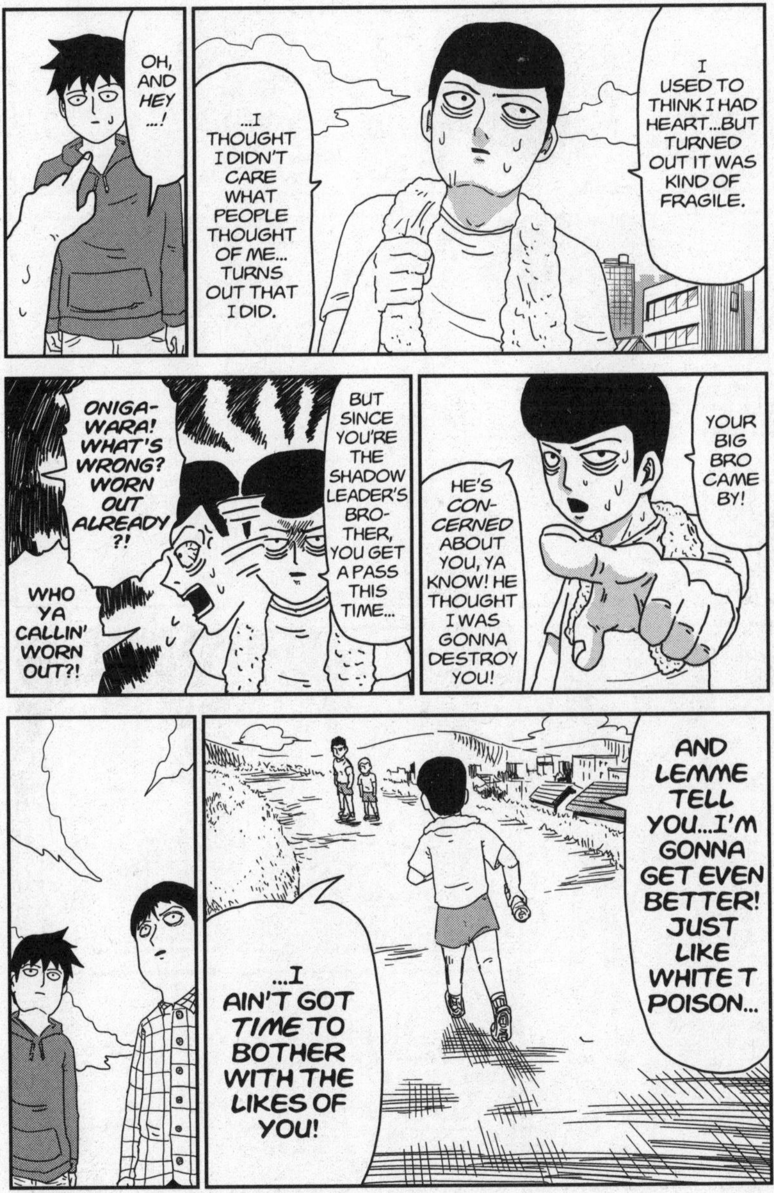
I USED TO THINK I HAD HEART...BUT TURNED OUT IT WAS KIND OF FRAGILE.
...I THOUGHT I DIDN'T CARE WHAT PEOPLE THOUGHT OF ME... TURNS OUT THAT I DID.
OH, AND HEY ...!
YOUR BIG BRO CAME BY!
HE'S CONCERNED ABOUT YOU, YA KNOW! HE THOUGHT I WAS GONNA DESTROY YOU!
BUT SINCE YOU'RE THE SHADOW LEADER'S BROTHER, YOU GET A PASS THIS TIME...
ONIGAWARA! WHAT'S WRONG? WORN OUT ALREADY?!
WHO YA CALLIN' WORN OUT?!
AND LEMME TELL YOU...I'M GONNA GET EVEN BETTER! JUST LIKE WHITE T POISON...
...I AIN'T GOT TIME TO BOTHER WITH THE LIKES OF YOU!

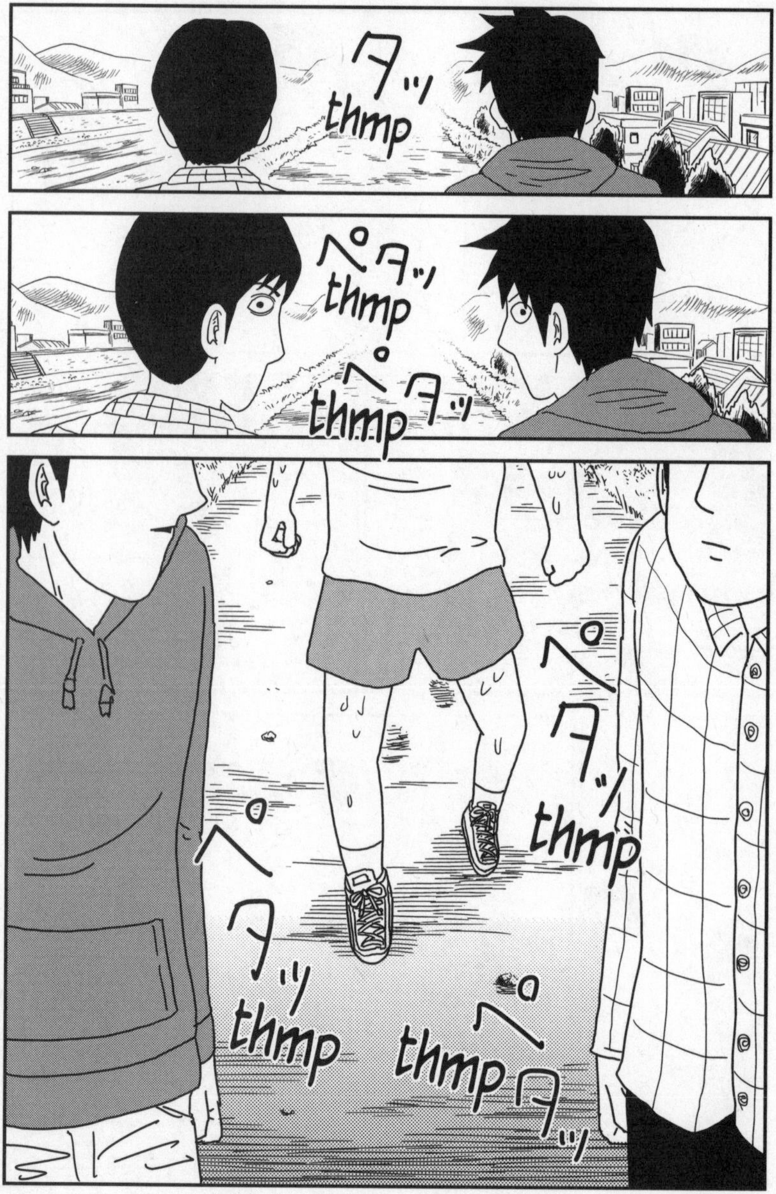
タッ
thmp
ペタッ
thmp
ペタッ
thmp
ペタッ
thmp
ペタッ
thmp
ペタッ
thmp

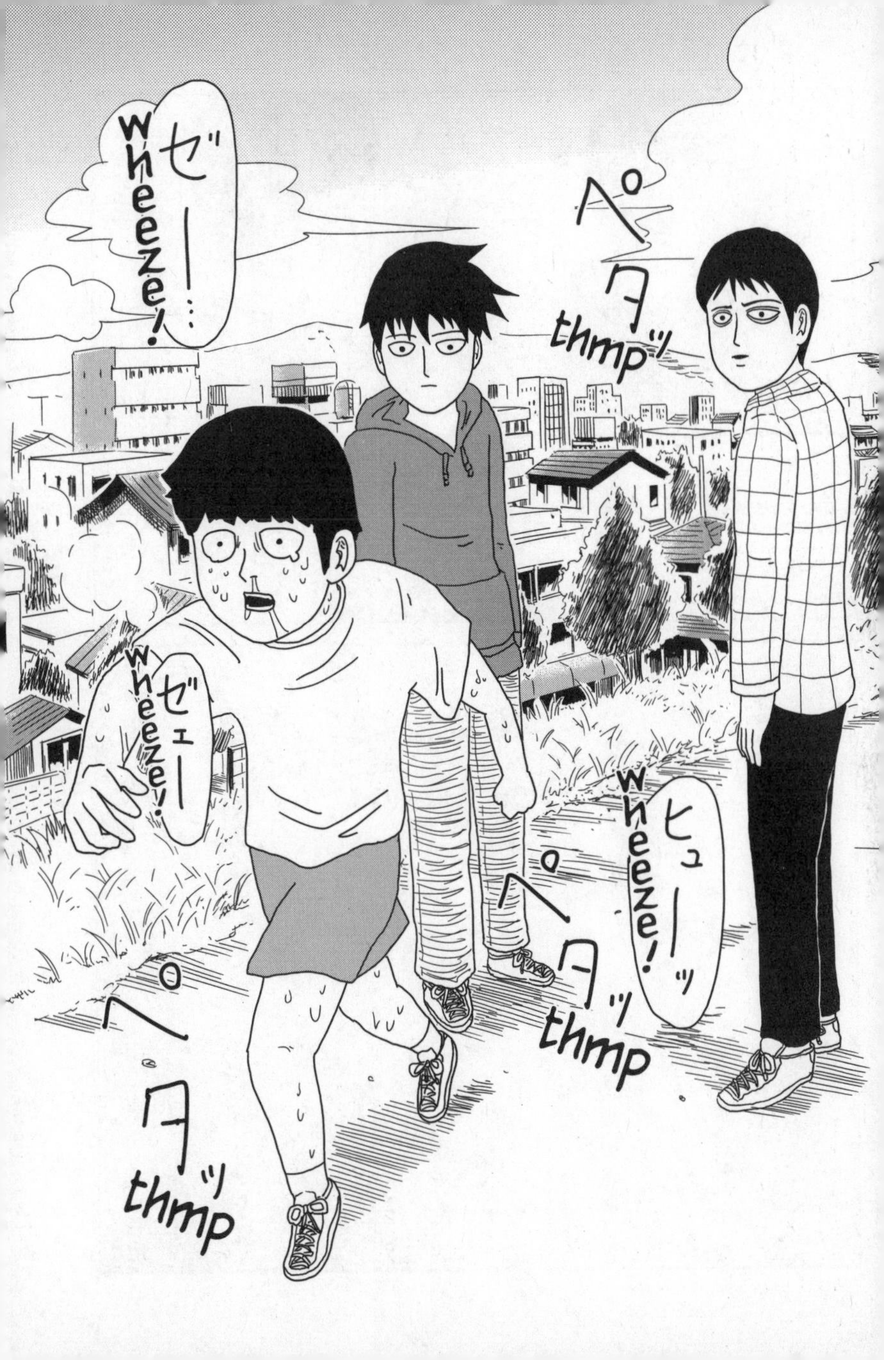

ペタッ
thmp
ゼー…
wheeze!
ヒューッ
wheeze!
ペタッ
thmp
ゼェー
wheeze!
ペタッ
thmp

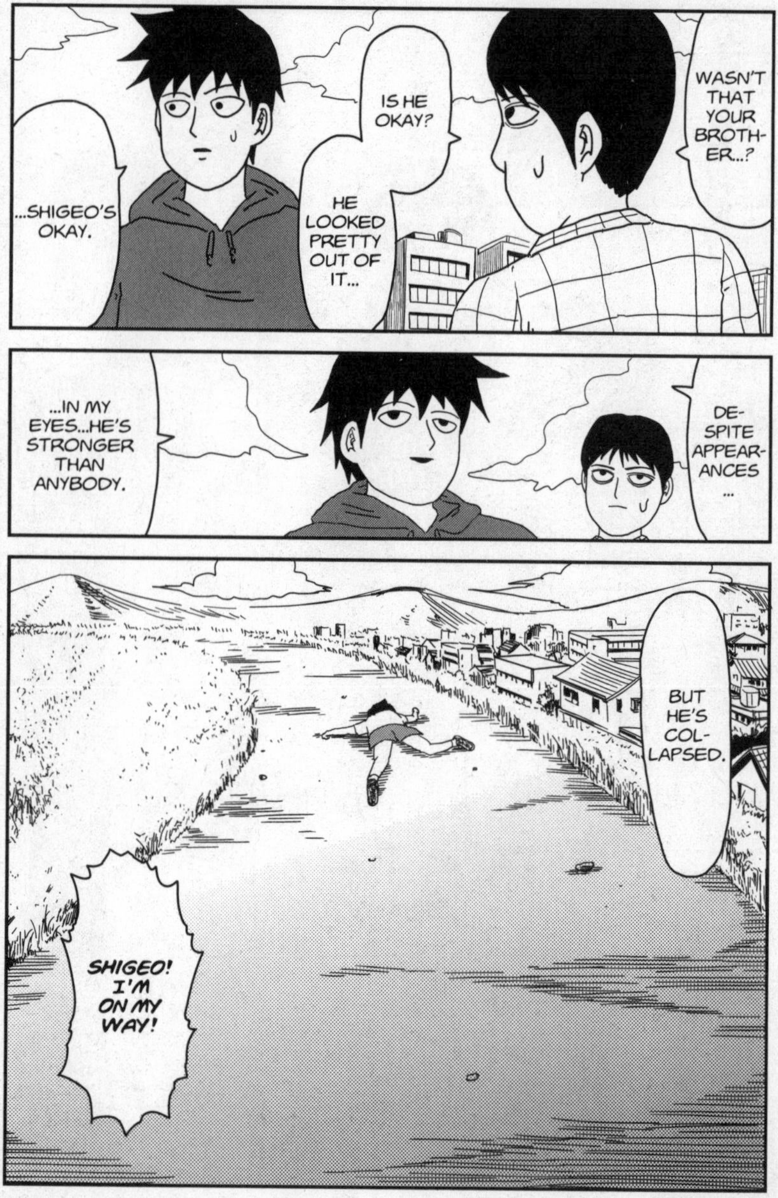
WASN'T THAT YOUR BROTHER...?
IS HE OKAY?
HE LOOKED PRETTY OUT OF IT...
...SHIGEO'S OKAY.
DESPITE APPEARANCES...
...IN MY EYES...HE'S STRONGER THAN ANYBODY.
BUT HE'S COLLAPSED.
SHIGEO! I'M ON MY WAY!

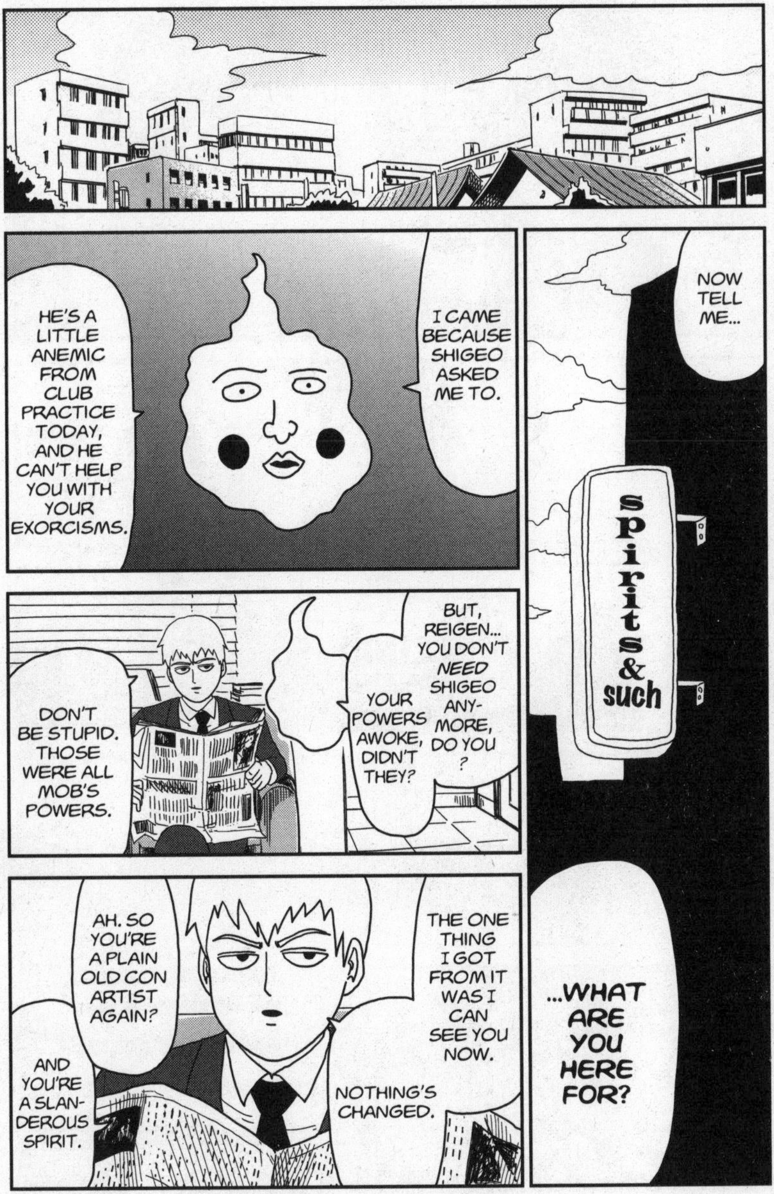
NOW TELL ME...
spirits & such
...WHAT ARE YOU HERE FOR?
I CAME BECAUSE SHIGEO ASKED ME TO.
HE'S A LITTLE ANEMIC FROM CLUB PRACTICE TODAY, AND HE CAN'T HELP YOU WITH YOUR EXORCISMS.
BUT, REIGEN... YOU DON'T *NEED* SHIGEO ANYMORE, DO YOU?
YOUR POWERS AWOKE, DIDN'T THEY?
DON'T BE STUPID. THOSE WERE ALL MOB'S POWERS.
THE ONE THING I GOT FROM IT WAS I CAN SEE YOU NOW.
AH. SO YOU'RE A PLAIN OLD CON ARTIST AGAIN?
NOTHING'S CHANGED.
AND YOU'RE A SLANDEROUS SPIRIT.

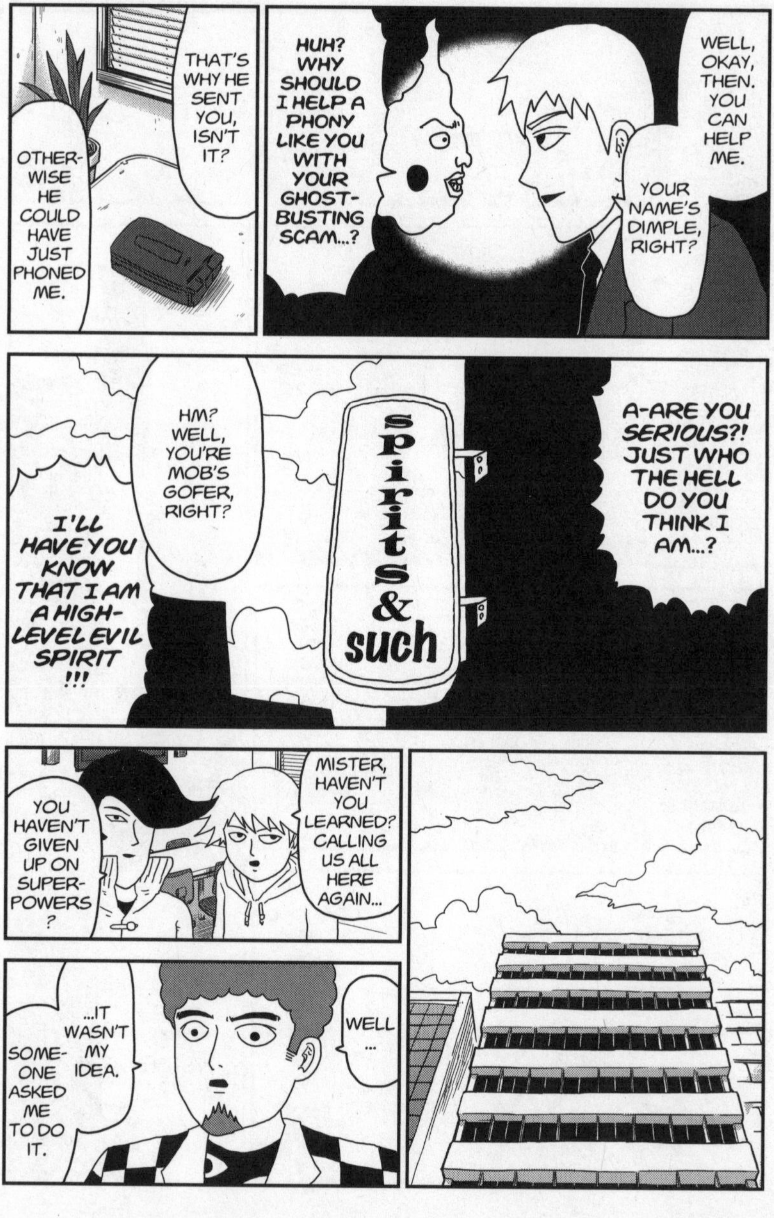
WELL, OKAY, THEN. YOU CAN HELP ME.
YOUR NAME'S DIMPLE, RIGHT?
HUH? WHY SHOULD I HELP A PHONY LIKE YOU WITH YOUR GHOST-BUSTING SCAM...?
THAT'S WHY HE SENT YOU, ISN'T IT?
OTHER-WISE HE COULD HAVE JUST PHONED ME.
A-ARE YOU SERIOUS?! JUST WHO THE HELL DO YOU THINK I AM...?
spirits & such
HM? WELL, YOU'RE MOB'S GOFER, RIGHT?
I'LL HAVE YOU KNOW THAT I AM A HIGH-LEVEL EVIL SPIRIT!!!
MISTER, HAVEN'T YOU LEARNED? CALLING US ALL HERE AGAIN...
YOU HAVEN'T GIVEN UP ON SUPER-POWERS?
WELL...
...IT WASN'T MY IDEA.
SOME-ONE ASKED ME TO DO IT.

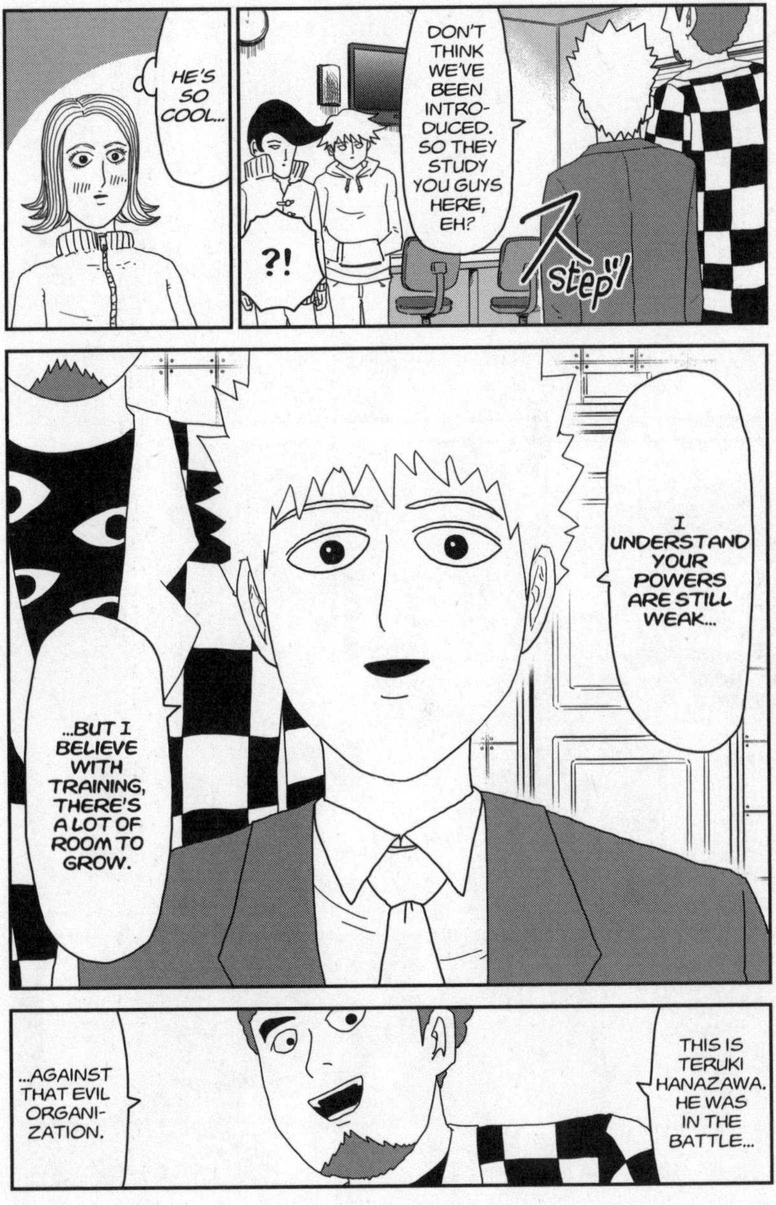
DON'T THINK WE'VE BEEN INTRO-DUCED. SO THEY STUDY YOU GUYS HERE, EH?
STEP!!
?!
HE'S SO COOL...
I UNDERSTAND YOUR POWERS ARE STILL WEAK...
...BUT I BELIEVE WITH TRAINING, THERE'S A LOT OF ROOM TO GROW.
THIS IS TERUKI HANAZAWA. HE WAS IN THE BATTLE...
...AGAINST THAT EVIL ORGANI-ZATION.

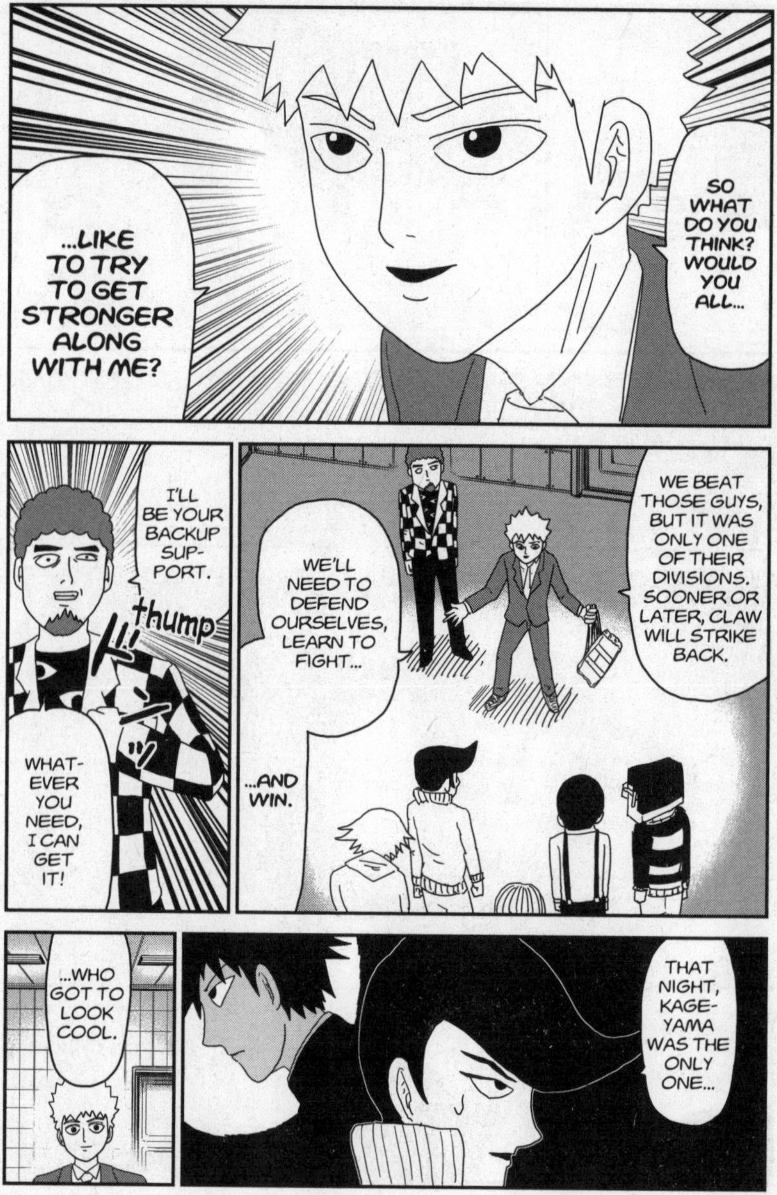
SO WHAT DO YOU THINK? WOULD YOU ALL...
...LIKE TO TRY TO GET STRONGER ALONG WITH ME?
WE BEAT THOSE GUYS, BUT IT WAS ONLY ONE OF THEIR DIVISIONS. SOONER OR LATER, CLAW WILL STRIKE BACK.
WE'LL NEED TO DEFEND OURSELVES, LEARN TO FIGHT...
...AND WIN.
I'LL BE YOUR BACKUP SUP-PORT.
thump
WHAT-EVER YOU NEED, I CAN GET IT!
THAT NIGHT, KAGE-YAMA WAS THE ONLY ONE...
...WHO GOT TO LOOK COOL.

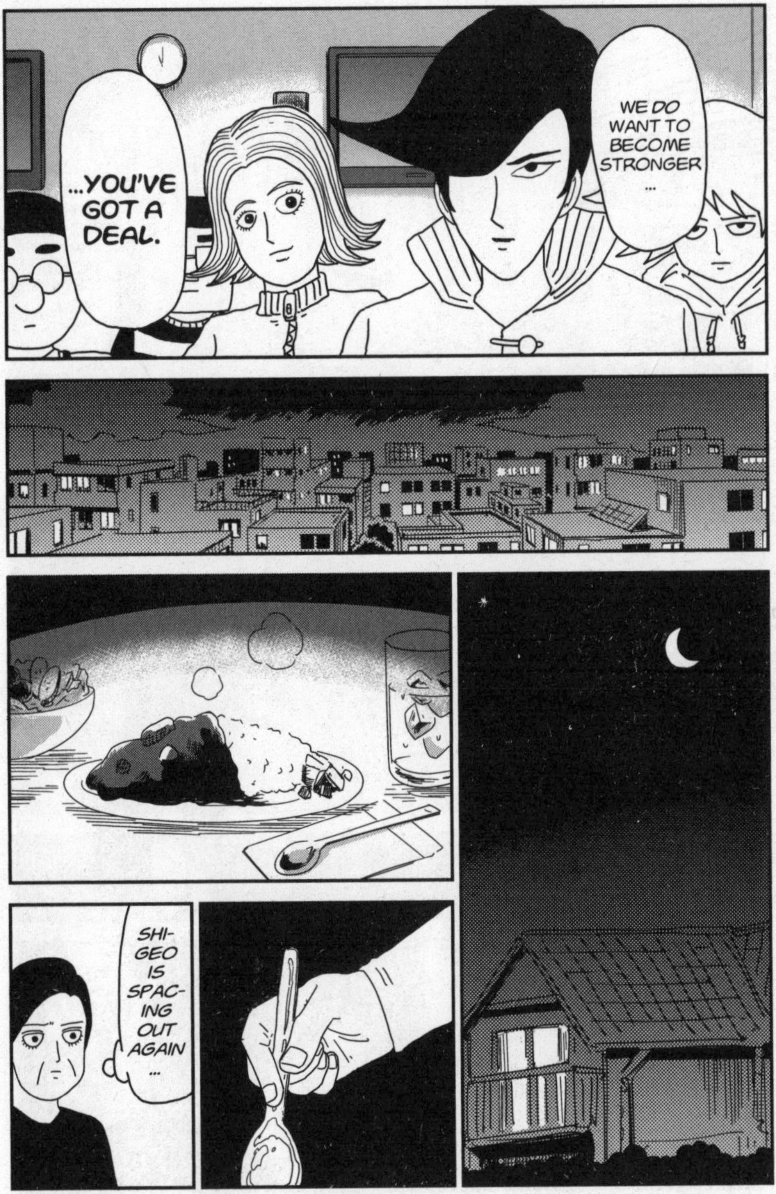
WE DO WANT TO BECOME STRONGER ...
...YOU'VE GOT A DEAL.
SHI-GEO IS SPAC-ING OUT AGAIN ...

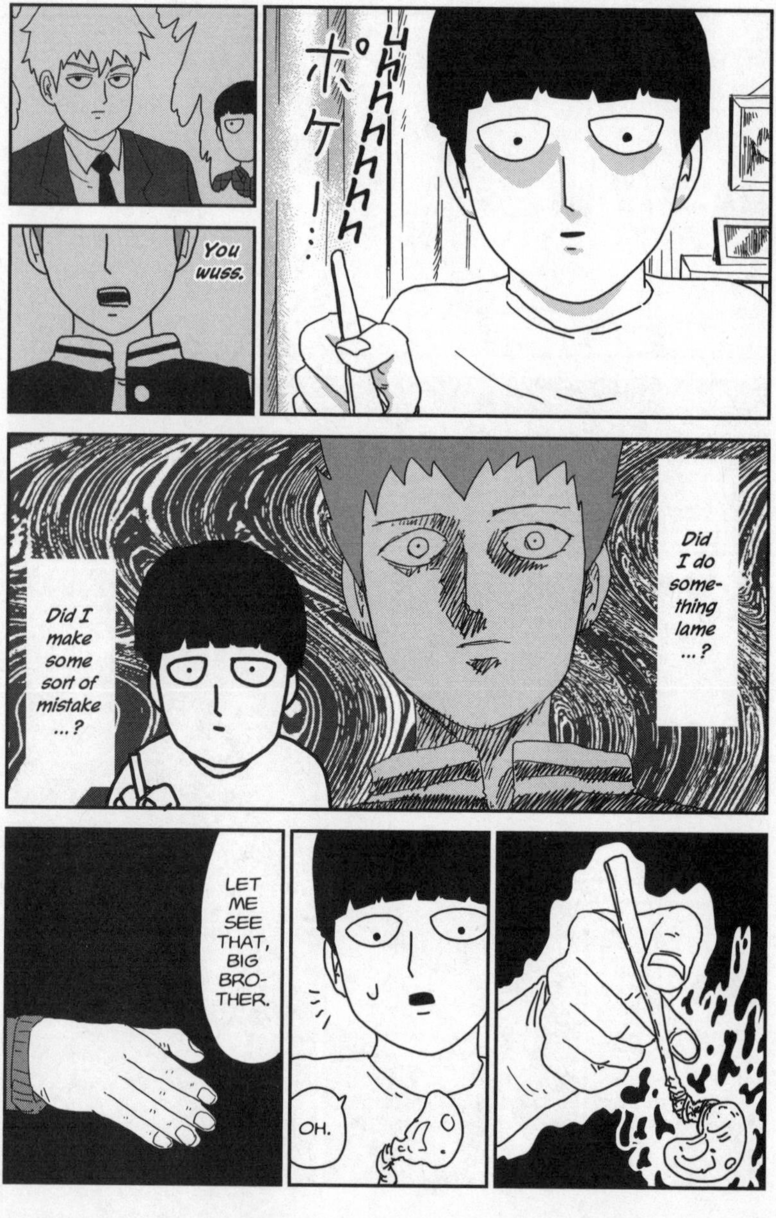
ポケー…
You wuss.
Did I do something lame...?
Did I make some sort of mistake...?
OH.
LET ME SEE THAT, BIG BROTHER.

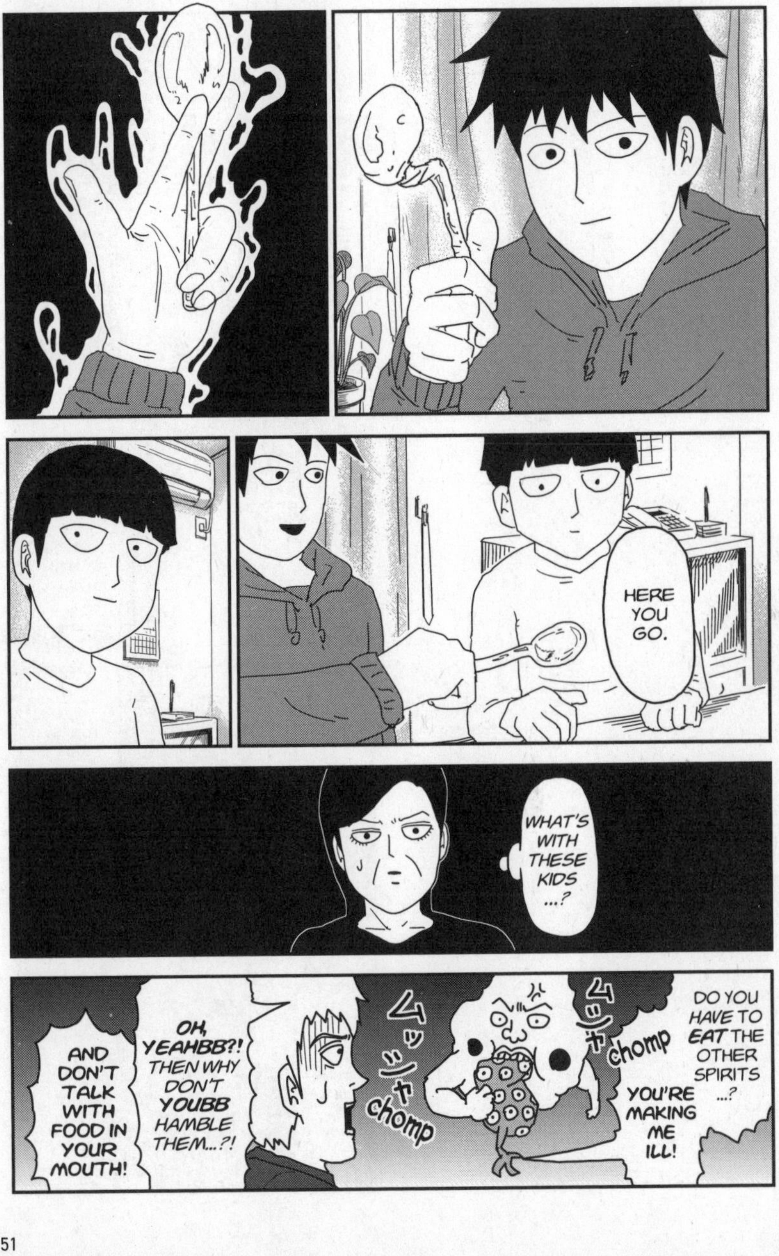
HERE YOU GO.
WHAT'S WITH THESE KIDS ...?
DO YOU HAVE TO EAT THE OTHER SPIRITS ...?
ムッシャ
chomp
YOU'RE MAKING ME ILL!
ムッシャ
chomp
OH, YEAHBB?! THEN WHY DON'T YOUBB HAMBLE THEM...?!
AND DON'T TALK WITH FOOD IN YOUR MOUTH!

Matsuo's Evil Spirit Observation Log (#7)

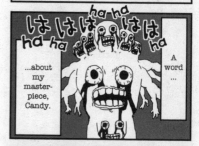

はは ha
ha ha
ははは ha ha
A word ...
...about my master-piece, Candy.
He has a wild temperament, so if I let him out along with my other evil spirits, he cannibalizes them.
And so...
...at feeding time, I'll let Candy go into a dangerous haunted area by himself.
After all, he's a big boy.
ズ thump
ズ thump
But when he comes back...
ズゥン thoom
...he's a bit more of a big boy.

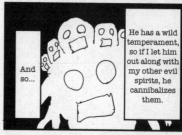

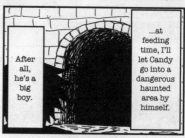

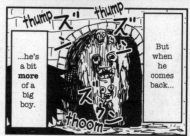

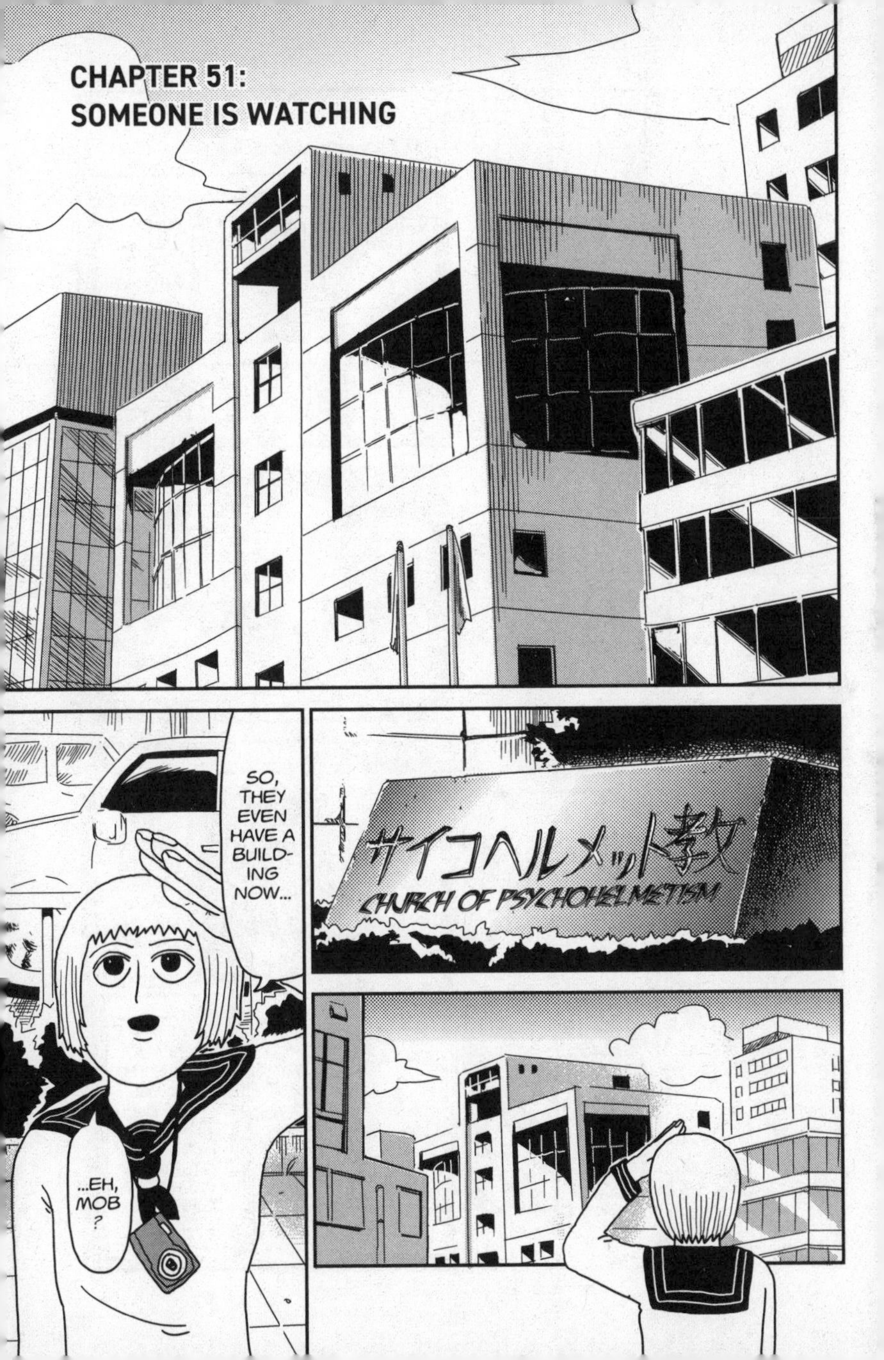
CHAPTER 51:
SOMEONE IS WATCHING
サイコヘルメット教
CHURCH OF PSYCHOHELMETISM
SO, THEY EVEN HAVE A BUILDING NOW...
...EH, MOB?

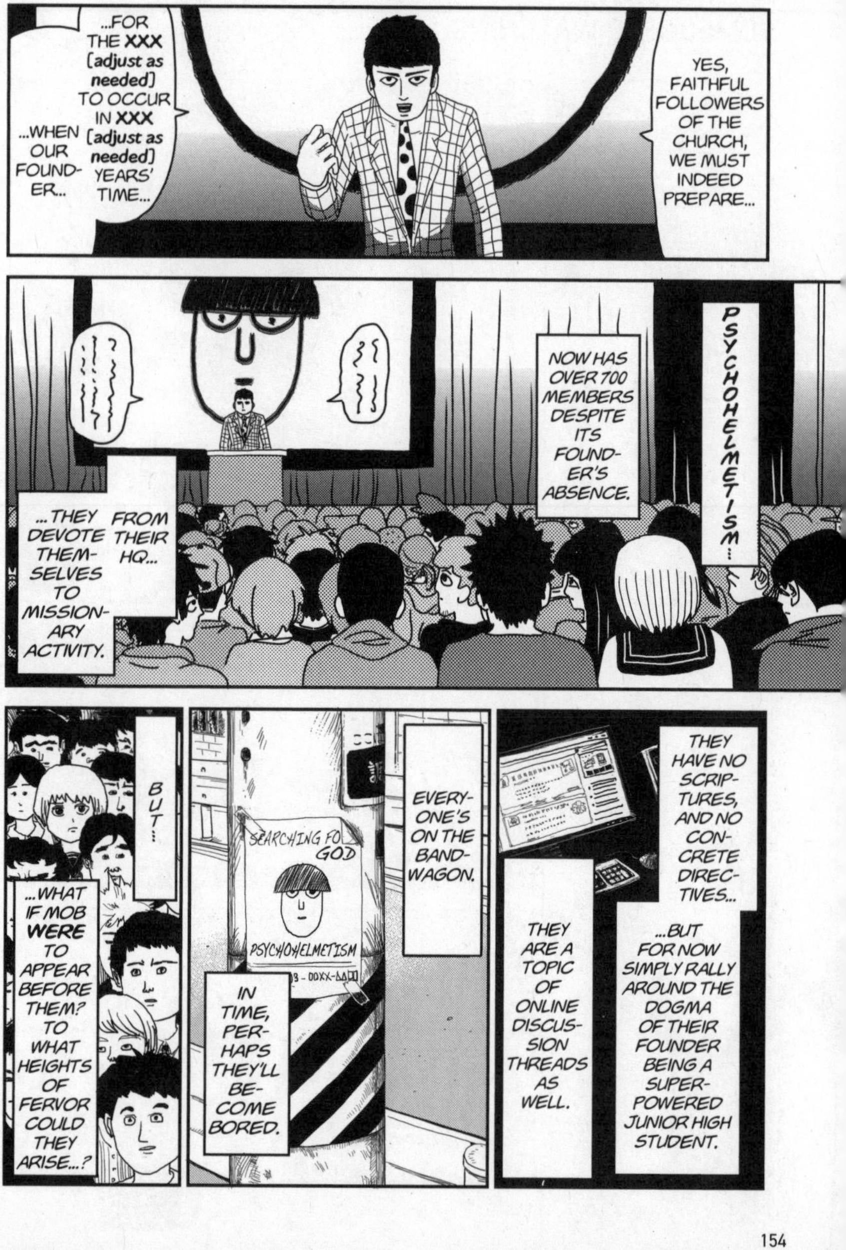
YES, FAITHFUL FOLLOWERS OF THE CHURCH, WE MUST INDEED PREPARE...
...FOR THE **XXX** [adjust as needed] TO OCCUR IN **XXX** [adjust as needed] YEARS' TIME...
...WHEN OUR FOUNDER...
PSYCHOHELMETISM...
NOW HAS OVER 700 MEMBERS DESPITE ITS FOUNDER'S ABSENCE.
FROM THEIR HQ...
...THEY DEVOTE THEMSELVES TO MISSIONARY ACTIVITY.
THEY HAVE NO SCRIPTURES, AND NO CONCRETE DIRECTIVES...
...BUT FOR NOW SIMPLY RALLY AROUND THE DOGMA OF THEIR FOUNDER BEING A SUPERPOWERED JUNIOR HIGH STUDENT.
THEY ARE A TOPIC OF ONLINE DISCUSSION THREADS AS WELL.
EVERYONE'S ON THE BANDWAGON.
SEARCHING FO GOD
PSYCHOHELMETISM
IN TIME, PERHAPS THEY'LL BECOME BORED.
BUT...
...WHAT IF MOB **WERE** TO APPEAR BEFORE THEM? TO WHAT HEIGHTS OF FERVOR COULD THEY ARISE...?

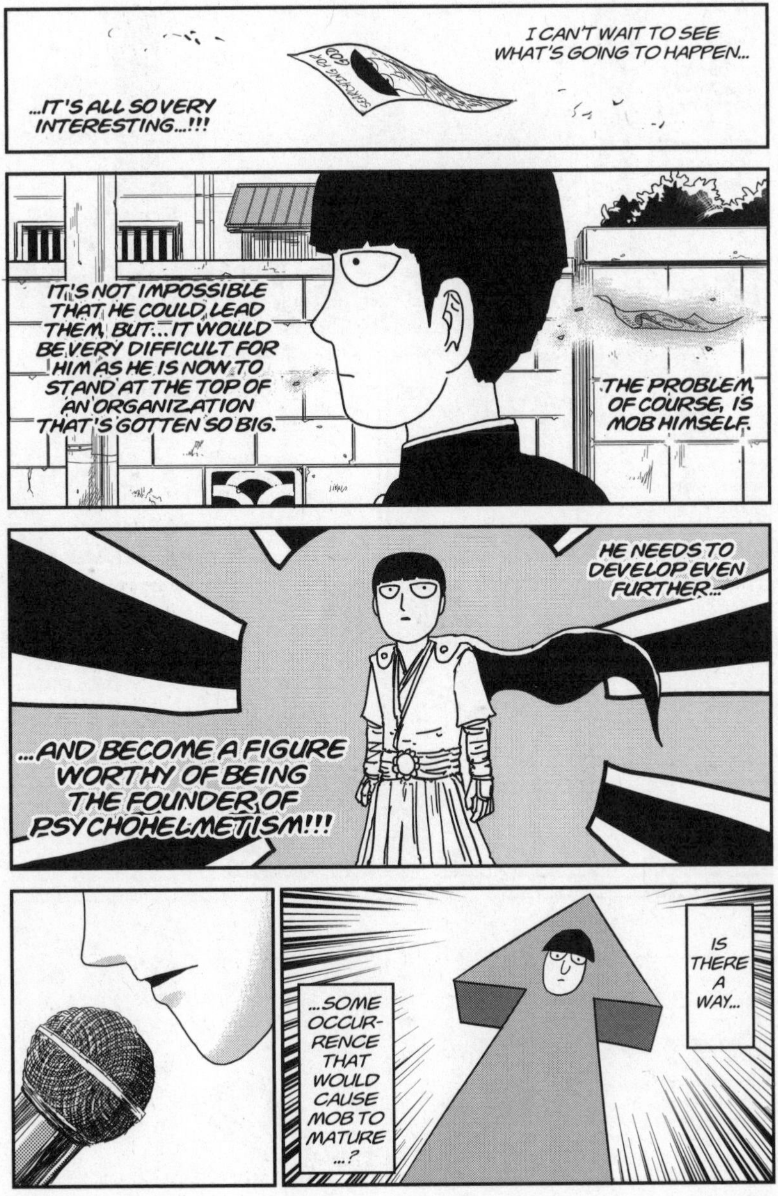
I CAN'T WAIT TO SEE WHAT'S GOING TO HAPPEN...
...IT'S ALL SO VERY INTERESTING...!!!
THE PROBLEM, OF COURSE, IS MOB HIMSELF.
IT'S NOT IMPOSSIBLE THAT HE COULD LEAD THEM, BUT... IT WOULD BE VERY DIFFICULT FOR HIM AS HE IS NOW TO STAND AT THE TOP OF AN ORGANIZATION THAT'S GOTTEN SO BIG.
HE NEEDS TO DEVELOP EVEN FURTHER...
...AND BECOME A FIGURE WORTHY OF BEING THE FOUNDER OF PSYCHOHELMETISM!!!
IS THERE A WAY...
...SOME OCCURRENCE THAT WOULD CAUSE MOB TO MATURE ...?

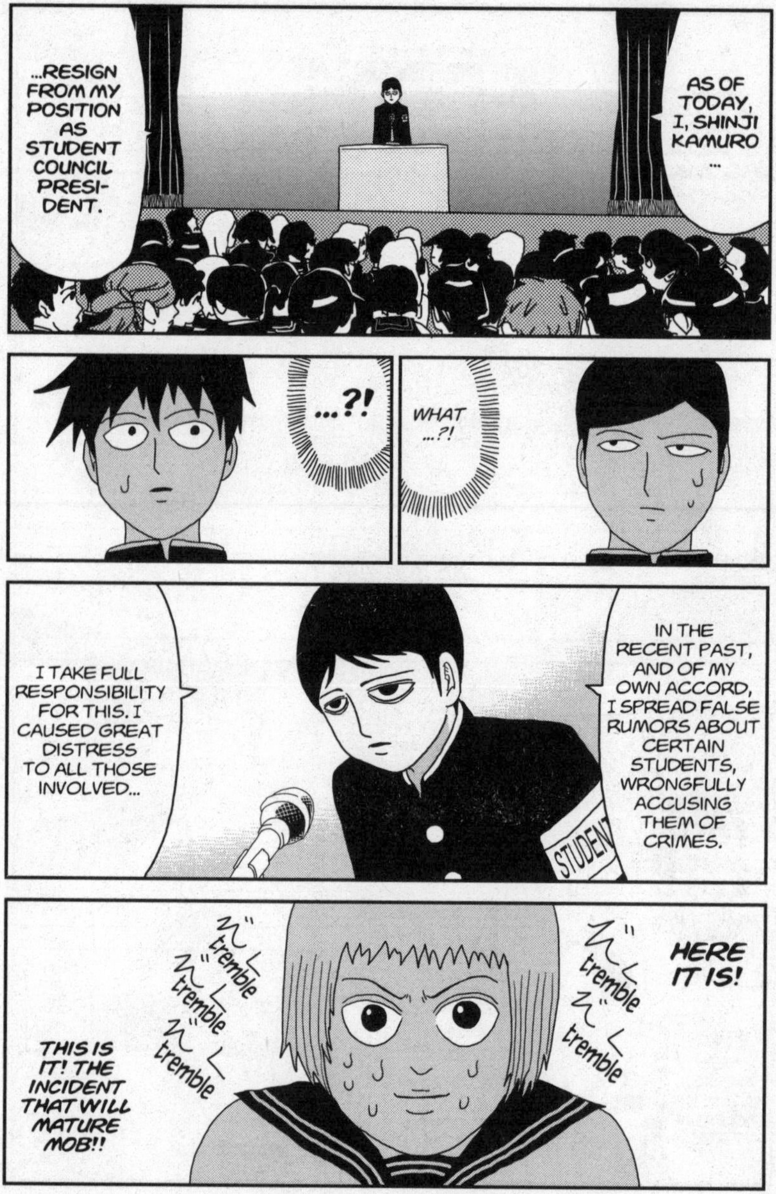

AS OF TODAY, I, SHINJI KAMURO ...
...RESIGN FROM MY POSITION AS STUDENT COUNCIL PRESIDENT.
WHAT ...?!
...?!
IN THE RECENT PAST, AND OF MY OWN ACCORD, I SPREAD FALSE RUMORS ABOUT CERTAIN STUDENTS, WRONGFULLY ACCUSING THEM OF CRIMES.
I TAKE FULL RESPONSIBILITY FOR THIS. I CAUSED GREAT DISTRESS TO ALL THOSE INVOLVED...
STUDENT
HERE IT IS!
tremble
tremble
tremble
tremble
tremble
THIS IS IT! THE INCIDENT THAT WILL MATURE MOB!!

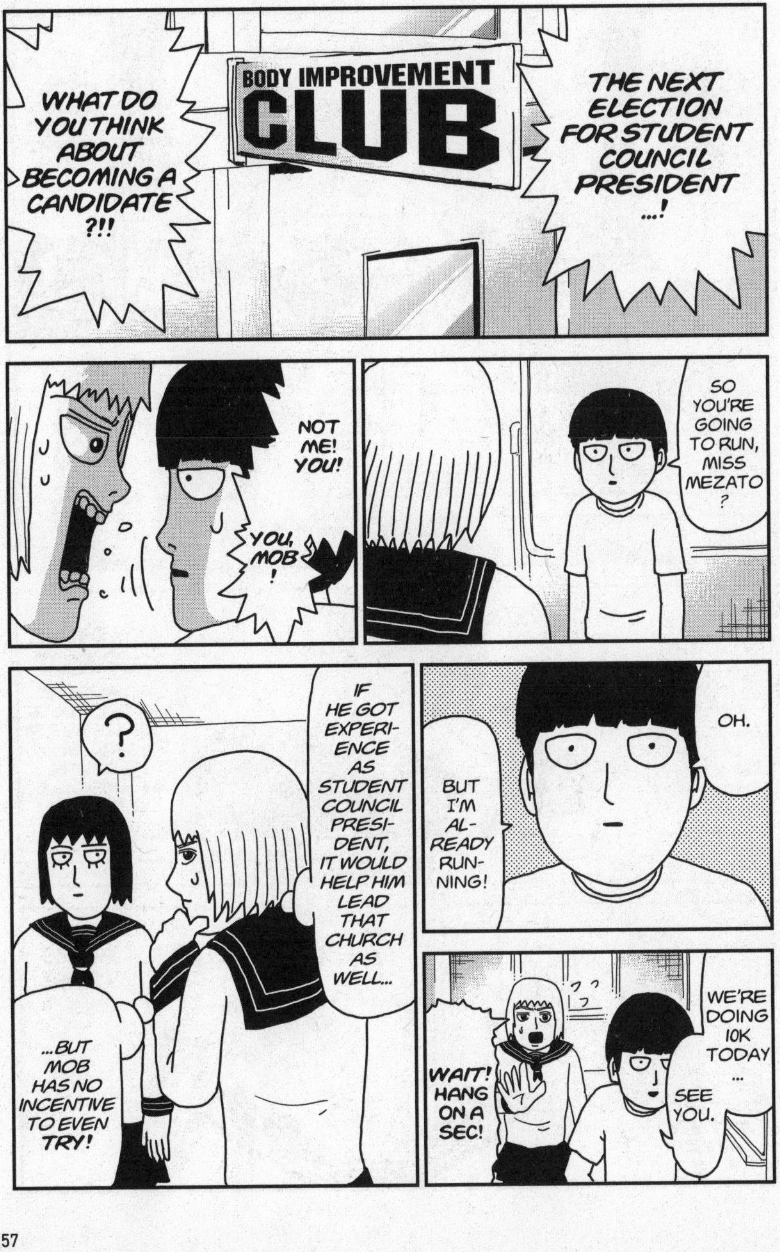
THE NEXT ELECTION FOR STUDENT COUNCIL PRESIDENT ...!
BODY IMPROVEMENT CLUB
WHAT DO YOU THINK ABOUT BECOMING A CANDIDATE ?!!
SO YOU'RE GOING TO RUN, MISS MEZATO ?
NOT ME! YOU!
YOU, MOB !
OH.
BUT I'M AL-READY RUN-NING!
WE'RE DOING 10K TODAY ...
SEE YOU.
WAIT! HANG ON A SEC!
IF HE GOT EXPERI-ENCE AS STUDENT COUNCIL PRESI-DENT, IT WOULD HELP HIM LEAD THAT CHURCH AS WELL...
?
...BUT MOB HAS NO INCENTIVE TO EVEN TRY!

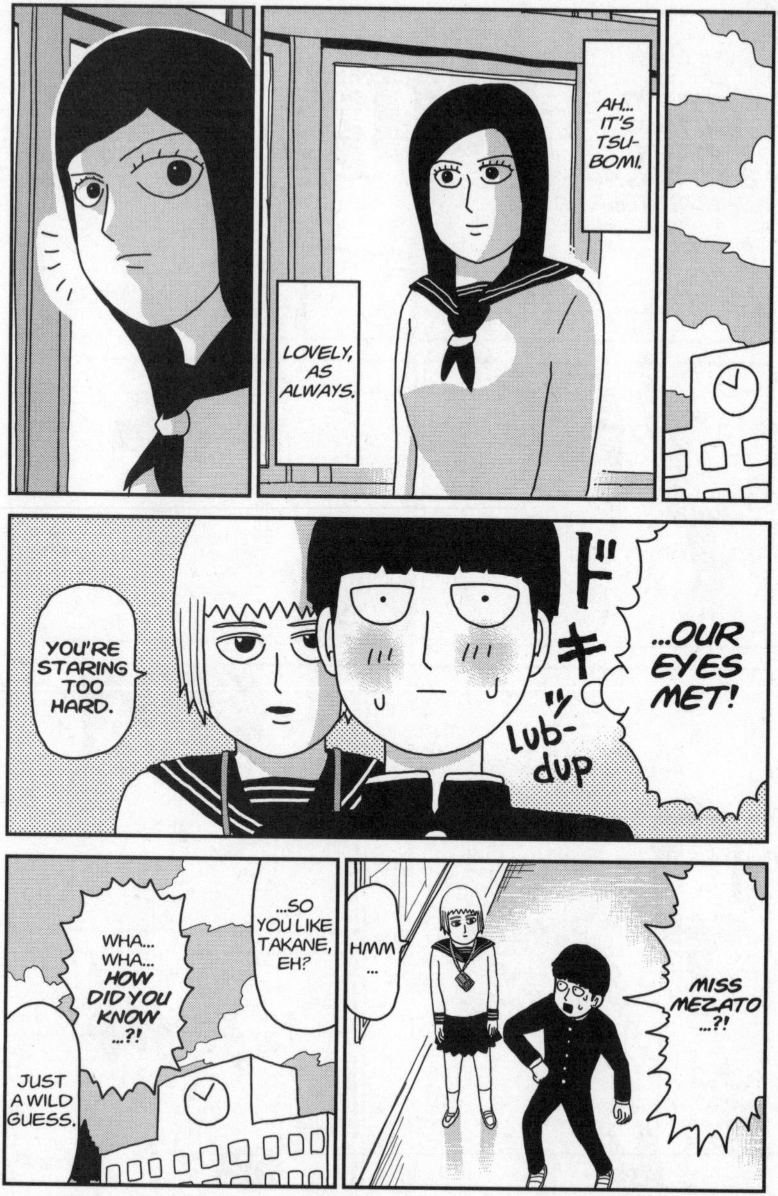
AH... IT'S TSU-BOMI.
LOVELY, AS ALWAYS.
...OUR EYES MET!
ドキッ
lub-dup
YOU'RE STARING TOO HARD.
MISS MEZATO ...?!
HMM ...
...SO YOU LIKE TAKANE, EH?
WHA... WHA... ***HOW DID YOU KNOW*** ...?!
JUST A WILD GUESS.

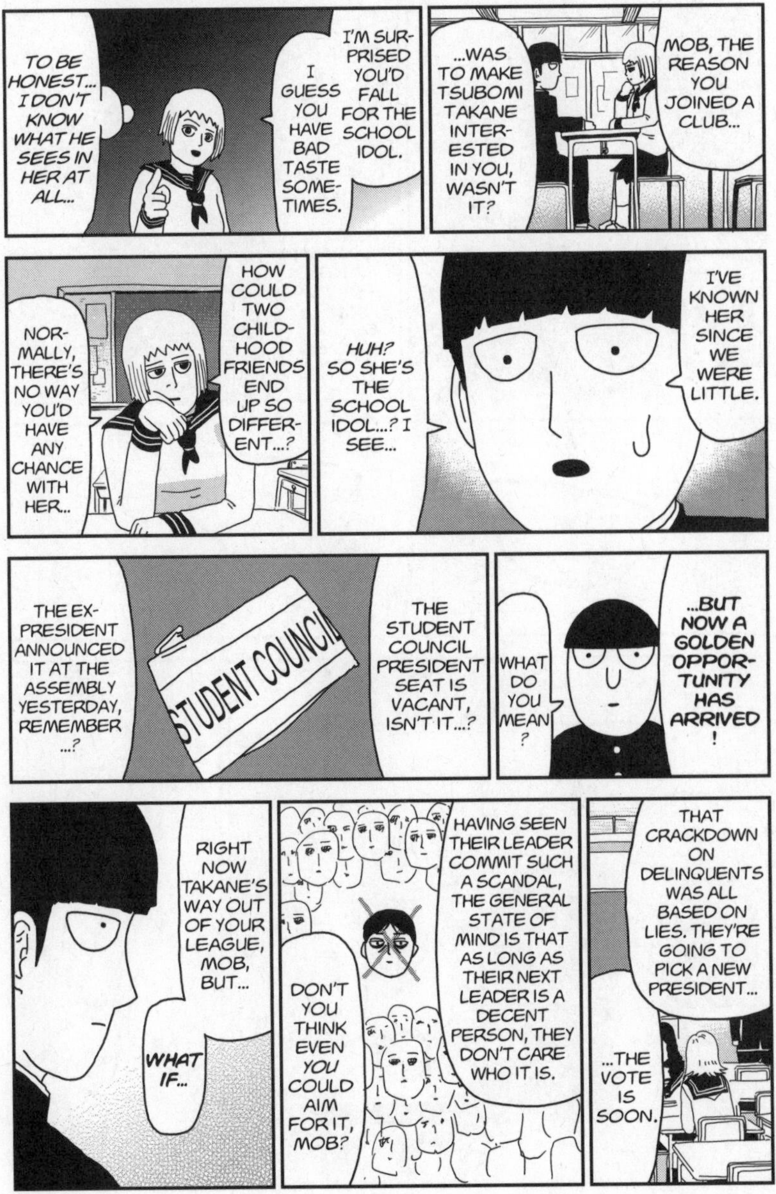
MOB, THE REASON YOU JOINED A CLUB...
...WAS TO MAKE TSUBOMI TAKANE INTERESTED IN YOU, WASN'T IT?
I'M SURPRISED YOU'D FALL FOR THE SCHOOL IDOL.
I GUESS YOU HAVE BAD TASTE SOMETIMES.
TO BE HONEST... I DON'T KNOW WHAT HE SEES IN HER AT ALL...
I'VE KNOWN HER SINCE WE WERE LITTLE.
HUH? SO SHE'S THE SCHOOL IDOL...? I SEE...
HOW COULD TWO CHILDHOOD FRIENDS END UP SO DIFFERENT...?
NORMALLY, THERE'S NO WAY YOU'D HAVE ANY CHANCE WITH HER...
...BUT NOW A GOLDEN OPPORTUNITY HAS ARRIVED!
WHAT DO YOU MEAN?
THE STUDENT COUNCIL PRESIDENT SEAT IS VACANT, ISN'T IT...?
STUDENT COUNCIL
THE EX-PRESIDENT ANNOUNCED IT AT THE ASSEMBLY YESTERDAY, REMEMBER...?
THAT CRACKDOWN ON DELINQUENTS WAS ALL BASED ON LIES. THEY'RE GOING TO PICK A NEW PRESIDENT...
...THE VOTE IS SOON.
HAVING SEEN THEIR LEADER COMMIT SUCH A SCANDAL, THE GENERAL STATE OF MIND IS THAT AS LONG AS THEIR NEXT LEADER IS A DECENT PERSON, THEY DON'T CARE WHO IT IS.
DON'T YOU THINK EVEN YOU COULD AIM FOR IT, MOB?
RIGHT NOW TAKANE'S WAY OUT OF YOUR LEAGUE, MOB, BUT...
WHAT IF...

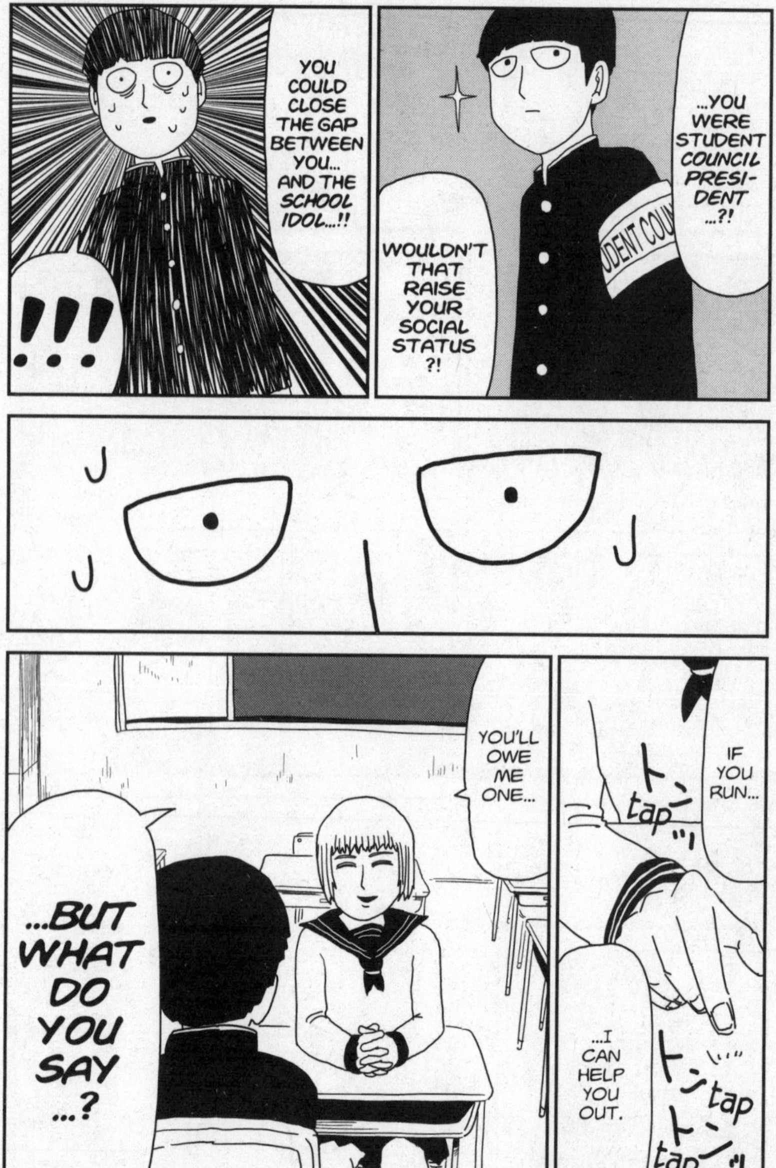
...YOU WERE STUDENT COUNCIL PRESIDENT...?!
UDENT COU
WOULDN'T THAT RAISE YOUR SOCIAL STATUS?!
YOU COULD CLOSE THE GAP BETWEEN YOU... AND THE SCHOOL IDOL...!!
!!!
IF YOU RUN...
tap
...I CAN HELP YOU OUT.
tap
tap
YOU'LL OWE ME ONE...
...BUT WHAT DO YOU SAY...?

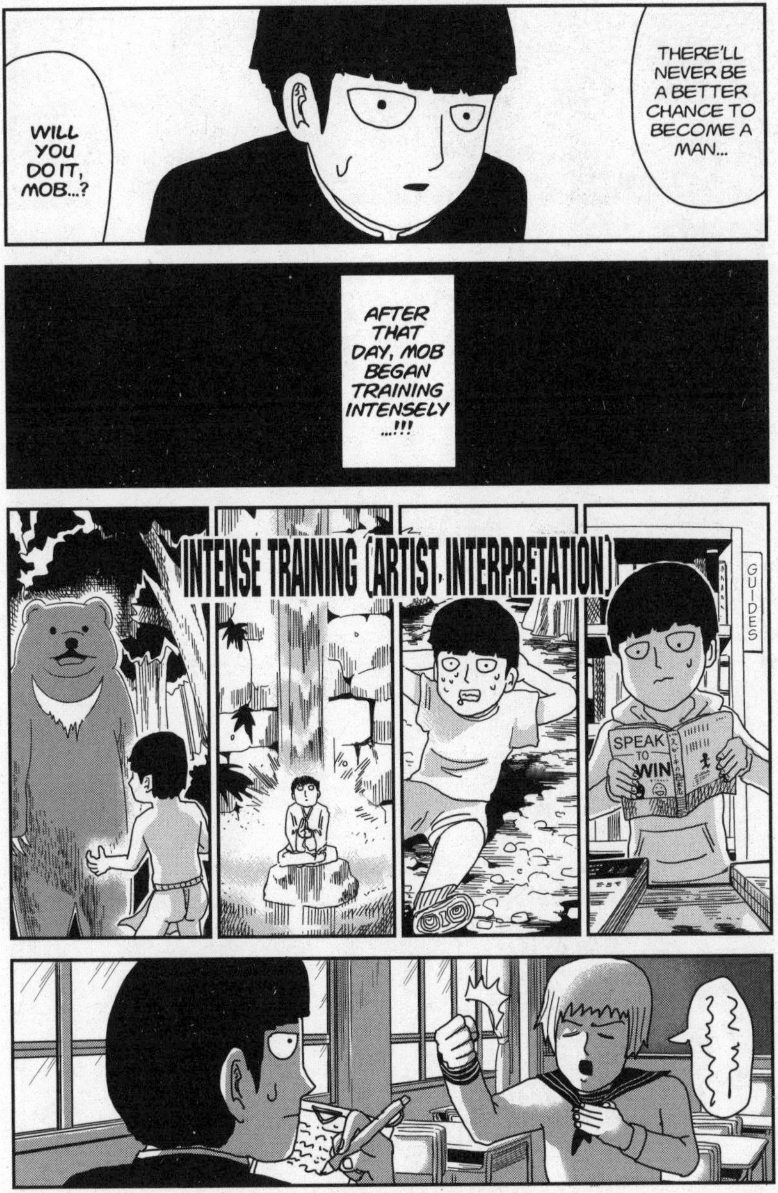
THERE'LL NEVER BE A BETTER CHANCE TO BECOME A MAN...
WILL YOU DO IT, MOB...?
AFTER THAT DAY, MOB BEGAN TRAINING INTENSELY ...!!!
INTENSE TRAINING (ARTIST INTERPRETATION)
GUIDES
SPEAK TO WIN

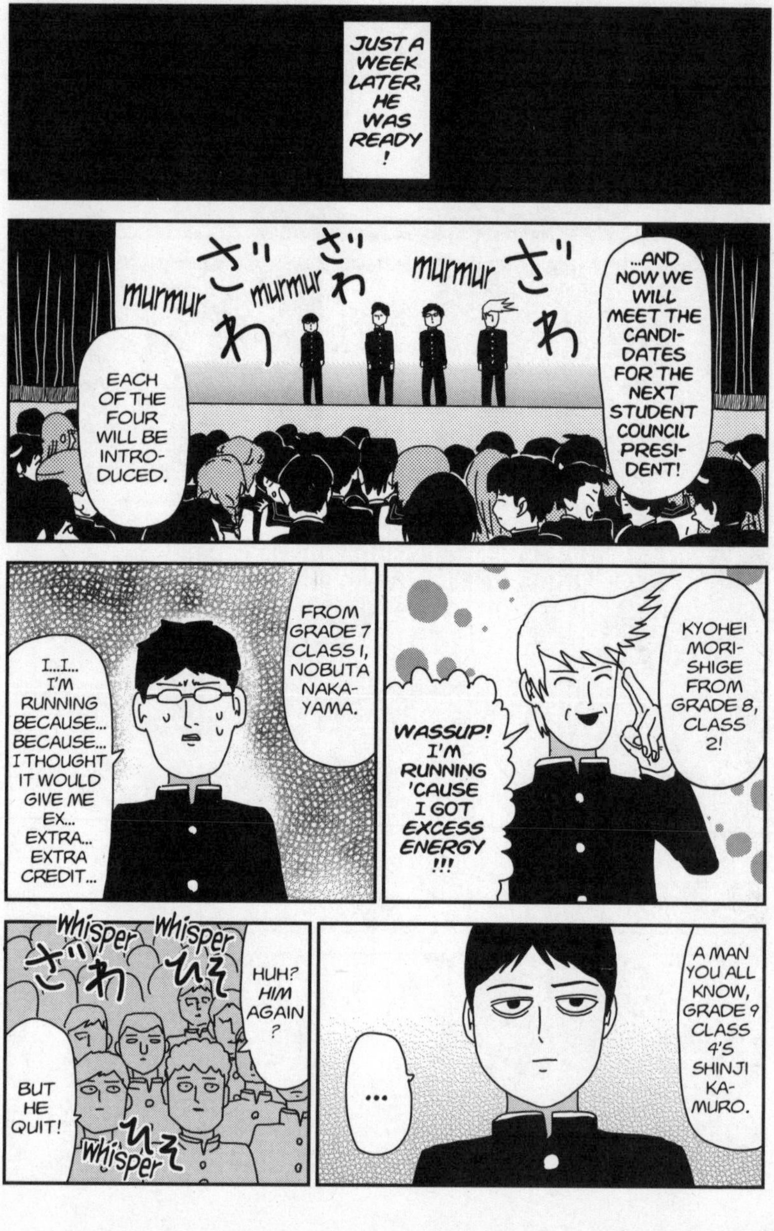
JUST A WEEK LATER, HE WAS READY!
...AND NOW WE WILL MEET THE CANDIDATES FOR THE NEXT STUDENT COUNCIL PRESIDENT!
ざわ
murmur
ざわ
murmur
ざわ
murmur
EACH OF THE FOUR WILL BE INTRODUCED.
KYOHEI MORISHIGE FROM GRADE 8, CLASS 2!
WASSUP! I'M RUNNING 'CAUSE I GOT EXCESS ENERGY!!!
FROM GRADE 7 CLASS 1, NOBUTA NAKAYAMA.
I...I... I'M RUNNING BECAUSE... BECAUSE... I THOUGHT IT WOULD GIVE ME EX... EXTRA... EXTRA CREDIT...
A MAN YOU ALL KNOW, GRADE 9 CLASS 4'S SHINJI KAMURO.
...
whisper
ひそ
whisper
ざわ
HUH? HIM AGAIN?
BUT HE QUIT!
ひそ
whisper

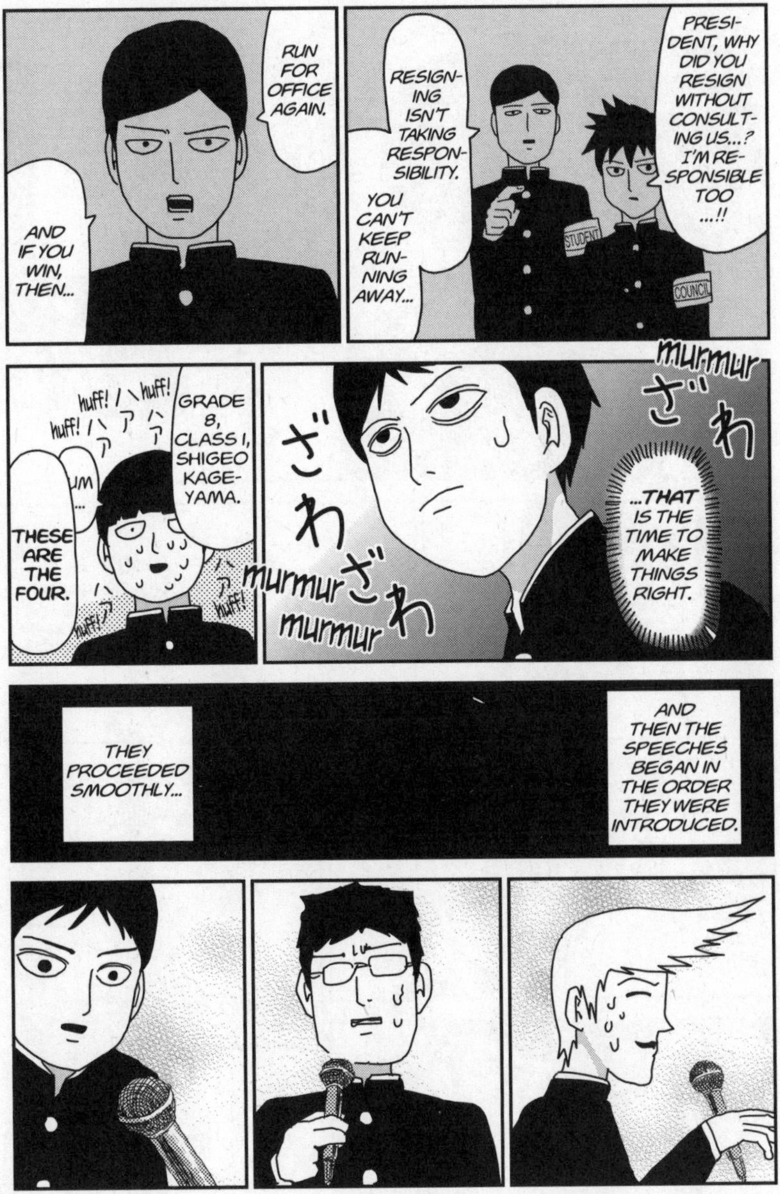
PRESIDENT, WHY DID YOU RESIGN WITHOUT CONSULTING US...? I'M RESPONSIBLE TOO ...!!
STUDENT
COUNCIL
RESIGNING ISN'T TAKING RESPONSIBILITY.
YOU CAN'T KEEP RUNNING AWAY...
RUN FOR OFFICE AGAIN.
AND IF YOU WIN, THEN...
murmur ざわ
...THAT IS THE TIME TO MAKE THINGS RIGHT.
ざわ
murmur ざわ
murmur
GRADE 8, CLASS 1, SHIGEO KAGEYAMA.
huff! ハ huff!
huff! ハア ハア
UM ...
THESE ARE THE FOUR.
ハア huff!
ハア huff!
AND THEN THE SPEECHES BEGAN IN THE ORDER THEY WERE INTRODUCED.
THEY PROCEEDED SMOOTHLY...

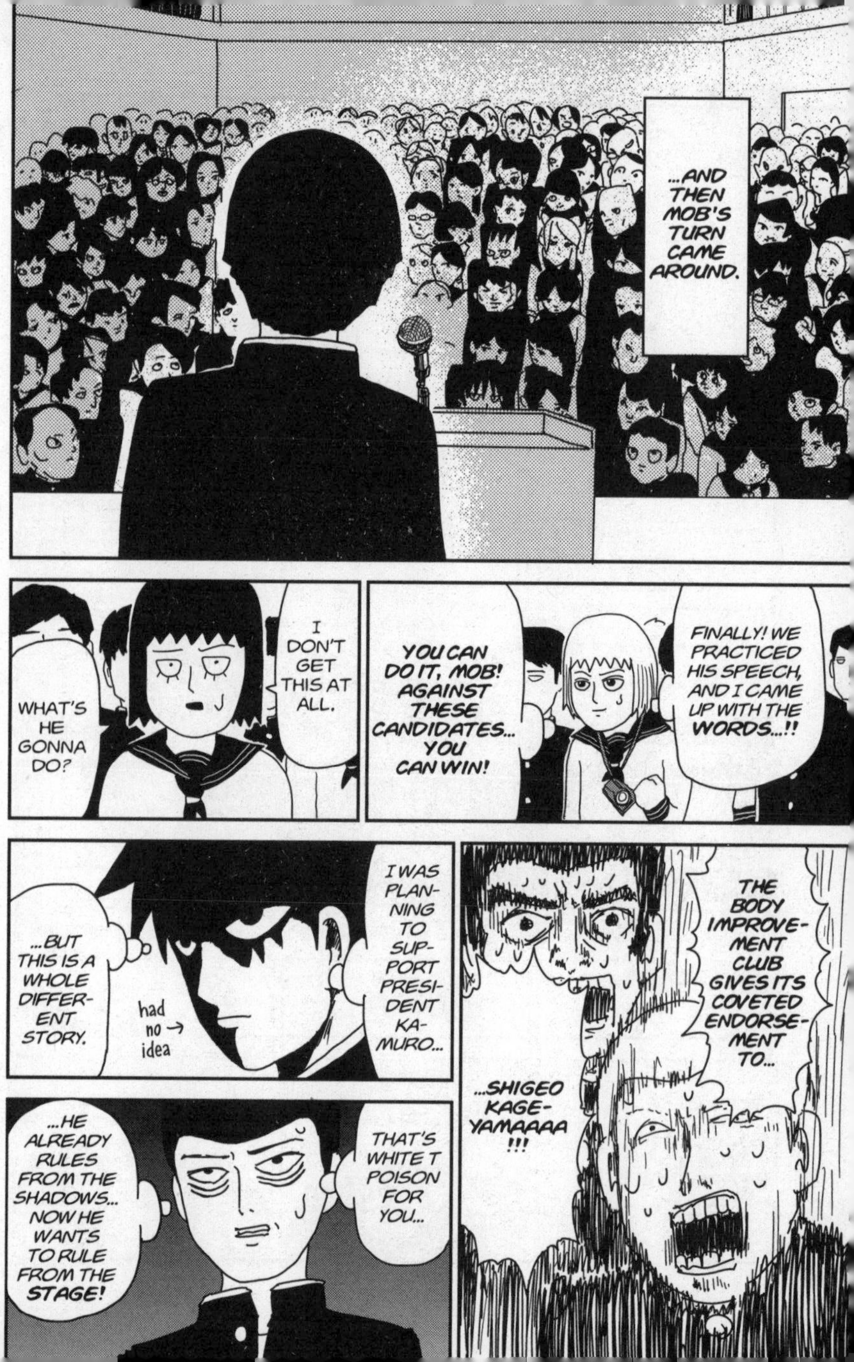
...AND THEN MOB'S TURN CAME AROUND.
FINALLY! WE PRACTICED HIS SPEECH, AND I CAME UP WITH THE WORDS...!!
YOU CAN DO IT, MOB! AGAINST THESE CANDIDATES... YOU CAN WIN!
I DON'T GET THIS AT ALL.
WHAT'S HE GONNA DO?
THE BODY IMPROVEMENT CLUB GIVES ITS COVETED ENDORSEMENT TO...
...SHIGEO KAGEYAMAAAA!!!
I WAS PLANNING TO SUPPORT PRESIDENT KAMURO...
...BUT THIS IS A WHOLE DIFFERENT STORY.
had no idea
THAT'S WHITE T POISON FOR YOU...
...HE ALREADY RULES FROM THE SHADOWS... NOW HE WANTS TO RULE FROM THE STAGE!

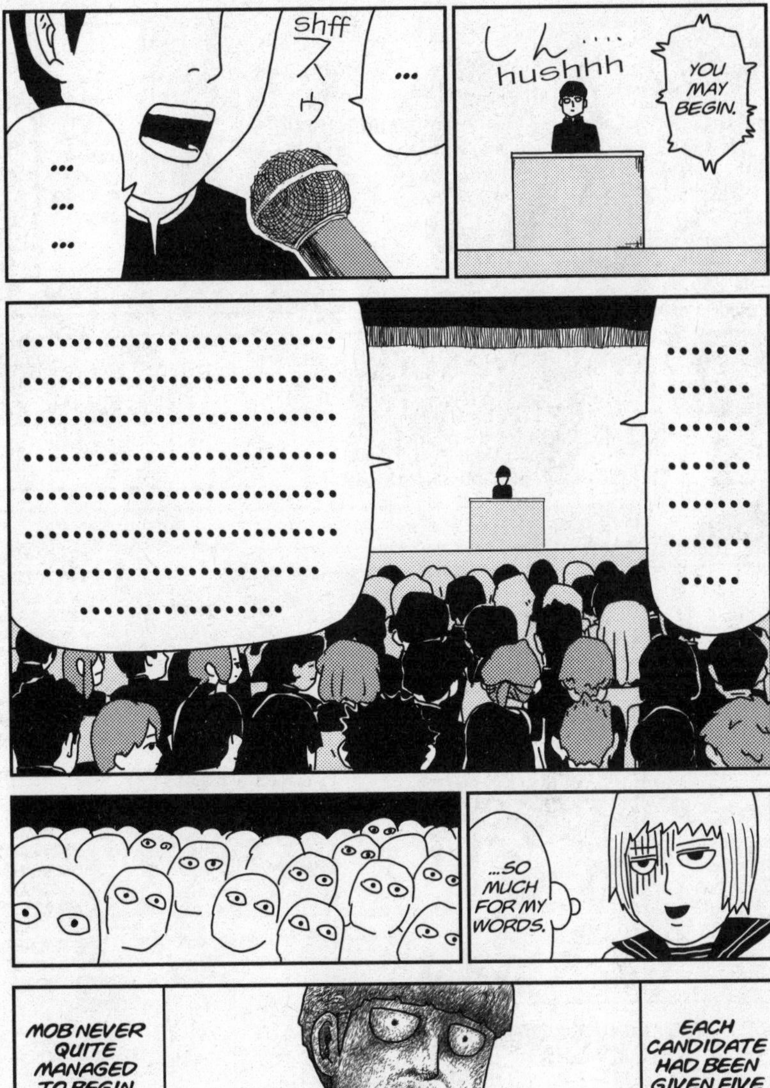
しん……
hushhh
YOU MAY BEGIN.
shff
スゥ
...
...
...
...
....
....
....
....
....
....
....
....
....
....
....
....
....
....
....
...SO MUCH FOR MY WORDS.
EACH CANDIDATE HAD BEEN GIVEN FIVE MINUTES FOR THEIR SPEECH.
MOB NEVER QUITE MANAGED TO BEGIN BEFORE HIS TIME RAN OUT.

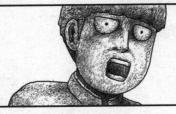

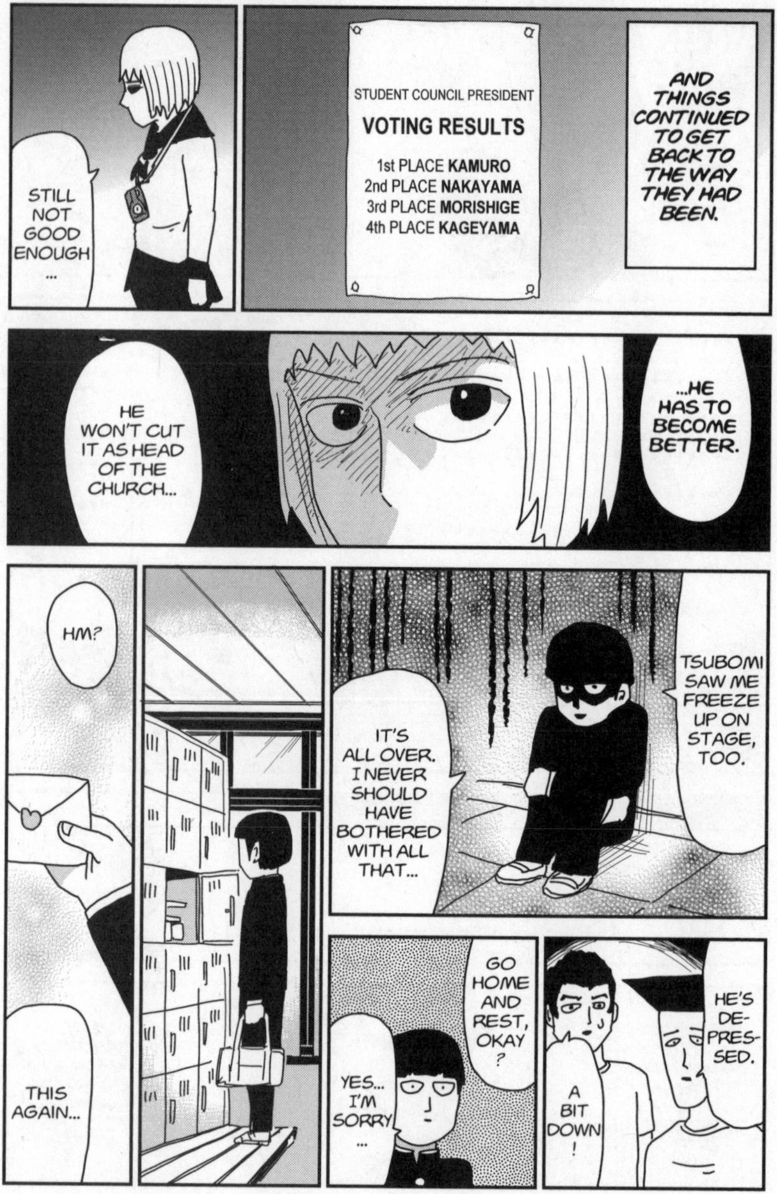
AND THINGS CONTINUED TO GET BACK TO THE WAY THEY HAD BEEN.
STUDENT COUNCIL PRESIDENT
VOTING RESULTS
1st PLACE KAMURO
2nd PLACE NAKAYAMA
3rd PLACE MORISHIGE
4th PLACE KAGEYAMA
STILL NOT GOOD ENOUGH...
...HE HAS TO BECOME BETTER.
HE WON'T CUT IT AS HEAD OF THE CHURCH...
TSUBOMI SAW ME FREEZE UP ON STAGE, TOO.
IT'S ALL OVER. I NEVER SHOULD HAVE BOTHERED WITH ALL THAT...
HE'S DE-PRES-SED.
A BIT DOWN!
GO HOME AND REST, OKAY?
YES... I'M SORRY...
HM?
THIS AGAIN...

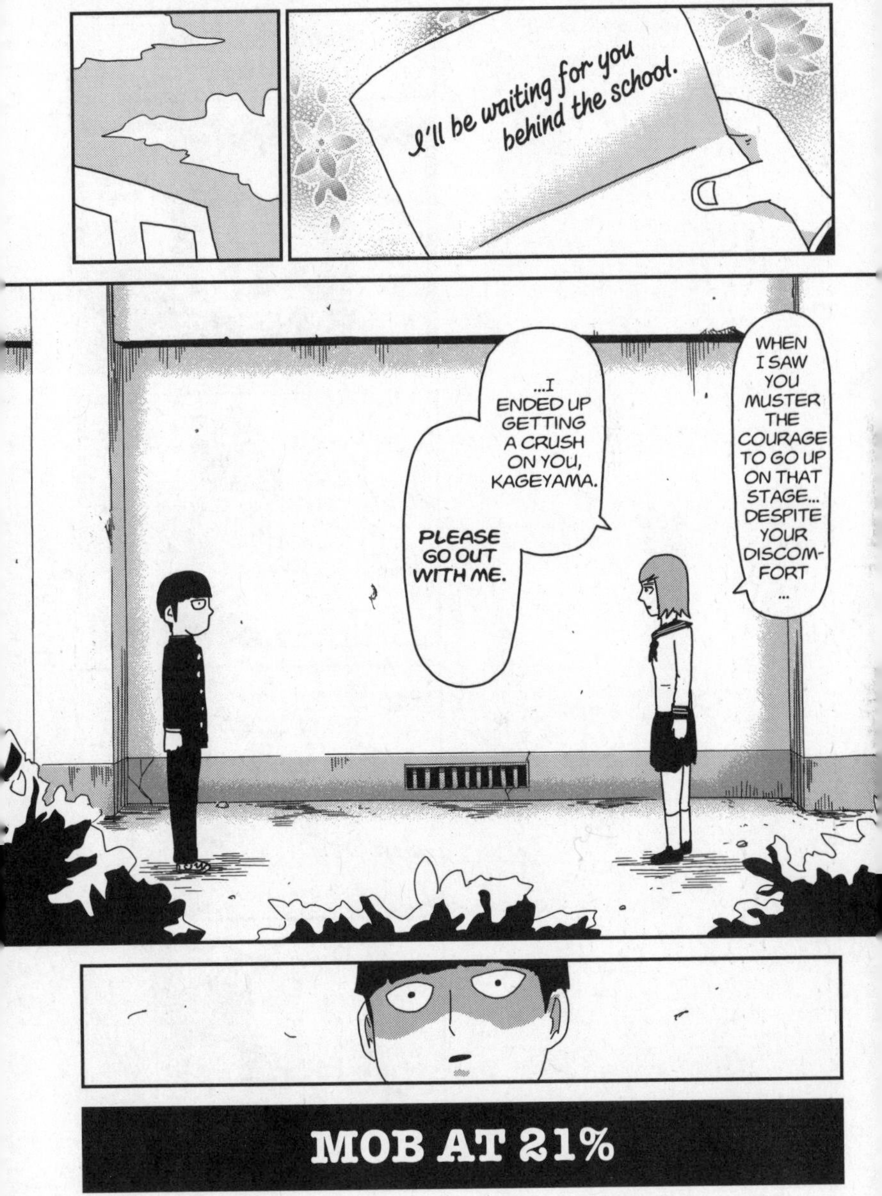
I'll be waiting for you behind the school.
WHEN I SAW YOU MUSTER THE COURAGE TO GO UP ON THAT STAGE... DESPITE YOUR DISCOMFORT...
...I ENDED UP GETTING A CRUSH ON YOU, KAGEYAMA.
PLEASE GO OUT WITH ME.
MOB AT 21%

Mob's Evil Spirit Observation Log

This is Dimple. He's moved in.

He can be classified as an evil spirit.

Apparently he normally gets energy by consuming the "spirit element" found all around us.

THERE'S DUST IN THE CORNER OF MY ROOM.

YEAH...

HERE YOU GO.

ス ッ swiff

HUH?

WHAT AM I, A ROOMBA...?

YOU CAN EAT IT.

KYMM

GRMM KYMM

CHAPTER 52: SHRED

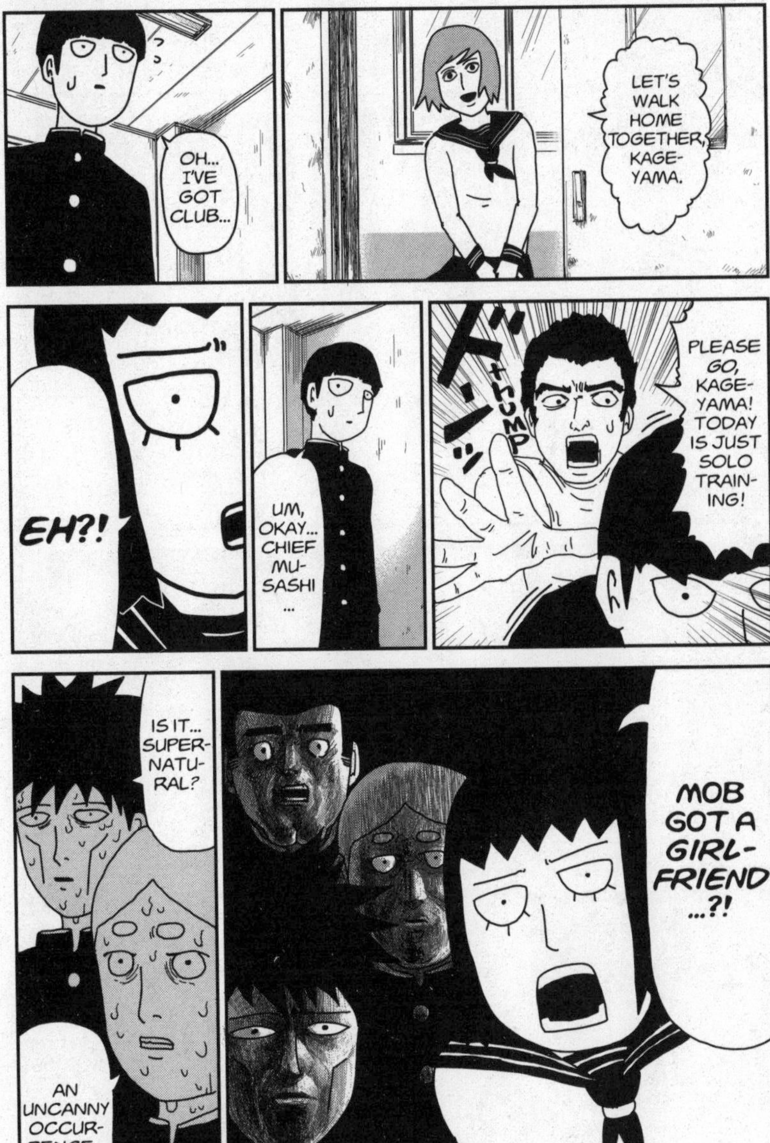

LET'S WALK HOME TOGETHER, KAGE-YAMA.
OH... I'VE GOT CLUB...
PLEASE GO, KAGE-YAMA! TODAY IS JUST SOLO TRAIN-ING!
THUMP
UM, OKAY... CHIEF MU-SASHI ...
EH?!
MOB GOT A GIRL-FRIEND ...?!
IS IT... SUPER-NATU-RAL?
AN UNCANNY OCCUR-RENCE...

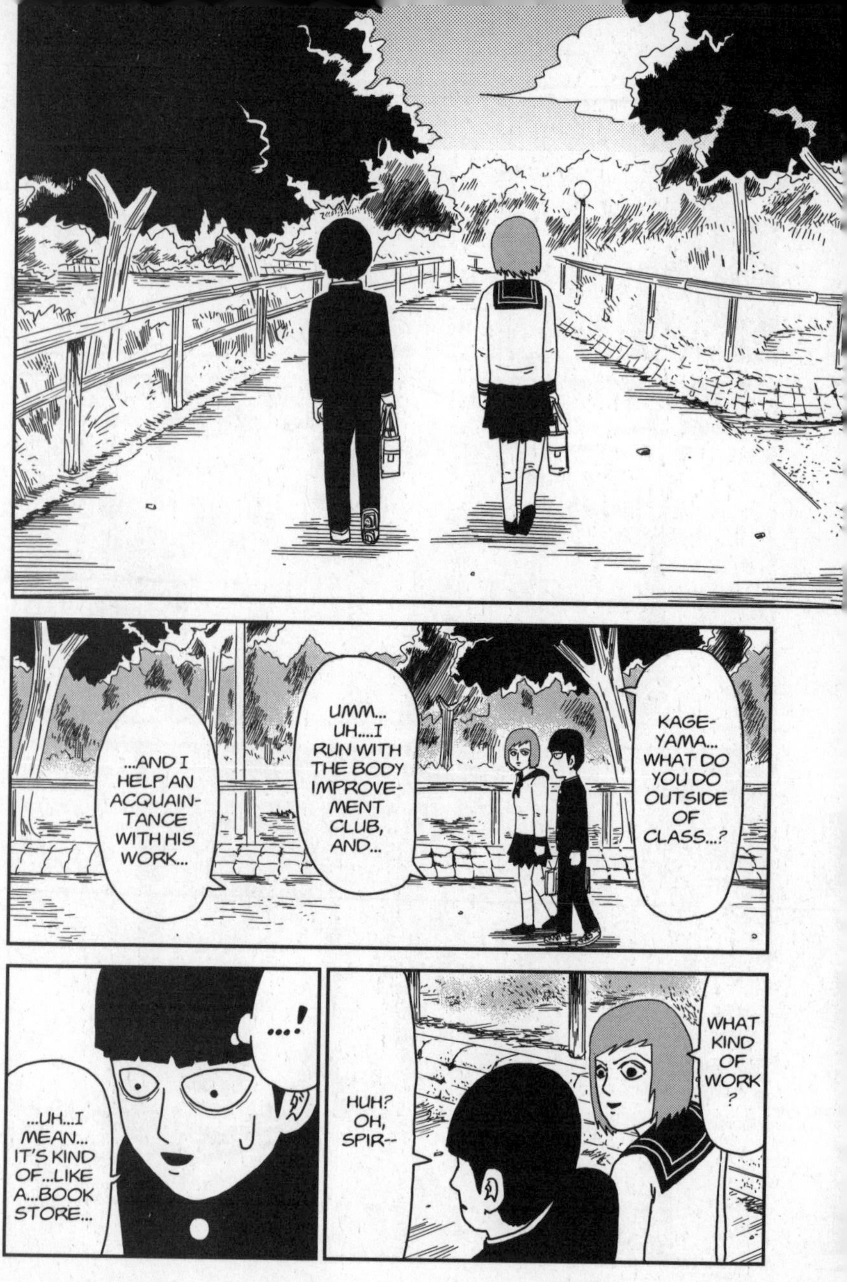
KAGE-YAMA... WHAT DO YOU DO OUTSIDE OF CLASS...?
UMM... UH....I RUN WITH THE BODY IMPROVEMENT CLUB, AND...
...AND I HELP AN ACQUAINTANCE WITH HIS WORK...
WHAT KIND OF WORK?
HUH? OH, SPIR--
...!
...UH...I MEAN... IT'S KIND OF...LIKE A...BOOK STORE...

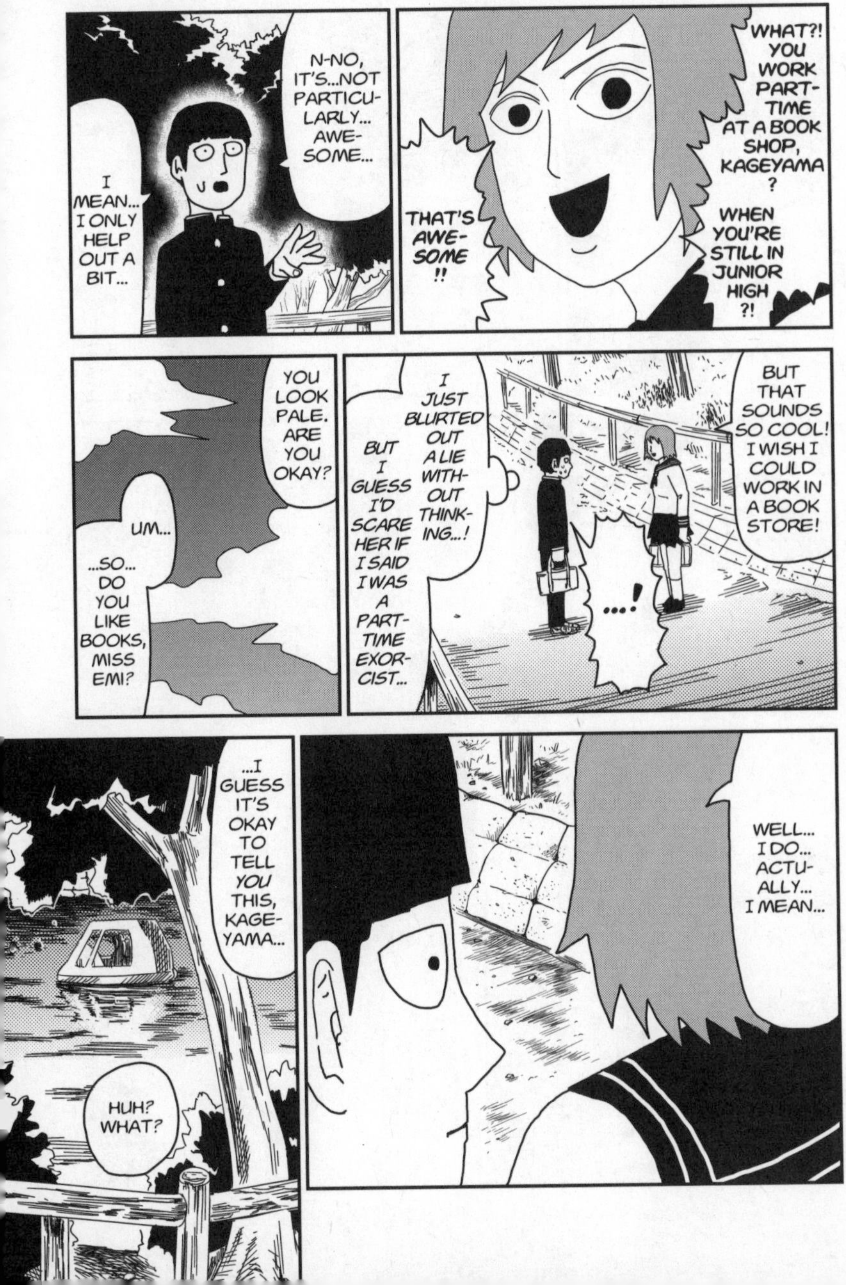
WHAT?! YOU WORK PART-TIME AT A BOOK SHOP, KAGEYAMA? WHEN YOU'RE STILL IN JUNIOR HIGH?!
THAT'S AWESOME!!
N-NO, IT'S...NOT PARTICU-LARLY... AWE-SOME...
I MEAN... I ONLY HELP OUT A BIT...
BUT THAT SOUNDS SO COOL! I WISH I COULD WORK IN A BOOK STORE!
...!
I JUST BLURTED OUT A LIE WITH-OUT THINK-ING...!
BUT I GUESS I'D SCARE HER IF I SAID I WAS A PART-TIME EXOR-CIST...
YOU LOOK PALE. ARE YOU OKAY?
UM...
...SO... DO YOU LIKE BOOKS, MISS EMI?
WELL... I DO... ACTU-ALLY... I MEAN...
...I GUESS IT'S OKAY TO TELL YOU THIS, KAGE-YAMA...
HUH? WHAT?

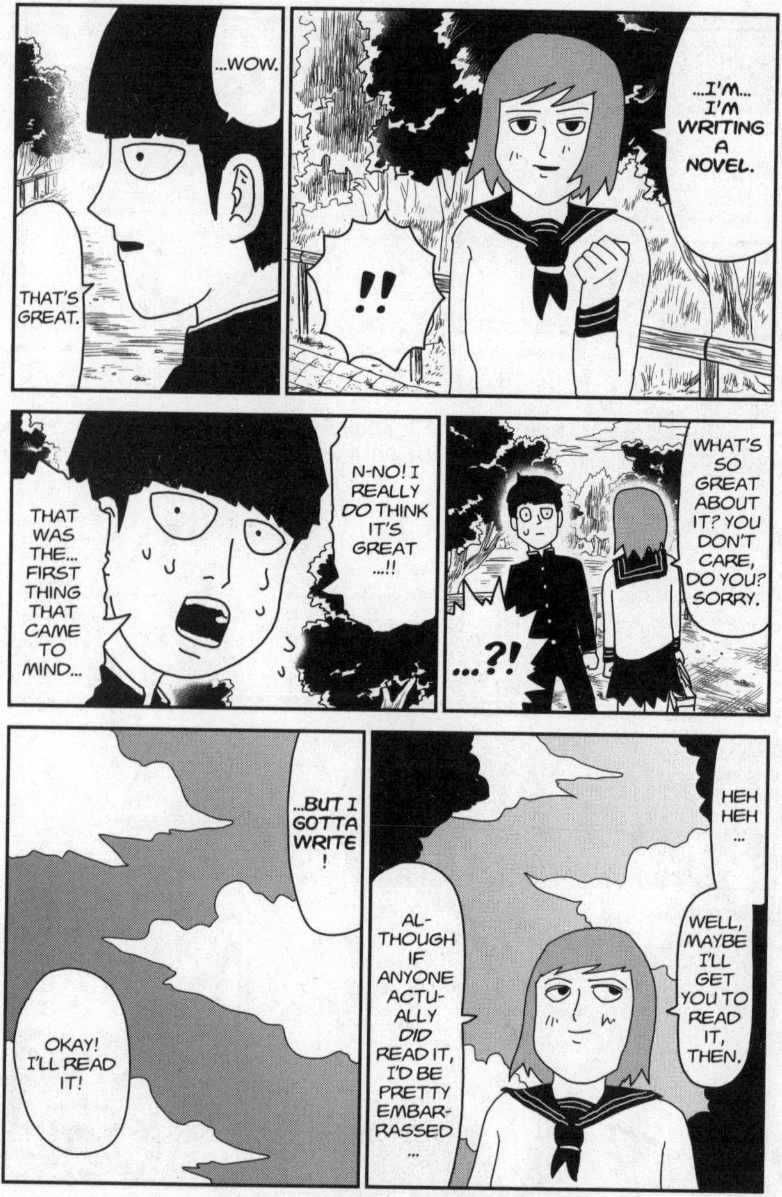
...I'M... I'M WRITING A NOVEL.
!!
...WOW.
THAT'S GREAT.
WHAT'S SO GREAT ABOUT IT? YOU DON'T CARE, DO YOU? SORRY.
...?!
N-NO! I REALLY DO THINK IT'S GREAT ...!!
THAT WAS THE... FIRST THING THAT CAME TO MIND...
HEH HEH ...
WELL, MAYBE I'LL GET YOU TO READ IT, THEN.
ALTHOUGH IF ANYONE ACTUALLY DID READ IT, I'D BE PRETTY EMBARRASSED ...
...BUT I GOTTA WRITE!
OKAY! I'LL READ IT!

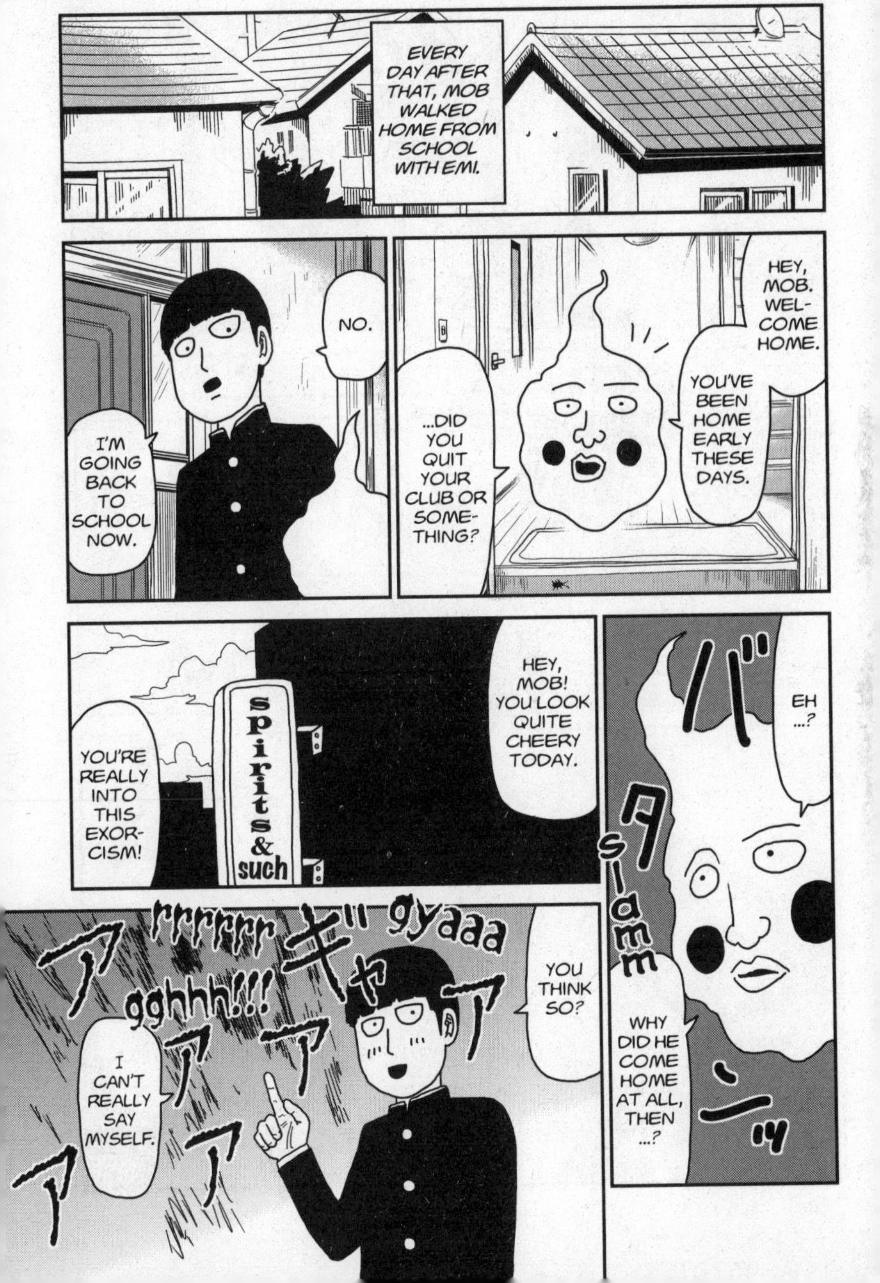
EVERY DAY AFTER THAT, MOB WALKED HOME FROM SCHOOL WITH EMI.
HEY, MOB. WEL-COME HOME.
YOU'VE BEEN HOME EARLY THESE DAYS.
...DID YOU QUIT YOUR CLUB OR SOME-THING?
NO.
I'M GOING BACK TO SCHOOL NOW.
EH ...?
slamm
WHY DID HE COME HOME AT ALL, THEN ...?
HEY, MOB! YOU LOOK QUITE CHEERY TODAY.
spirits & such
YOU'RE REALLY INTO THIS EXORCISM!
YOU THINK SO?
gyaaa rrrrrrr gghhh!!!
I CAN'T REALLY SAY MYSELF.

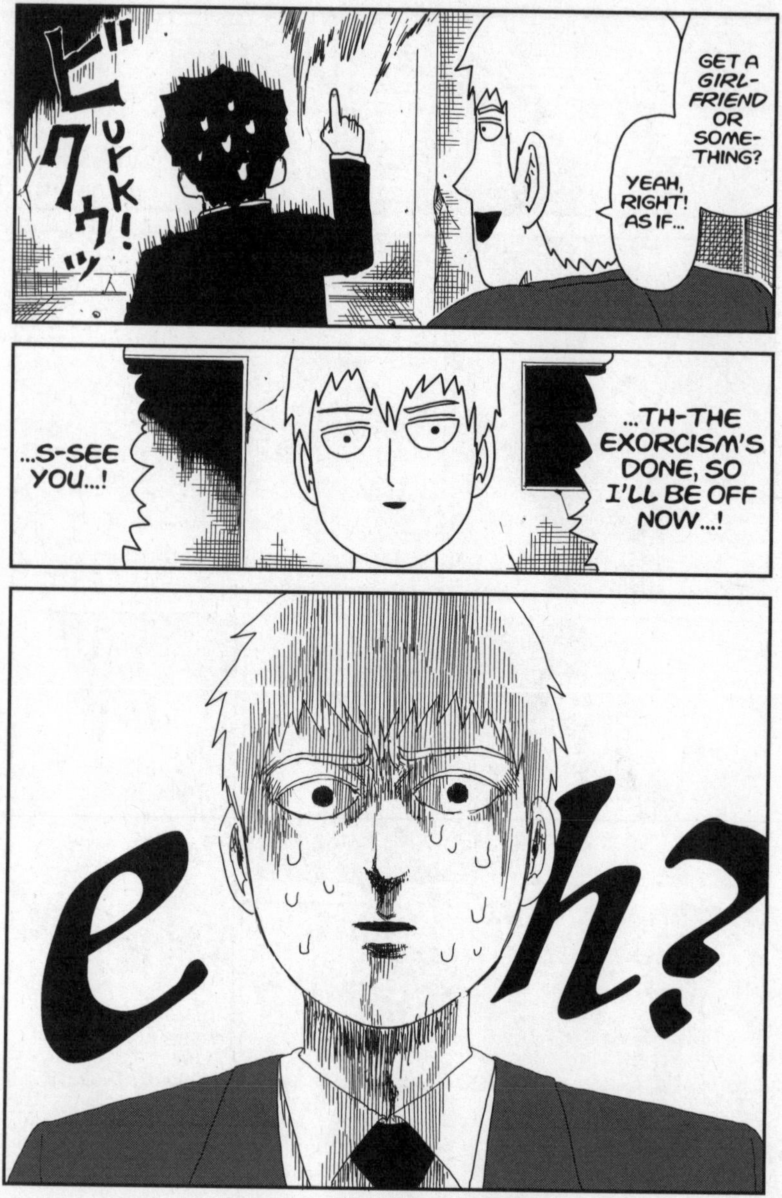
GET A GIRL-FRIEND OR SOME-THING?
YEAH, RIGHT! AS IF...
ビクウッ
URK!
...TH-THE EXORCISM'S DONE, SO I'LL BE OFF NOW...!
...S-SEE YOU...!
eh?

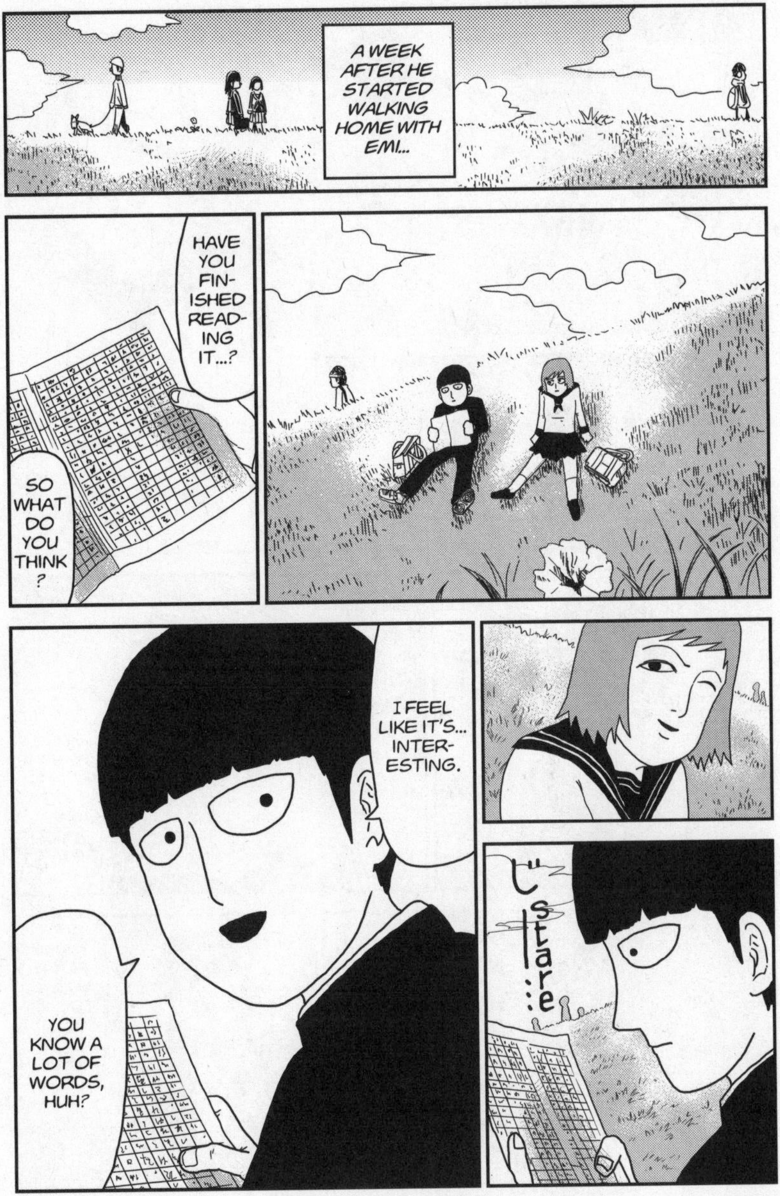
A WEEK AFTER HE STARTED WALKING HOME WITH EMI...
HAVE YOU FIN-ISHED READ-ING IT...?
SO WHAT DO YOU THINK?
じ stare...
I FEEL LIKE IT'S... INTER-ESTING.
YOU KNOW A LOT OF WORDS, HUH?

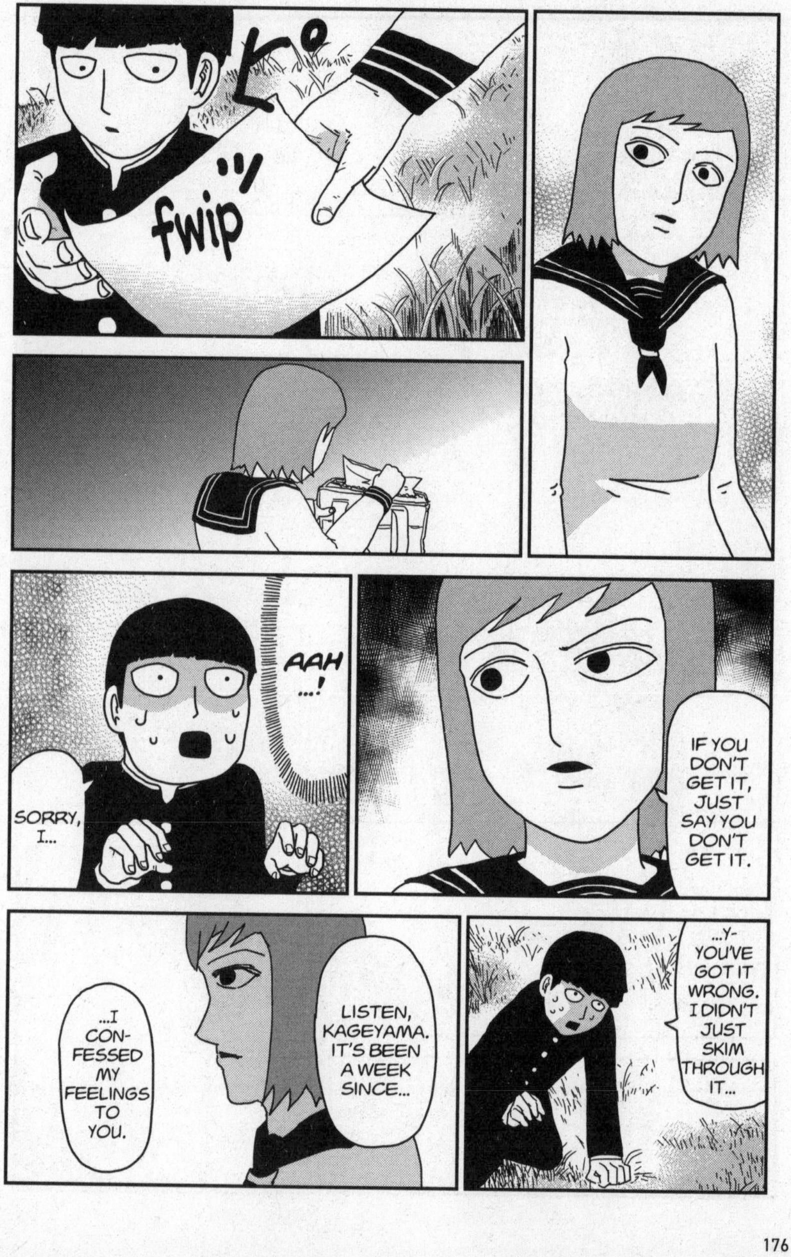
fwip
IF YOU DON'T GET IT, JUST SAY YOU DON'T GET IT.
AAH ...!
SORRY, I...
...Y- YOU'VE GOT IT WRONG. I DIDN'T JUST SKIM THROUGH IT...
LISTEN, KAGEYAMA. IT'S BEEN A WEEK SINCE...
...I CON-FESSED MY FEELINGS TO YOU.

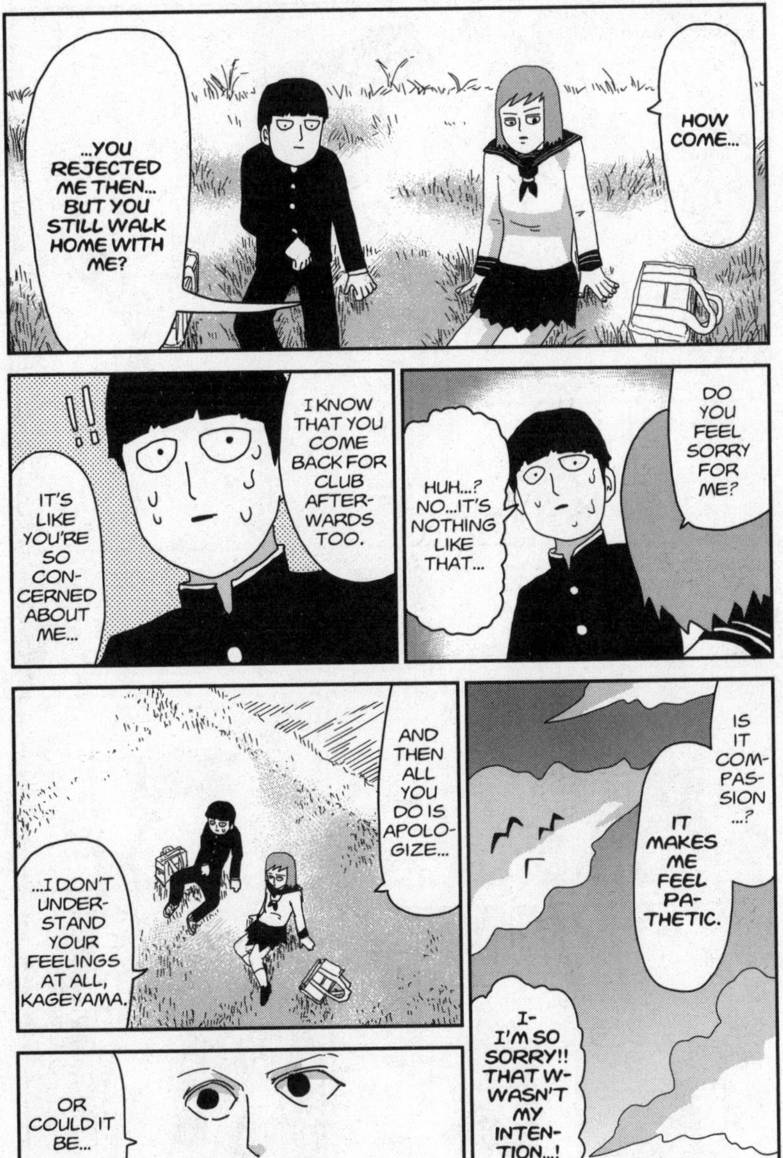
HOW COME...
...YOU REJECTED ME THEN... BUT YOU STILL WALK HOME WITH ME?
DO YOU FEEL SORRY FOR ME?
HUH...? NO...IT'S NOTHING LIKE THAT...
I KNOW THAT YOU COME BACK FOR CLUB AFTERWARDS TOO.
!!
IT'S LIKE YOU'RE SO CONCERNED ABOUT ME...
IS IT COMPASSION...?
IT MAKES ME FEEL PATHETIC.
I- I'M SO SORRY!! THAT W-WASN'T MY INTENTION...!
AND THEN ALL YOU DO IS APOLOGIZE...
...I DON'T UNDERSTAND YOUR FEELINGS AT ALL, KAGEYAMA.
OR COULD IT BE...

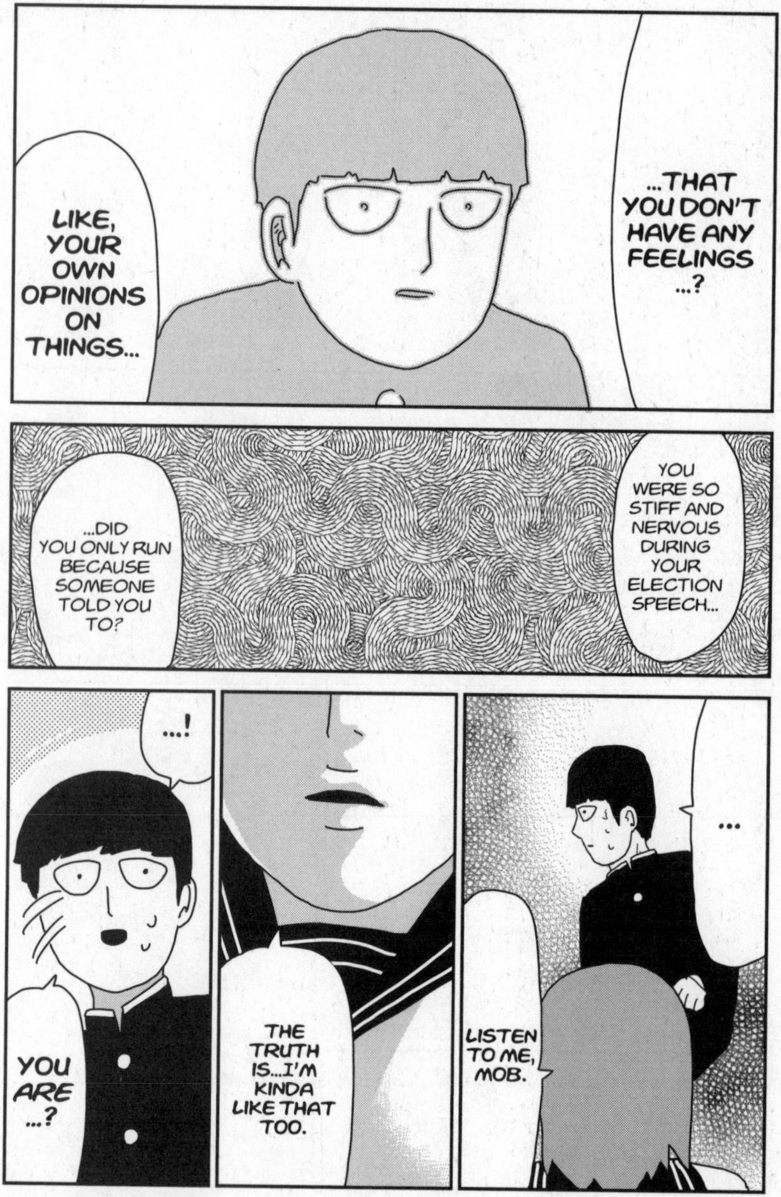
...THAT YOU DON'T HAVE ANY FEELINGS ...?
LIKE, YOUR OWN OPINIONS ON THINGS...
YOU WERE SO STIFF AND NERVOUS DURING YOUR ELECTION SPEECH...
...DID YOU ONLY RUN BECAUSE SOMEONE TOLD YOU TO?
...
LISTEN TO ME, MOB.
THE TRUTH IS...I'M KINDA LIKE THAT TOO.
...!
YOU ARE ...?

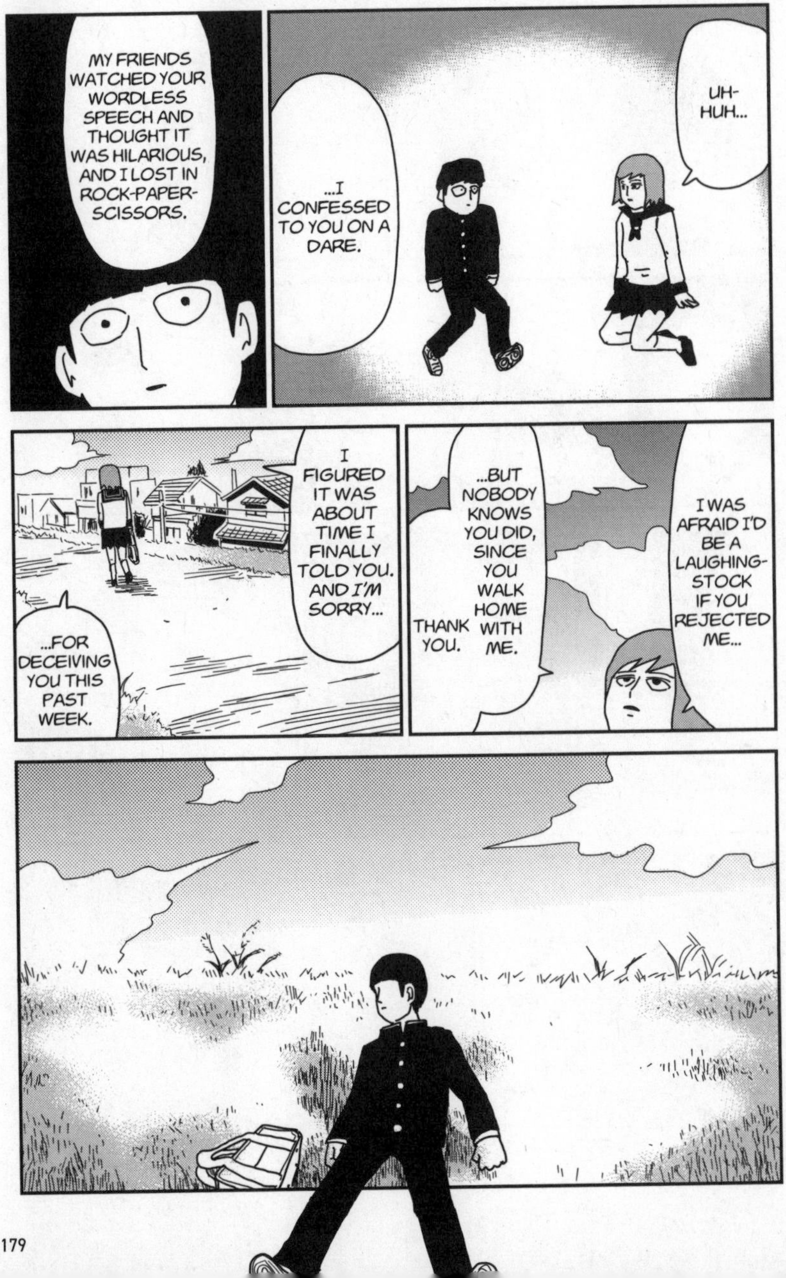
UH-HUH...
...I CONFESSED TO YOU ON A DARE.
MY FRIENDS WATCHED YOUR WORDLESS SPEECH AND THOUGHT IT WAS HILARIOUS, AND I LOST IN ROCK-PAPER-SCISSORS.
I WAS AFRAID I'D BE A LAUGHING-STOCK IF YOU REJECTED ME...
...BUT NOBODY KNOWS YOU DID, SINCE YOU WALK HOME WITH ME.
THANK YOU.
I FIGURED IT WAS ABOUT TIME I FINALLY TOLD YOU. AND *I'M* SORRY...
...FOR DECEIVING YOU THIS PAST WEEK.

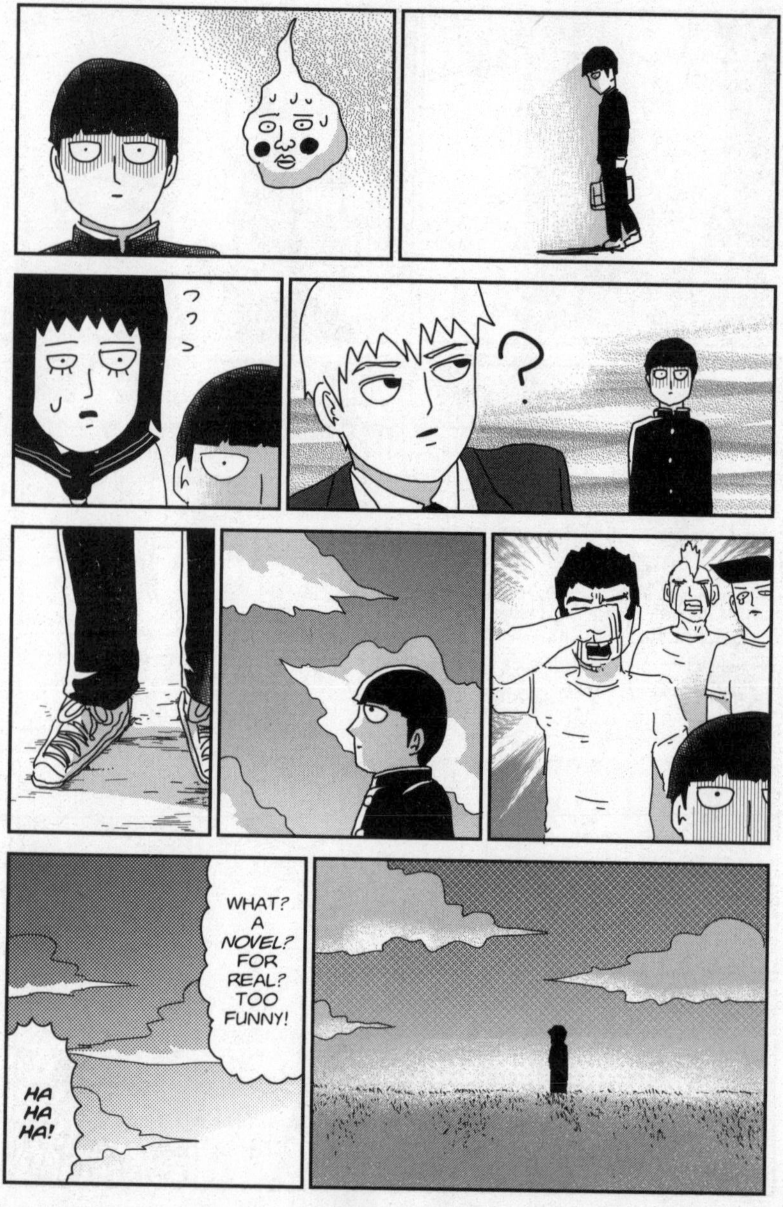
?
WHAT? A NOVEL? FOR REAL? TOO FUNNY!
HA HA HA!

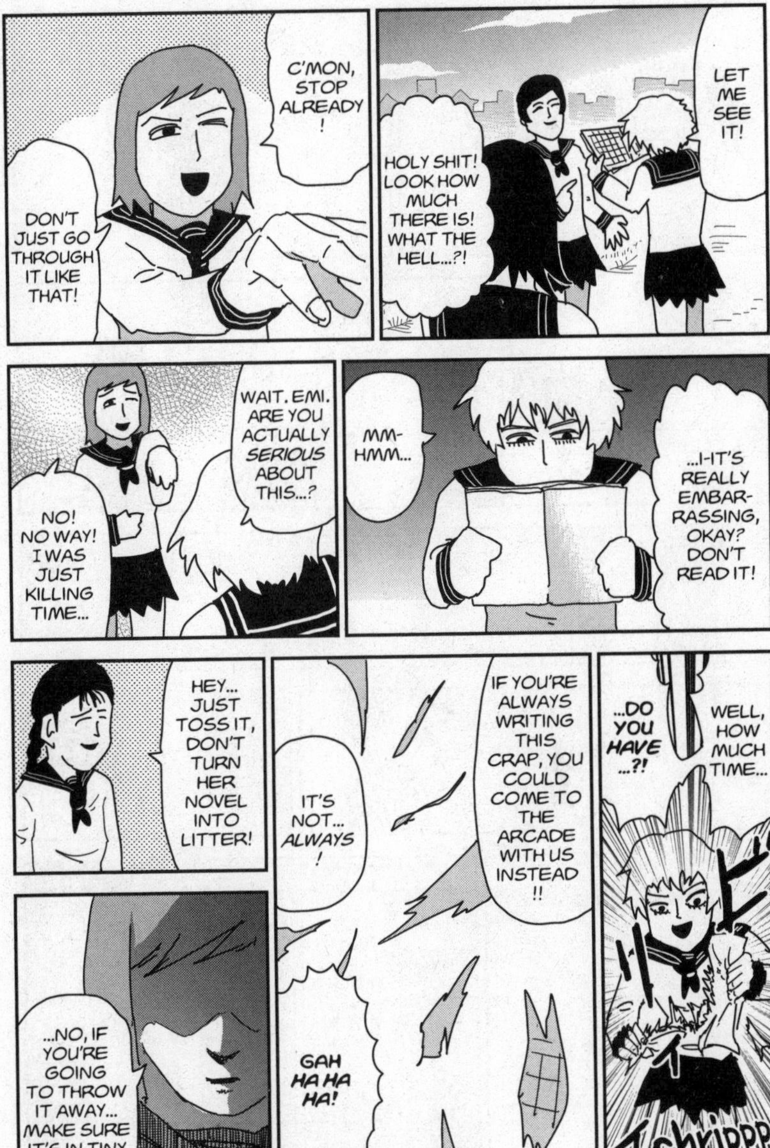
LET ME SEE IT!
HOLY SHIT! LOOK HOW MUCH THERE IS! WHAT THE HELL...?!
C'MON, STOP ALREADY!
DON'T JUST GO THROUGH IT LIKE THAT!
...I-IT'S REALLY EMBAR-RASSING, OKAY? DON'T READ IT!
MM-HMM...
WAIT. EMI. ARE YOU ACTUALLY *SERIOUS* ABOUT THIS...?
NO! NO WAY! I WAS JUST KILLING TIME...
WELL, HOW MUCH TIME...
...DO YOU *HAVE*...?!
Tshrippp
IF YOU'RE ALWAYS WRITING THIS CRAP, YOU COULD COME TO THE ARCADE WITH US INSTEAD!!
IT'S NOT... *ALWAYS*!
GAH HA HA HA!
HEY... JUST TOSS IT, DON'T TURN HER NOVEL INTO LITTER!
...NO, IF YOU'RE GOING TO THROW IT AWAY... MAKE SURE IT'S IN TINY PIECES...

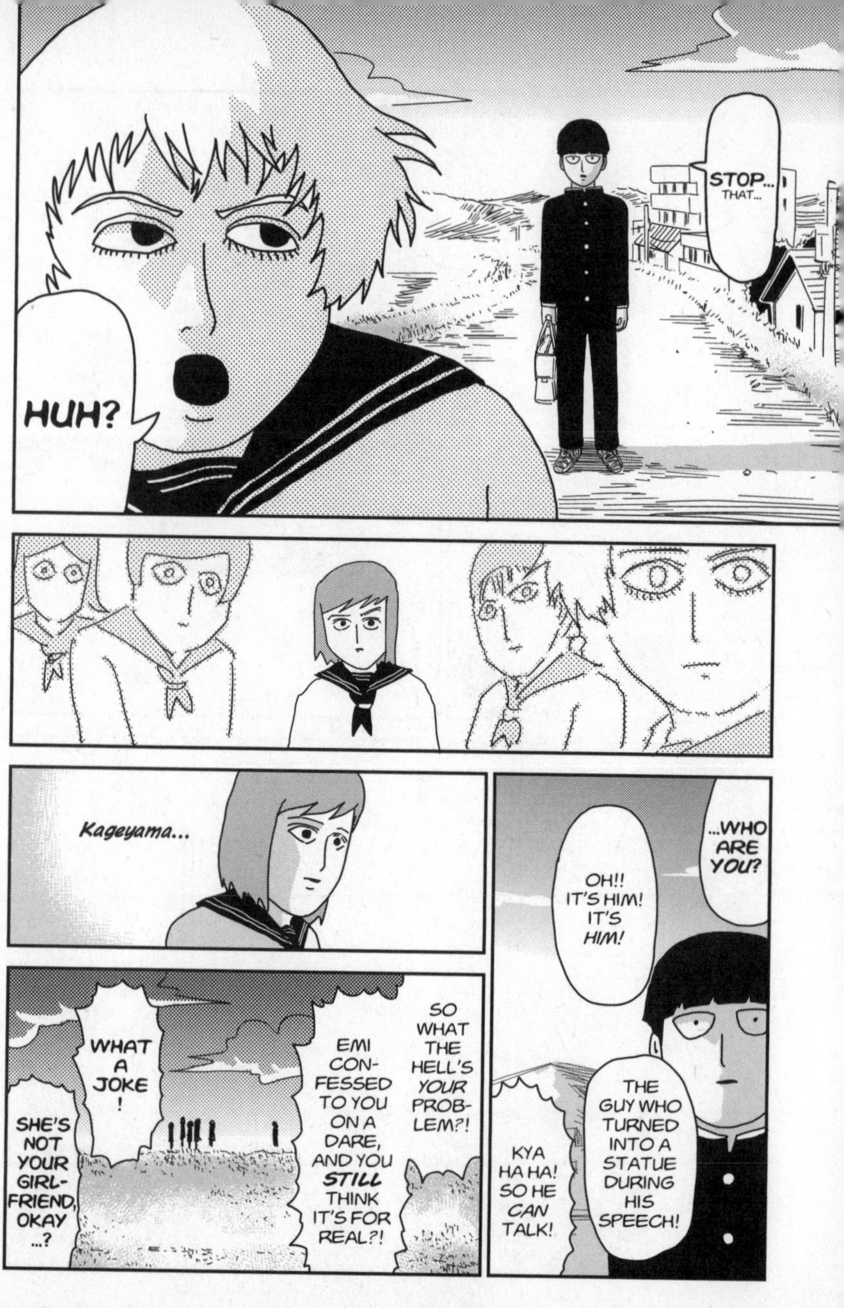
STOP... THAT...
HUH?
...WHO ARE YOU?
OH!! IT'S HIM! IT'S HIM!
THE GUY WHO TURNED INTO A STATUE DURING HIS SPEECH!
KYA HA HA! SO HE CAN TALK!
Kageyama...
SO WHAT THE HELL'S YOUR PROBLEM?!
EMI CONFESSED TO YOU ON A DARE, AND YOU STILL THINK IT'S FOR REAL?!
WHAT A JOKE!
SHE'S NOT YOUR GIRLFRIEND, OKAY...?

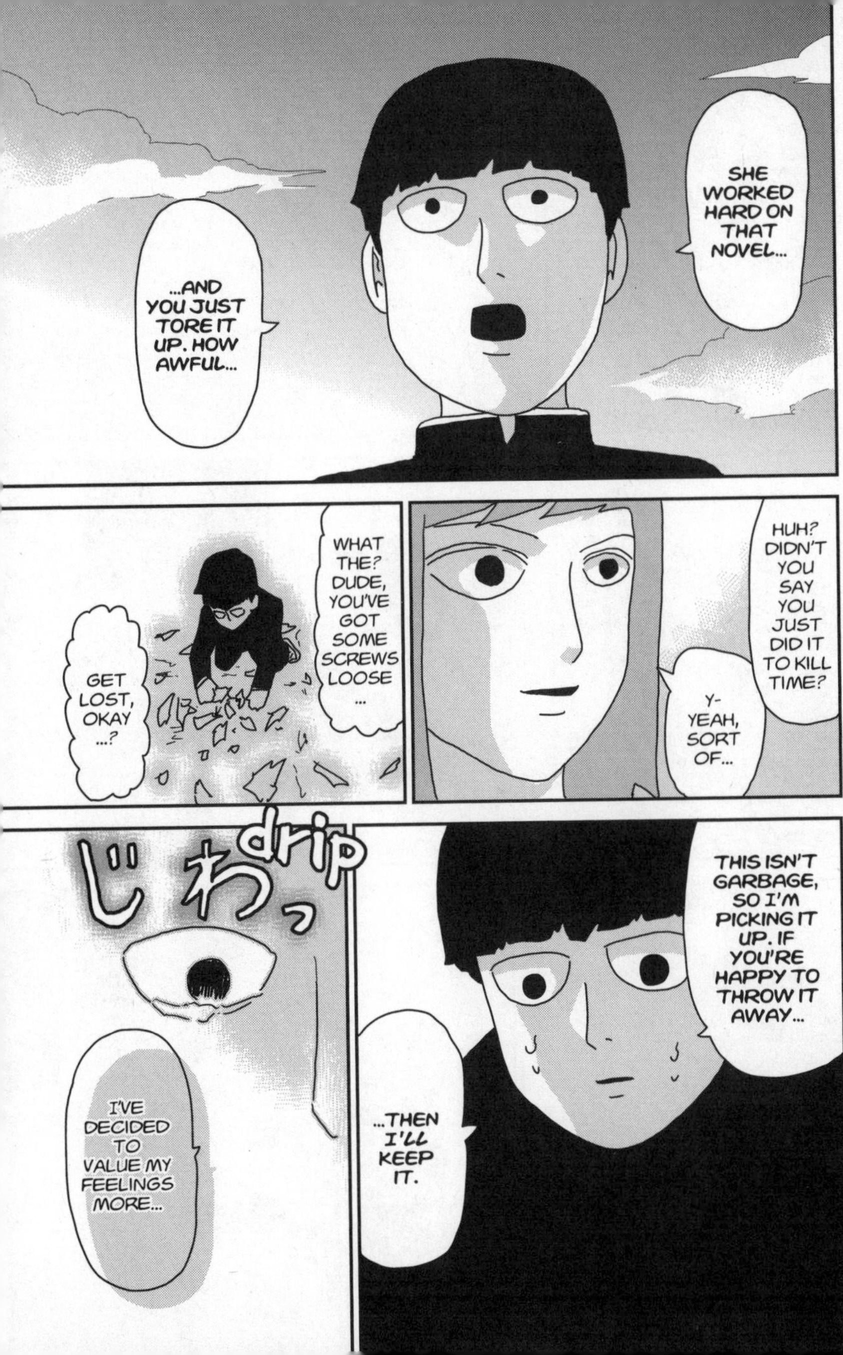
SHE WORKED HARD ON THAT NOVEL...
...AND YOU JUST TORE IT UP. HOW AWFUL...
HUH? DIDN'T YOU SAY YOU JUST DID IT TO KILL TIME?
Y-YEAH, SORT OF...
WHAT THE? DUDE, YOU'VE GOT SOME SCREWS LOOSE...
GET LOST, OKAY...?
THIS ISN'T GARBAGE, SO I'M PICKING IT UP. IF YOU'RE HAPPY TO THROW IT AWAY...
...THEN I'LL KEEP IT.
じわっ
drip
I'VE DECIDED TO VALUE MY FEELINGS MORE...

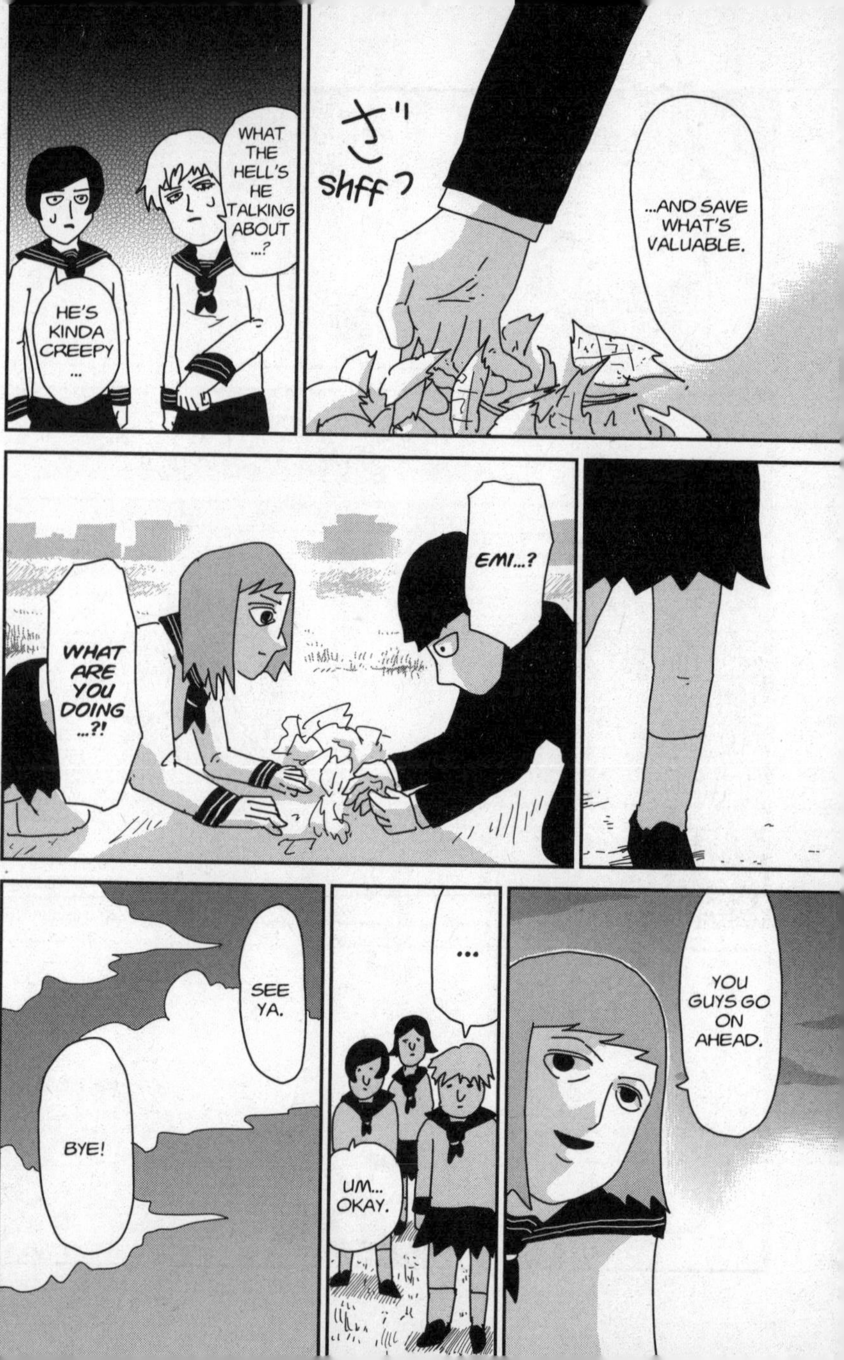
...AND SAVE WHAT'S VALUABLE.
ざっ
shff
WHAT THE HELL'S HE TALKING ABOUT...?
HE'S KINDA CREEPY...
EMI...?
WHAT ARE YOU DOING...?!
YOU GUYS GO ON AHEAD.
...
UM... OKAY.
SEE YA.
BYE!

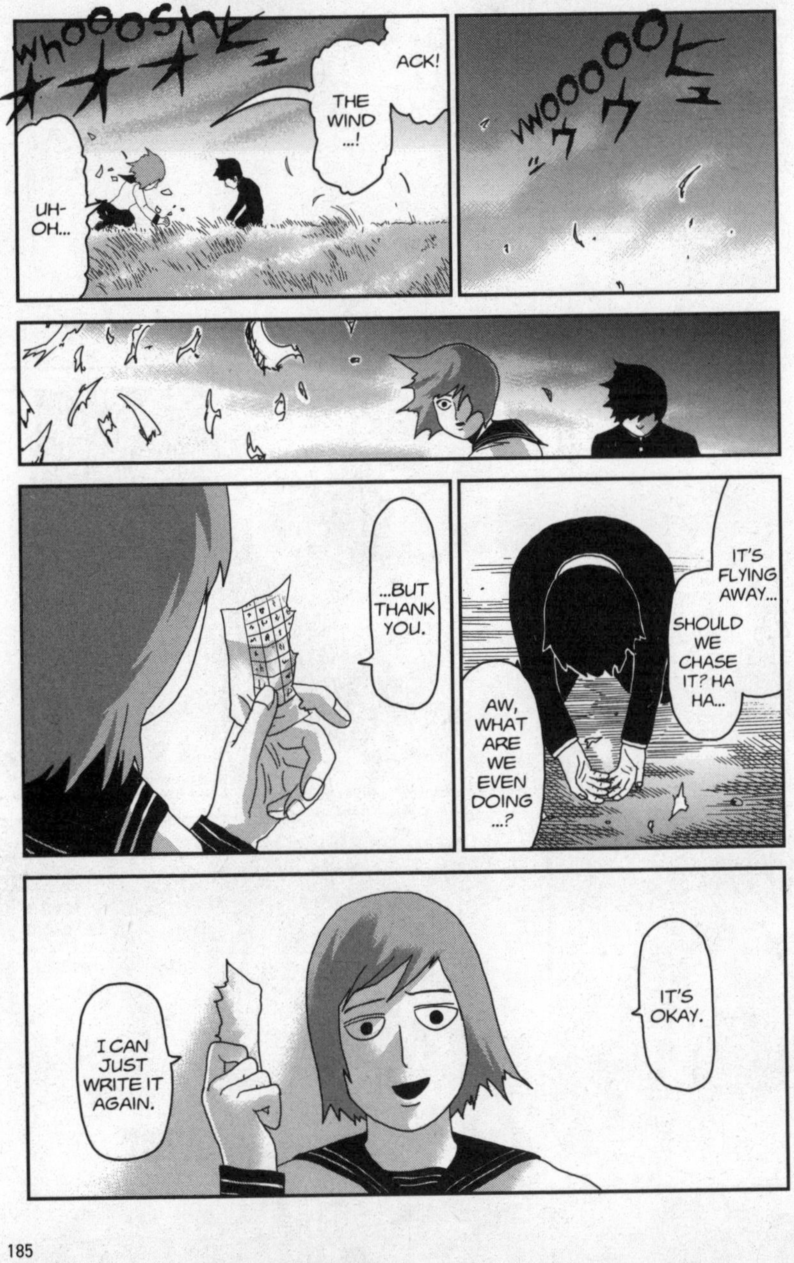
VWOOOOO
WHOOOSH
ACK!
THE WIND ...!
UH-OH...
IT'S FLYING AWAY...
SHOULD WE CHASE IT? HA HA...
AW, WHAT ARE WE EVEN DOING ...?
...BUT THANK YOU.
IT'S OKAY.
I CAN JUST WRITE IT AGAIN.

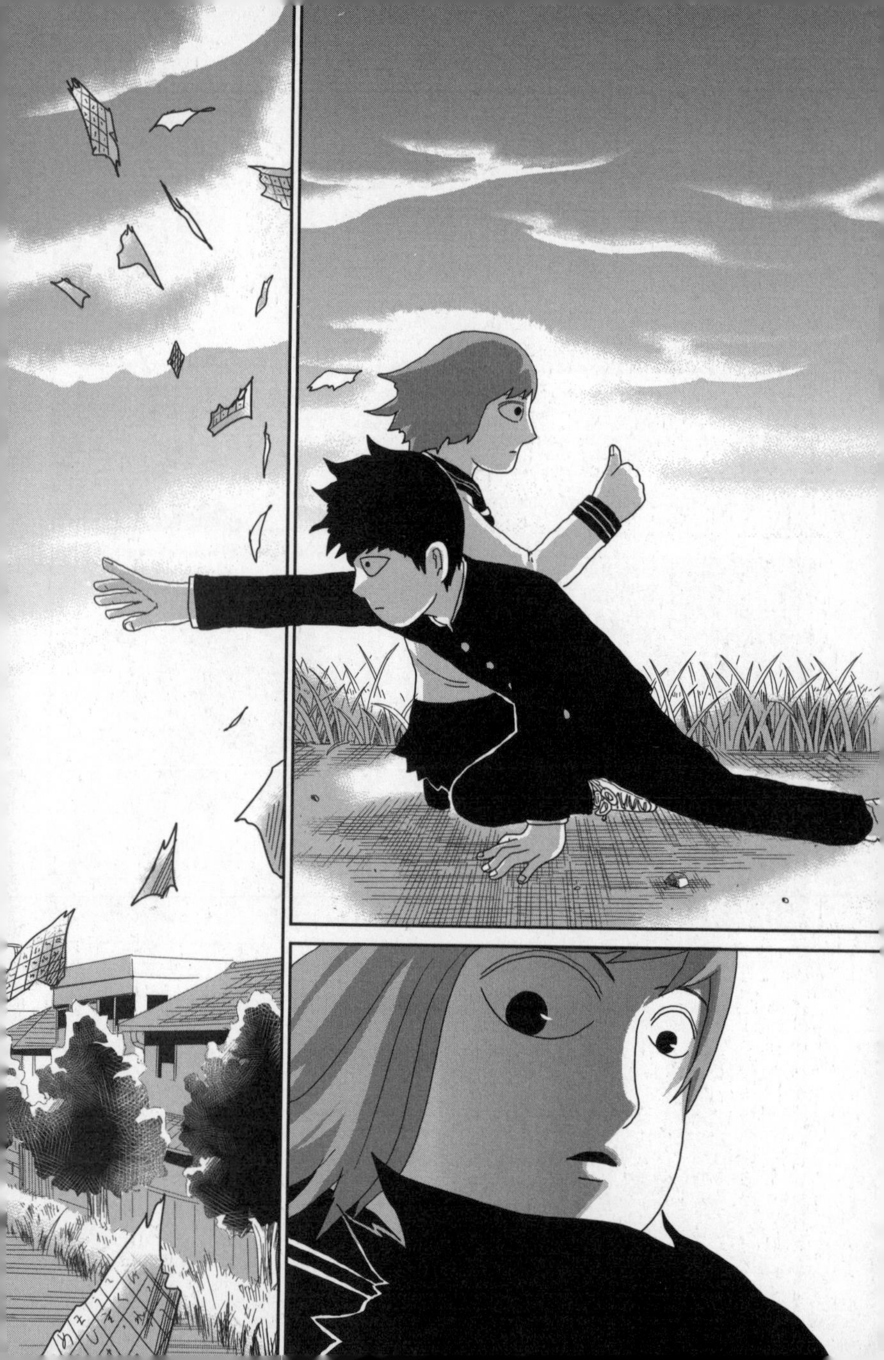

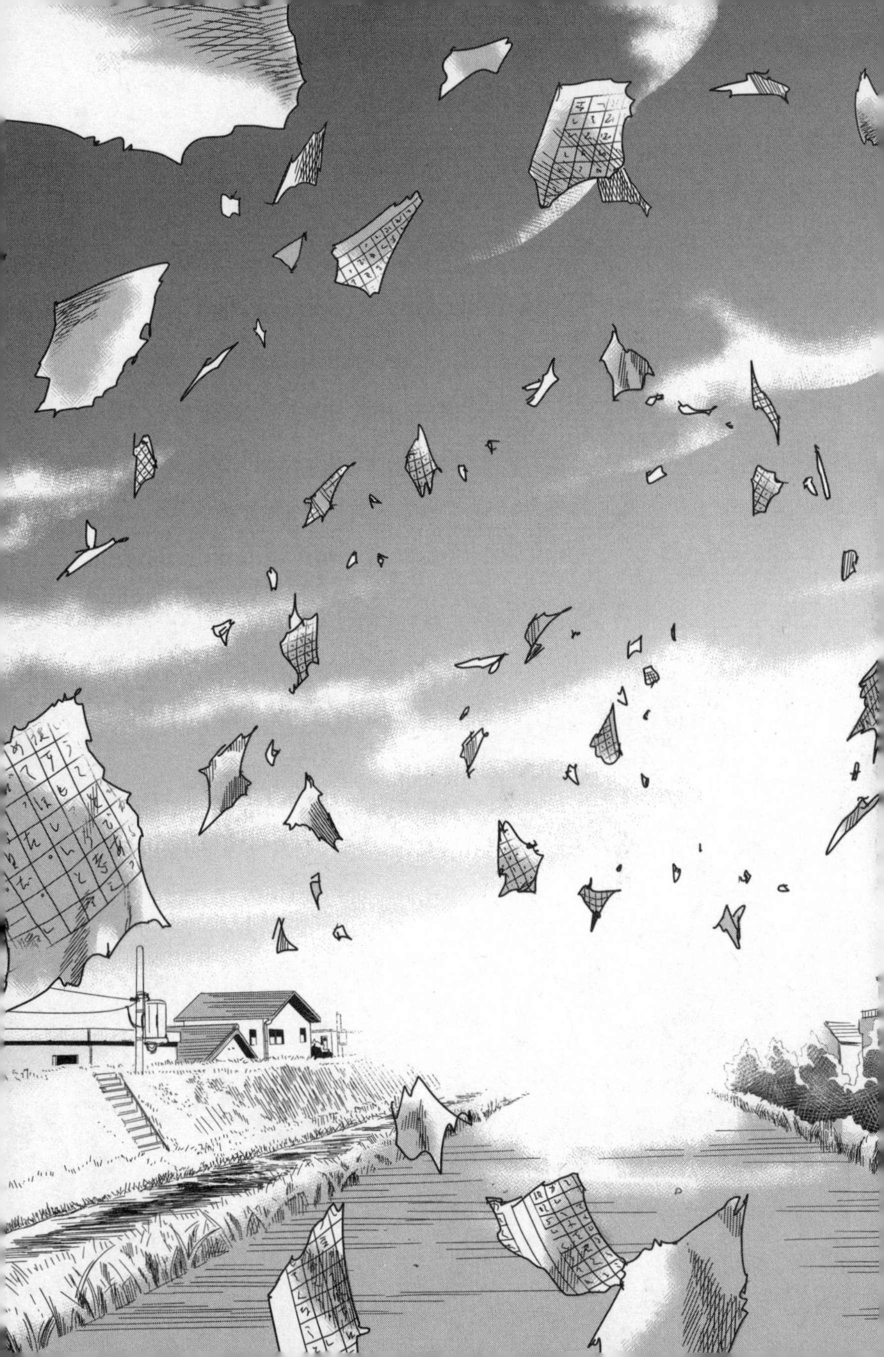

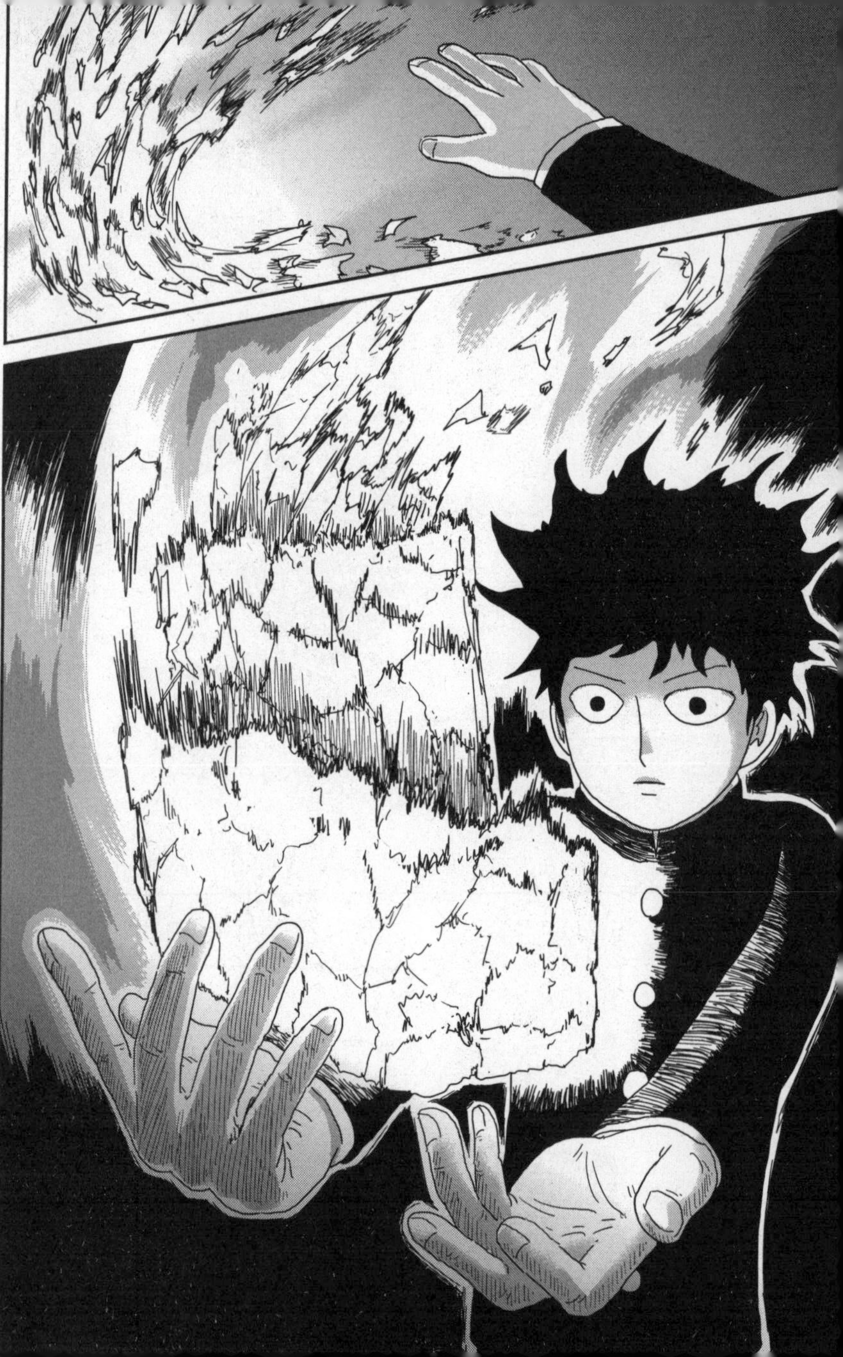

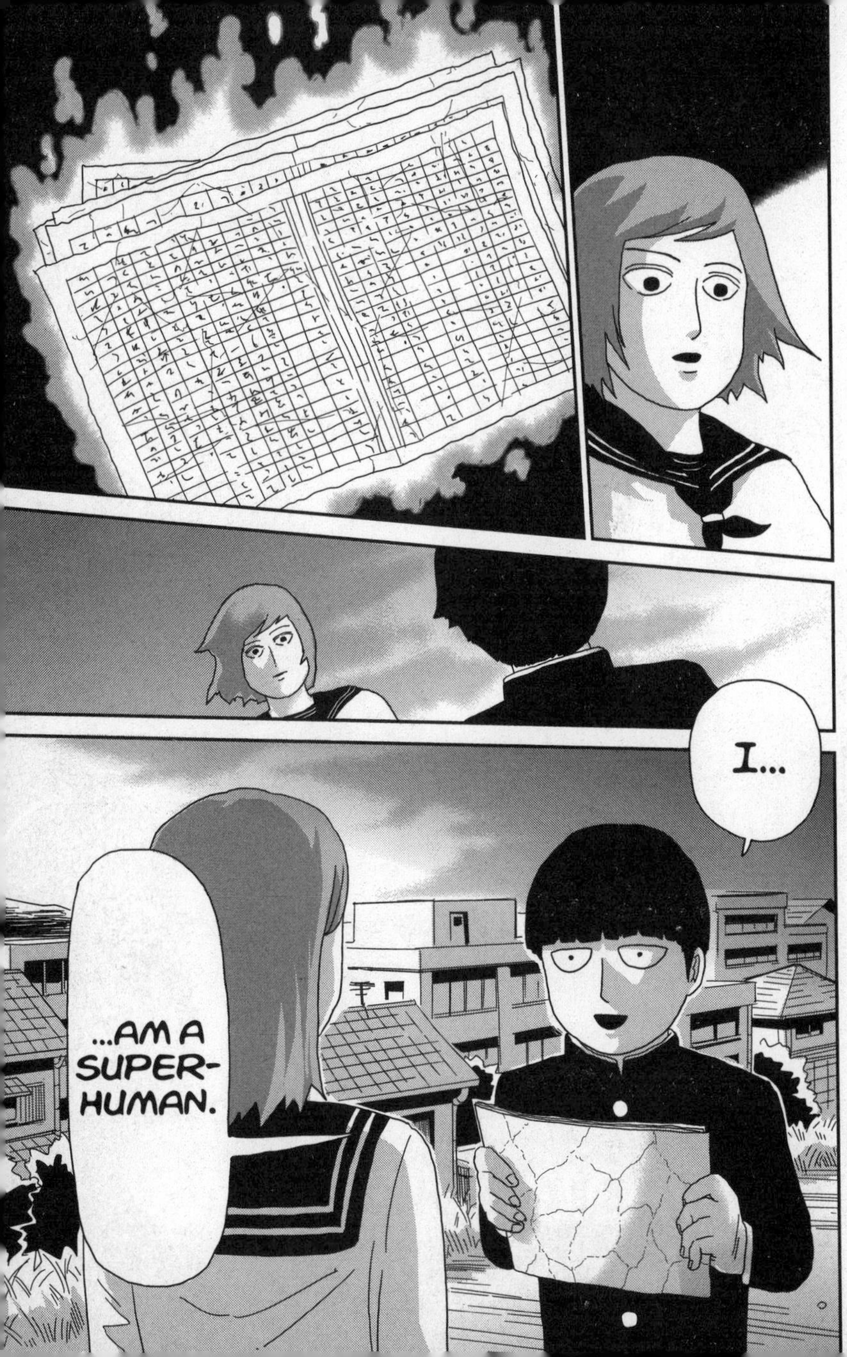
I...
...AM A SUPER-HUMAN.

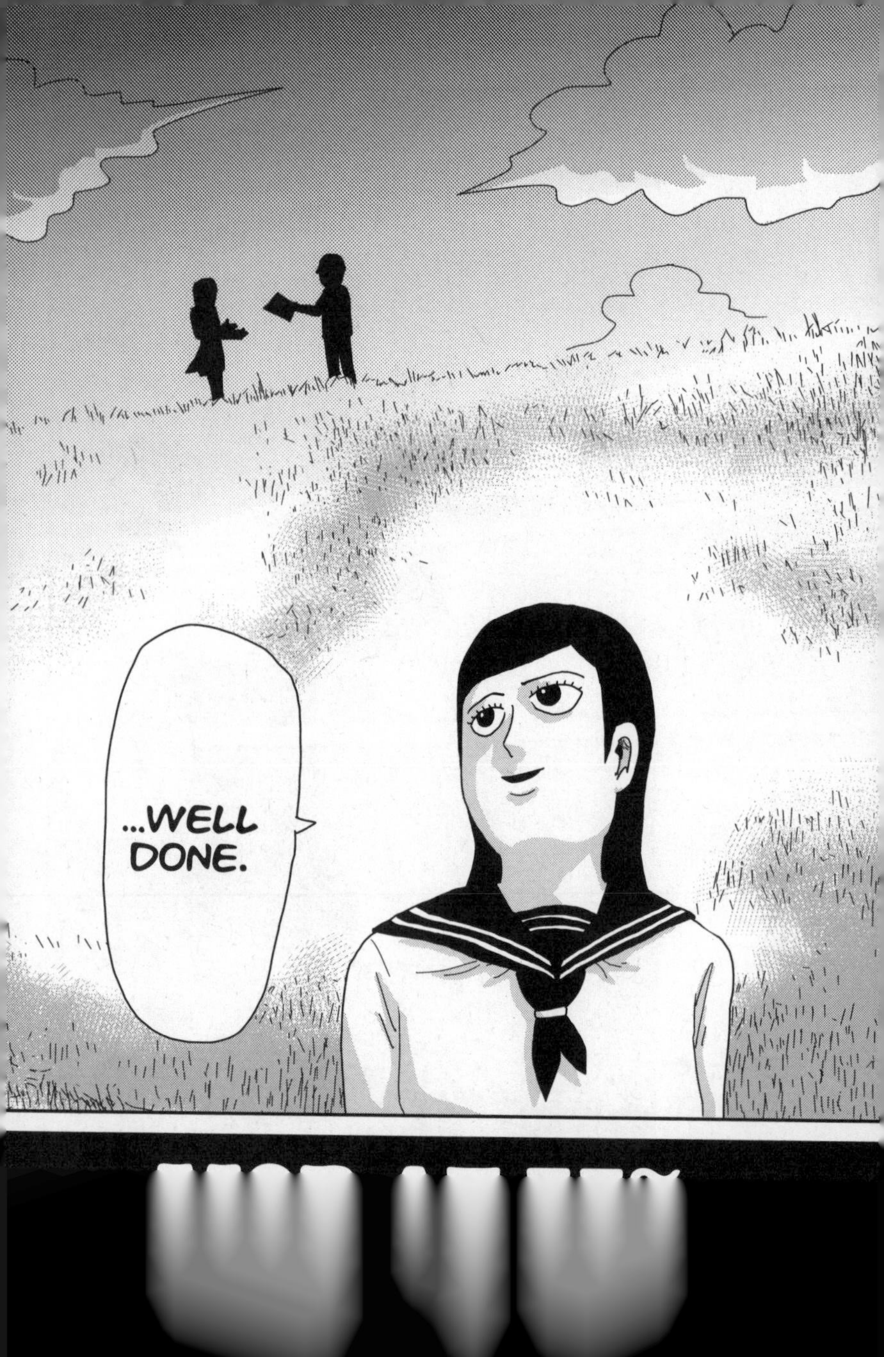
...WELL DONE.

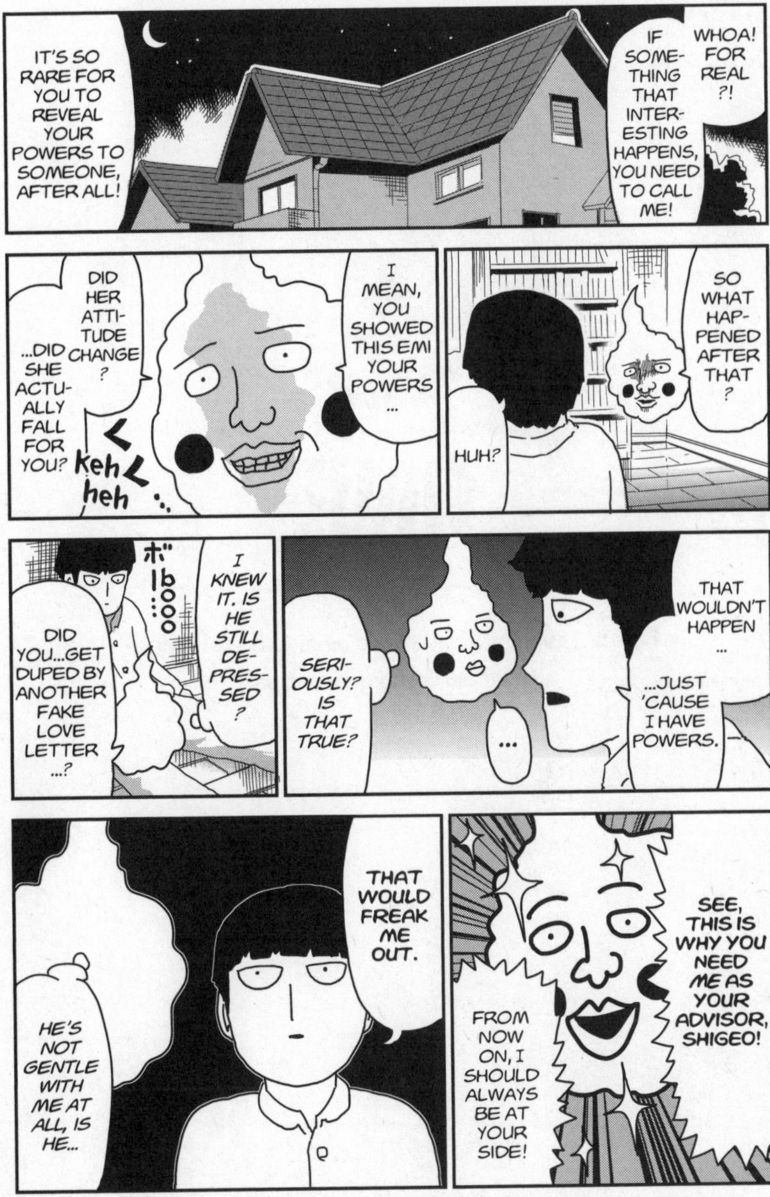
WHOA! FOR REAL?!
IF SOMETHING THAT INTERESTING HAPPENS, YOU NEED TO CALL ME!
IT'S SO RARE FOR YOU TO REVEAL YOUR POWERS TO SOMEONE, AFTER ALL!
SO WHAT HAPPENED AFTER THAT?
HUH?
I MEAN, YOU SHOWED THIS EMI YOUR POWERS...
DID HER ATTITUDE CHANGE?
...DID SHE ACTUALLY FALL FOR YOU?
keh keh heh...
THAT WOULDN'T HAPPEN...
...JUST 'CAUSE I HAVE POWERS.
...
SERIOUSLY? IS THAT TRUE?
I KNEW IT. IS HE STILL DEPRESSED?
ボ booo...
DID YOU...GET DUPED BY ANOTHER FAKE LOVE LETTER...?
SEE, THIS IS WHY YOU NEED ME AS YOUR ADVISOR, SHIGEO!
FROM NOW ON, I SHOULD ALWAYS BE AT YOUR SIDE!
THAT WOULD FREAK ME OUT.
HE'S NOT GENTLE WITH ME AT ALL, IS HE...

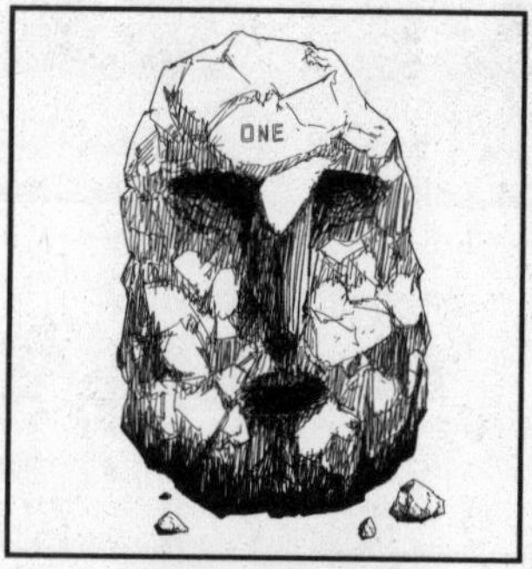
ONE

ONE

Before I even realized it, it's been two years since I started doing this manga.

president and publisher
MIKE RICHARDSON

editor
CARL GUSTAV HORN

designer
BRENNAN THOME

digital art technician
CHRIS HORN

English-language version produced by Dark Horse Comics

MOB PSYCHO 100

Published by Dark Horse Manga
A division of Dark Horse Comics LLC
10956 SE Main Street, Milwaukie, OR 97222

DarkHorse.com

To find a comics shop in your area, visit comicshoplocator.com.

First edition: October 2020 | ISBN 978-1-50671-371-7
Ebook ISBN 978-1-50671-878-1

1 3 5 7 9 10 8 6 4 2

Printed in the United States of America

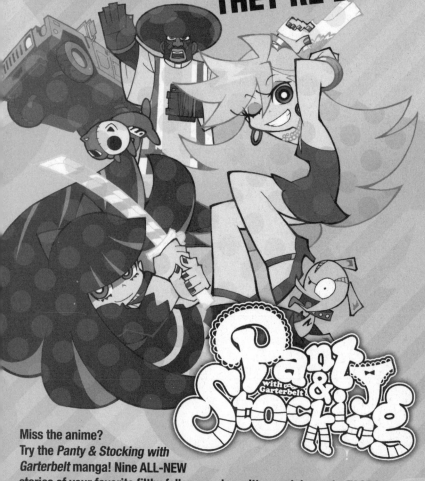

QUITE POSSIBLY THE MOST *fabulous*

EVANGELION MANGA EVER.

"IT'S A TRULY LAUGH-OUT-LOUD BOOK THAT *EVANGELION* FANS SHOULD BE SURE TO PICK UP. **RECOMMENDED.**"—CHE GILSON, OTAKU USA

DON'T BE CONCERNED THAT THERE'S NO REI OR ASUKA ON THIS COVER. THERE'S PLENTY OF THEM INSIDE. OH, YEAH, AND THAT SHINJI DUDE, TOO.

VOLUME 1
978-1-50670-151-6 • $11.99

VOLUME 2
978-1-50670-375-6 • $11.99

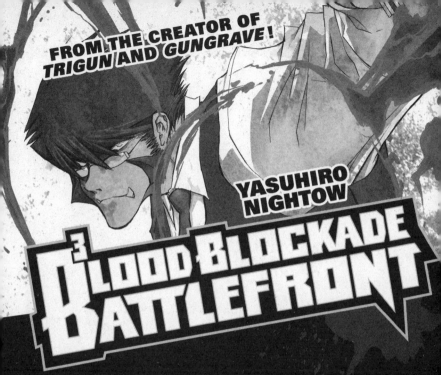

FROM THE CREATOR OF TRIGUN AND GUNGRAVE!

YASUHIRO NIGHTOW

BLOOD BLOCKADE BATTLEFRONT

Three years ago, a gateway between Earth and the Beyond opened over New York City. In one terrible night, New York was destroyed and rebuilt, trapping New Yorkers and extradimensional creatures alike in an impenetrable bubble. New York is now Hellsalem's Lot, a paranormal melting pot where magic and madness dwell alongside the mundane, where human vermin gather to exploit otherworldly assets for earthly profit. Now someone is threatening to breach the bubble and release Hellsalem's horrors, but the mysterious super-agents of Libra fight to prevent the unthinkable.

Trigun creator Yasuhiro Nightow returns with *Blood Blockade Battlefront*, an action-packed supernatural science-fiction steamroller as only Nightow can conjure.

VOLUME ONE
ISBN 978-1-59582-718-0 | $12.99

VOLUME TWO
ISBN 978-1-59582-912-2 | $12.99

VOLUME THREE
ISBN 978-1-59582-913-9 | $10.99

VOLUME FOUR
ISBN 978-1-61655-223-7 | $12.99

VOLUME FIVE
ISBN 978-1-61655-224-4 | $12.99

VOLUME SIX
ISBN 978-1-61655-557-3 | $12.99

VOLUME SEVEN
ISBN 978-1-61655-568-9 | $12.99

VOLUME EIGHT
ISBN 978-1-61655-583-2 | $12.99

VOLUME NINE
ISBN 978-1-50670-705-1 | $12.99

VOLUME TEN
ISBN 978-1-50670-704-4 | $12.99

AVAILABLE AT YOUR LOCAL COMICS SHOP OR BOOKSTORE
To find a comics shop in your area, visit comicshoplocator.com • For more information
or to order direct, visit DarkHorse.com

Kekkai Sensen © Yasuhiro Nightow. All rights reserved. Original Japanese edition published by
SHUEISHA, Inc., Tokyo. English translation rights in the United States and Canada arranged by SHUEISHA,
Inc. Dark Horse Manga is a trademark of Dark Horse Comics LLC. All rights reserved. (BL 7099)

DRIFTERS

KOHTA HIRANO

Heroes from Earth's history are deposited in an enchanted land where humans subjugate the nonhuman races. This wild, action-packed series features historical characters such as Joan of Arc, Hannibal, and Rasputin being used as chess pieces in a bloody, endless battle!

From Kohta Hirano, creator of the smash-hit *Hellsing, Drifters* is an all-out fantasy slugfest of epic proportion!

VOLUME ONE
978-1-59582-769-2 | $13.99

VOLUME TWO
978-1-59582-933-7 | $12.99

VOLUME THREE
978-1-61655-339-5 | $12.99

VOLUME FOUR
978-1-61655-574-0 | $13.99

VOLUME FIVE
978-1-50670-379-4 | $13.99

VOLUME SIX
978-1-50671-546-9 | $14.99

SOMETHING'S WRONG HERE . . .

You sense it, somehow. You suspect this story doesn't really go the way it should. You're suspicious! But a smooth talker like Reigen would know what to say at this point. *"Just flip the book around and start reading it the other way instead."* Aha! So this was really the last page of the book. You're saved! Thank you, Reigen-sensei! *"Now, about my fee . . . "*

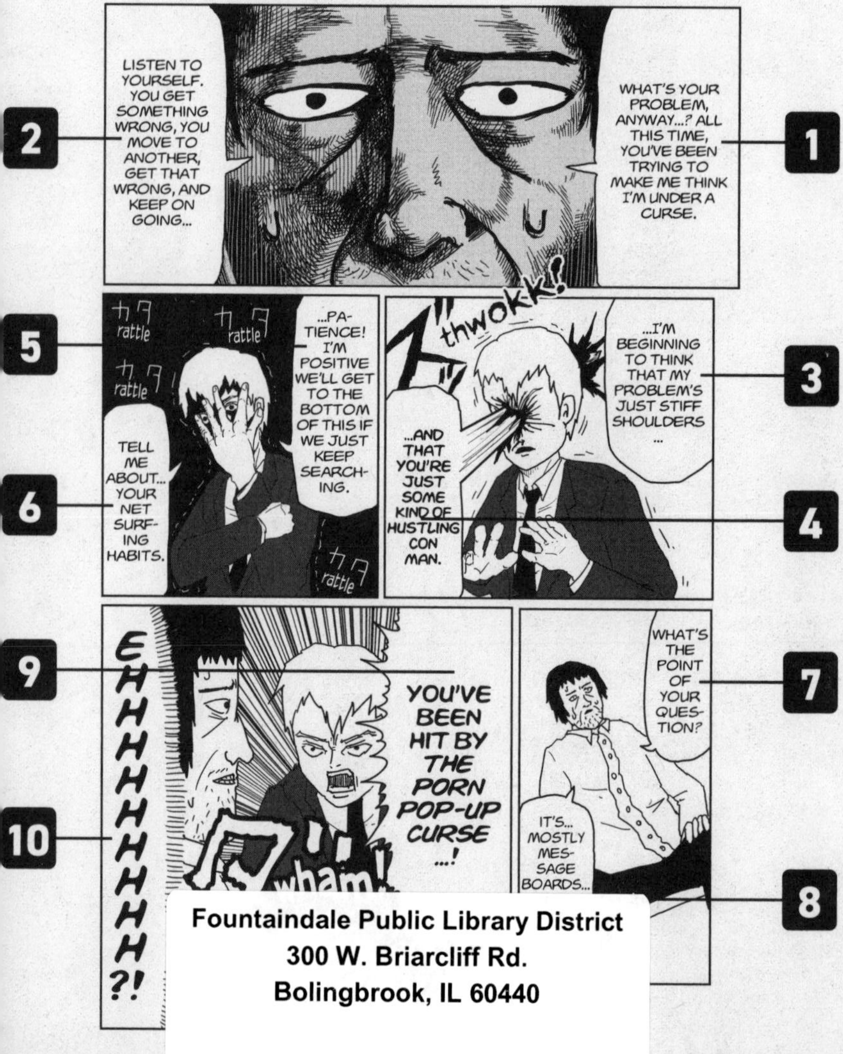
1
WHAT'S YOUR PROBLEM, ANYWAY...? ALL THIS TIME, YOU'VE BEEN TRYING TO MAKE ME THINK I'M UNDER A CURSE.
2
LISTEN TO YOURSELF. YOU GET SOMETHING WRONG, YOU MOVE TO ANOTHER, GET THAT WRONG, AND KEEP ON GOING...
thwokk!
3
...I'M BEGINNING TO THINK THAT MY PROBLEM'S JUST STIFF SHOULDERS...
4
...AND THAT YOU'RE JUST SOME KIND OF HUSTLING CON MAN.
カタ rattle
カタ rattle
カタ rattle
5
...PA-TIENCE! I'M POSITIVE WE'LL GET TO THE BOTTOM OF THIS IF WE JUST KEEP SEARCH-ING.
6
TELL ME ABOUT... YOUR NET SURF-ING HABITS.
カタ rattle
7
WHAT'S THE POINT OF YOUR QUES-TION?
8
IT'S... MOSTLY MES-SAGE BOARDS...
9
YOU'VE BEEN HIT BY THE PORN POP-UP CURSE ...!
wham!
10
EHHHHHHHHHH?!